THE LIVING PAST

IVAR LISSNER

THE LIVING PAST

Translated from the German

By J. MAXWELL BROWNJOHN, M.A. (Oxon.)

G. P. PUTNAM'S SONS NEW YORK

LIBRARY OF CONGRESS CATALOG
CARD NUMBER: 57-12213

MANUFACTURED IN THE UNITED STATES OF AMERICA

VAN REES PRESS • NEW YORK

CONTENTS

CONTENTS

CAMBODIA

CHINA

CENTRAL ASIA

JAPAN

AUSTRALIA

POLYNESIA

MELANESIA

NORTH AFRICA

SOUTH AMERICA

CONTENTS

CENTRAL AMERICA

CRETE

GREECE

ITALY

CARTHAGE

ROME

INDICES

FOREWORD

EACH DAY OF YOUR LIFE HAPPENS BUT ONCE, AND CAN *never be recalled. Will you waste this day? Only when you recognize what generations before you have striven for, thought, and achieved, will you recognize and best employ the opportunities your own short life affords.*

And only then will you realize that you are set upon a veritable mountain of human history and civilization which others have built for you over thousands of years.

You who live in the twentieth century—do you ever reflect upon this?

IVAR LISSNER

A WORD OF THANKS

I SHOULD LIKE TO EXPRESS MY SINCEREST GRATITUDE TO *the eminent scholars who have aided me in my work by offering advice and many valuable suggestions, and also by checking the sections dealing with individual civilizations.*

DR. HANS STOCK, *Professor of Egyptology at Munich University, Director of the Egyptian State Collection, Munich, for checking and amplifying the sections on Mesopotamia, Egypt, Phoenicia and Persia.*

DR. KAMENHUBER, *First Assistant of the Institute for Indo-Germanic Languages, University of Munich, for going over the chapter on the Hittites so thoroughly.*

PROFESSOR DR. LUDWIG ALSDORF *of Hamburg, for looking over the chapters on the Indian and Persian civilizations and offering valuable suggestions on the sections about Mohenjo-Daro and Harappa.*

DR. RICHARD SCHRÖTER, *Departmental Director at the Museum of Ethnology, Hamburg, for his hints on planning the chapter on the Khmer civilization of Cambodia.*

DR. PETER WILHELM MEISTER, *Museum of Arts and Crafts, Hamburg, for supplementing the chapters on China and Japan.*

PROFESSOR DR. ANNEMARIE VON GABAIN, *Lecturer on Turkish at Hamburg University, for looking over the chapter on Mongolia.*

A WORD OF THANKS

DR. HERBERT TISCHNER, *Curator and Director of the Indo-Oceanic Department at the Museum of Ethnology and Prehistory, Hamburg, for looking over the sections on Australia, Polynesia and Melanesia.*

DR. HANS DIETRICH DISSELHOFF, *Director of the Museum of Ethnology, Berlin, for his interesting hints on the treatment of early American civilizations.*

PROFESSOR DR. ERNST SITTIG, *for manifold suggestions on dealing with the language and script of ancient Crete.*

DR. W. BRANDENSTEIN, *Professor of Comparative Philology at Graz University, for his perusal of the chapter on Troy and his important information on the stratification of the Homeric city.*

DR. REINHARD LULLIES, *Chief Curator, Munich, for valuable interpretations of certain examples of the Greek plastic arts.*

DR. SIEGFRIED LAUFFER, *of the University of Munich, for checking the chapters on classical Greece and Rome.*

DR. HANS L. STOLTENBERG, *Professor of Sociology, authority on German etymology and elucidator of the Lycian language, for his help in composing the chapters on the Etruscans, Hannibal, and Carthage.*

All these scholars have contributed to the success of my work, and if there are instances in the text where my wording does not precisely correspond with their interpretations, they have done their best to insure that my picture of the great civilizations of mankind is not at variance with scientific thought.

INTRODUCTION

Now the first men, since none of the things useful for life had yet been discovered, led a wretched existence, having no clothing to cover them, not knowing the use of dwelling and fire, and being totally ignorant of cultivated food. And though the sounds which they made were at first unintelligible and indistinct, yet gradually they came to lend articulation to their speech.

Diodorus Siculus (c. 25 B.C.), *Universal History*

"There's a whole city down there," the fisherman said. He was right: you would only have had to step out of the boat into the water to find yourself standing on broad slabs of marble, the remnants of balconies, walls, and houses. The old man told me that on clear nights he had often seen the dim outlines of the submerged city below the surface.

We were off Comacchio, where the calm waters of the Valle del Mezzano lagoon cover the ruins of the ancient metropolis of Spina. Legends thousands of years old tell us about this important Etruscan city, which reached its prime five hundred years before the birth of Christ and once dominated the Adriatic. The low-lying area at the mouth of the Po, a land of endless marshes and lagoons, has already yielded up vast quantities of Etruscan-made articles: vases, mirrors, candlesticks, clay figurines, bronze vessels, jewelry, examples of goldsmith's work, and a Greco-Etruscan cemetery of some thousand graves. All these things can be seen in the Museo di Spina at Ferrara, yet the city of Spina itself still lies buried, its site guessed-at but as yet unexcavated.

I had a strange feeling, standing there above the ruins of this once highly developed and pampered civilization. How many of the Etruscans' cities still lay hidden and undiscovered? Where exactly in Asia Minor was Tyrsa, their legendary city of origin? Where had they come from, these men who called themselves Tyrseni or Tyrrheni, after the name of their city? A whole sea, the Tyrrhenian, bears their name; yet Tyrsa itself still remains lost to us.

The Etruscans or Tyrrhenians who emigrated from Lydia in Asia Minor and settled in Italy have provided us with a clear indication, in their burial places, of the magnificent results which can spring from a meeting between East and West. Rarely has there been an art which gave a more human and dramatic impression or implored eternity to spare it from oblivion more fervently than the Etruscan.

By far the greater part of mankind's thoughts, dreams, deeds, and material achievements lies beneath the ground: under marshes, like the vanished city of Tartessus in the estuary of the Guadalquivir River; or under the seas, like Gondwana, the erstwhile bridge of land between South Asia and Australia.

When will we discover Wasukanni, capital of the Mitanni empire, which must have stood somewhere on the southern slopes of the Armenian mountains? When will we excavate Kussara, the erstwhile seat of Anittas, first king of the Hittites? Who is going to discover the city of Nessa, entombed in the soil of eastern Anatolia, or identify the location of Arzawa, the kingdom which flourished in western Asia Minor about 1400 B.C.? And when will Sodom and Gomorrah or the other cities in the Vale of Siddim at the southern end of the Dead Sea be excavated?

About the year 400 B.C. a man arrived in Athens who had already, even in those days, won a considerable reputation. Hard-working and hungry for information, he was steadfastly resolved to acquire a wide knowledge of the workings of Nature. But he was so indifferent to fame and so anxious to avoid being recognized in Athens that he frequently withdrew into solitude, one of his favorite haunts being a graveyard. He discoursed with Socrates, the greatest Greek philosopher, yet not even Socrates recognized him. He taught that the world was composed of innumerable, infinitesimal atoms. These atoms were only quantitively definable, but the shapes which they could assume were infinitely variable, and they whirled about unceasingly in boundless space. They could either unite or disperse: they could even become so dense that they formed whole stars.

The man who had evolved this theory was Democritus, who was born at Abdera in Thrace and lived from 460 to 370 B.C., dying at the age of ninety. His many attainments included a knowledge of perspective and the technique of building a true arch, and he was a brilliant engineer and inventor. He raised the status of natural science to hitherto undreamed-of heights, a task in which he was greatly aided by his wide knowledge of mathematics and astronomy. What won him the most fame, however, was his atomic theory. He actually used the term "atom" or *atomos*, the Greek for indivisible, and held that these atoms whirling through the universe, could produce every imaginable combination of matter, including fire, water, air, and earth.

Democritus had taken over the rudiments of his atomic theory from Leucippus of Miletus, but he had a more restless mind and was a greater scientist than his former teacher. Eager to know the world, he collected information from all quarters, spending the bulk of his private means on traveling expenses. He saw Babylon, visited Egypt, and roamed across large tracts of Asia, probably reaching Persia, the Red Sea, and even India. In fact, most of Democritus' scientific knowledge was acquired from Chaldean theologians in the temples of Mesopotamia, and from the astronomers of Babylon and Egypt.

Another man who traveled widely in the East was Thales of Miletus, who lived about 600 B.C. He adopted the Egyptian division of the solar year into 365 days and learned how to foretell solar eclipses from the Babylonians. It was he who accurately forecast an eclipse of the sun for May 28th, 585 B.C. Anaximander imported the idea of the sundial from Babylon about 560 B.C., and was the first man to attempt to draw a map of the known world.

Pythagoras armed himself with a letter of introduction to the Pharaoh Amasis and traveled to Egypt, where he learned the Egyptian language. He also spent some time with the Chaldeans and the Magi in Babylon and Persia. Hipparchus, who was probably the most important of all the Greek astronomers, identified more than 850 stars. He was born in Bithynia, part of what is now modern Turkey, and the East had a decisive influence upon his scientific researches. Ptolemy, who lived between A.D. 100 and A.D. 178, was born in Egypt, and was the last great natural scientist of antiquity.

The number of notable Greek scholars who acquired the fundamentals of their knowledge from the East is extraordinarily large, and it was this knowledge which, developed and amplified, Greece and Rome handed on to the Western world. The Greeks and Romans were our masters, yet it was they who in a sense paid for our schooling, for they exhausted and weakened themselves so much in the process of exchanging and giving away ideas that they ultimately brought about their own downfall. Christ spoke Aramaic, a Semitic language, and his teachings conquered the West on the wings of Hellenism. In literature, we are still using the same themes which men evolved, expounded, and performed long ago in ancient Greece, and Euripides is a mute and constant collaborator in all our modern playwrights' most "original" ideas. Plato and Aristotle laid the foundations for our philosophy and ethics, and Athens and Olympia the home of our ideals of sport.

We have all been linked together for many, many thousands of years now, and the ties which bind us are not only ancient but remarkably far-reaching: they stretched nearly all the way around the world, long before the great age of discovery arrived. The gulf between Mesopotamia and China, for instance, was bridged by the Asiatic steppe civilization of the Scythians, who made use of Mesopotamian and Chinese examples in evolving an art of their own. Not only was it very long-lived, but it traveled over enormous distances, borne along in the Scythians' carts and on the backs of their pack animals. Between the eighth and third centuries B.C. the Scythians dominated the greater part of what is now Russia. It is an astonishing thought that the golden fish, sixteen inches long, which was found in Germany in 1882 at Vettersfelde, Brandenburg, was a Scythian work of art dating from about 500 B.C., and that these same Scythians were in cultural communication with countries as far away as Turkestan and China.

In China, the history of copper and its alloy, bronze, goes back to 1400 B.C. What is interesting, however, is that the idea of casting bronze was actually imported into China from the "Far West." In other words, East and West were interchanging cultural ideas 3,500 years ago.

But there are still greater surprises in store. During the Shang Dynasty, an era of great culture lasting roughly from 1500 to 1050 B.C., we repeatedly come across the image of Tao-tie on sacrificial bowls. The same Tao-tie was also reproduced by the magnificent bronzesmiths of the Chou emperors, whose line survived for almost a thousand years until 249 B.C., when the last of the dynasty abdicated. The Tao-tie is the head of an unidentified beast whose origins lie far in the prehistoric past and may perhaps have stemmed from a vague memory of some ogre or long extinct man-eating monster. Astonishingly enough, the likeness of this monster traveled as far as America, where Tao-tie reappears as Quetzalcoatl, the plumed serpent. More than that, the mysterious animal is to be found not only in the Olmec civilization on the coast of the Mexican Gulf, but also in the Chavin civilization of ancient Peru, where it recurs unmistakably as a gold mask in the shape of a beast of prey.

Five hundred years before the birth of Christ, the Pythagoreans taught that the earth neither occupied a central position in the cosmic system nor enjoyed any special privileges over other heavenly bodies: it was a mere speck of dust in the universe, like millions upon millions of others. The middle of the universe, so they said, was occupied by a "central fire," from which the inhabited parts of the earth were averted, and toward which the sun and moon were turned. Aristarchus of Samos declared about 260 B.C. that the sun remains motionless, while the earth circles about it on its own axis. This startling discovery was forgotten for two thousand years, until the sixteenth century, when Copernicus, closely following out the ancient Pythagorean line of thought, defied the whole of contemporary ecclesiastical opinion by expounding his heliocentric system.

In this manner ideas, discoveries and inventions have traveled back and forth across the world. Our whole Western way of life is descended from civilizations which once flourished in Mesopotamia, Egypt, Central Asia, and the islands of the Aegean. Yet the life span of the advanced civilizations known to us is incredibly brief. Ten thousand years are like a day in the lifetime of human evolution. We are in possession of sewing needles, pipes, flutes, harpoons and magicians' wands, for instance, which date back twenty thousand years to the Magdalenian period, so called after Abri la Madeleine near Tursac in Dordogne, France. Man has been roaming the earth as a two-legged creature endowed with intellect since the first Ice Age, or for about 600,000 years. We of today are not only burdened with the countless afflictions and everlasting mistakes of past millennia, but are also heirs to the discernment and knowledge which they have brought in their train. We owe the brief happiness of what we call our existence to countless millions of men who have long since crumbled to dust.

Each era fancies that it is the most important in world history. Because of this obvious fallacy I have developed a dislike for such phrases as "We have now reached a turning point. . . ." or, "We live in a time of drastic change. . . ."—the stock-in-trade of public speakers. For when has there been a time without a "turning point" or "drastic change?" The golden ages of the great civilizations were only the peaks that emerged from the infinite ocean of the primitive. And even the greatest creative ages have no inkling of their own towering sublimity so that the loftiest art and the greatest naïveté very often live side by side. We need the distance of centuries or millennia before we can recognize when and where Homo sapiens scaled the steepest cliffs of human achievement. I am speaking of artistic, not scientific, accomplishments, for a work of art is unique and can never be duplicated. When it comes to scientific accomplishments, mankind has time enough: what one generation does not achieve will probably be mastered by the next. And, were there no such thing as danger or man as the enemy of his own kind, technological discoveries would always occur exactly when they were needed.

There is nothing very new about our way of life or the age in which we live, nothing very new about our ideas or scientific methods. We have taken over much more from the East, from Greece and Italy, than we realize. All our modern sciences move along the same lines, concerning themselves almost exclusively with the nature of material things and living creatures. We imagine that our wide knowledge in these spheres represents progress, and pay far too little attention to man's inner self, his mind and soul. Yet I submit that the nations and eras which did not merely strive for material comfort, but constantly thought in terms of eternity, were probably more "progressive" and certainly wiser than ourselves.

The Greeks were fond of telling lies, a trait which explains why they were highly imaginative poets. They knew the fundamental secret of how to blend imagination and reality to produce a work of art. To them the exploration of the human mind with its intellectual and spiritual possibilities was more important than anything else, and in this respect they were always truthful and sincere. Whether we of today, with our "exact sciences," are pursuing more perilous chimeras than the ancient world did remains to be seen. The only certainty is that if the intellectual development of the West continues lagging, as it has, behind our indisputably great scientific achievements, we shall one day be like small children playing with large and dangerous toys which they do not understand, or will become specialist technicians pressing buttons and unleashing forces whose moral implications we no longer are capable of assessing.

What would happen if we could look back and see with our own eyes all the sufferings and struggles which man has experienced during his hundreds of thousands of years as a human being? Would we turn to salt, like Lot's wife?

I do not think so. For it was not Sodom and Gomorrah that brought us through the ages to our present state, but nations and individuals, endowed with an endless store of patience, who always built anew upon the ruins of yesterday, accumulating a vast treasury of ideas which their descendants one day committed to stone, clay, and parchment.

This book was not written in a day; it was not written in haste nor from the desire to exploit our contemporary appetite for the historical past. When I began to gather the materials that went into the making of this volume, people were interested in totally different matters. I have worked on this project for many years, trying to condense the enormous bulk of material, to crystallize it, to highlight it—for we know too much and, therefore, as it were, too little. And I have at all times taken into account the latest available scientific data. I express my gratitude to the many specialized scholars who have checked each one of my chapters and given me numerous stimulating suggestions. Not a thought or date was written down lightly—although I aimed at readability—and I learned that even the greatest scholars hold widely differing opinions when it comes to the population of many an ancient city or to the date of birth or death of many a ruler of antiquity.

Beginning in 1949 excerpts from this book were published in European periodicals, which enabled me to consider certain scholarly objections and make amendments to the text. In fact, it took me many years to gain a comprehensive and living picture of this earth, with its diversity of peoples, their driving motives, their failures and successes.

In my view, the known span of human history is so brief that we may for once be pardoned if we try to isolate and define the essential features of the past, its nations, countries, and civilizations. We only learned how to write four or five thousand years ago, but the most important events in our history occurred at widely separated points in that tiny portion of earth-time. Every civilization, every race, has furthered at least one side of human development in its own inimitable fashion; and in the prime of every civilization lie the seeds of its death.

This is not a history book, nor is it exclusively concerned with ancient civilizations. All past history once lay in the present, and all present history is rooted in the past. If I were asked which I considered the most important landmarks in the history of mankind, I should probably reply: the invention of writing by the Sumerians; the Book of Job and the Prophets' wealth of ideas; democracy in Athens during the Periclean Age; the life and death of Socrates; the art of Japanese wood engraving; and the poems of Li Tai-po. These all seem to lack cohesion and to vary a great deal in comparative worth, I admit, but when you have wandered several times around the world as I have, things take on a different perspective.

We must always be on our guard against the temptation to apply the restless, progressive standards of the West to civilizations which should be assessed by quite different criteria. Our Western standards are not by any means applicable to every race on earth. Neither dynamism nor progress, in the Western sense, necessarily make for human happiness. The slumbering, dreamy existence of the Pacific races, for instance, with its careless tranquillity and unconsciousness of sin, its elemental rhythms of joy and sorrow, is probably much closer to the secret of living. Arrested civilizations appear to have a much longer expectation of life than dynamic civilizations, which is why the Polynesians have survived for so long. The whole of humanity has made much greater and faster advances in the past seven thousand years than ever before; yet Homo sapiens managed to survive 600,000 years of slow and undisturbed existence without writing, chemistry, or machines. Progress, in our sense of the word, is probably a poor guarantee of mankind's longevity: hence the greater wisdom of men like Li Tai-po and the Japanese masters of wood engraving who painted "the rhythm of the world."

I am not saying that the West is likely to meet its doom any sooner than the East. That would be a contradiction in terms, for the East is appropriating all the most dubious achievements of the West and furiously copying them. China, Japan, India, and Asiatic Russia are even more obsessed with progress today than the West. There seems to be little to choose between any of the sections of modern humanity: they have all lost the art of living.

It was in 1932 that I first set out to visit all the places whose past history has most contributed to our own way of life: Athens, Carthage, Rome and Constantinople. I traveled along the Nile, the Euphrates and Tigris, the Indus, the Yangtze, and the Hwang-ho, for the ancient world's most advanced civilizations were born in these river valleys. They are still inhabited by farmers and merchants with the experience of thousands of years behind them, enlightened men who are wise in the ways of the world and sometimes even of eternity, thrifty and not over-hospitable men who know that a tide of invading humanity may one day make them poor.

And I got to know other races, too: warm-hearted, generous people like the wandering Polynesians of the Pacific and the nomadic inhabitants of the endless steppes, grasslands, and deserts of the world;

people who never cling to their possessions because their herds keep them constantly on the move, people who look up at the starry skies more often than we, hence realize the ultimate futility of material things. I talked to nomads in Arabia, drank many bowls of tea in the tents of Mongolia, and lived among the wandering Tungus in the forests of the North Manchurian *taiga*.

We are a tenacious and inventive species. Perhaps our modern technology will enable us to survive the next Ice Age in 50,000 or 100,000 years' time. Who knows? There have been four Ice Ages and three temperate periods during the past 600,000 years, so men have already managed to survive eras of cold lasting up to 100,000 years on four separate occasions, each time without the help of modern science.

Yet, in another respect, our ideas are imperfect and limited. We forget that we are only an insignificant link in the endless chain of people who have made us what we are and brought us as far as we have come, men who survived not because they strove for success, but because of their immense reserves of fortitude and endurance. Our horizons are alarmingly restricted because we always greatly overestimate the significance of the convulsions, upheavals, and so-called "new orders" of our own limited age.

We should always remember that man is by no means indispensable to the cosmos. The earth would still go on rotating about the sun even if he ceased to exist.

THE LIVING PAST

7,000 YEARS AND 4,000 GODS

Without the ancient Orient we would not be what we are; without understanding it we shall never know ourselves. Many features of civilization have come down to us from the Sumerians via the Assyrians, Babylonians, Egyptians, Greeks and Romans. The excavations in Mesopotamia—'Land of the Two Rivers'—have revealed to us the roots of our own intellectual and spiritual growth. Our alphabet, our religion, our legal system, our arts—they are all predicated on a long process of evolution. From Mesopotamia and the Sumerians came what is perhaps the most decisive starting point for all civilization: the art of writing.

"OF THE history of the Sumerians we know nothing." This is stated in Helmolt's *History of the World*, a work comprising nine volumes published in Germany in 1913.

Yet, in the space of a mere forty years, we have succeeded in unearthing human civilizations that have added several thousand years to our knowledge of history. It is in the valleys of the Tigris and Euphrates—in modern Iraq—that the secrets of one of the two most ancient advanced civilizations we know have been wrested from the desert—a fascinating, almost fabled world which had long lain buried and forgotten.

The Greek historian Herodotus had never heard of the Sumerians. Berossus, a Babylonian scholar who lived about 250 B.C., knew of them only from dim legends. He wrote about a race of monsters who supposedly had emerged from out of the Persian Gulf, led by a man called Oannes. It was not until 2,000 years after Berossus that the Sumerians were rediscovered.

Only a hundred years ago, scholars were still gazing uncomprehendingly at the mysterious characters chiseled in stone which the Sumerians had left behind. The German scholar Georg Friedrich Grotefend was the first to devise a method of deciphering this picture writing. The wedge-shaped, or cuneiform, script of the Sumerians is in fact the earliest known system of writing in the world. It was practiced by many Mesopotamian peoples living in the Tigris-Euphrates valley, as well as by the Elamites, the ancient Persians, and others.

From 3500 B.C. on, the Sumerians lived in the region between the two rivers, their land stretching from the Persian Gulf as far north as modern Baghdad. Their own records, which reach back into remotest times, never mention any other land of origin. It was here that they invented their picture writing. In time, and with clay tablets as a writing surface and hollow stems as graving tools, this script developed into cuneiforms. It happened here—and here alone—because the Sumerians have suggested nowhere that they borrowed the idea from others. The beginnings of this writing date from about 3000 B.C. when with specially fashioned hollow reed stems the symbols were pressed into clay tablets that were subsequently hardened.

In Sir Henry Rawlinson the English possessed a man who, like Lawrence of Arabia, had wide interests, a rich imagination and great gifts. He had worked as a political agent in Afghanistan and Arabia; he was also an indefatigable traveler and explorer. During a stay in Persia he studied the cuneiform inscription of Behistun, and when he was consul at Baghdad, in 1844, he managed to decipher this ancient tablet which also contained a Babylonian translation.

In 1854 the Englishmen Taylor and Loftus started digging in the ancient cities of Ur, Eridu, and Erech (Uruk). Erech, allegedly a royal capital before the Great Flood, apparently was the seat of King Gilgamesh. Then at the end of the nineteenth century, French archaeologists digging at Tell Loh brought to light what remained of ancient Lagash. In this city they found tablets bearing the first clues to the history of the Sumerian kings.

Sir Henry Austen Layard uncovered ancient Nineveh under the hill of Kouyunjik on the right bank of the Tigris, opposite present-day Mosul. Amid the ruins of the palace of the Assyrian king, Assurbanipal (668-626 B.C.), he unearthed a large library of clay tablets, among them whole "dictionaries" listing Sumerian words along with their Semitic-Assyrian meanings. King Assurbanipal's library was very old indeed, and the clay tablets contained transcripts and compilations of tests dating back to about 2000 B.C.

Among the tablets was a particularly precious find—the Gilgamesh Epic, the story of the Flood, which proved to be an astonishing confirmation of what the Book of Genesis tells us about Noah. The Gilgamesh Epic was inscribed upon twelve tablets, each one recording a different adventure. The whole work consisted of about three thousand lines. Fragments of all twelve tablets were found in these ruins, and of the full text about one thousand five hundred lines have been preserved either wholly or in part.

Shortly after the first World War, Professor (later Sir Leonard)

▲ = RUINS
0 MILES 190
TURKEY
IRAN
(PERSIA)
MESOPOTAMIA
SYRIA
IRAQ
LEBANON
ISRAEL
JORDAN
SAUDI ARABIA
Mediterranean
Persian Gulf
TIGRIS
EUPHRATES
SIVAS
MUSCH
VAN
LAKE VAN
TABRIZ
TEHERAN
MALATYA
DIYARBAKIR
MARDIN
URFA (EDESSA)
ANAZARBA
ISSO
CARCHEMISH
TEL HALAF
ARPAD
ATCHANA
ALEPPO
ANTIOCH
RAS SHAMRA
SIFFIN
HARAGLA
BALIS
SURJA
ARBAN
MARGADA
SELEBIJE
ED DEIR
CIRCESIUM ?
MÂRI
HOMS
PALMYRA
BAALBEK (ELIOPOLI)
BEIRUT
SIDON
TYRE
DAMASCUS
DUR SARRUKIN (KHORSABAD)
TEPE GAWRA
ASKI MOSUL
NINEVEH
MOSUL
NIMRUD
ERBIL
CALAH
HASSUNA
KIRKUK
ASSUR
KALAAT-MAKHUL
ABU CHALCHALAN
KHAFAJE
BAGDAD
SELEUCIA
CTESIPHON
GEMDET NASR
SIPPAR
KISCH
BABYLON
THEMAIL
BORSIPPA
NIPPUR
ADAB
KISURRA
ISIN
KUFA
ERECH
LARSA
SHURUPPAK
KUTALLA
LAGASH
TELLOH
AL UBAID
UR
ERIDU
BÉJAT
SHUSH
SHUSTAR
BASRA
ABADAN
KUWAIT
N
E
S
W

Woolley directed an Anglo-American team of archaeologists working jointly for the University of Pennsylvania and the British Museum. They excavated the small site at Al-Ubaid (Tell el'Obed), northwest of Ur, and unearthed temples, residential districts, pottery and sculptures. It was then realized that the Sumerians had attained a high level of civilization as long ago as 5,000 years. These explorations lifted the veil from an ancient race whose history is probably twice as long as the history of the West from the birth of Christ to the present day.

Christ's contemporaries never ventured to think back that far into the past. In their day Sumer had long been forgotten: it lay in that twilight of past millennia, and mountains of desert sand covered what remained of the brilliant mosaics, fine sculptures, mighty temples, vases, pots, ornaments and cosmetic articles once created by human beings very much like ourselves. But more than that: this flourishing life reaches back into an age which even to the Sumerian scholars and priests of 2300 B.C. seemed immeasurably old. The priests, who also functioned as historians, compiled lists of their kings that went back for 432,000 years!

Now these priests had certainly exaggerated the facts, because the Sumerians did not arrive in the "Land of the Two Rivers" until about 3500 B.C. Of course it is possible these early settlers may have previously lived elsewhere for thousands of years and developed a rudimentary civilization. After all, Western civilization traveled from Mesopotamia and the Nile Valley into Palestine and Greece, from Greece to Rome, from Rome to Spain, France, Germany and England, and from England to North America. Perhaps the Sumerians had completed a similar westward migration before they finally arrived in the region which is probably the "Paradise" of the Bible.

To reach the bottom of the ruins at Nippur it is necessary to dig down to a depth of fully seventy feet, which exceeds the height of the average house in a modern metropolis. At Nippur, this seventy-foot depth points to an age of roughly 5,000 years.

Most recently, archaeologists have discovered something else: no matter how far they delve into this cradle of mankind, the beginnings of human settlements invariably are buried still deeper in the past. In 1927, E. A. Speiser, of the University of Pennsylvania, discovered a hill north of Mosul that rises some sixty-five feet above the plain of the Tigris. The villages of the neighborhood call this hill Tepe Gawra. After excavating it, Speiser laid bare no less than twenty-six strata, each belonging to a different period.

The latest excavations in the "Land of the Two Rivers" are taking us further and further back into time—into the fourth, fifth and sixth millennia B.C. For instance, the excavations near Hassuna, south of Mosul, have again pushed back appreciably what we used to regard as our prehistoric past. Near Hassuna, Iraqi archaeologists found clay vessels, as well as representations of a mother goddess, small amulets, remains of rush mats, and sickles of flint and bitumen. The first half of the fourth millennium B.C. is known as the "Halaf, Samarra and Eridu period," so named after the most important archaeological sites in northern, central and southern Iraq. One particularly interesting find belonging to this period is now in the Museum of Baghdad: the neck of a large earthenware vessel with a woman's head painted on it. She has three blue lines on each cheek, the same tattoo marks we sometimes see on the faces of Bedouin women in our own time. At Eridu the earliest houses known to mankind, as well as the oldest temple vault, were discovered. Above this temple were no fewer than thirteen other temples, piled up layer upon layer as they were carefully laid open.

When Jarmo, in northern Iraq, was excavated by the University of Chicago, the scholars discovered the oldest village we know, dating back to about 6000 B.C. Several small clay figurines found there must be the earliest existing examples of sculpture considering that they are almost 8,000 years old.

Probably the most interesting site of all was excavated not long ago in the central Euphrates valley, on Syrian soil, not far from the Iraqi border. People had passed the ruins on the hill of Tell Hariri for 2,000 years without giving them a second thought. And yet beneath, entombed in sand, lay the once mighty city of Mari. It was only after some Bedouins had stumbled on the fragments of a small statue that archaeologists began to be interested in the hill of Tell Hariri.

In January, 1933, the French set their shovels to work on a large excavation project. In the twenty-odd years since, they have uncovered the city of Mari and its history, a history which stretches from the beginning of our chronology to a point more than 2,000 years earlier—and even now the end is not in sight. Those layers of Mari's ruins that date back to 4000 B.C. lie at a depth which has yet to be reached.

The things that were unearthed here—made of stone, clay and shells—reflect a world so vivid that the time lapse between today and the year 2000 B.C. seems to shrink to nothing. There are the high dignitaries staring at us wide-eyed, and the grinning faces of the tiny caricature sculptures characteristic of the period; rulers pray with folded hands; a pious man leads a small goat to sacrifice; court stewards with sly, inquisitive expressions peer out of their world into our own. There sits the great singer Ur Nanshe in a perfect posture, as if she were about to break into song; a bronze lion gazes at us with a hint of disenchantment in his inlaid stone eyes, and the headless statue of a prince shows us the beautiful trimmings and tassels that adorned the court robes of Mari, almost 2,000 years before the birth of Christ.

We know that the people of Mari were Semites, and therefore not racially akin to the Sumerians. But Mari's civilization, like all great civilizations, surely must have been composed of many different elements. Hence we find that the grave and stern qualities of the Sumerians mingled with the humorous, subtle cynicism and a worldlier view of life that marked the people of Mari.

All the thoughts, actions and endeavors of the Sumerians were focused upon the future. Could they be happy if they always knew what was in store for them? The prophet-priests of the Sumerians, the *baru*, knew everything. They controlled the lives of their people for 3,000 years. Generation after generation they compared the course of events with the condition and appearance of sheep's livers, until finally they were able to predict the future "accurately" by means of such inspection. The whole life of Sumer was governed by this single-minded fatalism.

And fate was their god. To him belonged the city and all cultivable land. He could dispense happiness and plenty, or want and death. The Sumerians believed implicitly in the god of their own city and the numerous local gods; they served him and were prepared to sacrifice everything to him.

The god owned his city, and with it his state; and the political prototype of the city-state, next to the art of writing, is the most important single contribution the Sumerians made to the civilization of Mesopotamia and the ancient world in general. These independent city-states were strongholds of advanced civilization, and first among them was Uruk (the Erech of the Bible). German scholars have been digging in what is now known as Warkah, and in 1929 first published their scientific findings. No one who today stands among the lofty ruins of the ziggurat of Warkah can escape the feeling—even now, after 4,000 years—that here, long ago, the god and his children and his city formed a true unity. This is the only reason why the temple, or ziggurat, could become such a towering structure, and why the people of Uruk with their fanatical faith strove toward the heavens—to be nearer to him, their god Anu. Anu was the father and king of all other gods, but at Uruk his cult was closely associated with the worship of Inanna (or Innin), the mother goddess and Mistress of Heaven who later became more important to Uruk than Anu himself, and whom the Semites called Ishtar. Female deities held, indeed, great significance for the Sumerians.

In the temples of Nippur they worshiped Enlil, the god of the air, together with his consort Ninlil. But the Sumerians had a special feeling for the moon, because their seers foretold the future by observing the characteristics of the moon's phases. Indeed, the city of Ur at one time belonged to the important moon god Sin, whose sacred number was 30. Sippar and Larsa were cities of the sun god Shamash, while Eridu worshiped Ea the water god, whose son Marduk became the principal god of the Babylonians. There was even one city, Borsippa, whose god was Nebo the Scribe. Nebo's function was to record the decisions of the other gods. He also was the patron of the Sumerian scribes, mankind's earliest pen-pushers and stenographers.

It is possible that the Sumerians were the first to conceive the idea of building their god a house, or at least a terrace, where they could be near him and where he could reside. Every city possessed one or more such terraces. They dominated the scene; in time they were built higher and higher, one tier after another being added, until they finally became man-made mountains or towers—the "high places" of our Bible. Man felt it was his duty to build his god a sacred place. Only the power of true faith, only a strong yearning for the god could have accomplished those miracles in brick, those links between heaven and earth, those artificial mountains reaching into the sky, those temple towers we call ziggurats. The word means simply "pinnacle" or "hilltop," and was the Mesopotamian term for a temple or terraced tower. The Sumerians, and later the Babylonians, left us magnificent examples of these structures: at Uruk, Eridu, Al'Uqair, Khafaye, Ur, Assur and at Babylon. And because the great city gods of the Sumerians sprang from the darkness of prehistoric times, many a ziggurat has crumbled to dust.

The Sumerians were interested in astrology and also had an amazingly sound knowledge of astronomy. They undoubtedly believed in a resurrection after death—and thus it probably was not too terrible for the attendants of the Sumerian kings when they allowed themselves to be buried alive along with their dead masters.

Some two hundred miles south of Baghdad lie the ruins of the city of Ur. There, in the fall of 1922, Professor Leonard Woolley excavated a royal cemetery. During the following decade he and his assistant Mallowan, who meanwhile has become an authority in his own right, methodically dug up this burial ground, thereby revealing for the first time the true spirit of Sumerian culture. Woolley found 1,850 graves. From the burial offerings in these graves, the scholars were able to place most of them in their chronological order, for only 751 out of the 1,850 contained no objects of a datable nature.

Sixteen graves were distinguished from the rest by their special opulence, construction and manner of burial. In these "royal" graves Woolley found human sacrifices whose number varied between six and eight. Woolley established that in every case only one of the bodies had been *buried*, while the rest had been *sacrificed*. As we shall see later, this sacrifice was not made under duress.

Human sacrifices were found only in those graves which contained stone vaults, but they were by no means confined to graves provided with rich offerings. For instance, Prince Mes-Kalam-Dug's grave was far more sumptuous than the king's grave, which Woolley designated as PG/1054. But whereas no human skeletons were found in the prince's grave, PG/1054 contained eight. Woolley also unearthed the queen's burial chamber. This grave, too, has been catalogued; in the archaeological records it is entered as PG/800. The queen's name was Shub-ad.

Woolley determined her name from a cylinder seal on the queen's right shoulder. And we know still more: the queen was four feet, eleven and one-half inches tall, of delicate bone structure, and with small feet, small hands and a large, narrow head. Woolley also believes he can establish that the queen spent most of her time in a kneeling position, in the manner of Japanese women. Prince Mes-Kalam-Dug was about five feet, five inches tall, and Woolley has deduced from his skull structure that he was left-handed. According to Woolley, both queen and prince belonged to the "proto-Arabian" race. The graves are about 4,500 years old, and date from the first dynasty of Ur.

What was the manner of burial in those ancient days?

Queen Shub-ad was found stretched out on her back. Her body had simply been put on a wooden bier. At her head crouched a female attendant, while the remains of a second were found at her feet. These attendants died a sacrificial death, for the burial chamber had been ceremonially sealed.

Then, down the ramp leading to the chamber, there followed a procession of courtiers, soldiers and other male and female attendants. The latter had donned brightly colored robes, and wore golden hair ornaments and golden earrings, chaplets of lapis lazuli, cornelian and gold leaf, silver hairpins and ornamental combs, necklaces and large robe clasps. They all took up their positions around the grave pit, as carts drawn by oxen and donkeys followed them down. Each man and woman held a small receptacle of stone, earthenware or metal in their hands. In the middle of the vault stood a large copper vessel. Apparently, all beakers were filled and each person drank the poison. The animals, too, must have been killed in some manner or other. The whole grave was then filled up with earth. This is the only way in which Professor Woolley can explain why he found the victims ranged in tidy rows, looking completely calm, and why he was unable to detect any signs of violence whatsoever. Not even the women's coiffures had been disarranged. Probably all died in a prone or seated position, as though they had quietly and suddenly decided to take leave of life. Indeed, Woolley discerned that the musicians must have been playing up to the very end.

Every member of the king's retinue in every royal grave, without exception, was found holding a cup in his hand, and the copper vessel was always down there, too. This has convinced Woolley that the courtiers not only died peacefully, but also of their own free will. He thinks that the animals apparently died *after* their grooms, but they, too, died in their allotted places.

These live burials were certainly not bridal sacrifices to the gods, as many scholars have supposed, for actually, more men than women were found among the principal victims. A bride for a deity would have had to be young and beautiful, yet Woolley ascertained that Queen Shub-ad was about forty years old. It should of course be remembered that he based this opinion on the examination of a woman who had been dead for almost 5,000 years.

The other treasures that Woolley brought to light from the royal burial ground stagger the imagination. Queen Shub-ad's shell powder box, her little reticule of blue malachite, golden pins, rings, bracelets and necklaces, the lovely bright-colored amulets, the queen's diadem, the many different head ornaments made of finest gold leaf—all these things are so unique, even by present-day standards, that no modern jeweler could even begin to duplicate them. Woolley found massive golden bowls of beautiful design in the queen's and the prince's graves, as well as innumerable other precious objects: harps and lyres, checker boards, figurines of wood, metal, shell-encrusted stone and lapis lazuli, miniature boats, an ornamented royal standard of white marble, goblets of lapis lazuli, bowls and basins. All these things are designed with an exquisite simplicity which gives them a timeless elegance.

Woolley found many other objects: golden daggers, axes, lance heads, carriage shafts and bridle rings, and, finally, the famous "Ram in the Blossoming Tree," a magnificent work of art made of precious metals and colored stones.

It is difficult to imagine how it must feel to discover such untouched graves. There lie the dead, undisturbed, their servants still inside the tomb, soldiers still guarding the entrance, grooms holding their animals' bridles, musicians at their instruments, and the ladies-in-waiting still grouped respectfully near the royal chamber—the mass burial of a whole retinue, loyal to their sovereign lord even in death. These people entered the vault firmly believing in a life after death; they must have felt completely secure in the close proximity of their god-prince, and immune to the dread of eternal night.

Among the other city-states which flourished in central Sumer early in the third millennium B.C. was Lagash (now Tello), city of the god Ningirsu. Lagash was only a provincial town, but since a number of clay tablets were discovered there we know a little more about this particular place. The citizens spoke Sumerian; they were cattle breeders, fishermen, merchants or artisans. Like every other city in Mesopotamia, Lagash was built around its temple. Its citizens cherished their freedom, owned property, and obeyed their city-god and his priesthood only to the extent that was necessary for maintaining the public water supply, the drainage system and other utilities.

About 2500 B.C. disaster overtook Lagash as foreign rulers conquered the city and overran all Sumer. It is interesting to read the clay tablets written by a contemporary historian describing the conditions which then came to prevail. The boat official took over the boats, the cattle officials took over the cattle, and fishery officials appropriated the fisheries. Any citizen who took a white sheep to the palace gate for shearing had to pay a tax of five shekels. Every divorce brought five shekels for the ruler and one shekel for his ministerial adviser. The best soil belonging to the city-god was earmarked for the foreign usurper's onions and cucumbers. Death itself became taxable, and innumerable priestly officials robbed the bereaved relatives. The whole country was teeming with tax collectors.

The palace became rich, its harem grew fat.

Then, when things were at their worst, a new ruler came to power in Lagash: the famous king Urukagina. He eliminated the many overlapping offices and priestly officials who were exploiting the citizenry. The priests once more became the servants of the god, and the city's governor, the Ensi, was again the first servant of his realm. The great king and social reformer looked after the property and well-being of all, and no doubt could truthfully say in his old age that he had really restored his people's freedom.

Unfortunately, his reign lasted less than ten years. Then, from the neighboring country of Umma, came the Sumerian ruler Lugalzaggisi. He overthrew Urukagina, destroyed much private property, slaughtered many inhabitants, pillaged the temples and founded a new empire in Uruk. But there was no weeping, no complaining. The people accepted their fate: the gods knew what they were doing.

When did the bell toll for the Sumerians? Actually they never did die. They were merely assimilated, just as the Tungus by the Chinese, or the Etruscans by the Romans. For at the zenith of their civilization, about 2350 B.C., the Sumerian city-states were succeeded by nomadic tribes of a Semitic people who had settled in the region of Akkad after their immigration from the Arabian Peninsula.

Sargon I, an historical figure of legendary fame, was the first great leader to unite these Semites, and one by one he conquered the Sumerian cities. He thus founded the Akkadian Empire, and his era, the Akkadian period, lasted from 2350 until 2150 B.C. The king now became the godhead, and the Akkadian Empire a divine kingdom. This Semitic dynasty produced a succession of extremely able men for Sargon, his sons Rimus and Manistusu, and his grandson Naramsin, were all rulers of great competence. But though the Semites conquered and ruled, it was the Sumerian culture which prevailed.

Sargon himself was the son of La'ipu the Semite, while his mother is said to have been a priestess. Indeed, what Sumerian legend relates about her is reminiscent of the Moses legend: the priestess placed her new-born child in a little wicker basket calked with clay, set it afloat on the Euphrates, and then went calmly back to her temple duties. A gardener called Akki found the little basket, and the boy later became cup-bearer to King Ur-Zababa of Kish, only to dethrone his master and make himself ruler of Kish in his stead. This done, he defeated Lugalzaggisi and exhibited him alive in a cage in front of the temple of Enlil at Nippur. Then Sargon subjugated the whole of Sumer, finally rinsing his weapons in the waters of the Persian Gulf. Before he was finished he had reached the Mediterranean and even Anatolia and founded the first large empire in world history.

But the Semitic kingdom of Akkad was in turn destroyed by a foreign people, the Guti, and in the end we are back in the city-states, and in Lagash, where a late Sumerian dynasty held sway. Many diorite statues of Gudea, the king who ruled at that time, are now in the Louvre and other museums in the world. Sometimes the prince is portrayed in a sitting posture and sometimes standing, but always he appears composed and coldly aloof, with hands folded and feet pressed firmly together. Gudea was a builder of the first order, as many cornerstones attest, and the crowning glory of his life was the new temple of Ningirsu, the city-god of Lagash.

At the beginning of the third millennium B.C., the Sumerians began to write on clay tablets, and by the latter half of the third millennium this art was fairly advanced. About fifty years ago, several thousand clay tablets dating from this period were dug up near ancient Nippur, about a hundred miles from Baghdad. Most of them are now in the University Museum at Philadelphia, and in the Museum of Oriental Antiquities at Istanbul; several hundred others, mostly bought up by dealers in antiquities in the East, are in the British Museum, in the Louvre, and at Berlin. They are an amazingly rich treasure, ranging from short textual fragments to hymns, myths, prose narratives, proverbs and fables. In a mere fifty years Sumerologists have of course deciphered only a few of the tablets. Many are smashed, but others fortunately exist in several identical versions, so that the experts could piece them together, restore them, and finally were able to read them. The whole work will take decades, but several good translations of Sumerian literature are already available.

King Ur-nammu, the founder of the III Dynasty of Ur, reunited the Sumerian-Akkadian kingdom, about 2100-2050 B.C. He was probably the first to convert a terraced temple into the towering structure we call a ziggurat. It is very likely that a ziggurat of this type gave rise to such a story as the Tower of Babel.

Professor Samuel Noah Kramer, of the University of Pennsylvania, tells us how, in 1951-52, when he was in Istanbul, he came upon an extremely interesting law promulgated by this king. F. R. Kraus, Professor of Cuneiform Studies at the University of Leyden, suggested that Kramer "read" clay tablet No. 3191 from the Nippur collection at the Istanbul Museum which Kraus at one time had reconstituted from two broken pieces. Kramer put the small sun-baked, pale-brown clay tablet, which measured a mere eight inches by four, on his desk, and after days of arduous work the scholar realized that before him lay one of the earliest laws ever found. Here we read that the king dismissed corrupt officials, introduced honest weights and measures, looked after orphans, widows and the needy, for "He who has a shekel shall not fall prey to him who has a mina [sixty shekels]." Any man who cut off another man's foot had to pay him ten shekels, while a man who broke another man's bones had to pay a silver mina. But anyone cutting off another's man's nose had to pay only two-thirds of a silver mina. Professor Kramer was right when he added that this law must have been preceded by even more ancient codices.

As the Sumerian-Akkadian peoples lost their vigor, another Semitic people, the Amorites, had been spreading their sway from a small town upriver named Babylon. Within a century they had become the masters of all Mesopotamia under a great legislator-king, Hammurabi. Again, peace and plenty were restored to the valleys of the Tigris and Euphrates.

Hammurabi reigned for forty-two years and it was under him that the supremacy of the Semites was securely established in the ancient "Land of the Two Rivers." The history of the Sumerians, however, began to fade further and further into the past, only to be brought to light again in our own century. And even as you read these lines, printed in characters which, in the last analysis, owe their existence to a Sumerian invention, the digging is still going on.

CITY LIGHTS–1000 B.C.

I came to Babylon and saw you not.
Ah, I am so sad.
From a Babylonian clay tablet

THE region that once comprised Babylonia and Assyria is today known as Iraq. This name, meaning "land of the river banks," is particularly appropriate because the country has literally been created by the rivers Euphrates and Tigris. Thanks to their alluvial silt deposits, the region produced rich harvests, flowering civilizations, thousands of cities and, in fact, marked the beginning of our Western history.

At one time the two rivers entered the Persian Gulf in separate places. But through the millennia they deposited such enormous masses of mud and pushed so much new land into the sea that their lower courses finally united to form an estuary which today lies some ninety-five miles farther to the southeast than it did in the golden age of Babylon and Assur. Anyone looking for ancient cities should not dig for them in this new ground. However, the soil "between the rivers" is so rich in buried cities, temples and art treasures, that valuable finds will be made for years to come.

Even today we have a fairly good idea of life among the Babylonians and Assyrians, *i.e.*, of an era that is anywhere between 2,500 and 4,000 years in the past. Yet, only about one per cent of all buried cities has been excavated. The remaining ninety-nine per cent are still waiting for the field archaeologist and his pick and shovel. Magnificent royal graves still slumber beneath the ground, filled with gold, jewels and precious stones. Between thirty and sixty feet below the surface there are hundreds of fortresses, towns and temples. Whole libraries wait for the scholars, who nowadays could easily read their contents if only they were unearthed. It is fortunate for us that the Babylonians and Assyrians wrote in cuneiform characters on fairly durable clay tablets; of our own literature, printed on perishable paper, not the slightest trace will have remained after 4,000 years.

As one travels through the arid desert country near the Euphrates and Tigris it is hard to realize that here cities once flourished, mighty kings reigned and gods in their temples were worshiped by hundreds of thousands of people. Today it is a land of infinite loneliness, ruled by death. Not a single pillar, not a single archway, remain standing—everything has crumbled to dust. Only the fox peers from his den and the deathly hush is broken only now and then by the plaintive howl of a jackal. No one—unless he were familiar with archaeological excavation techniques—would suspect that the secrets of thousands of human habitations are buried beneath this waste land, or that the graves underneath have remained undisturbed for thousands of years. But the plain is dotted with hills wherever one looks, and under each hill there is a town. But why under a hill?

Towns grow vertically. All the wood, stone and other material that people have amassed in one particular place, all the refuse and rubble, form a large mound when the town is destroyed or sinks into decline. But often on top of the doomed city a new one is erected, and the hill grows. That is why excavations must be conducted with the utmost care: the historical periods lie right on top of each other, the oldest layer at the bottom, and on the surface, perhaps, a modern village.

Thriving civilizations become prone to destruction once they have reached their zenith and are weakened and vulnerable. What is civilization anyway if not the breathing space between the two dominions of jungle and steppe?

When an urban civilization has reached its peak and its people no longer care for anything save their comforts, when they have become peaceable and law-abiding and are tired of the game of war, then, invariably, a race of nomads falls upon them—usually from the east—and destroys all their pomp and splendor. This rise and fall of civilizations has been going on for thousands of years.

A visitor to Babylon, some 3,000 years ago, would have seen from a distance a mighty pyramidal edifice rising two hundred feet into the air, its seven stories towering loftily above the city. The glazed bricks of its walls sparkled in the Mesopotamian sun. Directly below the pinnacle was a shrine which contained, so Herodotus informs us, a golden table and a sumptuous bed, and at night a young girl would recline there to welcome the god of the Babylonians. This structure was the Tower of Babel, which Biblical tradition has it the Babylonians originally intended to build as high as the sky (Genesis 2.4), until God in His wisdom would not sanction such a plan.

To the south of the pyramidal tower was the gigantic temple of the god Marduk, and below this temple sprawled Babylon, a city of wide thoroughfares and narrow lanes, of rubbish-strewn streets, of fetid smells mingled with the scent of myrrh, of noise and bustle, a city with bazaars and a sacred avenue flanked by one hundred and twenty brazen lions. One end of this avenue led through the famous Gate of Ishtar, which German scholars transported to the Pergamon Museum in Berlin.

The golden age of Babylon lasted, with interruptions, from about 1700 to 562 B.C., and two particularly outstanding kings marked the beginning and the end of this epoch: Hammurabi and Nebuchadnezzar. The succession of the Babylonian kings was broken early by the domination of the Kassites, a savage non-Semitic people from the mountains and steppes of eastern Iran. The Kassites overran Babylon after Hammurabi's death and thirty-six of their kings reigned altogether for 577 years over the metropolis on the Euphrates. During that period Babylon lost its hegemony over western Asia; Syria and Palestine remained independent, and the high priests of Assur made themselves kings of Assyria.

It was Hammurabi who left behind a code of laws which, though it no longer rates as the oldest, is certainly one of the most famous of its kind. He informs us that, like the Moses of our Bible, he received his laws directly from the god. On the famous diorite stele, or stone pillar, that contains his code, Hammurabi is depicted with a long beard, wearing a toga-like robe and a turban, sitting opposite the sun god Shamash who is giving him divine inspiration. Hammurabi had this massive diorite block placed in the temple of Marduk at Babylon, but later—during the twelfth century B.C.—it was carried off by the Elamites to Susa, where it was dug up by French archaeologists between 1897 and 1899. Today, the stone is probably the most valuable monument in the Louvre Museum at Paris.

Hammurabi was not only a legislator but also a fine stylist and letter-writer, a great city builder and conqueror. But he also destroyed cities, for it was he who laid Mari in ruins.

This most outstanding personality of his time reigned over the whole of Sumer, Akkad and Assyria for forty-two years, around 1700 B.C. Apart from the diorite stele, there also exists a remarkable sculpture of the king's head, done in black granite. The bearded countenance, the furrowed brow and the sharp lines about the eyes, the intelligent mouth—all these features combine to create the impression of a truly great ruler, a man of vast experience and wisdom. The ancient artists did not strive for photographic accuracy of detail. Yet even today the king's spirit speaks to us with powerful directness from the black granite, which can also be admired in the Louvre.

As for his laws, they were actually "legal verdicts" or court decisions, no longer written in the old Sumerian tongue but in Akkadian—"law and justice in the language of the country." His penal code was literally based on the principle of retaliation—"an eye for an eye." The putting out of an eye was punishable by blinding, and severe physical injury by punishment of the same order. A man who struck his father forfeited his hand. A man who boxed the ears of his superior received sixty lashes with a cowhide whip. If a doctor performed a successful operation, he got his fee, but if the patient died the physician had one of his hands chopped off. Slaves were branded, and any surgeon who removed such a branding mark without instructions from the slave's owner, also lost a hand. Furthermore, doctors were obliged to perform operations for high-ranking officials at a lower fee than for ordinary citizens. If a house collapsed and its owner lost his life, the architect was put to death. If the owner's son died, the architect's son likewise forfeited his life. Anyone who killed a strange girl had to pay with the death of his own daughter, and anyone who bore false witness or made unfounded accusations was called severely to account. Unfortunately we also read that people could be indicted for witchcraft. The accused person was forced to undergo the "water ordeal," which meant submitting to divine judgment. Hammurabi strove to protect the poor, the widows and orphans, but generally speaking his "legal verdicts" are every bit as hard as the stone on which they are inscribed.

By this time the Babylonians had already made great achievements in astronomy, mathematics and literature. They catalogued the stars, and by 1200 B.C. their system was known in the Mediterranean. By 800 B.C. Babylonian astronomers had attained sufficient accuracy to begin to give the stars positions and heliacal settings. In mathematics they adopted 60 as a unit of measure, a unit still used in modern timepieces; and their epic poems and religious poetry were being carried to the known world which was adopting their cuneiform writing.

By the time we get to Nebuchadnezzar, at the end of Babylonian history, we can recognize the first signs of decadence. This king ruled over the entire known world as far as Egypt, and made Babylon one of the wonders of antiquity. He built many palaces and temples, and, using the waters of the Euphrates and Tigris, he built canals far inland to make the soil fertile. Even today, from an airplane, one can see the traces of the former Babylonian irrigation system, long since dried out.

Toward the end of his reign, in 562 B.C., however, Nebuchadnezzar became intoxicated with his own power. Tormented by delusions and insomnia, he imagined he had turned into a beast. Bellowing, he crawled through his palace on all fours, and ate grass.

His successor, Nabonidus, was no longer a warrior but a scholar. He spent his time in archaeological pursuits and studied the culture of Sumer, already ancient in his time.

The Book of Daniel in the Old Testament tells us about King Belshazzar, whose story clearly demonstrates the weaknesses and fears of a dying dynasty. When Belshazzar saw the fiery letters appearing on the wall he interpreted them as the end–and death. That very night he was murdered.

For hundreds of years the Assyrians struggled with the Babylonians for the hegemony of western Asia. A tough, hardy race, the Assyrians lived in the valley of the upper Tigris and its mountainous borders. Their pillagings, burnings and massacres belong among the bloodiest chapters in the history of mankind. King Sennacherib, for example, razed eighty-nine towns and eight hundred and twenty villages to the ground, carrying 208,000 prisoners off into exile.

He fought a bitter battle for Babylon, captured the city, and burned it down to its foundations. Men and women, young and old, he slaughtered them all–until the corpses lay piled so high in the streets that any would-be fugitives found themselves trapped before the city was set afire.

The Assyrians were a peculiar-looking people who wore great beards and long, ringleted hair, tall conical hats and long robes. In all history few peoples were more dedicated to bloodshed than they. Their kings were generals, their nobles were warriors, their only interest was war. The little culture they possessed they borrowed from the Babylonians and their main contribution to man's knowledge and progress was their preservation of much of the "literature" of ancient Babylon in the royal libraries of her kings. Through most of their history they warred continually with the peoples surrounding them–not only with the Babylonians but also the Hittites to the west, and even with the Egyptians against whom Sennacherib led a mighty army that was decimated by pestilence (a disaster described in the Bible in the Second Book of Kings). They developed the military arts to a very high degree and became merciless conquerors who extorted vast tributes from their victims. Under Shalmaneser I, they conquered Babylon about 1300 B.C., but their hold on the older city was not secure and for the next few centuries power swayed between Nineveh and Babylon as to which should rule the Mesopotamian world.

It was in the middle of the eighth century B.C. that Tiglath-Pileser III founded the so-called new Assyrian empire when he reconquered and ruled Babylon. Under this king, his son Shalmaneser, the usurping Sargon II who first armed the Assyrians with iron weapons, and, above all, under the mighty Sennacherib II the Assyrian empire was most powerful, although it reached its greatest extent, even including Lower Egypt for a time, during the reign of Sennacherib's grandson, Ashurbanipal.

The second Assyrian empire lasted only a brief century and a half before fresh Semitic wanderers from the southeast, the Chaldeans aided by the Indo-European Medes and Persians, conquered both Babylon and Nineveh (the latter fell in 612 B.C.). The last Assyrian army was wiped out at the Battle of Carchemish in 606 B.C. But this Chaldean, or second Babylonian, empire with its capital at Babylon was itself short-lived, and in 538 B.C. the Persian armies of Cyrus the Great spelled the end of the Semitic dominance of the Tigris-Euphrates valley.

The Assyrians were in most ways a self-contained people, preferring their cold stone capital of Nineveh even after they had conquered Babylon. Of all their kings only Ashurbanipal, who received a Babylonian instead of a military Assyrian education, was a truly learned man.

History is usually passed on to us at second hand, which is why it so often seems dry and uninspiring. In the case of Babylonia, however, we have an eyewitness account: Herodotus the Greek lived about 450 B.C. and saw the city of Babylon only 150 years after the death of Nebuchadnezzar. We know that Herodotus was inclined to embroider the facts, but his descriptions do have the merit of direct—if occasionally exaggerated—experience. According to him the city wall was fifty-three miles long, and wide enough on top for a team of four horses to be driven easily on it. Through the center of the city, bordered by palm trees, flowed the Euphrates, spanned by a number of bridges. There was even an underwater tunnel leading from one bank to the other. Large numbers of bricks were found in the ruins of Babylon, for, like the Sumerians, the Babylonians built largely with clay, while the Assyrians used stone. In ancient times, bricks were marked with the name of their royal builder, and many of Babylon's bricks are marked "Nebuchadnezzar, King of Babylon." It was under him that the city had its last flowering before the Persians conquered it.

Herodotus also tells us about Queen Semiramis of Babylon about whom even in ancient times so many fables and legends were spun that it is nowadays difficult to distinguish between fact and fiction. Some scholars have expressed doubt that this Chaldean princess even existed. On the other hand, how could the Greeks have counted her famous hanging gardens among the seven wonders of the world if Semiramis herself was but a legend?

Semiramis is the Greek version of the Babylonian name "Shammuramat," and a pillar discovered in 1909 describes Shammuramat as "a woman of the palace of Shamsi-Adad, King of the World, King of Assyria..." The inscription proves that Shammuramat enjoyed a unique position and that she survived a change of government. She lived about 800 B.C., and probably conducted a military campaign against the Indo-European Medes, as well as against the Chaldeans.

So much, apparently, for the facts. Legend, as usual, knows more. The princess, it is said, was a Mede who could not get used to the burning sun of Babylon, and yearned for the mountains of her northern homeland. She therefore had heaps of earth piled on the upper terrace of her palace for many kinds of plants and flowers. Even the tallest trees could take root, and the entire airy botanical gardens were supplied with water pumped up from the Euphrates by machines concealed in the supporting pillars and kept working day and night by slaves. It was there, high above the city in the shade of her trees, that the princess sat, an imperious lady attended by the women of the harem.

Babylon was well lit at night, for the Babylonians had already discovered how to extract petroleum from the Mesopotamian soil. And Babylon must have had its garden suburbs. For example, let us quote from a letter sent to King Cyrus of Persia in 539 B.C.: "Our property seems to me the most beautiful in the world. It is so close to Babylon that we enjoy all the advantages of the city, and yet when we come home we are away from all the noise and dust."

In spite of all this—or perhaps because of it—slavery existed in Babylon as, indeed, it did everywhere else. The purchase price of slaves was fixed according to age and ability, but female slaves were cheaper than male slaves. Masters often handed slaves over to their creditors, to have this human property returned when the debt was paid. Debtors could also "hire out" their wives or sons until their indebtedness was worked off. Persons could be slaves for several reasons: because their parents were slaves; because they were prisoners of war; as a form of punishment, or because they voluntarily sold themselves. Slaves were completely in their master's power: their labor, their property and their children were all at his disposal. He could sell them and punish them, but he was not allowed to kill them. Most slave-holders also had children by their female slaves, and these children remained slaves until their father died, when they became free. However, they could not inherit anything from their father unless he had publicly declared them to be his legitimate children during his lifetime.

It was considered proper for a slave owner to look after the feeding and housing of his slaves, to pay their doctor bills and provide for them in times of unemployment and old age. And it sometimes happened that slaves whose services had won them particular favor with their master were manumitted. But only very few achieved this dubious distinction, fraught with the hazards of economic insecurity. Actually most slaves were fully reconciled to the loss of their freedom; they bore their lot like people who had never known any other, and did not even regret that their children were born as slaves. In the course of time these apathetic and underprivileged masses grew larger and larger; as they became more educated they also became more recalcitrant and menacing, particularly in times of external danger.

The Babylonians solved the problem of arranging marriages so ingeniously, according to Herodotus, that it almost deserves to be copied today. On a given day, all marriageable girls were gathered in the market place. A crier bade them stand up one by one, and auctioned each in turn. The most beautiful was the first to be sold, and naturally brought the most money. Then came the second most beautiful, and so on, down to the ugliest. The proceeds were placed in a chest, and when the first half of the auction was over, each man who was willing to marry an ugly girl received a "dowry" along with her. The uglier the girl, the more money for her future husband. To quote Herodotus: "In that way, the beautiful girls secured a man for the ugly and deformed ones." He closes this interesting chapter with the words: "This, then, was their wisest custom."

But now, as Herodotus puts it, we come to "the Babylonians' most unattractive practice." Every girl in the land was obliged, at least once, to sit in the temple of Malitta and "accommodate" a complete stranger. The daughters of the well-to-do drove to the sacred grove in closed carriages, taking their women servants along. All the girls seated themselves in neat rows, separated by paths going in all directions. "Then the strangers strolled by and picked out the one they wanted." The first man who tossed a coin into a girl's lap could take her with him. After that, she was consecrated to the goddess, went home and never did it again, as Herodotus puts it, unless she got married. "Girls who were pretty and shapely soon went home. But the ugly ones had to stay a long time before they satisfied the requirements of the law. Many sat in the sacred grove for as long as three or four years."

Some of the clay tablets that were found contain love poems, songs and letters engraved in cuneiform script, and one of them has an amazingly up-to-date ring about it: it reveals the yearning and loneliness of a young heart in love. A young man has arrived in the vast, cruelly impersonal city, only to find that she, Bibiya, is not there.

To Bibiya. May the god Shamash and the god Marduk forever endow you with good health. I sent a messenger to inquire of your whereabouts. Please tell me how you are. I have come to Babylon—and saw you not. Ah, I am so sad.

What a tender ring there is to the first lines of this love song found at Assur: "I brought a girl hither. Her heart was like a stringed instrument. I thought of you—tonight." And what did the lovely girl look like whom the poet had in mind when he wrote: "You came to the gate, light of mine eye. Until this evening! Until tonight!"

FIRST-RATE SEWING NEEDLES—4,600 YEARS OLD

In prehistoric times Egypt looked considerably different. Whereas nowadays it is one of the most arid and treeless regions in the world, in the past there was still a good deal of wooded country, and large stretches of territory, especially in Lower Egypt, must have been almost like a jungle.

Alexander Scharff

THIRTY dynasties reigned in Egypt between about 2850 and 332 B.C., when Alexander the Great conquered the country. The famous German historian Eduard Meyer put the founding of the I Dynasty at 3200 B.C., while the German scholar Scharff, the Englishman Hall and other historians, date the start of Egypt's history from 3000 B.C. More recently, scholars are inclined to believe that Menes, the first king of the I Dynasty, ruled in 2850 B.C., and that this date marks the beginning of Egypt's amazing three thousand years of history. In this context the term "history" is rather arbitrary. There is clear evidence of Egyptian cultural achievements that go back even 2,000 years earlier.

Long before the official beginning of Egyptian history—15,000, 20,000 or even 30,000 years earlier—man lived on the high ground along the Nile, which then flowed through a marshy valley. What this man looked like we do not know, but we do know the tools he used. The tools of the Paleolithic period, the oldest stone implements known to mankind, that were found in the Nile valley or its neighboring deserts are similar to all those found in the whole of North Africa and Western Europe during the same period. Homo sapiens, 30,000, 50,000, or even 80,000 years ago, seems to have had a common civilization, regardless of whether he lived in Europe or Africa—a kind of unity which mankind has never again achieved.

During the mid-Paleolithic period—we are still in an age which lies about 15,000 years in the past—man developed a technique of chipping hand tools from flint, which is characteristic of the whole large region of North Africa and Egypt.

During the late-Paleolithic period, between 12,000 and 5000 B.C., the puzzling and still unexplained cultural unity in the Mediterranean area disintegrated.

Fireplaces of burned earth and "kitchen refuse" from this period were found along the former banks of the Nile and near prehistoric lakes. Fish bones, animal bones, shells, ivory and ashes were dug up. Stones hollowed out for corn grinding reveal that 10,000 years ago in Egypt, man was already making flour. He knew how to till the soil and harvest grain. He used the bow and arrow, as is proved by many arrowheads of stone, ivory and bone. But it appears that the early inhabitants of Egypt did not yet manufacture earthenware vessels.

In the Neolithic period, roughly between 5000 and 3000 B.C., man turned more and more to agriculture; he began to breed cattle, build houses, make pottery and weave cloth.

About 5000 B.C., there occurred a strange natural phenomenon. The land bordering the Nile began to dry out, and now man was forced either to succumb to nature or to become inventive—to create a civilization. Thus, in Egypt, nature made great demands upon the ingenuity of homo sapiens from the very start. For, once he left the drying banks of the river and settled in the Nile valley, he had to provide for the irrigation of his arable land. He had to fight floods, build dikes and canals. And so the powerful, capricious Nile compelled the weak human being to develop his natural gift for organization. Here the river introduced him to civilization a good deal earlier than elsewhere in the world. In fact, we may generally say that large rivers and their valleys apparently have always been the best teachers of humanity.

Neolithic graves found near Tása in Middle Egypt show that even the Egyptians of this prehistoric period believed in a hereafter, an existence similar to their daily life on earth. A dead man rested on his left side in an oval pit, with his knees drawn up, in a fetal position, as if he were sleeping in the womb. His head pointed south and his face was turned west. The body was wrapped in hides, mats or cloth, and the head was often supported by a leather cushion. His grave contained brown and gray-black bowls filled with food and drink, little palettes of alabaster or slate for rouge and eye makeup, ivory bracelets, necklaces, tiny cosmetic spoons, mortars for grinding grain, polished stone axes, stone knives, stone saws, and so on.

It is true that the broad skulls and jawbones of the Tása people distinguish them anthropologically from the later, historical Egyptians. But nevertheless it seems that the ideas about death and a hereafter, which became a part of Egypt's early culture—the ideas about permanent preservation which turned the Pharaohs into pyramid builders—stem directly from this dark dawn of prehistory.

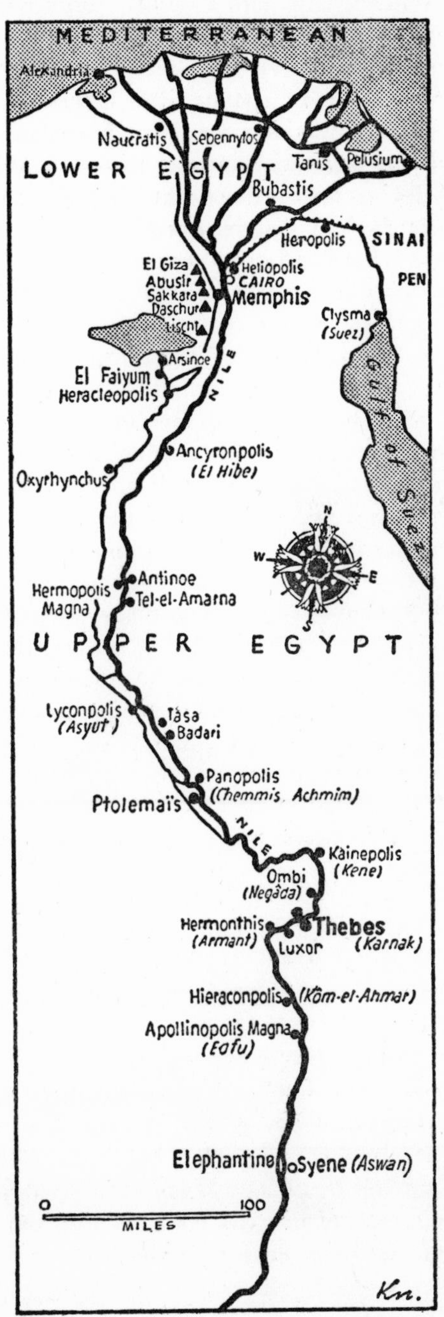
MEDITERRANEAN
Alexandria
Naucratis
Sebennytos
LOWER EGYPT
Tanis
Pelusium
Bubastis
Heropolis
SINAI
PEN
El Giza
Abusir
Sakkara
Daschur
Lischt
Heliopolis
CAIRO
Memphis
Clysma
(Suez)
Gulf of Suez
Arsinoe
El Faiyum
Heracleopolis
NILE
Ancyronpolis
(El Hibe)
Oxyrhynchus
N
W
E
S
Antinoe
Hermopolis
Magna
Tel-el-Amarna
UPPER EGYPT
Lyconpolis
(Asyut)
Tâsa
Badari
Panopolis
(Chemmis Achmim)
Ptolemaïs
NILE
Kainepolis
(Kene)
Ombi
(Negâda)
Hermonthis
(Armant)
Thebes
(Karnak)
Luxor
Hieraconpolis
(Kôm-el-Ahmar)
Apollinopolis Magna
(Edfu)
Elephantine
Syene (Aswan)
0
100
MILES
Kn.

In 1925, the indefatigable efforts of the archaeologists Gertrude Caton Thompson and G. Brunton at Badari brought to light a civilization dating from at least 4,000 B.C. advanced enough to bake clay pots in kilns and carve combs and spoons from hippopotamus tusk. These people were mainly hunters although they practiced agriculture in a primitive manner, and were acquainted with copper and gold, although they apparently did not know those metals could be melted and cast. They buried their dead in shallow graves in the sand and furnished them with weapons, food and drink, but with the bodies in a crouching position, unlike later Egyptians who buried corpses prone. The team even unearthed statuettes of women, the companions of the dead. But the civilization of Badari reached its perfection in the art of making jewelry. Here, for the first time, we find the technique of quartz cutting which later became so important for the Egyptian glass and faïence industries. But the Badari civilization teaches us more: it shows that the people of Middle Egypt were already in contact with Central Africa. Ivory was imported from the south and from Nubia, shells from the coast of the Red Sea, turquoise from the Sinai Peninsula.

Further excavations in the north, in Lower Egypt—carried out by E. W. Gardner and Gertrude Caton Thompson since 1925 at El Faiyûm, and by Junker and Menghin at Merimde-Benisalaam since 1928—have produced bone needles and fishhooks, ladles, spoons and jewels. Dwelling places were at that time made of wickerwork, wood and reed mats, and frequently of circular shape. The people buried their dead in "grave dwellings" above the ground, and shared their daily meals with them.

Between 3500 and 3000 B.C. there flourished the first Nagada civilization, named after the site of its discovery at Nagada in Upper Egypt. Here were found copper articles in the shape of a fishhook or a harpoon; also polished red ceramic ware with white ornamentation and drawings of people, animals, birds, ships and trees.

Even finer are the ceramics of the second Nagada period, also known as the Gerzeh period (after another archaeological site), which lasted 3000 to 2600 B.C. Now we find molded groups of people, beasts fighting, birds on trees, crocodiles, gazelles and giraffes; also, flatheaded copper axes, copper basins and some first-rate sewing needles, quite like the ones we use today! Among the most exciting finds were bowls with spouts, similar to the pitchers found during the same period in Mesopotamia, cylinder seals decorated with animal friezes, jars with corrugated handles molded onto each curved side, and vessels shaped like animals. All of this points to a contact between Egypt and Mesopotamia in the early part of the third millennium B.C.

At Hieraconpolis a tomb was found which measured eight by six and a half feet, and was divided into two parts. The first probably contained the body of the deceased, while the other housed various articles for his use. The walls of the chamber were decorated with river, hunting, battle and dancing scenes, very similar to those found on predynastic vases.

Many ancient royal graves have been found dating back to the close of the Nagada period. They are large, flat, four-cornered constructions of mud brick with slanting walls. A burial shaft leads down from the surface through the rocky floor into the subterranean chambers. It is certain that these graves were developed from their Neolithic prototypes. Nowadays, native workmen call these benchlike grave mounds "mastaba," an Arabic word meaning "bench." It is in such graves that the kings of the I and II Dynasties were buried: Horus Ahai, Horus Zer, Zer's wife Merjet-Neith, Horus Wadjet, Horus Kaa—in fact, most of the early Pharaohs known.

Let us digress for a second to explain the meaning of the prefix "Horus" to a king's name. In prehistoric times, Horus was the chief god of Upper Egypt, and the Nile delta had already been conquered by the rulers of Upper Egypt. From then on, the Pharaohs called themselves Horus, being the incarnation of their principal god. Thus god and ruler became identified. The symbol of Horus was a falcon.

The earliest historical figure in the Egyptian realm, and the founder of the I Dynasty, was Pharaoh Menes. This king is not a mythical figure, but his original name was not Menes. He was known by a glorifying epithet meaning "The Eternal," which caused this confusion about his identity. Menes lived about 2850 B.C., and it was he who unified Upper and Lower Egypt. He probably founded Memphis, and we also know that he conquered Lower Egypt from the south. A grave found near Negada has been attributed to him.

Two other prominent personalities of this general period in Egyptian history were Pharaoh Zoser, first king of the III Dynasty, and a scholar named Imhotep. The latter was an architect, a doctor, priest, magician, author, a composer of epigrams, and above all, Zoser's personal adviser. He lived about 4,600 years ago, and must have designed the plans for Egypt's oldest large monument, Zoser's step pyramid at Sakkara.

What is this step pyramid, and how did Imhotep the master-builder, or Pharaoh Zoser, conceive of erecting a "pyramid" from blocks of stone piled one on top of the other in tiers?

WHERE DOES PHARAOH SEKHEM-KHET LIE BURIED?

On his empty sarcophagus was a branch of giant fennel.

BENEATH the escarpment of the western desert, not far from Cairo, lies the village of Sakkara, whose inhabitants are descended from the people of Memphis, Egypt's earliest capital which lay directly across the Nile. The step pyramid of Sakkara stands high on the plateau, like a queen, near her much smaller sisters from later periods. Like all the pyramids, the one of Sakkara looks yellow-brown, but it differs from the others in one important respect: its walls are formed by steps. Before the time of Zoser, a ruler's grave was a large rectangular massif of bricks—the structure which the Arabs call a mastaba. Hence Zoser's towering construction of six such "benches" is not so much a pyramid proper as a step mastaba. The entire huge monument was built for Zoser by Imhotep during the nineteen years of the king's reign.

Zoser and his four successors are the Pharaohs of the III Dynasty. Zoser himself reigned about 2600 B.C, and he was the man who built the first vast stone monument in the world. Until his day, mud bricks were the only building materials people used.

In appearance, a pyramid is a colossal burial mound built of stone. Yet the pyramid and the whole grave precincts are far more than this: they are a reflected image of the city where the Pharaoh lived. Thus Zoser's tomb is a small scape reproduction of Memphis, his royal seat in the valley below. What down below was built of mud, wood and reed mats, here in the desert was built of stone.

This, then, is what distinguishes the great Zoser from all his predecessors: he was the first Pharaoh who tried to build a pyramid. The step pyramid was only a part of the grave: a tremendous wall enclosing government buildings, courtyards for festivals, vast store chambers, a second grave and a sacrificial temple—all this comprised the dead king's residence.

The step mastaba of Pharaoh Zoser today lies among thousands of other graves. He still rules over his dead subjects, in a land of the dead amid deathly silence.

Not too long ago, an aerial photograph revealed the outline of another burial precinct near Zoser's step mastaba in the desert sand.

These aerial photographs are the archaeologist's X-ray pictures. Especially after a rainfall they show the mysterious contours of cities, walls and graves long buried. For thousands of years two vast rectangular mounds had lain in the desert. But it was not until 1951 that Dr. Zakaria Ghoneim, Chief Inspector of the Antiquities Service at Sakkara, started excavating this new site.

Zoser's immediate successors reigned only for six years each. The Pharaoh who built the grave precinct discovered in 1954 did something very peculiar. At first, he followed Zoser's example and erected a step pyramid. When he had reached the third tier, however, he changed his mind and stopped short. He obviously did not want to lie beneath a mere mound, like the shepherds and nomads of Upper Egypt, but preferred to be buried in a regular house, like the peasant-kings of the Lower-Egypt delta. Therefore he filled in the whole area bounded by the perimeter wall, up to the third tier. In the process, he also covered a portion of the wall itself, namely, the long side to the north, and extended his grave beyond it. Thus he created a colossal mastaba, whose dimensions were roughly 760 by 215 yards. This area is vastly larger than that of the Cheops Pyramid, which is only 260 yards square.

The first surprise of Zakaria Ghoneim's excavations was the buried portion of the wall he discovered: it had been preserved unaltered and undamaged, just as it was when first built, 4,550 years before.

At about the same time, Ghoneim uncovered three of the slanting walls that once were part of the original step mastaba. These were now below the desert level: 4,000 years of wind and weather had completely covered it with drift sand. The great problem now was to find the entrance to the subterranean chamber beneath the mastaba massif. The burial chamber had to be somewhere in the depths below the immense earthwork. But where?

In the winter of 1953-54 Ghoneim finally discovered, about 130 feet north of the mastaba massif, a passage which led downward through the rock. This discovery was in itself an immense achievement, for the ground area is vast, and the passage or tunnel is but a small slanting crack in the monumental construction. However, it must be remembered that only 500 yards away lies Pharaoh Zoser's burial ground, the step mastaba whose familiar ground plan could serve as a guide to the investigation of the new grave. And just as Zoser's step mastaba provided his successor with a model, it now helped the archaeologists in their work.

Ghoneim began by clearing the passage into the burial chamber, being interrupted only when part of the ceiling caved in and killed one of his workmen. Deeper and deeper into the rock face burrowed the archaeologist, until he reached a depth of more than 120 feet. At last he came to the burial chamber. An uncomfortable, clammy heat was down there, but in the middle of the vault stood a massive sarcophagus of solid alabaster.

Two circumstances were noted right away: first, the sarcophagus was not in the exact center of the vault; secondly, it stood at a slight angle. Did this indicate that the sarcophagus might be empty? Certainly the ancient Egyptians were extremely meticulous in such important matters as their burial cult.

The fact that the sarcophagus was closed caused great surprise since nearly all royal sarcophagi hitherto discovered in Egypt had been forced open and rifled. Out of hundreds, only very few were found intact, as, for example, those of Tutankhamen, Osorkon, Psusennes and Queen Hetepheres.

On Saturday, June 26, 1954, the massive lid of the 15-ton alabaster sarcophagus was loosened. Anxiously the scientists peered through the first crack into the interior. Then they shone flashlights inside. The sarcophagus was not only empty, but immaculately clean. There was not the slightest trace of any object inside.

How was this to be explained? Was the Pharaoh buried elsewhere? Was this merely a sham grave? Certainly this was possible, for the Pharaohs of that period used to build one grave each for Upper and Lower Egypt, just as Zoser had done a while earlier.

Now we come to a find that brings the time of this particular Pharaoh uncannily close. We do not know what took place in this burial vault, but the people who lingered down there 5,000 years ago left a curious momento: the remnants of a large branch. After 5,000 years it has decayed to the point of disintegration on touch, but botanists have clearly established that it came from a giant fennel (*ferula*), a thorny plant yielding a kind of resin for medicinal purposes, which may well have been used in the embalming process.

Why should there be a branch on the empty sarcophagus? Perhaps the burial was merely symbolic. Perhaps the Pharaoh continued to reign and was eventually buried in another tomb.

There is an unfinished look about the interior of the whole grave, a hint of improvisation and inexplicable haste. One is automatically reminded of the brief reign of the Pharaoh. But *which* Pharaoh?

We know the most important title of the Pharaoh who built these burial precincts, for some clay jug stoppers found in the new vault all bore the same title: Sekhem-khet.

And here is another remarkable fact about this 5,000-year-old greeting from the beyond. The title of Sekhem-khet was completely new and unfamiliar to us, although its form and composition clearly place it in the III Dynasty. For example, Zoser's title was Neter-khet, the word "khet" in both cases meaning "body."

We may assume that Sekhem-khet was Zoser's successor and that he died in 2575 B.C., which would explain why his tomb is so close to, and shares certain features with, that of Pharaoh Zoser. If all this is correct, the king whose title is Sekhem-khet would have been called Zoser-Atoti, for this follows Zoser's in the tables of Egyptian kings.

As in all pyramids, the chute or ramp down which the sarcophagus was originally transported into the vault was sealed in two places by stone blocks. In front of one of these obstructions, deep in the rock, the scholars found a small jewel case. The case itself had crumbled to dust, but the jewels were intact: twenty-one golden bracelets, a golden necklace, a pair of golden tweezers and a golden sea shell. The two halves of this shell, beaten out of pure gold, fit perfectly and are joined by a hinge. Certainly this shell represents the most beautiful example of earliest Egyptian goldsmith's art, the most enchanting as well as the oldest product of such craftsmanship in the world. Its incredibly delicate filigree work must make it the finest exhibit in the Cairo Museum. The shell has a diameter of four and a half inches.

Who was the queen, or delicate princess, who carried this trinket? Who was the graceful woman who used the shell as a little container for jewels, perfumes or cosmetics? And how strange that such a find should have been made precisely here, in a passage leading to an empty sarcophagus! The shell, like the branch of fennel, would seem to indicate that a king *must* be buried here somewhere—or perhaps a queen.

Explorations and research will continue for years to come, but we shall probably never fathom all the mysteries of this remarkable tomb.

ETERNAL SUN–SOURCE OF LIFE

And this civilization was once alive, sustained by beating hearts and rooted in the human soul, springing from true faith, and for that reason so strong and sublime. For where there is no seed nothing can grow.

WITHIN an incredibly short space of time the Egyptians learned how to shift the most gigantic stone blocks ever known in the entire history of architecture, and how to erect their amazing pyramids. A mere fifty years separate Pharaoh Zoser's, who built the huge step mastaba–the earliest monumental stone construction in history–from the Pharaohs who reared the great pyramids at Giza. In this brief period the Egyptians abandoned brick and became master-builders in natural stone such as the world has never seen before or since. In less than a hundred years Egypt's twin cult of the god-Pharaoh soared from the level of the desert, from the slab graves and unpretentious mastabas, to Zoser's miracle structure and the summit of the Cheops Pyramid, almost 500 feet high. From then on, the pyramids diminished in size.

Facing Old Cairo, across the Nile, is the village of Gisa. Nearly five miles to the west, on the edge of the desert, three pyramids, lonely and enormous, reach into the deep blue sky. These world-famous tombs were erected by three Pharaohs: Khufu, Khafre and Menkaure. Khufu means "khnum," or "protect me." Khafre translates as "The sun god [Ra] rises aglow." Menkaure means "Eternal is the essence of Ra."

During a visit to Egypt, the Greek historian Herodotus inquired about Pharaoh Khufu, who even then had been dead for 2,000 years. In the vernacular, the king's name sounded like "Cheops" to the visitor, which is why Herodotus calls him by that name. Khufu placed his pyramid near the precipitous northeastern edge of a rocky plateau. Khafre's stands further to the southwest, on higher ground. The third pyramid, that of Menkaure, is the smallest.

"All the world fears time, but time fears only the pyramids," so says an Arabic proverb.

Those who visit these pyramids would do well to reflect that Herodotus, the "father of history," once stood here in 450 B.C., gazing in wonder at these titanic monuments; that Mark Antony strolled here with Cleopatra; and that Julius Caesar, Emperor Septimius Severus and Napoleon all stood here, too. Two thousand years are as nothing, and 4,500 years like a mere second in the evolution of mankind. It is as if the ancient Pharaohs and the modern Caesars, who lived during that breath of time we call "history," were shaking hands. The mighty Pharaoh Cheops, Herodotus the Greek with his all-encompassing imagination and gift for observation, the unbending Emperor Severus and the ambitious little Corsican—are they not all of one family with you and me, when we consider the 30,000, 50,000 or 80,000 years of prehistorical past which the people on the banks of the Nile can look back on? For the pyramids were built only 4,500 years ago, when the first homo sapiens who shaped a chisel out of flint was already "old."

Half lion, half king, the legendary Sphinx crouches motionless on its limestone base to the right of the road leading from the valley temple up to the funerary temple of Khafre's pyramid. It was probably this outcropping of rock which induced the Pharaoh to hew from it the giant sculpture he had in mind. The man-beast creature gazes out over the ephemeral landscape, seeming to smile but keeping its eternal secret. The Sphinx has been painted, measured and photographed. Its total length is 230 feet, and it is more than 65 feet high. Its ear measures four and a half feet, and its mouth is almost eight feet wide. This much we know. What until recently we did not know, however, was the identity of the man who created this largest sculpture in the world. The Sphinx stands near the valley temple of Pharaoh Khafre, below and to the east of his pyramid. The latest investigations seem to confirm that Khafre himself built the Sphinx. What is the basis for this conclusion? The pyramid of Pharaoh Sahure, who reigned during the V Dynasty about 2430 B.C., provided the clue. A relief found in the adjacent temple of worship portrayed the king as a Sphinx slaughtering his enemies. If Pharaoh Sahure was depicted as a Sphinx near his pyramid, it is reasonable to assume that the Sphinx near the valley temple of Khafre depicts none other than Pharaoh Khafre himself, and that it was he who built it. Thus the great Sphinx is not an embodiment of the sun god Ra, as some authorities believe. It represents King Khafre, whose pyramid still overshadows him.

King Cheops, Khafre's father, in his desire to defeat Time itself and to build for eternity, erected Egypt's largest pyramid. One hundred thousand of his subjects had to labor continuously for twenty-three years to assure their King's eternal life. They handled no less than two and a half million huge blocks of dressed stone, some of them weighing 150 tons—when the largest modern trucks can carry only 40 to 50 tons at the most! These immense loads had to be transported to the site over large distances. Some of them were floated downriver for hundreds of miles before they were finally hauled up a series of ramps. The granite freestone quarry at Assuan lies 500 miles away.

The base of the pyramid, however, was built of stone taken from the surrounding country. Today we cannot visualize the effect of the pyramid's white facing which must have endowed it with an almost unearthly beauty. Imagine such glorious radiance beneath the sunny skies of Egypt! This facing consisted of snow-white limestone which was brought from the east clear across the Nile valley during the flood season. The gigantic edifice reaches a height of about 500 feet and contains just under 5,300,000 cubic yards of masonry.

Even today anyone who reads about the pyramids seems to hear the cracking of whips, the harsh commands of overseers, and the sound of curses and groans. But actually this is not what happened. In the golden age of the "ancient kingdom" the individual's life centered upon the god-Pharaoh figure. Through the Pharaoh, man's life had a purpose, and through the Pharaoh's continued existence after death man's life held a hope. Thus the 100,000 labored not only under the threat of the whip, but out of religious devotion, for no beating or violence could have engendered the fanaticism which freely and willingly translated the god-Pharaoh concept into stone. In those days there was no other goal, no other task, nothing that so completely absorbed the energies of the Egyptian people as the building of the pyramids. Of course there was a certain degree of coercion. The priests and officials saw to that, for the eternal city of their dead god-king was worth absolutely any sacrifice. And if the individual did break down during the work, the eternal life of the Pharaoh was nevertheless assured, and, through him, the life of the individual laborer. Thus the helpless individual could hold his own in a rounded, well-organized concept of the world, where everything had a good reason, where nothing was wasted, and where death lost its terrors. Needless to say, this constructive outlook did not last long, because throughout the history of mankind periods of irresolution, doubt and impotence have always been more enduring than the creative periods when man knew his place in the universe.

The Pharaohs never dreamed of gaining fame through their pyramids. They had no desire to be admired by posterity for their monumental buildings. They had no idea of creating "eternal architecture." But they wanted to live, to live on after their death—not just modestly and in any old style, but in grandeur and security, undisturbed and imperishable. The Pharaohs believed—and later every Egyptian came to share this belief—that the body was inhabited by a second being, the Ka. The body might die, but the Ka lived on, no matter what happened. If the Ka had no body, however, it merely rested and became inert; hence the lifeless body had to be preserved, no matter at what price, and secured against desecration and decay. This, then, was the purpose of the pyramids and their burial chambers. The embalmed body was supposed to rest there, eternal and unchanging, and the pyramids would last through the generations. Did the Pharaohs succeed in their fantastic plan?

In the passage of 4,500 years, the Pyramid of Cheops has lost some twenty-two feet in height. The wind takes its time, but it works away conscientiously, and the original surface of the huge structure has already disappeared. It was, and still is, being burned up literally by the natives who reconvert its limestone to lime. This dismantling process is going on to this day. The fellaheen are forbidden to remove any limestone from the funerary temples or the cemeteries, and stones bearing inscriptions are also protected. But limestone fragments without inscriptions may be carried off.

Anyone today who walked down the many steps to the burial chambers in the heart of the pyramids (in Cheops' case the steps lead upward) will recognize the futility of man's struggle against the ravages of time and nature. There he stands with a pounding heart in the dead, musty stillness of the vault, in the silence of the grave. At one time Cheops rested in this impenetrable darkness, shut off from the world by walls which even today cannot be shattered by bombs. The Pharaoh's granite sarcophagus is still there, but it is open—the vault was plundered and the body of the king stolen, never to be found. Other Pharaohs who, like Cheops, wished to escape the eyes of man for all time have also been torn from their graves, robbed even in death, and left to wither somewhere in the desert, where perhaps the winds bore them up to heaven after all. Still others lie in the shabby glass cases of some museum, where frightened human eyes stare at them.

Egypt's 3,000 years of history may seem an amazing achievement in the art of living, self-preservation and culture, but there are other races that exhibit the same peculiar 3,000-year rhythm. Invariably a people's history starts with the art of writing. It reaches its cultural zenith and goes through periods of foreign domination. It is defeated, assimilates with other races, and, somewhere about the middle of its lifetime—after 1,500 years or so—it enters upon an era of dictators and generals. Again, it plunges into the depths, comes back to new greatness, and ends its history after about 3,000 years. We find the historical life span among the Greeks, if we date the beginning of their history at about 1400 B.C. and the end as 1453 A.D. with the conquest of Byzantium by Mohammed II. The same applies to Europe and America if we assume that the history of Western civilization started in 451 A.D. with the Battle of Châlons, when Detius and the Romans, with their Visigothic allies, defeated Attila and his Huns, and saved the West from the barbarians of the steppes of Asia. If we accept this premise, then we are now at the halfway mark of our own historical 3,000-year cycle. We have reached the age of generals and dictators. We may expect wars and destruction, followed by a golden age. According to this theory, Europe is still far removed from her final plunge into decadence and her hour of death—we still have 1,500 years before us.

Ancient Egypt produced great rulers; some were vicious, and others benign; some were cruel, and others gentle; some Pharaohs were robust conquerors, and others men of great sensibility like Nebkaure, Sesostris I and Amenhotep IV, all of whom had a high regard for literature and art. The statue of Khafre shows a proud, fearless man with penetrating eyes. Sculptured in stone, it is now in the Cairo Museum. Khafre's pyramid is also a memorial to an inflexible will.

Then there is Amenemhet I who ushered in an age of artistic greatness, and lived about 2,000 B.C. In the twentieth year of his reign, in 1971 B.C., this wise Pharaoh made his son Sesostris I co-regent, and father and son ruled together for ten years. Amenemhet I honored Amon, the god of Thebes, by making him part of his own name. After the Pharaoh was murdered, his son Sesostris established the following principles: "Be harsh with your subjects. The people obey only those who use force. Draw close to no one unattended, and make no one your brother. Do not believe in friends. When you retire to bed, have yourself well guarded, for a man does not have a single friend in times of danger."

These sentiments have come down to us via the famous Millingen Papyrus authored by Pharaoh Sesostris. But he attributes them to his father Amenemhet.

Sesostris erected his pyramid some thirty miles south of Memphis, a little to the west of the village of Lisht. It was a brick structure whose interior was built of blocks taken from the funerary temple of Cheops. Sesostris' mummy was never found—his grave had been ransacked.

At about the same time the Egyptians built a canal from the Nile to the Red Sea—the "Suez Canal" of the pre-Christian era.

It is interesting to note that vast quantities of foodstuffs, stores and flowers were found in Sesostris' funerary temple. Similar arrangements were made for all other departed Pharaohs, but here alone these stores have remained intact up to the present day: fowl, both plucked and unplucked, sides of beef, garden lettuce, cucumbers, numerous loaves of bread, and white and blue lotus lilies. Here were found some representations of the royal butchers slaughtering and preparing oxen. A wooden statue of Sesostris, standing about two feet in height, shows the king with a red crown and a scepter, wearing a short apron that left the upper part of his body and his legs bare. The statue is so lifelike, natural and, one is tempted to say, modern, that one can only marvel at the superb craftsmanship displayed by the artists of that period, and at their talent for capturing the spirit of their models.

Every advanced human civilization is like an island in a sea of barbarity. There came a day—about 1675 B.C.—when nomadic tribes came storming out of Asia and conquered Egypt. They overran the Nile valley just as the Kassites had overrun Babylonia shortly before, just as the Romans would conquer Greece, as the Huns would invade Italy, as the Mongols would sack Peking.

Who were these conquerors? The Egyptian priest and historian Manetho, who lived about 300-280 B.C., has recorded this foreign invasion, which was followed by the empire of the peasant kings. The most complete account can be found in the writings of Josephus, although this historian unfortunately rewrote a good deal of it from Israel's viewpoint. More reliable account of the *amu*—the nomads from the city of Auaris, who plundered northern Egypt—stem from the Egyptian kings Kamosi and Ahmosi, and from Queen Hatshepsut. If the Hyksos really were *amu*, or Syrian Semitic kings, then they were probably either Canaanites or the same Khurrites who invaded Mesopotamia in 1680 B.C. and founded the great empire of the Mitanni on the Euphrates and Tigris. The fact that the Hyksos were able to conquer Egypt at all was due to the decades of anarchy which preceded their arrival.

It is a truism that as soon as conquerors have settled down in a fertile river valley they become fat, lazy and weak. Under the last rulers of the XVII Dynasty from Thebes, the Egyptians began their struggle for liberation, and at the beginning of the XVIII Dynasty the Pharaohs finally chased the Hyksos out of the country and founded a large and powerful kingdom.

One of the most prominent personalities of this era was a woman—the above-mentioned Queen Hatshepsut, who reigned from 1501 to 1479 B.C. Since all of Egypt's rulers had to be the sons of the god Amon, the idea of a female Pharaoh was inconceivable. Queen Hatshepsut solved this difficulty by declaring herself to be a man and the son of the god. She even had herself portrayed in masculine attire, wearing a beard. She adorned and enlarged the temple at Karnak, where she erected two large obelisks. She also built a magnificent funerary temple for herself at Der el Bahari, and eventually did what her father and grandfather had done before her: she had a second, secret, burial place hewn out for herself in the rocks of the sand-swept western hills on the Nile, a region which later was known as the "Valley of Kings." Sixty royal graves are carved into these rocks, and in time there arose on both sides of the Nile, at Thebes, an enormous city—that of the living on the east bank, and that of the dead on the west bank.

The half-brother of the famous Queen Hatshepsut, Thutmose III, founded an empire which extended from the Sudan to the Euphrates. The most powerful Pharaoh of his time, Thutmose was married to Hatshepsut when he was very young. She was so greedy for power that she seized the reins of government. But after a number of years she died, or was murdered, and Thutmose then erased all memory of his "beloved sister." It really looks as if this act released all his pent-up energy. He conquered the whole of Palestine and Syria, and all the countries up to the Euphrates. His sixteen years of military campaigning are recorded in stone on the walls of the temple at Karnak.

Amenhotep II was a great archer and hunter. He personally put down a revolt in Syria, and provides a startling example of the severity which the Pharaohs exercised toward their enemies. It is reported that he brought seven Asiatic kings in chains to Thebes. Six of them he hanged right away from the city walls, and the seventh was hanged later, at Napata in the Sudan. This Pharaoh seems to have been a regular daredevil, and to the authentic exploits recorded during his twenty-six years on the throne he must have added a good many which he boastfully invented. A stele standing between the paws of the great Sphinx shows Amenhotep II as a bowman.

Amenhotep III ruled after 1400 B.C., and during his reign the empire reached the height of prosperity, wealth, luxury and splendor. Thebes was then as magnificent a city as modern Paris. Goods from all over the world were sold in the markets of the metropolis, and its vast, towering temples can match even the giant buildings of the largest city.

Dozens of subject states paid tribute to the Pharaoh, and the rulers of the great Asiatic kingdoms of Mitanni, Assyria, Babylonia and of the Hittites sent their daughters to Amenhotep's harem, and considered themselves fortunate to be his friends. The temples of Thebes were bursting with gold, and the city's sumptuous villas, vast palaces and artificial lakes outshone anything the world had ever known. Amenhotep III built the temple at Luxor and the Colossi of Memnon which guarded his huge funerary temple (now completely disappeared), overlooking the plain west of Thebes.

The most interesting character among all the Pharaohs, however, was the son of Amenhotep III and his wife Tiy, who incidentally was not of noble birth. Amenhotep IV acceded to the throne in 1330 B.C. when he was just fourteen years old, and his competent mother Taia temporarily handled all affairs of state in his stead.

From his earliest youth, Amenhotep IV was an ardent worshiper of Ra, the sun god of Heliopolis. It is possible that there existed an early, long-standing rivalry between the priesthood of Ra at Heliopolis and that of Amon at Thebes. The sun god Ra was certainly older than Amon, whose importance dates only from the XII Dynasty. There was as yet no overt struggle between the two gods, both of whom had a place in the Egyptian pantheon. But Amon grew in stature because he was regarded as an embodiment of Ra. He now became Amon-Ra.*

The young Pharaoh venerated the sun god particularly in his visible manifestations as the sun's disk, or Aten. To him, Aten was

* Pre-dynastic Egyptians worshiped innumerable gods—every tiny settlement along the Nile having one or more of its own. Over two thousand of these primitive gods have been recorded, but of them a few such as Ra the sun god of Heliopolis, Horus the falcon-headed god, Amon the principal god of Thebes, and Osiris the god of the dead and his wife-sister Isis became most important. There was also Seth, the wicked god. The local gods never lost their appeal, however, even when from time to time the state prescribed the worship of Ra, Amon or Osiris, and all attempts by the priesthood to organize a single theological system proved fruitless.

the visible source of all life, all creation, growth and action. The king erected temples everywhere for his sun god, in whose honor he even adopted the name of Akhen-Aten, today known as Ikhnaton. Then, after years of tension and continuous friction with the priesthood of Amon, the Pharaoh abandoned his capital of Thebes and established his new residence near El Amarna, calling it Akhet-Aten, "City of the Horizon of Aten."

Ikhnaton composed the most beautiful poem we know in the whole of Egyptian literature:

> Lordly thou climbest the heavenly mountain of light, eternal sun, origin of life.... Thou hast created the world after thy liking. Thou gavest sustenance to all living creatures for ever. Thou apportionest to each his span of life. Thou art the pounding of my heart. All that we perceive in thy light shall perish, but thou shalt live and prosper for ever more.

We continually come across this hymn to Aten, on the walls of graves and temples and, indeed, wherever Ikhnaton built in Egypt.

One can imagine what it must have meant to the people of ancient Thebes when the Pharaoh moved away, taking his retinue with him. One can understand the fear and anger of the priests of Amon at the prospect of losing the reflected glory they had enjoyed in the king's presence. As if that were not enough, Ikhnaton ordered the god's name to be erased from all the holy places. Everything which, by virtue of belonging to Amon, did not serve Aten, was to be destroyed. Amon's name was obliterated everywhere. The state archives were combed, and the Masters of the Rolls had to make sure that the proscribed god's name was deleted from all papyrus documents. The priests of Amon lost their official positions and emoluments. Only the visible sun god could now be worshiped. It was a fury of iconoclasm such as Egypt had never witnessed before.

How did the young Pharaoh come to carry out such a fundamental reform? Was he a religious fanatic? Was the priesthood of Ra behind it all? Or his mother Tiy? Was he motivated by shrewd political considerations?

None of these speculations does justice to Ikhnaton's personality. He was the harbinger of a new era, an idealist within whom a mysterious spark of genius was at work. Thus he embodied a historical period which, on the brink of decline, nevertheless produced one last burst of creative energy. For now arose an utterly new era of artistic achievement. The products of the workshops at Akhet-Aten during

Typical Assyrian physiognomy. A thousand years before Christ they contested with the Babylonians for sovereignty of the Land Between the Rivers (Mesopotamia).

Iraqi archaeologists laid bare the foundations of this house at Eridu, originally occupied in about 4000 B.C. A raised fireplace is visible in the foreground (center), and to the right of it is a large clay oven roughly six feet in diameter. The foundations of the house consisted of mud bricks and the walls of reeds coated on both sides with clay.

A Basalt statue, about 4,500 years old, found in Northern Iraq. A cuneiform inscription on the back of the figure indicates that it portrays Dudu, the court scribe. It is among the finest sculptures of the early Sumerian artistic period.

Brewing beer in Egypt almost 5,000 years ago. Beer used to be made out of water and fermented bread. Small models like these accompanied the Egyptian dead into their graves. Height: 15¾ inches.

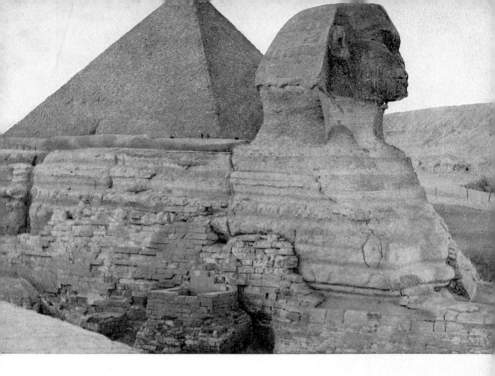

The Sphinx, a personification of Pharaoh Khafre (IV Dynasty) probably erected by himself. In the background is the Pyramid of Khufu (Cheops).

►

Ground plan of the Pyramids of Chephren (Khafre) and Cheops (Khufu) and their boats. Previous to 1954 all the boats excavated were carved from rock but in that year a large wooden boat was found.

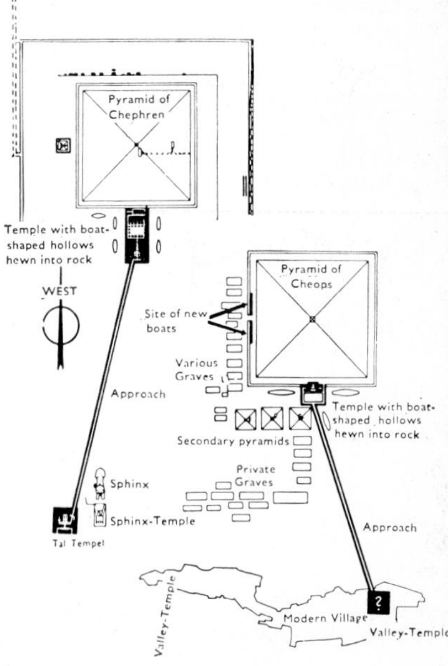

◄

Babylon shortly after its excavation at the turn of the century. In the left foreground can be seen the Gate of Ishtar. The ruins of Babylon yielded thousands of clay tablets whose cuneiform inscriptions throw light on contemporary history.

◄

The Temple of Luxor at Thebes, built by Amenhotep III between 1413 and 1377 B.C.

▲

Amenhotep IV (Ikhnaton) was only twelve years old when he married ten-year-old Nefertiti. He is here shown kissing one of his small daughters, while Nefertiti holds the other two in her arms. Pharaohs had hitherto been unapproachable in their sanctity, and it was quite a new departure for them to be portrayed with their families. This "humanization" of Egyptian art is known as the Amarna Period.

◀

130 feet below the level of the desert lies the burial-chamber of Pharaoh Sekhemkhet. His sarcophagus, hewn out of solid alabaster and weighing nearly fifteen tons, was empty. On it lay a branch of giant fennel which had almost crumbled away to dust. The stone slab (facing) could be let down.

The magnificent funerary temple built at Der el-Bahari (Thebes) by Queen Hatshepsut (1501-1479 B.C.), the wife and half-sister of Thutmose III.

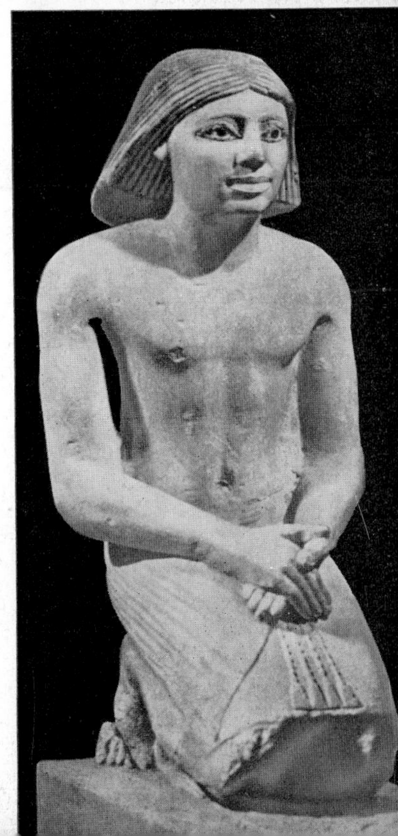

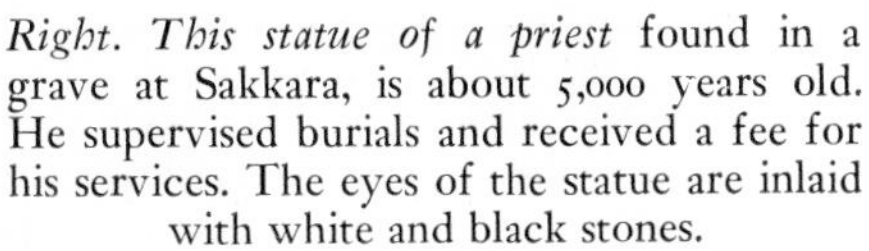

Right. This statue of a priest found in a grave at Sakkara, is about 5,000 years old. He supervised burials and received a fee for his services. The eyes of the statue are inlaid with white and black stones.

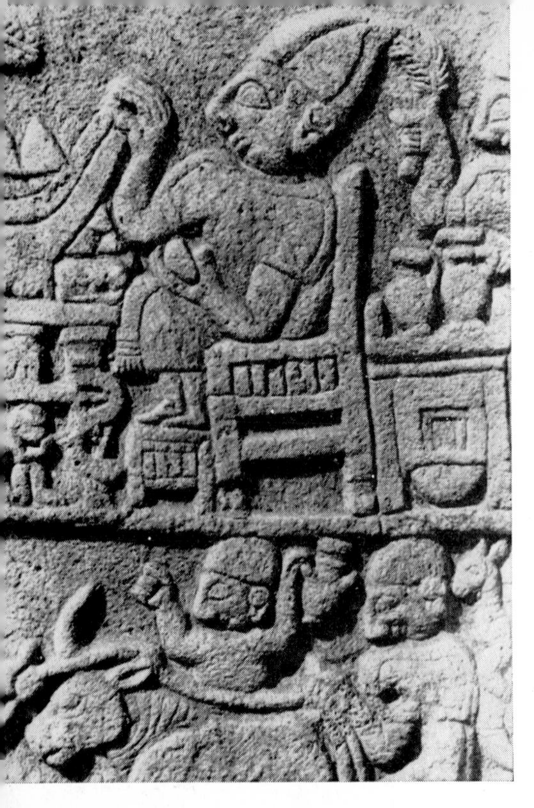

8th century B.C. *bas-relief* from a banqueting scene on one of the panels of a stele at the late Hittite site of Karatepe, excavated under the direction of Prof. H. T. Bossert. The enthroned figure is a queen or a goddess. At the upper left is a vessel holding loaves of bread. Below are two men leading an ox to sacrifice and holding a jug for the offering. © Therese Goell. By courtesy of Prof. H. T. Bossert.

Musicians in a procession attending a ceremony. This bas-relief is also a panel on a stele by the southern entrance to the late Hittite citadel at Karatepe. © Therese Goell. By courtesy of Prof. H. T. Bossert.

this period are among the finest known examples of Egyptian sculpture. We have now reached the Amarna period.

This Amarna period rediscovered Nature, enhancing and revitalizing all media of expression. Amarna humanized Egyptian art, strongly influenced by Crete, and broke many strict and hitherto inviolable laws. The Pharaoh, who had been sacrosanct and unapproachable, suddenly became a human being, whose life was, as it were, in the public domain, and who could even be portrayed performing state functions. The veil of secrecy which had screened the royal apartments of the Pharaoh's wife was lifted, and the famous Nefertiti emerged. Many portrayals of her still exist, all beautifully executed. Now the artists were permitted to be true to nature, to paint and sculpt what they really saw. That is why we possess such magnificent sculptures of Nefertiti in all her exquisite perfection, sculptures of unexcelled beauty and delicacy, painted in glorious colors.

Who was Nefertiti?

We already know that Ikhnaton's father, Amenhotep III, had several princesses of Mitanni in his harem. Mitanni was the country between the Euphrates and Tigris, in the region where the two rivers are farthest apart. It was then ruled by King Tushratta, and the Indo-European princesses he sent to the Pharaoh's court were called Tadu-Khepa and Gilo-Khepa. On the death of Amenhotep III, both princesses were taken over into his son's harem, and it is within the realm of possibility that one of them had a daughter who later became the wife of the Pharaonic reformer, and that this daughter was the world-famous Nefertiti. If this is correct, Nefertiti would have been of Indo-European descent.

Amenhotep IV was only twelve years old when he married Nefertiti, then a little girl of ten. Throughout his reign she was always at his side, sharing the burden of government. Thus she bore no resemblance to our usual conception of an Asiatic queen, whose principal duty was to remain in the harem and out of sight.

The happiness of the young couple was not destined to last. Akhet-Aten, the new royal residence (the modern Tel-el-Amarna), was from the start a city of parvenus, and nobility and tradition, property and rank all remained vested in Thebes. The king was too high-strung and weak for his immense task, and the opposition of the priesthood of Amon did not subside but grew in secrecy. What was more, the Pharaoh took absolutely no interest in foreign affairs, and as soon as the tributary countries discovered that the throne of Egypt was no longer occupied by a ruthless tyrant but by a sensitive reformer, they suspended their payments. Egypt's hegemony in the Near East began to crumble.

Ikhnaton soon became lonely as one after another of his friends deserted him. He died when he was scarcely thirty years old, in 1358 B.C. A bust of the Pharaoh found at Tell el Amarna shows a remarkably fine profile and a gentle, almost feminine face of great sensitivity and intelligence. He had large, dreamy eyes, and a decadent body.

With Ikhnaton dead, Nefertiti believed that the only way to preserve the throne for her children, and perhaps for herself, was to turn to the king of the Hittites for aid. She appealed to him to send her a Hittite prince, whom she planned to marry in order to use Hittite power to secure her own throne. Her project failed, however, for the prince was murdered on his way to the lovely queen. We do not know how Nefertiti died. In all probability her overtures to the Hittite king were regarded as high treason, and she was assassinated. The fact that Nefertiti turned to the Hittite king—a man who was an Indo-European—is in itself extremely interesting. This might well be an additional indication that she was of similar origin, namely, the daughter of one of the Mitanni princesses. Neither Ikhnaton's nor Nefertiti's mummy has ever been found.

The reign of the imaginative religious reformer was followed by a period of great confusion. First came Semenkh-ka-Re, Ikhnaton's son-in-law. But few men lived very long in those days, and shortly afterward Semenkh-ka-Re died—certainly not a natural death. His successor Tutankhamen, the Pharaoh who became world-famous through Howard Carter's excavations, was likewise a son-in-law of Ikhnaton. Indeed his original name was Tutankh-Aten, but the priesthood of Amon at Thebes forced him to change it. Furthermore, he was obliged to transfer the royal residence from Amarna back to Thebes and to renounce the cult of Aten. He, too, died early.

For decades, the Egyptologists have racked their brains for some indication of Tutankhamen's age when he died. Then when his grave was discovered, in 1922, the young Pharaoh's name swept the world. On opening his sarcophagus, Howard Carter found a second one inside which he unsealed carefully—to find it held a third, this one of pure gold. This coffin was in the shape of a man, and in it lay the young Pharaoh's mummy. At last it was known . . . Tutankhamen was a youth of no more than eighteen when he died.

The big traitor and intriguer of this period was a man named Ay, an official and priest of Amon's cult at Thebes. He had been forging his dark plans even during Ikhnaton's lifetime. He eventually managed to become Pharaoh, but he was not allowed to enjoy the fruits of his intrigue for long, for he, too, had a strong rival: Har-em-hab, commander-in-chief of the army of Lower Egypt. After four years, General Har-em-hab succeeded in assassinating Ay, and mounted the throne in his turn.*

Anyone who nowadays travels along the Nile will discover abundant evidence of one particular Pharaoh. For Rameses II was, so to speak, a mass producer. To some extent he destroyed the over-all effect because he erected too many statues of himself. An egoist and a monomaniac, this Pharaoh was so fond of building that almost half the ruins found in Egypt today originated during his reign. He completed a gigantic hall at Karnak and expanded the temple at Luxor. He built himself a vast funerary temple, known as the Ramaseum, and erected colossal statues of himself all over the country. He rebuilt the canal from the Nile to the Red Sea. He had at least a hundred wives, a circumstance less remarkable in ancient Egypt than it would seem today since most of the Pharaohs married many women. Rameses II is reputed to have had a hundred sons and fifty daughters; some of these daughters he married himself—again nothing unusual in ancient Egypt.

A mere hundred years after his death his name was anathema, and his dynasty died out on the demise of his successor. However, his mummy has survived—a fine-boned face which neither sixty-seven years of rule, nor ninety years of living, nor more than three thousand years of oblivion have materially affected.

Under his successor, Rameses III, the wealth and power of the god Amon reached staggering proportions. Amon's priests now lived in luxury. Their storage chambers were crammed, and they commanded the services of 107,000 slaves. Like many old statistics, the latter figure may be exaggerated, but it does explain what the ancients meant when they said: "There were many of them." If we put the population of ancient Egypt at five to six million, then one out of every fifty or sixty persons must have been temple property. The British Museum now contains the longest ancient Egyptian manuscript in existence, the famous *Harris Papyrus*. It is more than one hundred and thirty feet long. The

* Another theory has it that it was not Nefertiti who wrote the aforementioned moving appeal for a husband to the King of the Hittites, but rather Tutankhamen's widow Ankhesnamen in the period after her husband's death when Ay and Har-em-hab were vying for the vacant throne.

text, which is extremely well preserved, contains detailed lists of all the gifts and bequests which Rameses III made to the temples of Egypt during his reign. According to these reports Amon and his priests owned one-seventh of all cultivable land, 169 cities in Egypt, Syria and Kush, a fleet of 88 ships, 53 dockyards large and small, and 500,000 head of cattle.

In those days there were as many feast days as workdays, an arrangement which swelled the coffers of the priests of Amon. The king was reduced to a servant of the priests. The power of the king had to suffer so that the gods might live. The Pharaoh's circumstances thus had grown increasingly precarious until he was compelled to rely on an army largely composed of mercenaries.

The details relating to the attempted assassination of Rameses III—a plot, like so many others in the history of the East, whose threads were spun in the harem—are very characteristic of this period. Wishing to secure the throne for her son, one of the harem queens managed to enlist the aid of the wives of six officers of the harem guard in her plan to remove the Pharaoh, as well as the support of other influential persons. When the conspiracy was betrayed and Rameses summoned a high court to mete out due punishment, the accused harem ladies actually succeeded in visiting two of the judges in their homes and won them over. Then it was the turn of the judges to be tried. Their ears and noses were cut off, and one of the men so punished committed suicide. Thirty-two officials of varying rank received a very lenient sentence: they were permitted to take their own lives. However, the old Pharaoh did not survive all this excitement for long, and died in 1167 B.C.

These, then, were the signs of the times: domination by the priesthood, harem intrigues, treachery and foreign influence. Thus Egypt gradually began to decline. The country was invaded: by the Libyans, by the Ethiopians (or Nubians), then by the Assyrians. It was conquered by the Persians under Cambyses. Alexander of Macedon conquered it, but made it a province of Macedonia. Under Ptolemy I it was soon independent again. In 48 B.C. Julius Caesar took the Egyptian capital, Alexandria, and gave Cleopatra the son who was never to sit upon Egypt's throne. In the end, Egypt became a mere province of the metropolis on the Tiber, and the granary of the Roman Empire. A vast kingdom and three thousand years of history were virtually extinguished.

What remains is the pyramids, temples, rock graves, royal statues of limestone, alabaster and diorite, the pictures, inscriptions and rolls of papyrus. What remains is the rainless, burning sky and the annual flooding of the Nile beginning July 19, a date which the ancient Egyptians adopted as their New Year's Day. What remains is the river's fertile mud, whose color caused the ancient Egyptians to name their land "keme," or "the black one"—the same word which, via the "black magic" of the Middle Ages, developed into the modern term "chemistry." The Egyptians, too, have remained much as they always were, in spite of racial intermingling and foreign invasions. But what these people, once so abundantly endowed with artistic and creative energy, have lost is the magnificent courage, the imagination, the striving for immortality and the urge toward that elemental art which marked their great religious epochs. They lost their god, and, with him, all striving for him. They lost their faith, and, with it, their creative strength. At one time the Nile was their greatest teacher. It was the Nile which compelled them to build dikes and canals. It was the overflowing waters of the Nile which led them out of poverty into abundance, inspired them to form a society, to organize public works, and so to create a state. That was how Egyptian civilization came into being. But the floods—that whip of nature which once provided such a cultural impulse—have long lost their effectiveness with the coming of enormous power dams and their efficient machinery.

The value of Egypt's bequest to humanity, and to Western civilization in general, is well-nigh inestimable. She gave us the smith's trade, architecture, the stele, the art of stonemasonry, some aspects of the religious concept of the West, monasticism, the principles of governmental organization (some of which were assimilated by the Roman Empire), the civil service, chronology and geometry, glassmaking, fine clothing and jewelry, furniture and houses, a postal service, and medicine. All these things were passed on to us by the Egypt of the golden age when we still lived in forests and steppes. Sculpture and painting in Egypt attained heights which any other period has scarcely managed to scale again. Handed down to us via the Phoenicians, Syrians and Jews, the Cretans, Greeks and Romans, Egyptian culture has become an integral part of our lives. The astounding durability of Egyptian life once it had taken shape, the example as well as the inimitability of Egyptian art, the fanaticism and energy of Egypt's Pharaohs, craftsmen and artists, the people's devoted search for the "whence" and the "whither," the unbelievably high scale of values of what was, after all, merely a small people dwelling by a big, sluggish river—none of these things will ever again be achieved in the cultural history of mankind. Egypt provided the stage for the drama of a civilization that soared almost to the heavens and has not, even now, turned back to earth—perhaps the greatest civilization that ever flourished on our planet.

"DO NOT BE SAD WHILE YOU LIVE"

I lay abed—and I was awake.
From an ancient Egyptian papyrus.

IT IS strangely fascinating to examine the faces of mummies, as expressive in death as if they had but yesterday closed their eyes. Many mummies have waited 5,000 years for their resurrection, yet scholars have established that the soles of mummified feet 2,000 and 3,000 years old are still soft and pliable.

In death, most religions teach, the soul leaves the body. But the ancient Egyptians believed that when a corpse was buried, the soul was recalled by the officiating priest and reunited with it. Because the body had to be intact at this crucial moment, the Egyptians embalmed hundreds of thousands, even millions, of their dead—not only kings, but everyone who could afford it. Thousands of well-preserved mummies still lie in the graves of Egypt. The mummies of many Pharaohs repose in museums, but others have remained undisturbed. The body of Alexander the Great, who was embalmed in wax and honey, has not been found either.

There are three methods of preserving a dead body: by cold storage, by the modern method of injecting bacteria-killing agents into the blood vessels, and by desiccation and permanent dehydration. It was the latter method which was favored in ancient Egypt. Since three-fourths of the human body consists of water, it was not easy to dry it out completely. The Egyptians probably used fire for this purpose, or, less frequently, the heat of the sun. In the City of the Dead at Thebes, a chamber discovered inside the grave of a certain Hatiay contained a large number of mummies piled almost to the ceiling. The Egyptologist Yeivin thought that these mummies had been dried over a slow fire, an assumption which traces of soot on the walls of the vaults would appear to substantiate. According to a second theory, however, the soot stains may have been caused by brushwood fires kindled at the entrance to the burial chamber by people who had surprised tomb robbers at work: the desecrators were simply "smoked out."

There are other methods of desiccation, such as the use of dehydrating agents like chalk, salt or soda. Chemical analysis has established the presence of all three substances in Egyptian mummies, and in some graves the scholars found urns and pots filled with soda.

According to Herodotus' description, which in the main tallies with the results of modern research, the dead were embalmed in the following way:

First, the brain, intestines and stomach were removed, although the heart and kidneys were retained. The body was cleansed inside with wine and herbs, and then packed with myrrh, cassia and aromatic essences, linen cloths, sawdust, sand, soda and, occasionally, even a few onions. Chemical substances were injected into the arteries and blood vessels, and the skin of the body was anointed with oil of cedar and rubbed with myrrh and other fragrant essences. Even after several thousand years have passed, many mummies still exude the scent of these essences. The corpse was then swathed in linen cloths soaked in tar and other medicaments, while the face was often covered by a life-like mask of linen and plaster or of semiprecious stones, gold and other precious metals. The mummy was placed on its left side in a sleeping posture, its head resting on a support, and then the coffin was closed.

Specially designed embalming tables which were found testify to the care lavished on the embalming process; and these tables still showed traces of soda and salt. According to one inscription, the process sometimes took as long as ten months. In earlier times, the dead man was accompanied into the grave by all his household effects, and the grave itself resembled his house, or palace. Later, however, he was given only meat and beverages, and a miniature clay house complete with courtyard, granaries and figurines of laborers emptying sacks of grain. He was also accompanied by statuettes representing women servants who were supposed to spin, weave and wait on their master, just as they had during his lifetime. Other figurines—young girls in bright dress—brought their master his mirror or served his meals; and another woman would grind the grain. Small naked dolls, with the lower part of their legs missing, were also placed into the grave. There was a reason for this mutilation. In earliest times, the king's retinue was buried alive, along with the sovereign. Later on, these unfortunate victims were replaced by figurines which were fashioned without legs so that they could not "escape."

But the Egyptians were not only skilled in the art of preservation: they also knew how to live. Despite their funerary cult with all its superstitions, they were an extremely practical people. They combined a rich sense of humor—as shown by their brilliant caricatures—with remarkably few scruples about murder.

They amused themselves with games played on boards of twenty and thirty squares, examples of which have been found in graves. They also had a peculiar snake game, which they played on a circular board with pieces representing lions and dogs. They played dice and made fine toys for their children; they were fond of wrestling and sport. Servants and slaves often staged wrestling matches to entertain their masters, and prosperous households trained their own champions in the art of fighting with quarterstaffs. Here the opponents were not allowed to show each other mercy, and one of them was often carried out of the ring. Girls were trained in ball games and calisthenics, and artists, female dancers and musicians beguiled the time of the wealthy. They played the harp, the flute, the lute and the oriental lyre, an instrument not native to Egypt. Young girls fanned away the flies, and dwarfs looked after the household jewelry and clothing and also walked their masters' pet dogs and monkeys. Humpbacked jesters were very popular, and many a Pharaoh had his "court dwarf."

On feast days the Egyptians had themselves anointed and garlanded with flowers by their servants, and drank wine and beer, until they became, to quote a contemporary description, "like a broken ship's rudder, which no longer answers either to port or starboard." Indeed, one picture from the New Kingdom period shows an unfortunate woman of obvious social standing in the act of vomiting. A disconcerted woman servant is hurrying forward with a bowl, but already it is too late.

The Egyptians were a handsome race, whose aristocrats truly bore themselves like kings. The men were robust and muscular, with narrow hips and broad shoulders, full lips and serious, forceful expressions. Wealthy Egyptians set great store in being slim. We find many beautiful oval faces among the Egyptians, with long straight noses and wide, expressive eyes. Their skin was light at birth, but soon became so tanned under the hot Egyptian sun that artists always depicted men with reddish and women with yellowish skin, since the latter exposed themselves less often to the sun.

Fashions continued to change throughout Egypt's history, the changes being gradual, but perceptible enough to furnish clues for particular periods of history. In the Old Kingdom—about 3000 to 2270 B.C.—the men wore aprons only, and for at least 700 years (probably from time immemorial) the upper part of the body was bare. Sometimes the apron was worn short and tight; then again, as in the reign of Cheops, it became longer and wider. The apron was also draped in different styles, according to the prevailing fashion. During the Middle Kingdom, or roughly between 2100 and 1700 B.C., men wore a double apron: a tight-fitting, short one of stiff linen as an under-garment, and a longer one, of transparent linen, over it. Along with the newfangled double apron, a short, loose tunic made its first appearance. We also find a close-fitting striped robe reaching from throat to ankle and principally worn by the aristocracy. Later only the humblest servants and peasants wore the short apron, and during the New Kingdom—1550 to 700 B.C.—the men covered the upper part of their bodies.

There were of course differences in dress between the various social classes, and the lower classes—peasants, herdsmen, laborers and slaves—usually wore nothing but a short loincloth or girdle. Men who did hard work often went completely naked, for physical modesty was almost unknown. As Adolf Erman, the famous Egyptologist, says: "After all, some of the commonest hieroglyphic characters represent things which we ourselves are not exactly in the habit of depicting."

By comparison with the diversity of masculine attire, women's clothing was very monotonous. From the earliest beginnings of Egypt's history, or at least of her pictorial art, all women dressed alike in a long straight chemise which clung closely to the body and clearly revealed its outlines. This chemise began below the breast and reached to the ankles, the breasts being covered only by shoulder straps which held the garment in place. These shoulder straps were almost the sole article of female dress which was subject to changes in fashion. Sometimes they were worn straight, sometimes slanting or crossed; sometimes they covered the breasts entirely, sometimes in part, sometimes not at all; some straps were adorned with rosettes which fitted over the breasts. The chemises were usually white, less commonly red, yellow or green, and were practically always plain and unadorned. The most surprising feature about feminine fashions in Egypt, however, remains the fact that from the queen down to the poorest working girl there was little difference in dress. It was only later, early in the XVIII Dynasty, that it became *de rigueur* to wear two articles of clothing; now a flowing outer garment was added to the tight-fitting chemise. But both were made from such fine linen that the outlines of the body were clearly visible.

Women servants dressed almost exactly like their mistresses. If they did heavy work, however, they wore nothing but a short apron, like the men. Female dancers bared the upper part of their bodies and their legs, and in the New Kingdom the young girls were naked, except for an embroidered girdle about their hips, when they served meals at banquets.

The Egyptians kept their fine white linen scrupulously clean, and the washing, wringing and beating of clothes went on unceasingly under the eye of the laundry superintendents. Clothes stained by ointments and oils were cleaned by a special process, probably involving the use of soda. And one and all the ancient Egyptians went barefoot and wore sandals only if absolutely necessary.

The Egyptian aristocrat kept his hair clipped and wore either a close-fitting cap or a wig over it. Wig-making was a great art in Egypt, and the most intricate coiffures of plaits and ringlets were produced, but in many pictures one can often see where the natural hair peeps out from under the wig. Almost all the women of the Old Kingdom wore their hair long and straight, but women of the nobility who kept their hair slightly shorter occasionally were known to have it curled. The Egyptian wigs in our museums are not manufactured from human hair but sheep's wool.

The women painted their lips, lacquered their nails, and oiled their skins and hair. A variety of creams and rouges was a necessity to any Egyptian woman interested in her appearance, both while alive and in the grave. The lower eyelids were tinted with a green cosmetic made from malachite, while the upper lids and eyebrows were painted with a black preparation of lead sulphide, and the combined effect made the eyes appear larger and more lustrous. Samples of such cosmetics have been found in graves, and thus we know that they were applied with so-called cosmetic pencils—little sticks fashioned out of wood or ivory. Cosmetics were kept in small oblong boxes of ivory, stone, faïence or wood. Vast quantities of toilet articles have been unearthed: metal mirrors with handles of wood, ivory and faïence fashioned like slim, nude girls; mirrors of gold and silver with magnificent containers to match; ointment boxes of alabaster; combs, hair curlers and hairpins; powder boxes, razors and little ointment spoons made of wood, ivory, alabaster and bronze. And, of course, perfume was used lavishly in such a sophisticated civilization.

Men and women wore rich jewelry: necklaces of pearls, cornelian, malachite, lapis lazuli, amethyst and faïence; bangles of ivory, bone, horn, copper or flint; anklets; collars of strung pearls, as well as earrings. In the XIX Dynasty, the men gave up wearing large ear pendants and left them for the women to wear. From earliest times, Egyptians also wore rings of gold, silver, and blue and green faïence. The king wore a crown, and the noblemen of every Egyptian dynasty carried rods and scepters. In the field of cosmetics and jewelry there is little if anything we could have taught the ancient Egyptians.

The Egyptian aristocrats were keen sportsmen. They hunted water-fowl in boats, bringing the birds down with the throwing stick, a peculiar form of boomerang shaped like an elongated S with which they were extremely dexterous. Fowl for the kitchen were caught in outspread nets. Geese were caught in the same manner, and fattened in large hedged enclosures on country estates—pictures on the walls of graves show us the unfortunate birds being stuffed with paste balls. Curiously enough, the Egyptians also fattened cranes. Ducks and pigeons were captured in small clap nets which locked automatically.

The nobility liked fish-spearing, but fish were also caught with hand nets, baskets and dragnets. Fish were usually dried in the sun, and formed the staple diet of the poor, being cheaper than corn. Hunts were often organized for the king, the quarry including gazelle, ibex, antelope, maned sheep, deer, wild ox and hippopotamus. Wild animals were also captured by lassoing, and hyenas caught in this way were fattened, too. Thutmose III is supposed to have killed one hundred and twenty elephants in the course of a single hunt. Rameses II owned a tame lion, and an Egyptian nobleman of Pharaoh Khafre's court made much of his pair of pet baboons. Small long-tailed monkeys were also kept as pets, and tiny, dressed-up monkeys on leads were a common sight. Girls kept cats as playthings, and dogs could be found in every well-to-do household. Some murals even show Egyptians leading tame hyenas. Greyhounds were highly prized, and the dachshund was known. Even then, savage, stray mongrels roamed the streets of Egypt's cities.

We still have exercise books from Egyptian schools, although they are actually "exercise rolls," since all writing was done on papyrus which was rolled up. School discipline was very strict, and obedience was enforced by corporal punishment. Thus one pupil writes to his teacher: "You beat me. That is why your teachings have entered my ear." Then read: "The boy has a bottom. He listens when he is beaten," and: "Never be idle, or you will be thrashed."

"Paper" was manufactured by cutting papyrus plants into strips, laying them side by side, and placing other strips crosswise on top. The whole was then pressed, and produced a durable material which has in certain cases remained well-preserved and legible for 5,000 years.

The Egyptians probably became familiar with the script of the Sumerians when they first started trading with them, which inspired them to evolve a script of their own in addition to their hieroglyphs. This Egyptian script, called hieratic, was based on the use of pictures, a combination of which could be used for each word. Some words consisted of only one consonant and the accompanying vowel, others of two or three consonants. Since most Oriental writing systems use only consonants, the vowels being added only in the spoken language, it was possible to express a word of two or three consonants in terms of pictures. Thus the picture for the sacred dung beetle is used to designate, first, the beetle itself (three consonants: kh-p-r, and a given set of vowels), and also the verb "to become" (same three consonants: kh-p-r, but a different set of vowels), written by means of the beetle symbol but differentiated by a supplementary mark. An ancient Egyptian would immediately know which word was meant by the context; we would not, which is why it is difficult to decide how the Ancient Egyptian words were pronounced. Thanks to the one-consonant words we have been able to identify all the letters of the alphabet, although the Egyptians themselves never got that far. It was the Phoenicians who first collated the alphabet from the Egyptian script. This script contained no less than six hundred different symbols, each corresponding to an object.

Numerous writings have survived from the period between 2000 and 1000 B.C., for rolls of papyrus, labeled and arranged, have been found stored in jugs. These papyri contained the most remarkable adventure stories, travel diaries, fables and poems. One papyrus dating from about 1220 B.C.—the so-called *Orbiney Papyrus* in the British Museum—relates the story of an adulteress who turned two good brothers into enemies—a classic tale of jealousy and brother love and hatred. In another roll, the *Petersburg Papyrus*, we find the fascinating experiences of a shipwrecked sailor who is cast up by the stormy waves on a lonely island, where he has a strange encounter with a golden snake. The adventures of Sinuhe among the Syrian Bedouins read like an exciting modern travel story, even though the action takes place in the reign of Sesostris I, somewhere between 1980 and 1935 B.C. The complete text is preserved in a papyrus in the Berlin Museum.

Egyptian numerical notation and calculation were rather inconvenient, clumsy and slow. The Egyptians were familiar with the decimal system, however. One stroke signified 1, two strokes 2, nine strokes

9. The figure 10 was represented by a fresh symbol, derived from a curved contrivance for tethering grazing cattle. Two such symbols denoted 20 and so on up to 100, which was represented by yet another symbol. There was a new symbol for 1,000 (a lotus leaf), another for 10,000 (a finger), and another for 100,000 (a tadpole). The symbol for 1,000,000 was a man holding his hands above his head, as if he were amazed that such a large figure existed at all. In order to write a three-digit figure, people often used more than twenty individual symbols.

Multiplication was rather complicated: it was done by mentally doubling the basic figure, so that the sum 4 x 4 was reached in stages of 4, 8 and 16. Division was even more laborious, and fractions in terms of modern arithmetic were unknown. The Egyptians knew one-fifth plus one-fifth plus one-fifth, for example, but not three-fifths. For all that, the science of mathematics was highly developed in Egypt—otherwise there would have been no architectural achievements. The Egyptians observed the movement of the stars through thousands of years. Even in those days, they accurately distinguished between planets and fixed stars and recorded stars of the fifth magnitude, which are invisible to the naked eye. It was this which led to perhaps their greatest scientific achievement—the invention of the solar calendar which was passed on to us via the Romans.

Extremely interesting medical treatises have been preserved, among them two important rolls of the *Great Medical Papyrus* in the Berlin Museum and the *Ebers Papyrus*, formerly in the Leipzig Library. The Egyptians made a study of anatomy, the blood circulation and the functions of heart, stomach and spleen. They recognized that the heart "speaks in the vessels of every limb." One of the most interesting of the medical papyri, named after its discoverer Edwin Smith, is a roll about sixteen feet long and 3,600 years old containing descriptions of forty-eight surgical operations. It certainly indicates that ancient medical science clearly understood that the movement of limbs is controlled by the brain.

Egyptians were not exempt from the majority of our present-day ailments, although we come across no mention of syphilis or cancer, and dental decay seems to have appeared only during the last few centuries of Egyptian history, as a consequence of civilization. Astonishingly enough, accounts of atrophy of the little toe are found quite far back in Egyptian history, which seems to prove that this is not the result of wearing shoes since the Egyptians almost always went barefoot. Many hundreds of medicaments are listed in the *Ebers Papyrus*, one-tenth of all these being remedies for eye diseases which were probably widespread. Some of the prescriptions, such as human and animal dung, fly dirt and urine, today tend to make us shudder, but there were less repulsive remedies, like those for drawing blood out of a wound, which included wax, fat, date wine, honey and boiled corn. Whole medicine chests were found in some graves.

But apart from curing their ailments, the Egyptians also sought to preserve their health. Listen to them: "Most of what we eat is superfluous. Hence we only live off a quarter of all we swallow: doctors live off the other three-quarters." No wonder Herodotus the Greek wrote: "Next to the Libyans, the Egyptians are the healthiest people in the world."

In order to preserve the purity of the blood royal, the Pharaohs often married their own sisters. But whether or not this custom had any injurious effects in the long run, we cannot tell. In Arsinoë, marriage between brothers and sisters prevailed among three-quarters of the population until the second century A.D. Incidentally, the Egyptian mode of address between lovers was "brother" and "sister."

The Pharaoh invariably owned a large harem which included not only the daughters of the aristocracy, but also women captured on military campaigns. The great majority of Egyptians, however, practiced monogamy, and the stability of their family life is matched only by that of Christian countries. Divorce was rare, and the status of women was about the same as in our own day. There was perhaps no other people of antiquity who so honored and deferred to their womenfolk as the Egyptians. Greek travelers, accustomed to keeping the women of their native land on a short leash, were amazed to see the "progressive" women of Egypt. In fact, Diodorus Siculus, a Greek who lived in the latter half of the first century A.D., relates—somewhat indignantly—that on the Nile it was the man who was bound under the terms of the marriage contract to be obedient to his wife. Diodorus believed the woman courted the man and proposed marriage. Nor was she always particularly subtle about it, either. "Oh, my handsome friend," runs one letter, "it is my desire to become your wife and the mistress of all your possessions."

They were a hot-blooded people, these Nile dwellers. Girls were considered ready for marriage by the age of ten, and premarital promiscuity was rife. One courtesan is supposed to have built a whole pyramid from the proceeds of her amorous adventures!

The largest collection of Egyptian love poems still extant can be found on the obverse of the so-called *Harris Papyrus 500* in the British Museum. "The most wonderful thing to do is to go out into the field to meet one's lover," we read in one of them. Among the proverbs of Ptah-hotpe, chamberlain to Pharaoh Asosi about 2600 B.C., we find many a valuable precept that reminds us of the Proverbs of Solomon. This collection is preserved in the *Prisse Papyrus* in the Bibliothèque Nationale in Paris. "If a son accepts what his father says, none of his plans will go awry," we read. "When you speak, take care what you say." "If you wish to forge an enduring friendship with the household in which you are master, brother, or friend, take care to shun the women: the place where they abide is not good." "The truth endures for evermore. It goes down to the City of the Dead with him who practices it." This last passage comes from the "Story of the Eloquent Peasant," and dates back to about 2000 and 1800 B.C.

The following sentences deciphered from rolls of papyrus may serve to bring everyday life in ancient Egypt close to us for a moment. They are taken from letters, notes, jottings and the like.

Lovers longed to be always together, just as they do nowadays. And so "he" writes: "I go for a walk, and you are with me in every beautiful place, and my hand is in your hand."

One cannot help wondering what the man was thinking of when he wrote a few thousand years ago: "I lay abed—and I was awake." Or what annoyed the girl who scribbled: "Another time you need not come!"

A man called Anna addresses visitors to his tomb with the following words: "Hear ye! May ye do the good that I have done, that ye be likewise done by." And a nameless girl cries to her lover across thousands of years: "I am hateful to your heart—but why?"

A meditative poem—it is 4,000 years old—reminds us of the impermanence of human life:

"Nobody comes back from the other world to tell us how he fared. . . . Enjoy each day and celebrate. Do not be sad while you live. For see, no one takes with him what he owns, and none returns who has once departed."

And is not this a truly timeless little love poem:

"It disturbs me to hear your voice. My whole life hangs on your lips. To see you is better than all food and all drink."

ANATOLIA

THE HITTITES

"*Therefore the queen of Egypt . . . sent a messenger to my father and wrote to him thus: 'My husband died. A son I have not. If thou wouldst give me one of thine, he would become my husband. Never shall I pick out a servant of mine and make him my husband! I am afraid!' When my father heard this, he called forth the Great Ones for council saying: 'Such a thing has never happened to me in my whole life!'*" From *The Deeds of Suppiluliumas*, as told by his son Mursilis II (translated by H. G. Güterbock, Oriental Institute, University of Chicago).

THERE are many vanished races in the world whose names we know, but whose history and culture are still a mystery to us. Some 4,000 years ago, on the Anatolian plateau in the heart of what is now Turkey, there lived a race which was only rediscovered at the turn of the century. Hattusas, their capital, lay some hundred miles to the east of Ankara, near the modern village of Boghazköy.

The Hittites, who played a relatively brief role on the stage of world history, are nevertheless of great importance to us, for they left behind the oldest written documents in an Indo-European language that have so far been discovered. From about 1800 to 1200 B.C. they ruled the region in the great bend of the Kizel Irmar River, which enters into the Black Sea and was called by the Romans the Halys. They penetrated far to the east, south, and west, and then descended, like so many others before them, into the dark oblivion of peoples that collectively makes up the history of mankind.

The home of the Hittites, this third of the most important of the ancient civilizations, lay on a high plateau that rises eastward from the Mediterranean. To the south of the plateau the Taurus Mountains tower over the Syrian plain. To the north stretches the Black Sea.

They are strange people, these Hittites, strange because we do not yet know much about them, and because they are so different from those other ancient peoples who have become familiar to us over the last hundred years. Their own bas-reliefs show them as short and stocky, with prominent bones, sloping foreheads, long noses, slightly curved like a parrot's beak, and short chins. They wore long robes over short tunics, high conical caps, shoes or mocassins with upturned toes. As shown on the high relief on the so-called King's Gate at Boghazköy, their soldiers wore a belted kilt and a helmet with ear pieces, and carried both a short sword and a battle-axe. They borrowed their gods from Babylon and also their system of writing. They carved great bas-reliefs on massive blocks of stone on the fronts of their palaces and temples and also on the faces of the remote cliffs. Their history, as far as we know today, begins about 1900 B.C., at a time when the Cretans had already begun the palace as Knossos and the Pharaohs of the XII Dynasty ruled Egypt. Then the Hittites were divided into small independent cities under local kings, but gradually the country was united under one ruler. Some 400 years later the Hittites flooded southward from their mountain plateau and made vassals of the petty kings of Syria and Palestine and so threatened Egypt. Thutmose III defeated them and pursued them northward. But the Hittites recovered and continued to face Egypt as an equal and powerful rival for many years.

Our knowledge of the Hittites really began in 1902, when the Norwegian Orientalist J. A. Knudtzon examined two tablets from the royal archives at Tel-El-Amarna, Egypt. Both of the tablets were written in a completely unknown tongue, but Knudtzon ventured to suggest that he recognized in them traces of an Indo-European idiom. This was a bold theory in those days, and, needless to say, it was repudiated by all the Indo-European experts of the time. However, the lonely inscriptions on the walls, ruined buildings, and rockfaces at Boghazköy had long been an object of interest to scholars, and it was recognized, thanks to the work of the French scholar E. Chantre, that some of the fragmentary inscriptions there were inscribed in the same language as the two remarkable tablets at Amarna.

Between 1906 and 1912, the German Oriental Institute began excavating ancient Hattusas, under the direction of Dr. Hugo Winckler. No less than ten thousand cuneiform tablets were brought to light, and it was at last recognized that Knudtzon had been on the right track: the two Amarna tablets were inscribed in Hittite characters. The difficult task of deciphering them was undertaken by a very brilliant Czech scholar, Bedrich Hrozny, who finally proved beyond any reasonable doubt that the people who had left these written records were of Indo-European origin. This discovery was of the utmost importance, for it provided the earliest historical evidence of the penetration of the Near East by Indo-European settlers.

In 1931, long after the first World War, the excavation of Hattusas was resumed under the leadership of Professor Kurt Bittel. Nine years later, the ancient city's principal features had been unearthed.

The name of Boghazköy describes the place aptly since it means "village of the ravine." Hattusas is a fortress and its citadel of Buyukkale (which means "great castle") is its most important and spectacular architectural achievement. The highest point of the ancient city, occupied by the south gate, Yerkapu, is about 4000 feet above sea level. Why did the Hittites select this particular spot as the capital of their empire? The rough terrain with its deep gorges and rugged crags was an ideal site for a fortress: it was strategically located near the crossing of two important trade routes; it was highly defensible; and there was an abundance of water from the river. Furthermore, the high altitude and the steady wind provide a good and healthy climate. Kurt Bittel and Rudolf Naumann, the architect, have excavated and studied the remains of this mountain fortress and published an interesting report on it in 1952.

The city is probably the Indo-European prototype of all European fortified towns. The citadel Buyukkale which Hattusas contained was where the rulers of the Hittite empire used to live, and its walls were so closely integrated with the rock on which it was built that it must have been virtually impregnable. There was a massive temple, too, the Hittites' largest religious building, complete with vast storerooms and depots which housed the state treasury. The city's mighty walls enclosed a further four temples, residential quarters whose flat-roofed houses rose in terraces up the steep hillsides, massive towers, impressive gateways, a secret tunnel driven through the rock for sorties against the enemy in time of war, steep flights of steps, posterns, and paved streets. The skill with which the citadel was dovetailed into the landscape justifies one in regarding it as an example of advanced building technique. In Bittel's opinion, the massive, elemental nature of this architecture and the impression it gives of organic unity with the craggy countryside around make it something unique. Its originators brought their own individual conception of the world with them into the Orient. Excavations clearly show that Hattusas was the center of a large empire. Thousands of hands helped to build the city, thousands of stonemasons, laborers, and artisans. There are 200,000 bricks alone in the section of the city walls running from the King's Gate, via the lofty gate of Yerkapu, to the Lion Gate: and that does not take into account the bricks in the projecting battlements or the outlying walls. For all that, Bittel puts the total population of Hattusas during the Hittites' prime at no more than fifteen or twenty thousand.

Walls, battlements and turrets all conform to the landscape. Whole crags and sections of mountainside were removed, holes were drilled into the rock, blocks of stone pinned together with metal plugs, and deep embrasures carefully filled in. Whatever happened, the wall (which was 17½ feet thick around the citadel) was to constitute an impregnable fortification.

Within the citadel the archeologists found the building which housed the archives. Here were discovered 3294 clay tablets and literary fragments. Perhaps these tablets might have been kept in wooden cases like those at Amarna. They are flat on one side so they can be easily used, and many were inscribed with lists of royal possessions.

Very few graves dating from Hittite times have been found. In the corner of one house excavators dug up the bones of a very young girl, wearing a thin, flat, gold ring in her right ear and a fine bronze bracelet on each forearm. Near a fireplace was found the skeleton of a fully grown man, lying on his left side with his legs drawn up. His skull was smashed, unfortunately, and very few traces of his bones had survived. Another grave, also containing only poorly preserved bones, had belonged to a child. The German anthropologist Sophie Ehrhardt devoted a great deal of study to the lower jawbone of this child, who was between thirteen and fourteen years old, but the poor condition of nearly all the Hittite skeletons made them almost worthless for purposes of anthropological research. The Hittites sometimes buried their dead inside their houses, but they also practiced cremation.

Boghazköy yielded other secrets, too. Discoveries of bones enabled scholars to reconstruct the animal world of those days. Portions of seven canine skeletons indicate that the inhabitants of Hattusas kept medium-sized dogs, probably rather like the Australian dingo in build. Horses were used here as draught animals and beasts of burden, and the skeletons of six were discovered. The remains of other slaughtered and butchered beasts proved that oxen must have been the city's principal source of meat, but other animals identified included goats, sheep, pigs, and, among wild game, lions, aurochs, bison, elk, deer, onages, foxes and rabbits.

There is an indefinable atmosphere of tragedy about the ruins at Boghazköy. Hattusas was the capital of a large empire, yet archaeologists have always felt that the mountain city was never more than an artificial creation which could not have survived indefinitely, and that it was not really suitable as a road junction or as a link between the available oases in the Anatolian steppe.

This gigantic monument to human endeavor must have met a violent end. Wherever Bittel and his colleagues dug, whether in the residential quarters or in the walls of Yazilikaya, they found traces of a devastating conflagration. Every combustible object had been destroyed, brickwork had become fused by intense heat into a red, hard, slaggy mass, and limestone had burst or splintered. Bittel believes that the buildings would not normally have contained enough combustible material to account for such a degree of heat. In his opinion, some human agency had intentionally fed the flames, some unidentified enemy who had stormed the place during the Aegean migration, bringing inflammable materials with them. Not a house, not a temple or hut had escaped the all-consuming flames, and nowhere did the excavators find evidence of even the most modest attempt to rebuild the city during Hittite times. Many of the inhabitants must have been massacred, others were probably carried off and sold into slavery, and the remainder fled to northern Syria. From 1200 B.C. onward the city lay abandoned to the silence of death.

Whence did the Hittites come? By what route did they reach the Halys? What culture did they bring with them? What script did they use? And how far back can we trace their history?

The Hittites did not always live in the bend of the Halys. They were not, to put it scientifically, "autochthonous." Three clay tablets bring us some extremely interesting information on the matter. One of them was found in 1937, in the southeast store chambers of the Great Temple, while the other two date from excavations before 1914. The text in question owes its authorship to a certain King Anittas, and Heinrich Otten, the German authority on the Hittite language, regards the events described in it as historically accurate.

Anittas lived about 1800 B.C., long before the earliest Hittite kings previously known to us, and is separated from Labarnas, the first of them, by 100 to 150 years. The tablets have been translated as far as the ravages of time will allow, and the text, which is in an early Hittite idiom, reads like well-documented history.

King Anittas lived in a place called Kussara, and he tells us that his father Pitkhanas conquered the city of Nessa. (Kussara and Nessa may have stood in eastern Anatolia, perhaps in the interior of the

Halys bend, but they have not yet been located.) King Anittas further informs us that after his father's death, he followed in his footsteps by going to war, defeating all the lands which opposed him. He was twice attacked by Pijusti, king of Hatti, but took Hattusas by storm in the course of a single night. "In its place I sowed weeds. He who becomes king after me and peoples Hattusas again, him may the Storm God of Heaven strike down."

Did King Anittas originally write in Hittite (the tablets found were actually transcripts of a somewhat later date), and can his narrative stand as proof that even as early as this, in the nineteenth and eighteenth centuries B.C., Anatolia was inhabited by an Indo-European population?

Heinrich Otten brings forward ingenious arguments to prove that Anittas' text was, in fact, originally written in Hittite, and that the Indo-European Hittites were already resident in Anatolia in the nineteenth century B.C. Bittel, too, assumes that the king employed the Hittite language in recording his military and hunting experiences for posterity, and, consequently, that the Indo-European Hittite tongue was already known in central Asia Minor in the nineteenth and eighteenth centuries. And that is the present extent of our knowledge of the Hittites. We cannot at present trace their history beyond this point.

As we have read, King Anittas put a curse on anyone who would dare to recolonize Hattusas. Nevertheless, other Hittite rulers later made Hattusas their capital. Probably this means that Hattusas and King Pijusti existed long before the first Hittites arrived. Hattusas was not an Indo-European name and was not an Indo-European city. Nor was it Semitic, as far as we know. Its population spoke Hattili. The Indo-Europeans who conquered the city and settled there referred to themselves as "men and women of Hatti" or "sons of Hatti." Hence the name Hittite originated in Anatolia, but the people later called Hittites probably came from a different region.

It was long conjectured (and many scholars still cling to this theory) that these settlers came from the West, since many scholars believe that the original homeland of the Indo-European was in central Europe. On the other hand, Professor Ferdinand Sommer of the University of Munich believes that, in all probability, the Indo-Europeans entered Anatolia from the northeast, crossing via the Caucasian bridge between the Black and Caspian Seas. Probably this migration was not a sudden invasion but a gradual infiltration which lasted many years and appeared about the turn of the second millennium on the Anatolian plain.

From Kussara and Nessa they conquered the central towns and brought the older highland culture under their domination.

When the Hittites migrated into Asia Minor, they brought with them an archaic type of cuneiform writing which they had acquired in the course of their wanderings. The trading settlements of the East used an old Syrian cuneiform script considerably different from the Hittities', whose own script had an affinity with that of the third dynasty of Ur. All the records and correspondence in the archives at Hattusas were written in the Hittite mode.

The language of this cuneiform script was Indo-European, and there is no further doubt today about the Indo-European structure of the Hittite language. One can see at a glance how the Hittite word *uatar* became *water* in English, *Wasser* in German, and *woda* in Russian; or how *genu* became our own *knee;* or how *kardi* became *cor* (genitive: *cordis*) in Latin, *heart* in English, and *Herz* in German; or *pahhur* the English *fire*, the German *Feuer*, and so on. Admittedly, all the research carried out so far has shown that only a minority of Hittite words were actually Indo-European. But words are not the only decisive guides to the classification of a language. Inflexion, modes of declension and conjugation, etc., are much more important, permanent and invariable factors, and the inflexions in Hittite mark it unequivocally as an Indo-European language. It is quite certain, too, that it was a spoken tongue, not merely one that was employed for literary or official purposes.

There are two more languages which are closely related to Hittite: Luvian and Palaic. Luvian was spoken in the territories of the Taurus Mountains. Of Palaic, only about four hundred words have survived. All three languages, Hittite, Luvian, and Palaic, were about as closely related as English, Swedish, and German are today.

The Hittites also used a hieroglyphic script which was Indo-European. Remains of this pictographic writing, dating from the eighteenth through the fifteenth century B.C. have been found. After the fall of the empire in the twelfth century B.C. this type of writing is prevalent in the Late or Neo-Hittite city kingdoms in southeastern Anatolia, including Samal, Carchemish and other places. The discoveries at Carchemish have been particularly rich in tablets with hieroglyphic writing.

Why did the Hittites retain this second method of writing? It was only used for seals, monuments, and inscriptions in stone generally, and was thus of much less importance than the universally popular cuneiform script. Although our earliest examples of Hittite hieroglyphics date from the fifteenth century, they must certainly have been preceded by a long period of development, for they already exhibit a certain tendency toward the cursive, and their pictorial symbols are simplified and stylized. Bittel believes that the script was already in use during the latter half of the third millennium B.C. The simplest way to account for the script's invention is to assume that it was designed for a language related to Hittite. This is the theory held by Güterbock, and it seems a plausible one. Hieroglyphic Hittite is very probably a dialect related to Luvian. At all events, it is certainly a member of the Hittite-Luvian linguistic family.

The story of the hieroglyphic script's discovery and elucidation is an enthralling one. It has only recently been published, and even now not in its entirety. In the autumn of 1947, H. T. Bossert and his Turkish collaborators made a sensational discovery. On the mound of Karatepe, which stands in the foothills of the Taurus range in eastern Cilicia near the river Ceyhan, Bossert unearthed some inscriptions in Phoenician and hieroglyphic Hittite. Although the texts were not identical, they were similar enough to provide a means of deciphering the fundamentals of the Hittites' hieroglyphic script. Ambiguities still exist, of course, and much of the information had already been known, but Bossert's find, coming as it did after years of painstaking research by numerous students of the Hittite hieroglyphics, remains the most important landmark to date in this field.

In 1956 during the excavations of the royal palace at Ras Shamra on the Syrian coast a number of seals were discovered. They were highly productive for Hittite studies, because the Hittite hieroglyphic in the center was surrounded by a legend in Old Akkadian cuneiform script. From these the French scholar, E. Laroche, was able to clarify many additional hieroglyphic signs.

Cuneiform and pictographic texts alike point to Hittite as an Indo-European language, and the Hittites can, in fact, be classified as members of the Indo-European linguistic group. Their physical characteristics, on the other hand, were constantly subject to adulteration and alien admixtures, sometimes strong and sometimes less so. It would be interesting to know who were culturally more advanced, the invading Indo-Europeans or the indigenous population of Hattusas (known to science as "proto-Hattians"). We gather that newcomers and original inhabitants got on quite well and learned a lot from each other, but it is not certain which group made the more valuable contribution to their joint way of life. Moortgat and Sommer both think that the original, subjugated inhabitants were in many respects the cultural superiors of their new masters; and Bittel, who has spent years of research on the actual site of the ancient city, also surmises that although they speedily assimilated the old Anatolian civilization, the immigrant Hittites were at first culturally inferior.

The Hittites were foreigners from far away, yet once they had established themselves in eastern Anatolia, they took the indigenous civilization of the region and raised it to heights which received universal recognition, even in the world of that time. But despite all the fruits of the ancient Anatolian civilization which they adopted, the Hittites remained totally distinct from the Babylonians in their beliefs, ideas, and customs. They had their own individual style in everything: in dress, ornamentation, monumental sculpture, and town planning.

Hattusas was a fortified metropolis, and its crowning glory was its citadel, Buyukkale. The principal feature of the famous cities in Mesopotamia, by contrast, was always the temple of their city-god. Nor could the king of the Hittites exercise his authority as arbitrarily as other eastern potentates. He was supreme lord of his people both in war and peace, but his powers were circumscribed by the nobility. We find no indication that the Hittites persecuted and tortured defeated peoples, as was the habit of the Assyrians and Medes. Punishments were less severe, too. The practice of mutilation was unknown, and a sentence of death was only rarely passed on non-slaves.

The laws of the Hittites tell us a great deal about their civilization, and from their inscriptions we have gleaned something about their social and cultural life. They seem to have been a moderate-tempered people. When a Hittite wished to marry, he purchased a wife. Even a slave could buy a free woman. Unlike the Egyptians, the Hittites did not tolerate marriages between brothers and sisters. This is known from a tablet of King Suppiluliumas in the Late Empire who advises one Hukkanas from the land of Hajasa in the Armenian mountains; "The brother may not take his own sister or his own cousin for this is not right. Whoever does such a thing in Hattusas does not remain alive but dies."

Suppiluliumas remarked that while it might be quite customary in Hajasa to marry one's own brother, sister, or cousin, such a thing was prohibited at Hattusas. The king was justified in writing to Hukkanas in this fashion because he had ennobled the simple but able man and given him one of his sisters as a wife. He was therefore at pains to establish proper relations between his family, his court, and his new brother-in-law. The king strikes a very human note as he continues: "If, then, one of your wife's sisters or a half-sister or cousin comes to you, give her to eat and drink; eat and drink together and make merry. But do not lust for her. That is not allowed, and merits the death penalty: so do not try it. Even if someone should tempt you, pay him no heed and do not do it." There is something reminiscent of Solomon's shrewd proverb in this advice.

Suppiluliumas reigned from about 1380 to 1340 B.C., and was probably the most powerful ruler in the world at that time. He skillfully exploited Egypt's political weakness under Ikhnaton the reformer, incorporated the whole of northern Syria down to the Lebanon border into the Hittite empire, conquered the countries of Asia Minor, and destroyed the Mitanni nation. A man of his caliber naturally expected orderly behavior within his own household. Hence this additional warning on the clay tablet addressed to Hukkanas: that his new brother-in-law should not go too near any woman of the court, whether a free-born lady or a slave girl in the service of the temple. "Go not too near her, nor speak a word to her. Nor let your serving man or maid approach her. Be very wary of her. As soon as a lady of the palace approaches, leap out of the way and let her pass."

In the course of his covenant with Hukkanas, the able king told him a small story designed as an object lesson. It seems that, one day, a certain Marjas let his glance rest on a *hierodule*, or female temple slave, who was passing by. He, Suppiluliumas, the Father of the Sun, happened to be looking out of a window at the time, and saw the mild flirtation going on. Ordering the unfortunate Marjas to be arrested, he demanded: "Why did you look at that slave girl?" If the Father of the Sun asked such a question, it was tantamount to a sentence of death—and Marjas was, in fact, executed "on this account." But the king went a step further: he was determined that his new brother-in-law should not slip back into the old immoral ways even in Hajasa, his own country. There, too, he was in future to abstain from touching his brother's wives and his own sisters. On the other hand, he would be permitted to retain the women he already owned as concubines.

We have heard in a previous chapter how the widow of an Egyptian Pharaoh wrote to a Hittite king and asked him to send her one of his sons as a prospective husband. The Hittite, who incidentally must have been quite flattered by this suggestion, was none other than King Suppiluliumas, and the queen was probably Nefertiti, although we are not entirely sure if this unusual request was really made by Nefertiti or by the widow of Tutankhamen, Ikhnaton's successor. Eduard Meyer and Alexander Scharff both assume that it was actually Nefertiti who entertained these startling matrimonial plans. Heinrich Güterbock, however, believes that the author of the sensational proposal was Tutankhamen's widow, and the Egyptologist E. Edel shares this view.

The story of this dynastic scandal, which took place some 3,300 years ago and was certainly not made public at the time, is told in *The Deeds of Suppiluliumas*, written by his son Mursilis II. The fragmentary clay tablets bearing this extremely interesting text were carefully assembled by Güterbock between 1954 and 1956 at Frankfort and Ankara, and were then translated by him into English.

Let us go back three hundred years earlier to the time when the Hittite throne was occupied by Labarnas II, also known as Hattusilis I. This king left us a bilingual text in Hittite and Akkadian: his last will and testament, written as he lay dying. His queen consort and the heir-apparent seem to have been in league against him. His son shed no tears and showed his dying father no sympathy: "Cold he is, and heartless. I, the king, summoned him to my bedside, but he is my son no longer. Then his mother bellowed like an ox." But the king remained unmoved. "His mother is a serpent," he went on. "Time and again my disloyal son will heed the words of his mother, his brothers, and his sisters, and then he will wreak revenge. There will be a blood bath." The king warned against revolution and civil war. Then, instead of leaving his throne to the crown prince, he designated the latter's son, Mursilis, as his successor. Mursilis was still young, he said, "so bring him up to be a hero king." Hattusilis must have been an excellent psychologist, for he commanded that his young grandson have his grandfather's decree read to him once each month.

It is easy to deduce from the clay tablets of the Hittite kings that they were men who had accumulated the experience of many generations and applied it to their own circumstances. Where treaties were concerned, they were never satisfied with mere pacts of mutual assistance. They were able psychologists who were well aware of all the weaknesses and temptations to which even friends and relatives are prone. That was why they went much further in their security measures than our modern statesmen. They emphasized that their treaty partner must never waver in his loyalty, carefully laying it down in writing that he was not to let himself be influenced by any outside party. Anyone who was an enemy of the Sun (and the Hittite king was always referred to as "the Sun") must also be an enemy of his ally, and anything the ally heard which was to the king's disadvantage must always be reported to him. It is moving to hear Mursilis II, who reigned from about 1339 to 1306, address his ally Kupanta-Kal, enjoining him not to put any faith in false rumors. Here are his actual words: "Humanity is corrupt. If rumors fly, and someone comes to you and whispers that the Sun is doing you wrong, that he is going to take away your house or lands and do you a mischief, you must inform the Sun without delay."

In concluding pacts like these, the contracting parties always swore by the thousand gods of the Hittites. "We have called the thousand gods to the tribunal" ran the formula. The Sun God of the Sky, the Sun Goddess of Arina, the Storm God of Many Places, Ishtar the Queen of the Firmament, and countless other gods and goddesses were called to witness, and invoked to destroy anyone who disregarded the king's decree.

There came a time, however, when the gods of the Hittites failed. Hattusas went up in flames. Citadel, temples, store chambers and houses crumbled to the ground, and the sky glowed red as the Hittites met their downfall in the place which had once been the seat of their power. From 1200 B.C. onward, all reference to the Hittites in eastern Anatolia ceased abruptly, and the scene shifted to southeast Anatolia. This was a land of the Late or Neo-Hittite kingdoms which flourished until the end of the eighth century B.C. when they fell to Assyrian conquest.

The death of a nation is like the death of an individual: it is always hard to comprehend. Anyone who sees the truly remarkable fortifications of Buyukkale and allows his imagination free rein will recognize the elemental will power which must have belonged to the builders of Boghazköy. And he will recognize something else: that these men built for eternity. They sank wells, worked at their vineyards, tended their apple trees, tilled their fields, grazed their sheep, and, if the king so ordered, built chariots and went to war. They bought and sold slaves. Paragraph 14 of their legal code lays it down that anyone who punched a slave woman on the nose was fined three silver shekels, while the same assault upon a full citizen cost a whole *mina*, or sixty shekels. If a slave escaped and was recaptured for the owner by someone else, the finder received a reward.

If, after a man had paid the price of a bride, her parents subsequently decided not to part with the girl after all, they were obliged to repay the sum twice over. On the other hand, it also happened that a girl who had been promised to one man was suddenly married off to another. In that case, the successful bridegroom was only bound to repay his rival the equivalent of his expenditure to date. Perfumers and herdsmen were held in low esteem, apparently, for any girl who married one automatically became a slave for three years.

The Hittites' laws vividly illuminate their colorful way of life. A man who sneaked off after a woman into the lonely mountains and raped her was sentenced to death. But when another man assaulted a woman in her own home, her complicity was taken for granted, and she too had to die. (A slave woman's honor was not legally protected.) If somebody killed a snake, uttering the name of his enemy while doing so, this dangerous magic incurred a fine of one silver *mina*, and a slave who did the same thing forfeited his head. There must also have been at least one Hittite who was so enraged that he lifted a door off its hinges and carried it away, for a law was invented to cover such a contingency. The miscreant had to replace all the livestock which the owner of the house lost as a result of his act and pay a silver *mina* in addition.

No brief account of Hittite political and cultural history would be complete without something about their art. Specifically, their art might be divided into three periods. The first of about 1740–1460 B.C. is that of the Old Kingdom about which we know very little except for their highly developed skill in making pottery and figurines as shown from the excavations at Kül-Tepe in Cappadocia. The ancient name of this place was Kanesh and it was notable for having been the site of a settlement of Assyrian traders who were the medium of trade in copper and wool between Anatolia and Assyria.

The second phase of the Hittite art is in the Great Empire which lasted from about 1460 to about 1200 B.C. In this period we find the monumental sculptures, tablets and seal impressions which give us a vivid picture of their sculptural art. These sculptures are widespread from the west of Anatolia to the east, but the most important so far discovered are those at Alaca Hüyük with its sphinx gate and reliefs, and at Boghazköy with its Lion Gate, and reliefs of the king-god. The most dynamic and effective units are those from Yazilikaya two miles across the ravine from Buyukkale. There in natural recesses in the rock the walls are lined with processions of the gods, the kings and the queens designated by hieroglyphic symbols.

After the fall of the Empire and the decentralization that followed, we pick up their art in the kingdom states of southeastern Anatolia, especially at Carchemish, Sinjirli Sakegözii, and Marash, where rich remains were found. These were also characterized by processions and individual reliefs on stone panels at the bases of buildings, courts and stairways. Karatepe, the citadel city, in the land known as that of the Danunians, gave us a rich yield of sculpture which accompanied the bilingual text. They in turn give us a wide variety of subjects and clues to the life of the last part of the eighth century, such as scenes of banquets, hunts, boating parties, musical performances and adoration of the gods. They show a strong affinity between Mesopotamian, Assyrian, Syrian, Phoenician, Egyption and indigenous art.

The Hittites were a people of great vitality and created a unique culture, even though it was derived from many sources, giving them the reason to take their deserved place in the sun beside Assyria, Babylonia and Egypt.

They were a vigorous, hot-blooded race, and life seems to have been more eventful in the east Anatolian highlands in those days than it is now. We can visualize how the Hittite bridegrooms used to wade through the waist-high snow, lashed by the bitter north or northeast wind, to collect their brides; how the people used to rejoice when the plateau put on its bright mantle of green; how they celebrated the short-lived, tumultuous feast of color which only lasts until July and then yields once more to the grayish-brown monotony of the arid landscape; how they endured the scorching summers and the bitter winters with their heavy falls of snow; how they triumphed over the infinite loneliness of their mountain home, filling the melancholy Anatolian highlands with life and laughter. Yet there came a day when they succumbed to the most dangerous thing on earth, something far more implacable than Nature at its most destructive: the enemy in human form.

THEY NEVER HAD TIME...

Rogues, bringing countless trinkets with them in their dark ship.

Homer, circa 800 B.C.

WE KNOW exactly to what race the Phoenicians belonged, but we know very little about their history. And if we do know precisely where they came from, we know their cities, and we know where they went on their voyages. And we hope to learn more about them from the excavations now going on at Ugarit.

The most astonishing thing about the Phoenicians is that, although they were probably the greatest seafaring race of antiquity and built cities on every coast, scarcely any other race is so difficult to explore, for they left no large or enduring kingdom behind in their native land.

The Phoenicians were probably of Semitic origin, and were members of the Canaanite tribe of whom we read in the Bible. The name was then pronounced "Kinahni," and we find it in the *Amarna Tablets*, letters inscribed in clay and addressed to the Egyptian court in about 1400 B.C. and discovered at Tell el Amarna in Egypt.

If the Phoenicians were Semites, as their language would indicate, it is remarkable that they ever developed such an un-Semitic love of the sea. Fearless and infinitely patient, they sailed away across the seas to places where none had dared venture before them. Ancient Phoenicia comprised the coastal areas of modern Syria, Lebanon and Israel, and it was along these coasts that the Phoenicians built their seaports: Byblos, Tyre, Sidon, Marathus, Ugarit, Beirut and many others. The name "Phoenician" probably derives from the Greek word for the date palm (*phoinix*), or from the adjective *phoinos*, meaning red. Perhaps the Greeks called them by that name because the Phoenicians had a reddish or, rather, brownish-red skin. Or perhaps the name stems from the purple-dyed cloth for which the Phoenicians became famous.

When Herodotus the Greek visited Phoenicia, he stated that Tyre had been founded "2,300 years ago." If the date of his visit was about 450 B.C., as we believe, it would mean he believed that Tyre was founded around 2750 B.C.

Once these remarkable seafarers had freed themselves from Egyptian domination, they became the undisputed masters of the eastern Mediterranean. They manufactured articles of glass and metal, precious vases, weapons and jewelry. They traded in grain, wine and cloth, bartering these goods along all the coasts of the Mediterranean and transporting their wares to the most distant shores. Lead, gold and iron they obtained from the southern shores of the Black Sea; they loaded their ships with copper, cypress, timber and grain from Cyprus, ivory and gold from Africa, wine from southern France, tin from the lands along the Atlantic; and wherever they went they shanghaied foreigners for the slave trade. Indeed, almost singlehanded they supplied the harems of the contemporary world with the girls they seized. They traded with Tarshish (probably Tartessus in southwestern Spain), and imported so much silver from there that they allegedly made their ships' anchors out of that metal. And from Gadeira, the modern Cadiz, they sailed out into the Atlantic Ocean to the "Tin Isles," which were probably the Cornish coasts of England.

The Phoenicians are said to have circumnavigated Africa 700 years before the birth of Christ, which would mean that they discovered the Cape of Good Hope 2,000 years before Vasco da Gama! Their low, narrow galleys, often one hundred feet long, raced along in all weathers, the galley slaves who toiled at their oars being assisted by a large square sail. Soldiers were stationed on deck, and the Phoenician watchword was: "Trade or fight!" But the Phoenicians had a high regard for trade, and used their weapons only when other forms of persuasion failed. Ships like theirs, with a draught of only five feet and no compass on board, naturally had to hug the coasts whenever possible. Nevertheless, Phoenician helmsmen eventually learned how to steer by the stars, and the North Star later became known among the Greeks as the "Phoenician Star."

The Phoenicians established trading centers and garrisons at every strategic point along the Mediterranean: at Cadiz, Carthage and Marseilles, on Malta, Sicily and Corsica, and probably even on the distant shores of England and other islands in the Atlantic which were rediscovered only in our own time. The Phoenicians controlled southern and eastern Cyprus, Melos and Rhodes. They put slaves to work in their mines, and were not beneath combining business with robbery. They stole from the weak and swindled the gullible, and were honest only in their dealings with the ablest merchants. They also practiced piracy, inviting foreigners on board their ships, and then simply sailing off with them. The Greeks, who were not above practicing a little piracy themselves, used "Phoenician" as a general term for any pirate chieftain, and the poet Homer, who lived about 800 B.C., remarks pertinently in his *Odyssey:* "Then came the Phoenicians, renowned mariners, rogues bringing countless trinkets with them in their dark ship."

But the Phoenicians were not only merchants and pirates: they were also bearers of civilization in the truest sense of the word. They imported science and the art of writing from Egypt, Crete and the Near East into Greece, Africa, Italy and Spain. They linked East and West by trade, and acted as middlemen between Babylon and Egypt. Civilization traveled to Europe in their holds crammed with barrels and bales.

The commercial aristocracy of Phoenicia liked to do business and thought little of war, which was why their cities became so immensely wealthy. Byblos was probably the oldest of their metropolises, and papyrus, or paper, one of their most important trade goods. That was why the Greeks came to call any book *biblos*—the same word which, via the Greek *ta biblia*, became our word "*Bible*."

Some fifty miles south of Byblos, also situated on the coast, was the city of Sidon which provided King Xerxes with practically his whole fleet; and the sea battles of the Persians against the Greeks were fought mainly with Phoenician ships. Thus one may actually speak of Greco-Phoenician wars. When the Persians eventually besieged and took Sidon, the proud Phoenician merchants set fire to their own city, and 40,000 people died in the conflagration.

The most important Phoenician city, however, was Tyre. Built on an island some miles offshore, it possessed a magnificent harbor. Here slaves from every country in the Mediterranean carried bales, crates and barrels to warehouses and ships, and vice versa. King Hiram I of Tyre (969-936 B.C.) was a friend of the kings David and Solomon, and supplied them with cedar wood, carpenters and stonemasons. By 520 B.C., Tyre was so rich that it had silver "as the dust" and gold "as the mire of the streets" (Zachariah 9,3.).

The city had a circumference of just over two and one-half miles, but its buildings were tall enough to accommodate its population of 25,000 people. The total population of the city was larger still, for there was also a mainland city on the shore opposite the island, known as Old Tyre. We read that Nebuchadnezzar besieged Tyre for thirteen years, but there is no mention of his ever having captured it.

Alexander the Great finally succeeded in conquering the island citadel, but first he had to destroy the mainland city and then build a causeway from its ruins. During the course of centuries, alluvial deposits have built up a neck of land there which is today a third of a mile across at its narrowest point.

Carthage was another Phoenician foundation (878 B.C.), and the Carthaginians were a Phoenician people. Hannibal was a son of this unique race of merchants and seafarers. Phoenician ingenuity created the citadel of Carthage, with its tall buildings separated by narrow streets, like ravines. Carthage held out against Rome for a long time before her merchant inhabitants succumbed to the superiority of the Roman legions. The latest excavations show that the streets of Carthage ran at right angles, like those of New York. In the year 149 B.C., 700,000 people lived there.

The Carthaginians had a very simple method of insuring that the trade of northwest Africa flowed through their own port. They always permitted foreign merchants to come to Carthage–indeed, they made them most welcome. But if they ever found foreign merchants in any of their African colonies, they tied stones to their legs and threw them into the sea.

The Phoenicians worshiped many gods, and each of their cities had its own Baal. The Baal of Tyre, for example, was called Melqarth. He was as strong as the Greeks' Hercules, and performed feats which even a Baron Munchausen would have envied. The Phoenicians also adopted Ishtar, the goddess of fertility, from the Babylonians, and the handmaidens of Astarte at Byblos had to sacrifice their long tresses to the goddess and "accommodate" any strange passer-by in the court of her temple, just as the virgins of Ishtar-Mylitta did at Babylon. Finally, there was Moloch, the frightful god to whom the Phoenicians offered live children as a burnt sacrifice. When Carthage was besieged in 204 B.C., her inhabitants immolated one hundred boys of noble birth on Moloch's altar in a vain effort to propitiate the god and raise the siege.

Like the Egyptians, the Phoenicians placed great importance on the enduring burial of their dead. In 1921-23, French archaeologists under the direction of Montet dug up Ahiram's beautiful sarcophagus near Byblos (now Jebel). It bears one of the oldest Phoenician inscriptions we know.

The Phoenician merchants were practical men who were neither visionaries nor poets. Like the inhabitants of all large cities, they never had time, and that unfortunately is why so little pertaining to them has survived. Most of their monuments were destroyed or crumbled to dust through the generations. And whereas in the dry climate of Egypt rolls of papyrus have remained legible through thousands of years, everything decayed quickly on the humid coast of Syria. Scarcely more than a dozen inscriptions in stone have been unearthed in Phoenicia itself, and of the mighty sanctuary of Melqarth atTyre not one stone remains upon another. The cities are gone, and such few works of art as have been found almost invariably resemble those of Egypt and Babylon.

Since the Phoenicians introduced so many countries to the technical and artistic achievements of their day, it was long assumed that they themselves had invented glass, coinage, faïence ware, and even the alphabet. However, latest scientific research indicates that while they were great imitators and transmitters of culture, they were not great inventors. They marketed all these fine things, but the original ideas almost invariably sprang from elsewhere. Arithmetic, weights, measures and coins came from Babylon. The manufacture of glass and faïence was known to the Egyptians considerably earlier, and it was only later that the glass industry of Sidon became world-famous. The alphabet, too, had a long series of "editorial contributors" before it reached the Phoenicians, who at best "simplified" the more elaborate Egyptian writing to facilitate their commercial transactions.

It is not even certain whether the Phoenicians were the original manufacturers of the famed purple dyestuff, although their mastery of this art made them world-famous in antiquity. They extracted this much sought-after dye from a gland of the murex, or purple sea snail. Tyre's purple was not scarlet, as is frequently imagined, but rather a dark violet close to black, comparable to the color of congealed blood; if one looked at it from the side or from below, or in the glare of light, it took on a brighter tone. Egyptian women of the upper classes and, indeed, smart society throughout the Mediterranean, had a high regard for fabrics dyed at Tyre.

On the south side of the former island of Tyre thick layers, composed of the stone-hard conglomerations of waste matter from the former dye works, have been discovered. Indeed the Greeks used to wrinkle their noses at the very mention of Tyre, for the numerous dye works there produced a repulsive stench, somewhat like garlic. However, the supply was limited, so that cloth dyed with purple was very costly, and purple robes became a mark of royalty.

The Phoenicians would catch the live mussels in racks, rather like oyster-pots set in the sea; then they would open the shells and remove the glands. The juice was then left to simmer in cauldrons over a gentle fire for ten days, during which it was purified by constant skimming. When the liquid had sufficiently condensed, the fabrics to be dyed were dipped into it and left to dry in the sun. Then alone did the colors display their full splendor, and since their radiance appeared only when they were exposed to light, these colors never faded.

When Alexander the Great overthrew the city of Tyre in July of 332 B.C., the empire of the Phoenicians came to an end as 8,000 Tyrians were massacred and another 30,000 sold into slavery. The cities of Aradus, Sidon, Tyre and Tripolis experienced one more brief flowering in the time of Pompey (64 B.C.), but then their people adopted Roman customs, started to speak Latin and Greek, and married foreign women. And eventually, this mysterious race of courageous seafarers stepped from the arena of world history.

WHEN AHASUERUS COULD NOT SLEEP

When King Xerxes was reviewing his land and sea forces—in 480 B.C., *before the sea battle of Salamis—he wept, and said: Truly, it grieves me when I reflect on the brief span of man's life. For of all these men, not one will be alive a hundred years from now.*

Herodotus

THE known span of human history is so short that its most interesting questions are invariably lost in the twilight of the past. A complete history of the world would probably comprise a thousand volumes, but we can read only the last chapter of the last volume. This section deals with the gradual eclipse and domination of the Oriental peoples of the Near East by the Indo-Iranian, or Aryan, races. The original home of these Aryan conquerors may have been the great steppes of central Asia, or the plains of southern Russia, or the shores of the Baltic Sea. Certainly old legends tell of a lost land called Aryanem Vaejo and of nomadic peoples who migrated into Persia and India via Bokhara and Samarkand.

The Persian empire, the greatest empire of the ancient world, flourished only for some 225 years, from 559 to 331 B.C. During these 300 years, however, on the Iranian mountain plateau and throughout the Near East, unfolded a drama so fascinating, fabulous and incredible that we are still dazzled by the deluded genius, the abominations, the extravagance, but also by the greatness of some of the Median and Persian kings who made history there—more than 2,000 years ago.

The Persian empire was built upon the ruins of the supremacy formerly held by a people we call the Medes. But where did the Medes themselves come from?

Their wanderings evidently started somewhere in southern Russia, for they reached Persia by crossing the mountains between the Black and the Caspian Seas. Many of them trekked on further to India, while the others settled in what is now Iran. They were a tall, white-skinned race of nomads and herdsmen, and the most important cultural innovation they brought with them was the horse. They and their descendants soon held sway over the kingdoms of Babylonia, Assyria and Syria.

The first king of the Medes we know was Deioces who established Ecbatana, his capital city, on a hill, and crowned it with a temple that glittered in the sun. The city is said to have been enclosed by seven walls: the innermost of pure gold, the second of silver, the third of gleaming orange-colored bricks, and the others of blue, scarlet, black and white. Nothing is left of this fabled city, and we can only wonder whether the solid gold walls will ever be dug up. Ecbatana probably flourished at the site of the modern Hamadan, and Herodotus tells us that none of its inhabitants were ever allowed into their king's presence, so that it was commonly believed that he was of a shape different from other mortals.

The most important of the Median kings was Cyaxares, who sacked Nineveh and eventually besieged Sardis, where an eclipse of the sun is said to have put such dread into the hearts of besieged and besiegers alike that they forthwith made peace. They exchanged two bowls of human blood and ceremonially poured them out on the ground to symbolize the ending of the war.

Not a single stone, not a line of writing, and scarcely any works of art remain of the Medes.

In 585 B.C., Astyages assumed the reins of government from his father Cyaxares and settled himself on the Median throne at Ecbatana, determined to preserve and enjoy his dominion as long as possible. He introduced gorgeous fashions and every conceivable luxury. The gentlemen wore embroidered trousers, a garment which was then completely unknown and owes its invention to the Medes, while the ladies devoted much time and effort to taking care of their fine skin, and were mostly interested in cosmetics and jewelry. In a country constantly exposed to horse-borne invasions from the steppes to the north and east—in a country where horse and rider were an indispensable unit for defense—the animals were decked out with gold-trimmed blankets. The glittering capital, Ecbatana, was the scene of one festivity after another.

Such reckless splendor always carries a suggestion of the eleventh hour, inner doubts, impending doom and the fear of the coming nightmare, for man usually behaves in an unseemly way when he is at the height of his power. King Astyages had been told by seers that his daughter's son would one day rule all Media. Hence, when he arranged for the marriage of his daughter Mandane, he selected not a Mede but Cambyses, the Persian prince of a vassal state, for her. The child of such a marriage could be done away with later, Astyages reasoned, for the Medes, far from regarding the Persians with respect, were inclined to hold them in contempt. No sooner had Mandane presented her husband with a son—Cyrus—than Astyages ordered his chief councilor Harpagus to kill the child. Harpagus did not obey these orders, however, but instead gave the infant into the keeping of a cowherd. And it was in the bleak, windy country of the highlands north of Ecbatana that young Cyrus grew up—to become the greatest statesman of his age.

Herodotus tells us a horrible story in this connection. One day, Astyages found out that Harpagus had spared young Cyrus' life. As a punishment, he served him a joint of roast meat: it was Harpagus' own son, with his head, feet and hands lopped off, and while they were still at table Astyages showed the councilor the head of his dead son. Harpagus remained outwardly calm. "Everything the King does is good," he said. But from then on he bided his time until Cyrus grew up, then allied himself with him, brought the Persian armies into the land of the Medes and helped them to victory. It is interesting to note that right from the beginning of his career Cyrus showed himself to be magnanimous: he permitted Astyages to live out his life in honor and freedom after his defeat and subsequent capture.

And so the land of the Medes fell into the hands of their Persian cousins, who were likewise of Indo-European stock. The Persians had settled in Anzan in southern Elam, with Susa as their capital, and they traced their royal lineage back to the Achaemenidae, so named after their first king Achaemenes, who reigned sometime between 700 and 675 B.C. He was succeeded by Teispes, Cyrus I, Cambyses I, and Cyrus II. It is with this last-named king that the actual history of the Persians begins.

In 1928 E. Herzfeld, digging at Madar-i-Sulaiman, not far from the Pulvar River, about twenty-five miles from the modern town of Shushtar and some three hundred miles south of Susa, unearthed the ruins of Cyrus' royal residence at Pasargadae. Long before this Cyrus' tomb had been discovered, stark and lonely, still preserved in spite of centuries of blazing sun and raw winds. At one time the tomb had been surrounded by a park, by walls and colonnades, and on a pillar remain the words, inscribed in cuneiform lettering: "I am King Cyrus, the Achaemenid." But the grave had been empty for centuries; and the golden sarcophagus that once held the body of Cyrus the Great was stolen long ago.

With the conquest of Ecbatana, Cyrus at one fell swoop became master of all Media, and thus founded the Persian empire. To the Persians, he was the ideal of masculine beauty. However, it was probably not so much that they loved him because he was handsome as that they found him handsome because they loved him. Plutarch tells us that the Persians regarded a hooked nose as a mark of beauty. Why? Because Cyrus had this type of nose. We do not know very much about the great Cyrus, for Xenophon's *Cyropaedia*, or "Boyhood of Cyrus," is less of a work of history than a hymn in praise of monarchy and an educational treatise, typically Greek in character, and strongly colored by the philosophy of Socrates, who was a friend of Xenophon.

Cyrus' first step was to raise a powerful army, whereupon he proceeded to conquer Lydia with its famous city of Sardis. King Cyrus' triumphal reign seems like one of mankind's brightest hours, conducted with the mysterious magic of a statesmanship equal to Caesar's, carried by a spirit of emancipation, magnanimity and true greatness.

Caria, Lycia and Ionia surrendered to the Persian king's generals, while in the east, Cyrus protected his empire against the daring raids of the Saka tribes (Scythians) of the Turanian steppes. He laid his mighty hand on Bactria, Margiana and Sogdiana, and far away on the Jaxartes, north of modern Samarkand, he built the powerful frontier fortress of Cyreshata. He subjugated Babylon, discontented with its ruler Nabonidus, entering the ancient city on October 29, 539 B.C. amid scenes of public rejoicing. He liberated the captive Jews, sacrificed to the Babylonian god Marduk, and put an end to the Semitic domination of western Asia for a thousand years to come. Under his guidance the Persian empire became the greatest state organization of pre-Roman antiquity.

Cyrus seems to have been sympathetic toward the religions of other races. He respected their gods, made obeisance in their holy places, and apparently considered it advisable to place himself under the protection of their gods and idols, for he maintained their temples and stood in reverence as the incense rose before each sacred image. He never stooped to mass killings, but always tried to win the people's hearts. He was the new spirit of western Asia, and its most outstanding genius until Alexander the Great appeared on the world scene.

No wonder people hailed him with such jubilation; no wonder he occupied Babylon with the approval of most of its citizens; no wonder generals and princes and the people of Sumer and Akkad prostrated themselves before him and kissed his feet. He was a genuinely tolerant man and perhaps he had the intuition that, beyond his own religion and his god Ahura Mazda, the universe was ruled by a god whom he had not yet come to know. It is certainly worth noting that it was Cyrus who rebuilt the ruined temple of Yahweh in Jerusalem for the Jews.

Cyrus did not die in bed, at home, in his city of Ecbatana. He threw himself into the battle against invading Asiatic bowmen, the Messagetic horsemen of the north who stormed out of the steppes of Turkestan, incited by the Scythians. It was in his heroic struggle against this gravest menace to his beloved Persia that the great Achaemenid died in the summer of 529 B.C., presumably a victim of the wily tactics of his hard-riding adversaries and their dangerous bowmanship.

The statesmen of our own day could learn a great deal from Cyrus. He may have lived 2,500 years ago, but it is easily apparent that the intelligence of politicians has not appreciably increased since. For example, there was the King of Lydia, that renowned and envied man, Croesus, whose fabulous wealth rested on the output of his gold mines and other enterprises. Croesus' capital, Sardis, was a glittering center of the arts and sciences. Yet when Croesus asked the philosopher Solon what he thought of so much happiness and wealth, Solon quietly answered that no one should ever call himself happy until he had lived his life to the end.

Shortly afterwards Cyrus conquered Sardis, and the Persians prepared to burn Croesus at the stake. Hunched on his pyre, close to death, Croesus suddenly remembered Solon's prophetic words and murmured the philosopher's name. Cyrus himself heard him and asked for an explanation, and when Croesus told him the story, Cyrus in his wisdom freed the defeated king who had been Persia's arch enemy, gave him large tracts of land, a high position at court, and appointed him his personal adviser. Croesus served the wise king for thirty years, and his successor Cambyses after him.

Cambyses, Cyrus' son, corresponds more closely to our picture of a modern dictator. He was in every respect his father's opposite. He murdered his brother Smerdis, extended his empire to the Nile, slaughtering any prisoners he took on the way, and is reported to have thrown Egypt's gods into the dust. He even opened the Egyptian royal graves and took out the mummies, which then was considered a crime. His avowed intention was to cure the Egyptians of their "superstitions." However, since he ended up as a crazed megalomaniac, the Egyptians had the last laugh for they were convinced that their gods had punished him for his crimes.

Toward the end of his life Cambyses must have turned into something like a Nero. He killed his sister by hitting her in the stomach with his fist, murdered his wife Roxane, and mortally wounded his son Prexaspes with an arrow. Then, for a change of pace, he had twelve Persian nobles buried alive. He also sentenced Croesus to death, but he had scarcely pronounced the verdict when he regretted it and had a crying fit. However, on discovering that the execution had not been carried out, he flew into another rage and punished the officers who had not obeyed his orders. All this lunacy inevitably resulted in a revolution. A religious fanatic arrived on the scene claiming to be Smerdis, the brother whom Cambyses had murdered long before. But a second revolution soon overthrew the false Smerdis and put Darius on the throne.

Darius I is familiar to us from Greek history as the king who was defeated at Marathon in 490 B.C. Interestingly enough, Herodotus explains that Darius failed because, for once, he followed a woman's advice. The king, he relates, sprained his foot while leaping from his horse on a hunting trip, and sent for an Egyptian doctor. (Egyptian doctors were then still regarded as the best, although this was no longer true. When this happened, in 492 B.C., Greek doctors were patently superior to their Egyptian colleagues.) At any rate, the Egyptian doctors tried to wrench the king's foot back into place, causing him so much pain that he could not sleep for seven nights. It was at this point that the king heard of the Greek doctor Democedes of Croton, and speedily summoned him to his court. Democedes was brought to Darius, chained and in rags. Too much knowledge is a dangerous thing. Democedes was as much in demand as atomic physicists are today, and he feared that if Darius realized his great ability, he would never permit him to go home again. Thus he denied all knowledge of medicine. Darius, who knew that the physician was shamming, threatened to have him tortured. This did the trick: Democedes cured the king's foot, and Darius presented him with two golden chains as a fee. Democedes was the greatest surgeon of his day, and Crotonic medicine owed much of its fame to him. Now the doctor remained at the court of the Persian king, but he yearned for his native land. If Greece had been united with Persia, he could have traveled home, but now there was an "Iron Curtain" that prevented his return.

It so happened that Darius' wife, Atossa, was suffering from a cancer of the breast. At first she concealed the malady, but when the tumor grew she at last sent for Democedes who promised to cure her, on one condition: that she persuaded the king to conquer Greece. Atossa was cured, and one night in the royal bedchamber she began to wheedle her lord and master, reportedly as follows: "March against

Hellas," she said, "for I wish to have women servants from Sparta, Argos, Athens and Corinth. After all, you have a good adviser who knows conditions in Greece—our doctor Democedes." The king let himself be persuaded, and the result was the campaign against Greece, which ended with the battle of Marathon—or at least this is how the Greeks explained the event.

However, the defeated Darius was still a figure to be reckoned with. In western Asia he rebuilt the vast Persian empire again. He put down dangerous rebellions which smoldered and flared up in many of his provinces; he controlled the empire by a rigidly organized bureaucracy and unified the enormous administrative apparatus by the use of Aramaic, a diplomatic *lingua franca* which had been widely used during the days of the Assyrian empire.

In 520 B.C., near Behistun, overlooking the royal highway from Babylon to Ecbatana across the Zagros range, Darius had a steep cliff wall covered with reliefs and inscriptions. This chronicle of the king's achievements is situated so high up that it could never have been legible from the road, but Darius was primarily concerned with the future. And he actually created a vast memorial which has defied the ravages of time and weather up to the present day. Water has been trickling over the edge of the cliff for 2,500 years, but it has done little to affect the inscription on the rock face. It has rightly been called the queen of all inscriptions in the world. Composed in three languages—Persian, Elamitic and Babylonian—it is still quite legible today.

Darius was one of the greatest rulers in history, an organizer of the first order, and a better economist than any king before him. His pedantic insistence on collecting tributes won him a name of miserliness, but he was not a bad strategist, and in assessing the dangerous wastes of Russia he was a wiser general than Napoleon. He led his armies across the Bosphorus, northward through Thrace, and, crossing the Danube with a force of 70,000 to 80,000 men, he marched off into the uncharted wilderness, under constant attack from Scythian horsemen. It is uncertain exactly how far he pushed, but we know that it was lack of water which forced him to retreat without reaching the Dniester. Leaving the sick and the stragglers behind, he and his exhausted army recrossed the Danube without having inflicted a decisive defeat on the Scythians. Darius next marched on through Afghanistan down to the valley of the Indus, gaining gold for his coffers and many millions of foreign subjects for his empire.

In his homeland of Persia he founded a new capital, Persepolis. The ruins of this former residence—twenty-five miles southwest of Pasargadae as the crow flies, and the same distance from the modern town of Shiraz—were excavated between 1931 and 1934 by Ernst Herzfeld, working under the auspices of the Oriental Institute of the University of Chicago. Then from 1935 to 1937 Erich F. Schmidt took over the supervision of this work. These two distinguished archaeologists uncovered the huge artificial platform, or terrace, which Darius had begun to build in 518 B.C., and on which work was continued for more than fifty years, until 460 B.C., under the kings Xerxes and Artaxerxes.

In his own inscription, King Darius calls this terrace "citadel," or "fortress," but it may also be described as a royal residence with vast palaces; a "hall for a hundred thousand" houses for Darius and later Xerxes' harem; accommodations for the harem guard, quarters for officials and thousands of servants, administrative buildings, cisterns, fortifications and graves. The large network of subterranean tunnels probably served as a fresh-water supply system. Herzfeld found 30,000 clay tablets inscribed in Elamitic in the northeast corner of the terrace; they are now being catalogued and examined in the Oriental Institute of the University of Chicago. The tablets contain detailed bookkeeping accounts relating to the immense buildings, wages, expenditures for materials, and so on.

After the failure of his armies in Greece, Darius began preparing a new campaign against the Greeks, for as ruler of the largest empire in history and the undisputed master of millions of people of all races, he regarded Marathon merely as an accident. In the autumn of 486 B.C., however, in the midst of what was to be a decisive campaign, the conqueror died.

Darius had built an eternal resting place for himself during his lifetime, for the burial chambers of Darius the Great and his successors have been found in the steep rock face at Naksh-i-Rustam, not far from Persepolis. Each grave consists of three apertures carved into the rock; the central zone with the entrance being larger than the other two, so that the tombs look something like a cross hewn into the cliff. The trilingual inscription found in Darius' grave is one of the most interesting ancient texts we possess. Ernst Herzfeld has deciphered it, and it reads: "A great god is Ahura-Mazda, who . . . has done this work which . . . is manifest. By the will of Ahura-Mazda I am of this kind: that which is just, I love; injustice I hate. It is not my pleasure that the lowly should suffer injustice at the hands of his superior. . . ."

Darius' successor is known to us from the Old Testament as that

Ahasuerus who reigned at Susa and made Esther his queen. Herodotus has called him Xerxes. Like Cyrus, he was a very handsome man, tall and powerfully built. But handsome men are usually vain and in constant danger of falling victim to some woman's guile—and Xerxes had a whole harem of jealous women. In the end he no longer knew which one he loved, let alone which one loved him. Scandalous stories about his excesses were whispered in the streets of Susa, and it is no accident that the most impressive building he erected in Persepolis was his harem. Today any visitor to Persepolis may visit this harem that once belonged to this extraordinary king: using the plans drawn up by Ernst Herzfeld, the architect Friedrich Krefter has reconstructed the enormous building exactly as it must have looked about 2,500 years ago. It is remarkably modern and functional, and of great beauty in its simple, clean lines. Herzfeld knew that he had found the ruins of the King's harem when he first came across numerous small rooms of the same shape and size, sometimes connected by one long or two smaller chambers, and all connected by long corridors to rooms for the attendants of the harem ladies.

King Xerxes loved pomp and splendor, and devoted himself to wine drinking, banqueting and vast building projects. But then his fleet was vanquished by the Greeks at Salamis. This defeat coupled with the debacle at Plataea and, above all, the annihilation of a second large Persian army in the Mycale peninsula—the "victory of the spear over the bow"—served to confine the Persians permanently to Asia, and prevented them from becoming a European power. After twenty years of court intrigues and misadministration, Xerxes was—appropriately enough—murdered in his bedroom. He was buried with great pomp, because everyone was glad to be rid of him.

Cyrus and Darius built the Persian empire. Xerxes inherited it and began to let it go to ruin amidst debauchery and extravagance. Under his successors the empire fell apart, for now began an endless succession of violence and murder.

Xerxes' murderer was executed by King Artaxerxes, whose successor, Xerxes II, was murdered by a half-brother who was in turn murdered by Darius II. The blood flowed in torrents as Darius II put down a rebellion with extreme ferocity, had his wife hacked to pieces and his mother, brothers and sisters buried alive. Artaxerxes II killed his son and then died of a broken heart on learning that another son, Ochus, was in turn planning to murder him. Ochus reigned for twenty years, when he was poisoned by one of his generals. Thus the vast Persian empire literally drowned in a sea of assassinations, murders, cruelty, tears and blood.

Alexander merely had to smash what was already rotten to the core. Nevertheless, it was an immensely exciting moment in the history of mankind when, in November of the year 333 B.C., Darius III, the last of the Achaemenides and surnamed Codomannus, opposed Alexander at Issus. The Persians considerably outnumbered the Greeks, but Alexander won, thanks to his flank attack, his charge on the Persian center, and Darius' flight in his chariot, leaving his army leaderless. When the battle was over, Alexander had lost no more than four hundred and fifty men, while the Persians had lost perhaps ten times that number–certainly no more than that, for the figures handed down by the Greeks (a Persian army of 600,000, with losses amounting to 110,000) are grossly exaggerated, as is understandable since it made Alexander's victory seem even more impressive. In his flight, Darius abandoned his royal pavilion, leaving behind his mother, his wife, two daughters, his imperial carriage and all the golden jewelry, precious stones and treasures he had taken along.

If we can believe the accounts of Greek historians, the victorious Alexander behaved with all the chivalry of a Prince Charming, and treated Darius' relations with great courtesy.

Ancient Persia had fallen. Her fascinating history lies in ruins before our eyes, and patiently, stone by stone, the scholars are once again bringing this once glorious empire to light. It always spells the doom of a people and its rulers when the conqueror is so much greater and nobler than the conquered.

Darius was murdered by his own officers, but Alexander condemned the murderers of his enemy to death, and at Persepolis he gave Darius a state funeral of such splendor that the people of western Asia spoke of it with awe for centuries. The Persians flocked to Alexander by the thousands, dazzled by his manliness, his youth and magnanimity, and today his name outshines even Persia's most outstanding kings–Cyrus II and Darius I.

THE KINGS DIED—THE BUREAUCRATS REMAINED

What is the fifth most sorrowful thing in the world? Thereupon Ahura-Mazda answered: It is, O Zoroaster, if the wife or son of an innocent man be borne off as booty along dry and dusty roads, and the prisoners weep.
Avesta, Chap. 3 of the *Venidad.*

UNDER Darius I (Darius the Great, 521-485 B.C.), the Persian empire comprised twenty satrapies, each administered by a shatrapavan, or satrap, and reached its greatest extent. It stretched from Egypt—via Palestine, Phoenicia, Phrygia, Ionia, Cappadocia, Cilicia and Armenia—to Assyria. It extended across the Caucasus, Babylonia, Media, modern Iraq and Afghanistan, Baluchistan, India west of the Indus, Soctria and Bactria. It bordered on the steppes of central Asia. No one king had ever wielded his scepter over such a large area before. Many races, probably fifty million people, lived within the boundaries of the Achaemenid empire, while the inhabitants of Persia, its heartland, numbered no more than about 500,000. For two hundred years, this handful of Persians were the virtual masters of the world.

Many tongues were spoken in the Persian empire, but the court language at the time of Darius I was Old Persian. This language is related to the Indian Sanskrit, and it has long been established that many words, both in Europe and in the Indus valley, share a common derivation.

Who would think that, far away in an ancient river valley bordered by steaming jungles, the Old Indian equivalent of our word "brother" was "bhratar"? In the Old Persian of the Zend-Avesta this becomes "brater," in Greek "phrater," in Latin "frater," in Old Irish "brathir," in Old Slavic "bratru," in Old High German "bruoder," and in German "Bruder." The Sanskrit and Old Persian word "pitar" becomes "pater" in Greek and Latin, "Vater" in German, and "father" in English. "Mother" becomes "mater" in Sanskrit and Old Persian, "meter" in Greek, "mater" in Latin, "match" in Russian, "Mutter" in German.

The Persians adopted 36 letters out of some 300 Babylonian syllabic symbols for their cuneiform writing. They regarded writing as an unmanly skill, however, because war, hunting and the harem were far more important to them. To "degrade" themselves so far as to produce literature struck them as disreputable; hence they have left no written records of importance. All we have is the story of their great prophet, which has come down to us by word of mouth and in a few written accounts. Long before the birth of Christ there appeared in their ancestral homeland, Aryane-Vaejo, a man called Zoroaster. His desciples wrote down his prayers and precepts, and this Zoroastrian "Bible" later became known as the Zend-Avesta, which may be roughly translated as "Interpretation and Text."

The Roman historian Pliny informs us that this work originally comprised two million verses, and the Persians tell us that the original text was kept in the great library at Persepolis, written in golden letters on 12,000 cowhides. When Alexander the Great burned down the palace at Persepolis, this text is said to have gone up in flames. What has survived is five books of much-corrupted texts.

When did Zoroaster live? Modern research places him about 700 B.C., although the Greeks believed that he lived 5,500 years before their own time.

We do not know much about Zoroaster. His original home may have been in Eastern Iran or Bactria, and like Christ, he is supposed to have withdrawn into the wilderness, shunning the company of his fellow man. The Devil tempted him, but to no avail, and he was ridiculed and persecuted. But he won out, lived to a ripe old age, and finally ascended into heaven in a shaft of light.

Many words and phrases in the Avesta resemble those of the Indian Vedas, while others recall ancient Babylonian tradition. Thus we are told that the earth was created in six stages, that everyone is descended from a first man and a first woman, and that there was an earthly paradise. Zoroaster believed, like the prophets of our own Bible, in *one* supreme god. As a religious founder, he entered a world dominated by the ancient popular gods of the Indo-Europeans. Admittedly, these gods were invisible, like his; admittedly, they were probably never represented by the Aryans of ancient Iran in human or animal shape; but the idea of a *single* all-embracing and invisible god had not yet been conceived.

Before Zoroaster, divine worship was controlled by the Magi about whom we have only very scanty information. They were an extremely imaginative and deeply religious Median tribe from western Iran, and the capital of their priestly state was Rega, not far from the site of modern Teheran. Today we scarcely realize that whenever we use the

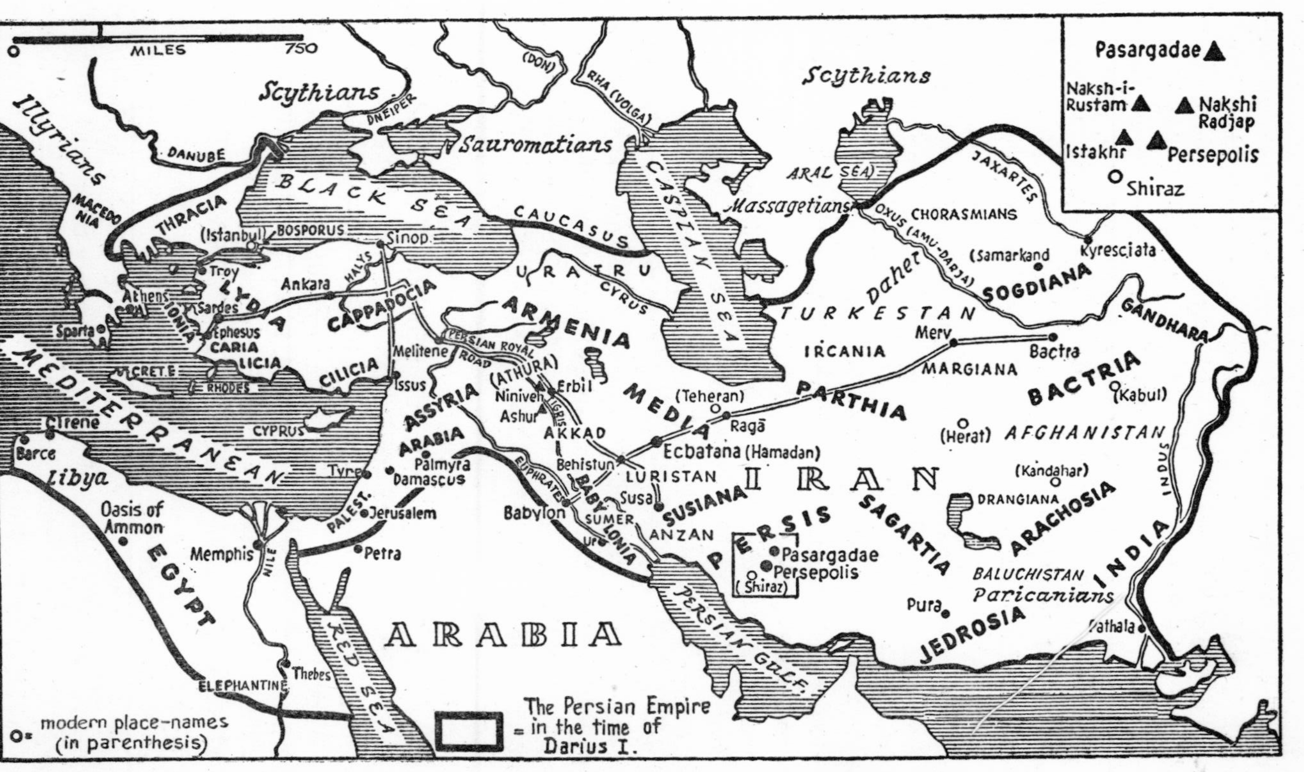

0 MILES 750
Scythians
Illyrians
DANUBE
DNEIPER
(DON)
RHA (VOLGA)
Sauromatians
Scythians
Pasargadae
Naksh-i-Rustam
Nakshi Radjap
Istakhr
Persepolis
Shiraz
MACEDONIA
THRACIA
BLACK SEA
CAUCASUS
CASPIAN SEA
ARAL SEA
Massagetians
JAXARTES
OXUS (AMU-DARJA)
CHORASMIANS
(Samarkand
Kyresciata
SOGDIANA
Dahet
TURKESTAN
GANDHARA
(Istanbul)
BOSPORUS
Sinop
Troy
LYDIA
Ankara
HALYS
CAPPADOCIA
URARTU
CYRUS
ARMENIA
Athens
IONIA
Sardes
Sparta
Ephesus
CARIA
LICIA
CRETE
RHODES
CILICIA
Melitene
PERSIAN ROYAL ROAD
(ATHURA)
Erbil
Issus
ASSYRIA
Niniveh
Ashur
TIGRIS
MEDIA
(Teheran)
Ragā
PARTHIA
IRCANIA
Merv
Bactra
MARGIANA
BACTRIA
(Kabul)
MEDITERRANEAN
CYPRUS
Cirene
Barce
Libya
ARABIA
Palmyra
Damascus
AKKAD
Ecbatana (Hamadan)
(Herat)
AFGHANISTAN
INDUS
Tyre
Behistun
EUPHRATES
LURISTAN
IRAN
(Kandahar)
Oasis of Ammon
Jerusalem
PALEST.
Babylon
BABYLONIA
SUMER
Susa
SUSIANA
DRANGIANA
ARACHOSIA
PERSIS
SAGARTIA
INDIA
EGYPT
Memphis
NILE
Petra
Ur
ANZAN
Pasargadae
Persepolis
(Shiraz)
BALUCHISTAN
Paricanians
Pura
JEDROSIA
Pathala
ARABIA
RED SEA
PERSIAN GULF
Thebes
ELEPHANTINE
O = modern place-names (in parenthesis)
= The Persian Empire in the time of Darius I.

word "magic" we are summoning the spirit of an ancient Iranian people. The Magi were priests, however, not sorcerers. Herodotus tells us that no one could make sacrifice without the presence of a Magus, who stood by and intoned the sacrificial liturgy. Also, the killing of certain creatures, in particular snakes and birds, was part of the religious cult of the Magi. On his death, a Magus was not encased in molten wax and buried like other people in Iran, but he was put out to be devoured by birds and dogs. Later Zoroaster's cult became identified with the Magi–or vice versa–even though his ideas originally were in sharp conflict with that priestly caste. Gradually differences were effaced, but the practice of exposing the dead has remained. Oddly enough, it is the former opponents of the Magi–the last surviving followers of Zoroaster, ninety million Parsees in India–who may still neither burn nor bury their dead. Instead they expose them on isolated towers–towers of silence–and leave them to the vultures. In modern Iran there are only some 10,000 Zoroastrians left.

Supreme among the ancient gods of Iran were Mithras, originally a god of war, and Anahita, the goddess of fertility, who probably had her origins in Semitic Babylon. But when Zoroaster arrived on the scene, about 700 B.C., he discovered that the people were also worshiping animals and a multitude of different gods. Zoroaster was outraged both at these "heathenish" customs and at the Magi, the priestly caste that lived off the proceeds of this polytheism. There was only one god, he taught, and that was Ahura-Mazda, the god of light and the heavens.

From the beginning of time to the present day, Zoroaster went on, Ahura-Mazda had been in conflict with the spirit of evil–Ahriman-Angramanyu. To one side were the principles of truth and goodness, light and fire, and Ahura-Mazda who incorporated them all; on the other side was the power of evil and darkness, Ahriman, forever eager for battle. From time immemorial the forces of good and evil had been fighting for the mastery of the world. It was an unremitting struggle, and the power of darkness was extremely resourceful.

The most interesting aspect of the Indo-European Devil was his creative power. And it was by adopting this idea of him that Zoroaster illuminated the quest for the origin of evil in all its complexity and diversity, and attempted to explain it. Thus Mazda's battle with the active and creative forces of darkness becomes the eternal struggle of the good against the unimaginable power of evil. Mazda and Ahriman are worlds apart. Nothing unites them, everything divides them. They have nothing in common, "neither thought nor doctrine, neither will nor beliefs, neither word nor deed, neither our self nor our soul."

But what did Zoroaster do with the old gods? In his teachings they became the demons, or "daevas," with Mithras and Anahita probably among them—the deities that rallied to the cause of evil and, like all false gods, corrupted the minds of men.

Man was placed in the middle of this spiritual battle between Ahura-Mazda and Ahriman. He was free to choose, but choose he *must*, and *go on choosing* until three days after his death when he stood before the tribunal of the living and the dead. There the godless, the evil and the liars could expect the eternal torments of hell; and the righteous, mercy and the immortality of his soul.

Besides this tribunal for the individual there was also an *end of the world*, a *resurrection* of the dead, and a *last judgment*. It was before this world court that the battle between light and darkness would ultimately be decided. The good spirit would prevail, mankind would be redeemed, evil would cease for all time, and all good men would enter Paradise with Ahura-Mazda, while the evil would fall into the abyss of eternal darkness. The duty of each man, as the Avesta describes it, is threefold: to befriend his enemy, to convert the evil man to goodness, and to bring knowledge to the ignorant.

This victory of Ahura-Mazda in Zoroaster's doctrine is of paramount importance. For in spite of its dualism, its twin powers of good and evil, Zoroaster's religion is essentially monotheistic. It proclaims the existence of a single god whom he regarded as the preserver of the firmament and the earth, the lord of all the winds, clouds and waters, the ruler of the suns and stars, the maker of plants and animals, and the creator of the soul. Prayers to this god could be said anywhere, and the religion had no room for idols or places of worship. No one ever built a temple for Ahura-Mazda, and no religious buildings were found in the citadels of Pasargadae or Persepolis, although fire altars on the surrounding hills may also have greeted Zoroaster's god with the smoke of their burnt offerings. We learn from the Greeks that the Persians of Darius' time looked down upon those races that represented their gods in human or animal form and compounded this indignity by confining them in a cramped little abode, quite unbefitting the god of all creation.

But the kings of Persia, the Achaemenidae, did not stick to the letter of Zoroaster's teachings and the commandments contained in the *gathas*

—the verses of the Avesta. They also recognized and worshiped the gods of subject peoples. While this was probably a matter of policy, it is more likely Zoroaster's religion took two hundred years to become firmly established. Darius I was the first king to accept Zoroaster's doctrines and suppress the ancient gods and the priesthood of the Magi. But he only partially succeeded, for the people certainly continued to cling to their natural religions and the Magi never did die out, even though Darius proclaimed the Zoroastrian faith as his state religion. To what extent the Persian kings before Darius believed in Zoroaster we do not know. Darius was the only one to speak of "the greatest of all gods," and Ahura-Mazda dominates his inscriptions. For Darius, Mazda was the creator of the earth, the sky and the universe, of mankind and, in particular, of his own personal welfare.

Darius' successors apparently drew away from Zoroaster, for Artaxerxes prayed not only to Ahura-Mazda but also to Mithras and Anahita. Indeed Berossus, the Babylonian priest of Bel, reports in 250 B.C. that Artaxerxes was the first king who taught the Persians to worship gods in human form. In his reign the cults of Mithras and Anahita received official state recognition; and once it had drunk its fill of the mystery cults that thrived in Asia Minor, the Mithraic faith eventually conquered most of the known world. Later, during Roman times, it became the soldiers' religion, and, ultimately, early Christianity's greatest enemy.

And Zoroaster? What happened to the doctrine of that spiritual giant who was so extraordinarily creative in the religious sphere?

Zoroaster had not evolved a national religion. His teachings were directed at the world in general, and everyone could embrace this one god. Ancient Persia's political history may have ended with Alexander's destruction of Persepolis, but her creative spirit lived on in the theology of the East and, later, of the West. According to the great Mithraic scholar Franz Cumont, the history of religion knows not only a Hellenism but also an Iranism, a mysterious and sometimes scarcely discernible creative force of great antiquity. Ahura-Mazda is perhaps the earliest religious synthesis of all those forces which regard moral values and the principle of justice as the supreme law, and the light of Zoroaster's teachings shines deep into the religious beliefs of the European peoples. The Jewish conception of Yahweh owes much of its essence to him, as does the idea of a universal god in heaven, the dualism of God and Satan, as well as redemption and the last judgment.

* * *

At the head of the largest pre-Christian empire was the king, and all other rulers were his vassals. That is why he called himself "King of Kings, King of the lands of many different peoples, King of this great wide world."

The king had many wives, as well as a very large harem of concubines —"as many as there are days in the year," the Greeks inform us. None of them ever visited the king's chamber twice unless "the King delighted in her," as we are told in the second chapter of the Book of Esther: "In the evening she went, and on the morrow she returned into the second house of the women, to the custody of Shaashgaz, the King's chamberlain, which kept the concubines." But first each woman went through a twelve-month beauty treatment, with oil of myrrh, balsams and other cosmetic preparations.

Herodotus reports that every Persian aristocrat had numerous legitimate wives, "but he took many more mistresses into his harem." The wealthy never went to war without a large company of women. There were many foreigners among the king's wives, and both Cyrus and Cambyses had Median and Egyptian princesses. Darius I even took over Cyrus' harem and married two of Cyrus' daughters, Atossa and Artystone, and Atossa, who previously had been married to her brother Cambyses, was the mother of Darius' successor, Xerxes. Artaxerxes II even took two of his own daughters into his harem.

The harem was guarded by eunuchs, and as a regular part of their tribute the Babylonians would castrate five hundred boys each year and send them as pages to the Persian king's court, to be instructed in their duties. And due to their influence on the women who were close to the king, the eunuchs became the greatest intriguers and gossip mongers at the Persian courts. Indeed, their influence became so great that they overthew kings, plotted palace revolutions, organized assassinations, and in general turned the petty jealousies among the women to their own advantage.

In the final years of the Persian empire, the succession to the throne was determined mainly by murder and revolution. The Persian kings based their power on huge armies which were unfortunately marked by an unprecedented linguistic confusion. And since they put their faith solely in numerical strength, they were often defeated. According to Herodotus, the expeditionary forces Xerxes led against Greece numbered 170,000 men. But even if this figure is grossly exaggerated (one-tenth would have been a powerful army in those days), we still can visualize the spectacle of this wild, frightened horde with its motley assortment of races as its endless columns spilled back into Asia Minor after their defeat. With such a heterogeneous army, even conducting a retreat became a great achievement.

The king was supreme judge and his word was law–his monarchy was absolute. Justice was administered in his name by royal judges appointed for life who could be dismissed only for crime or corruption, and frequently were succeeded in office by their sons. King Cambyses once stamped out corruption among his judges by having one of them beaten to death, covering the judge's chair with the dead man's skin, and placing his son upon it as supreme judge. Minor misdemeanors were punished by five to two hundred strokes with the horsewhip. Serious crimes were expiated by crippling, blinding, imprisonment or death. It was no laughing matter if a man molested one of the women in the king's harem, and anyone who thought of usurping the king's throne gambled with his life. Crucifixions, hangings, stonings, live burials, the application of hot ashes and worse cruelties–these were the punishments that held the Persian empire together.

Nevertheless, the empire was not merely a political organization devoted to injustice and cruelty. Herodotus points out that no one, freeman or slave, was sentenced to death except on adequate grounds, and a good king like Darius I never allowed himself to be swayed by personal caprice. He respected Ahura-Mazda's commandments and strove to safeguard the rights of his subjects. It is interesting to note in this context that Persian courts not only meted out penalties but also distributed rewards.

The twenty satraps who governed the various provinces were either members of the nobility or of the royal family. The satrap administered the provincial government, represented the interests of king and state, and looked after public order and safety. He was also the supreme judge of his province.

But power creates the thirst for absolute authority, and every governor of a distant province was a potential rebel, if only by virtue of his geographical location. Therefore, safety measures were devised: each satrap was given a royal secretary who was responsible for insuring permanent contact with the royal residence. It was he who supervised the receipt and dispatch of all royal correspondence and sent the dispatch riders galloping along the royal mail routes from one end of the empire to the other: from Ephesus and Sardis to the capital, Susa, more than 1,250 miles away; from Babylon across to Zagros range, past the cliffs at Behistun, to Ecbatana and the Bactrian and Indian frontiers, a total distance of more than 1,800 miles. Royal mail stations and hostels were established at regular intervals along the roads. Royal commands and government dispatches, carried by relays of riders, raced along night and day toward their destinations—"swifter than the cranes," as the Greeks put it. Supposedly there even existed a system of telegraphy operated by fire signals!

Each satrapy had a garrison and a fortress commander whose duty it was to keep an eye on the satrap, while the satrap in turn kept an eye on the general. Finally, there was the "king's eye," an official of highest rank—usually a brother or son of the king—who traveled from one satrapy to another with an armed body of men, turning up suddenly and unannounced to inspect the administration and check expenditures and other matters of government. Thus satraps, garrison commanders and royal secretaries alike had to exercise constant circumspection. These ingenious controls were remarkably successful in safeguarding the king's power in his vast empire. However, they only functioned as long as the supreme ruler was a statesman, and not the mere puppet of his harem.

In spite of enormous taxes and excessive expenditures, in spite of revolts and wars, the Babylonians, Phoenicians, Palestinians and other subject peoples were quite content to live under Persian domination. They felt that their own generals and tax officials would rob them even more effectively than the Persians. Under Darius I, the Persian empire became a brilliantly organized body politic such as the world would not see again until the great Roman emperors Trajan, Hadrian and Antoninus came on the scene.

Under the satraps, however, bureaucracy flourished. Kings might die, but the bureaucracy seemed everlasting. Not only did the satraps build sumptuous palaces and maintain large harems, but they also owned magnificent hunting preserves—parks which the Persians used to call "paradises." The cost of keeping a satrap's court and the administration in general was borne by the subject population, which also had to pay taxes to the king. Each satrapy sent him its tribute in the form of gold or silver talents, a Persian-Euboean gold talent containing about 55½ lbs. of pure gold, and a Babylonian silver talent 74 lbs. of silver. The combined satrapy of Babylonia and Assyria paid the largest tribute, pouring no less than one thousand silver talents annually into the treasure chests of the Persian king. Next came Egypt with seven hundred talents, the coastal satrapies of Asia Minor (i.e., Lydia and Mysia) with five hundred talents, and Caria with four hundred. The

Cilicians, who paid five hundred talents, were allowed to deduct one hundred and forty talents for the cavalry garrison stationed in their province, but in turn supplied the court with three hundred and sixty snow-white horses of the finest breed.

Since Persis, the heart of the empire, paid no tribute but probably sent the king only presents, the number of satrapies pouring their tributes into the royal exchequer was nineteen. Between them, they paid a grand total of 7,600 Babylonian silver talents, or, at about $700 to the talent, over $5,000,000—not such a vast sum, at that. Even after deducting the 8,000 talents which Darius III took along when he fled after his defeat by Alexander the Great, the Macedonian still received no less than 180,000 talents in minted and unminted gold and silver from the coffers of Susa, Persepolis and Pasargadae—a sum roughly equivalent to over a quarter of a billion dollars.

Apart from these financial tributes, each province paid the king taxes in kind. Cappadocia supplied a yearly quota of one thousand five hundred horses, two thousand mules and fifty thousand sheep, and Media supplied nearly twice that much. The Arabs were not obliged to pay any tribute; instead they sent "the King of the World" 1,000 talents' worth of incense. Interminable caravans of camels burdened with the precious commodity of the Gerrhaeans and Minaeans—the merchant tribes of Arabia—swayed along the famous incense roads toward the Persian metropolises. Newly purchased slaves straggled back over the same endless route. We have a Minaean inventory listing slave girls who were forced to dedicate their lives to the gods. We read that one each came from Ammon and Moab, three from Qedar, six from Dedan, seven from Egypt and twenty four from Gaza. Even far-off Ethiopia sent the Persian king two hundred trunks of ebony, twenty large elephant tusks—and five negro boys.

Within the framework of this extravagant, sanguinary, often cruel but, by and large, tolerable political organization, peoples of many different races lived more or less happily, more or less free, just as we do today. They were good-natured and extremely hospitable, just like the Persians of our own day. They loved, they hated, they laughed and they wept.

Persons of equal rank exchanged greetings by kissing each other on the lips, while inferiors kissed their superiors on the cheek and the citizenry prostrated itself before authority—a weakness which man has never been able to get out of his system since the days of Persian world rule. Spitting, blowing one's nose and eating in the street were forbidden, the pollution of rivers was strictly prohibited and infectious diseases were subject to quarantine. Up to the zenith of Persian world domination, i.e., up to the time of Darius I, the Persian lived a healthy life, partook of only one meal a day, and adhered strictly to his gods of nature or to Zoroaster's commandments, which branded lying as the most infamous of all sins. Horsemanship, archery and truthfulness—these were the things in which Persia's youth were indoctrinated, from their fifth to their twentieth year.

Gradually, however, the Persian empire fell prey to its own racial heterogeneity. The Persians took over every kind of luxury they found in their far-flung empire; temperamentally, so Herodotus tells us, they were susceptible to foreign customs in general. As time went on, the aristocracy began to ply themselves with ever-increasing quantities of food. They drank liberally and with gusto, and frequently transacted important affairs in a state of intoxication. When they sobered up, they reviewed the decisions they had made, and if they could not agree they discussed the whole matter all over—under the conciliatory influence of more wine!

Herodotus reports that the Persians regarded the abduction of a woman as an evil act, but looked upon any man who tried to avenge it as a fool. It was obvious, they reasoned, that no woman could be abducted against her will. Since the king needed soldiers, polygamy was allowed. Children were married off by their parents, and marriages between brother and sister, father and daughter, or mother and son, were not unusual. Women walked about unveiled and unmolested; they ran their households and could do business in their husbands' name. Only the wives of the nobility were not permitted to be seen in public in the company of men, or even to set eyes on their closest male relatives.

Sons were in greater demand than daughters, and a man who had many sons was rewarded by the king. Nobody prays for a daughter, the Persians used to say, and the angels did not number daughters among the blessings of mankind. Medicine was a combination of magic and medical skill but whenever a surgeon, an herbalist and a priest were all three available, people were inclined to consult the last—the doctor "who heals with the sacred word." Curing the mind was preferable to surgery: there was no danger involved in healing the soul, whereas the scalpel might prove fatal.

The Persians had beautiful houses and gardens, costly furniture, magnificent bed chambers, vessels of gold. But they bought most of these fine things from foreign craftsmen because they had enough to do running the government, making war and working the land. Only in the field of architecture did the Persians achieve anything of their own. The palace of Xerxes I at Susa must have been of phenomenal grandeur, as excavations and Old Testament descriptions in the Book of Esther would indicate. Excavations at Persepolis have also revealed the grandiose design of royal palaces; the pontoon bridges which the Persian kings threw across rivers and straits in their military campaigns stagger us to this day, even though wind and waves soon destroyed them. Yet Herodotus' description of the feats of engineering accomplished by slaves and soldiers some 2,500 years ago still borders on the fabulous.

Greek travelers returning from the Persian empire were filled with admiration. They told stories about marble halls and palaces, and about the wonders of Persian luxury. But as the Persians' extravagance, the splendor of their clothes and jewels increased from decade to decade—as their civilization grew brighter, richer and more magnificent—their kings became progressively weaker and more deluded. In the end this remarkable and glorious empire choked on its own luxury—an empire which already believed in *one* god, but did not survive long enough to witness the coming of Christ.

"O, ABSALOM, MY SON"

And the king . . . went up to the chamber over the gate, and wept: and as he went, thus he said, . . . would God I had died for thee . . . .

2 Samuel 18, 33

THE small country of Palestine has had a greater impact on humanity —on its ideas, ethics and beliefs—than mighty Babylonia, Assyria, Persia, Egypt, India or China. Palestine's cultural heritage has had more far-reaching effects than the whole of Greek culture. For this smallest of countries bequeathed to the world a religion filled with an unexampled dynamism: Christianity. The Bible, that "Book of Books," has outlived Egypt's Book of the Dead, India's Mahabaratha, the teachings of Confucius and of the Chinese, and the gods of the Aztecs. Flowing along without a break, the history of Yahweh and his chosen people lives on —generation after generation.

No other work has been burned so often as the Bible, no other work has been so widely translated, so often impugned, so greatly revered. It is the most frequently printed book of mankind, and the literature which has grown around it is like a vast ocean, whose waters man can drink only in mere thimblefuls.

The Jews—like the Babylonians, Phoenicians and Arabs—are a Semitic people who lived in Palestine back in ancient times. Originally they were nomads known as Khabiri.

The name "Jew" derives from "Judah," and the Jews claimed they were originally descended from Judah, the fourth son of Jacob and Leah. Although the word "Jew" appears as early as 516 B.C., the history of the Jews is several thousand years older.

Abraham, the ancestor of the Jews and described in the Bible as "the Hebrew" (Genesis 14,13), lived about 1700 B.C. and came from Ur in Mesopotamia. He built altars to the living gods, but he built no statues of them, a radically new idea: for Abraham had recognized the spirituality of God. He was no doubt a historical personality, a conclusion we may draw from modern archaeology which is constantly furnishing new proofs for the historical authenticity of the Old Testament. Abraham's name, in the Chaldean tongue of his native country, was Orham, and apparently he was a prince of Ur. And historically he is credited with a major accomplishment: that of replacing human sacrifice by the offering of rams.

When Abraham arrived in Canaan, he had conceived, after long years of spiritual torment and confusion, a firm belief in God which he did not abandon when he was put to the test. The story of Isaac appears to be a protest against the Canaanite custom of human sacrifice. In it God tested Abraham, saying: "Take now thy son, thine only son Isaac, whom thou lovest, and . . . offer him . . . for a burnt offering." Abraham bound his son, placed him on the altar and was about to take his knife to kill him when the angel appeared and absolved him from the sacrifice.

Later, Abraham made his eldest servant swear that he would not choose a Canaanite wife for his son Isaac. With ten camels the servant set off for the land of Abraham's birth, Mesopotamia, where he traveled about until he found the girl Rebecca, a daughter of the city of Haran. Isaac married Rebecca, and when his father died, he and his brother Ishmael buried him in brotherly harmony. He reaped a hundredfold, for the Lord blessed him, and his love of peace overcame his enemies. He dug two wells, left them to quarreling herdsmen, and dug a third for himself. After Isaac came Jacob, whose surname was Israel. It was he who had twelve sons—the ancestors of the twelve tribes of Israel.

After 1500 B.C., Palestine fell under Egyptian domination, and the *Amarna Tablets* cast some light on the conditions prevailing there sometime between 1400 and 1350 B.C. The 350 letters from Near Eastern princes to the Pharaohs Amenhotep III and IV were found at Tell el Amarna, Egypt, in 1887. After a period of slavery under the Egyptians, Moses welded the children of Israel into a nation and led them on a long and arduous desert march to Canaan. This migration stretched over forty years, with numerous halts on the way, and on it the Israelites lived like nomads, driving large herds of cattle, and donkeys burdened with goods and chattels. In the course of these forty years, Israel received the Ten Commandments at Sinai. It became "a priestly kingdom and holy nation," and Moses received the tables of the Covenant. Moses, who beheld Yahweh in a thundercloud or a burning bush, was undoubtedly one of the great geniuses of all time. General and preacher, organizer and historian, today he often strikes us as gloomy and irascible, viewing all civilization as a form of disloyalty to Yahweh.

Centuries before Christ was born, the religious literature of the Jews

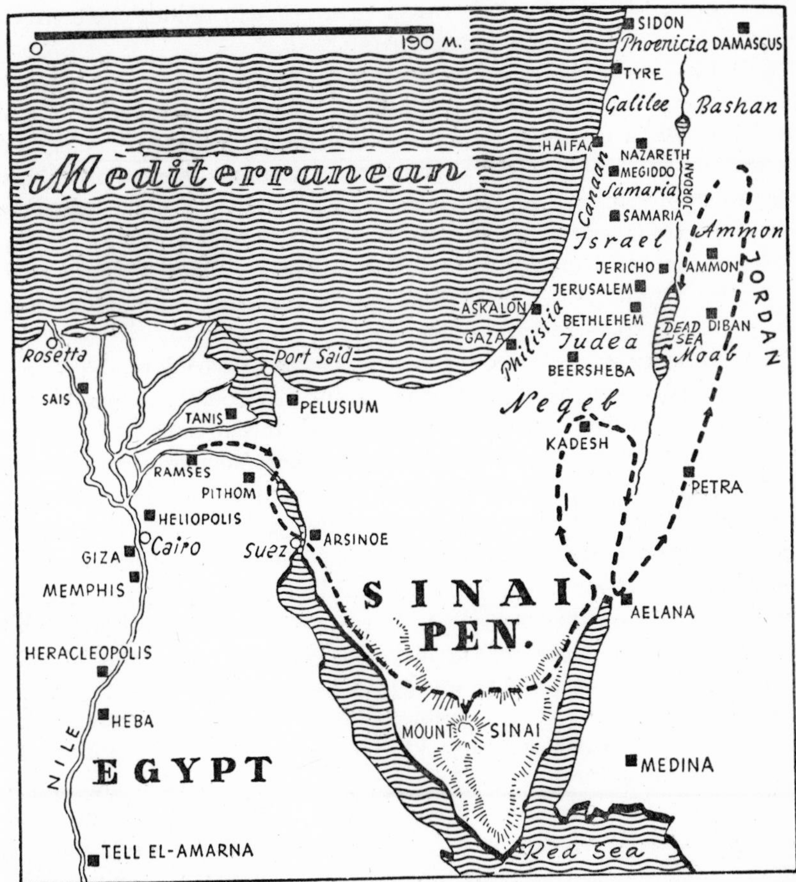

Sinai Peninsula, Egypt and the Holy Land. The broken line indicates the route followed by the Israelites in their migration under Moses from Egypt to the Dead Sea, where Moses died.

had been gathered in thirty-nine books written in Hebrew and Aramaic. This literature—the Old Testament—is divided into three large sections: the *Torah* (the Law), the *Nebiim* (the Prophets), and the *Ketubim* (the Holy Writings). The Torah consists of five books, and Moses is credited with authoring these five scrolls which later were collectively called the Pentateuch and which ranked as the law among the Jews. When, where and by whom were they written? This is a rather formidable question, and a literature of about 50,000 volumes has been written in an attempt to answer it! Let us here attempt to reduce these 50,000 volumes to their simplest possible form.

Scholars classify the oldest elements in the Bible—namely, the separate but similar versions of the Creation story—under the initials "J" and "E", because in one part the Creator is called Jehovah (Jahweh), and in the other, Elohim. The "Jehovistic" accounts were supposedly written in Judah, and the "Elohistic" in Ephraim. In 719 B.C., after the fall of Samaria, the two collections were made into one. A third group, classified as "D", contained the Deuteronomic Law, and a fourth element, "F", was later interpolated by the priests. The four works acquired their present form about 300 B.C.

The most ancient relics of Hebrew literature date back to about 1200 B.C.—inscriptions in the Old Canaanite script that contained twenty-two letters. The Hebrews probably brought their language and writing from Sinai into Canaan. In fact, there exists an ancient Semitic letter script which was in use in the Sinai Peninsula before 1600 B.C. But aside from the Bible, there are very few inscriptions with examples of the Old Hebrew script. One of these is found on the Mesa Stele of the King of Moab, who appears in the Bible. This inscription is composed in a script and language which is virtually identical with Old Hebrew and dates from the year 855 B.C. The stone was found in 1868 at Diban, Transjordan, and is now in the Louvre at Paris.

The God of the Jews is invisible; yet, his religion is founded upon civilizations thousands of years old. The Ark of the Covenant recalls the portable dwellings of the Nile gods. Traces of necromancy come from Egypt. The Flood and the mystique of numbers remind us of Babylon. The Babylonian god Gilgamesh becomes Nimrod, and the winged bulls of the Assyrians turn into the Hebrews' cherubim. The legend of Paradise, the figure of Satan (Ahriman), and the dominion of angels and archangels are reminiscent of Persia. We recognize Baal, the god of the Phoenicians and Canaanites, in the names of Saul's sons, Eshbal and Meribaal. The Syrian Philistines, who probably originally hailed from Crete, regarded the dove as a divinity; the fish that was worshiped at Askalon turns up in the story of Jonah. And the Semitic Aramaeans revered a "Mother of the Living" called "Khavva," from which the name "Eve" appears to be derived.

In the tenth century B.C., Israel became a monarchy, and the Old Testament describes the personages of that era in the books of Samuel and Kings. Grandiose and reckless, often moved by a childlike, primeval fervor, they are drawn so true to life, with all their human weaknesses revealed, that all poetry or historiography pales beside them. It is certainly not the historicity of the Old Testament that we should doubt, for seldom has history been painted with such true and vivid colors as in these Sacred Books.

Saul was a handsome and chivalrous man who in 1025 B.C. was called by the prophet Samuel to become king of Israel. Calm and magnanimous, deeply religious, valiant and triumphant, he always obeyed his God. But as he grew older, he became increasingly impatient, irresolute, restless and hot-tempered, until at the end of his life he was as vindictive as a raging demon. When he found that God no longer answered him, he began consulting soothsayers, and eventually died by his own hand.

Saul was succeeded not by his son Jonathan, but by David, who became the greatest king of Israel. David unified his people, vanquished neighboring tribes, founded Jerusalem, and forged the link between throne and altar. He appears as a titanic figure, possessed of many good qualities but also afflicted with all human weaknesses, an extremely able sovereign who ruled for forty years. Yet he was the man who abducted the beautiful Bathsheba into his large harem, and then sent her husband Uriah into battle to get rid of him; who forgave his ungrateful son Absalom for plotting against him, and wept when he heard that he had been killed, crying: "O, my son Absalom, my son, my son!"

David reigned from 1012 to 972 B.C. He was a historical personality, in a sense still a barbarian, but already an impressive oriental potentate and one of the greatest poets and singers the world has ever known. For modern scholarship has confirmed the ancient assumption that this royal bard composed many of the Psalms.

Solomon, who succeeded him, truly must have been one of the wisest kings in the history of mankind. Who but a wise man could have combined a life of fantastic opulence and exquisite luxury with such punctilious fulfillment of all royal duties? The name Solomon derives from *shalom*, meaning peace, and King Solomon lived up to it—not only by teaching his people law and order, but also by assuring them peace. Under his wise administration, Jerusalem became one of the wealthiest cities in the Near East. Phoenician merchants brought their caravans through Palestine to Jerusalem, and Israel's produce was bartered at Tyre and Sidon. Solomon's fleet sailed the Red Sea, and he traded with Africa and Arabia, where he started mining gold. Even the powerful Queen of Sheba courted his friendship. He recruited armies of forced laborers. But he also brought the Ark of the Covenant into the Temple, spoke the prayer of consecration and blessed the congregation. For all that, he loved life and had few men before him. He gathered many wives, and his passionate vitality seems scarcely diminished when modern scientific research tells us that the traditional estimates crediting him with seven hundred wives and three hundred concubines should be reduced to sixty and eight respectively.

Beginning with 1925 the Oriental Institute of the University of Chicago started extensive excavations at Megiddo, Palestine. The first layer disclosed ruins of Babylonian and Persian times; the second produced ruins of Assyrian palaces. Layers three and four were, however, of Israelitic origin, and the latter stratum revealed traces of Solomonic architecture, for the king had made this city the capital of Israel's fifth administrative district. Royal stables came to light; also, the palace built for Baana, at one time governor of Megiddo, as we learn from the Bible (I Kings 4,7 and 12). The excavations were continued between 1935 and 1938 and it was established that Megiddo must have been originally founded about 3500 B.C. Three temples and one altar for burnt sacrifices were discovered, all dating back to about 1700 B.C.—the time of Abraham and his successors. This was the first altar found in Palestine which was more or less intact.

After Solomon's death, in 932 B.C., a revolution broke out, and ten of the twelve tribes of Israel broke away from Solomon's son Rehoboam and established the kingdom of Israel. Rehoboam stayed in Judea with the remaining two tribes, while Jeroboam became king of Israel and ruled over the ten rebel tribes.

From then on there were two kingdoms—Judea and Israel. Israel, the larger of the two, existed only for 200 years and its history ended in 721 B.C. with the conquest of Samaria by the Assyrian king Sargon II when twenty-seven thousand people belonging to the ten tribes were deported to central Asia, and vanished from the historical scene. We have never heard what became of them, and their fate remains one of history's unsolved riddles. It is, in fact, a favorite pastime of historians to "rediscover" the ten lost tribes. When stones with Jewish hieroglyphics were found in China, some scientists believed that it was there that these tribes finally settled; their traces were also allegedly found in India, while other scholars regard the Anglo-Saxons as the latter-day descendants of these "deportees," and the Anglo-Israelite theory has its own extensive literature.

The final destination of the ten lost tribes has been "discovered" almost everywhere in the world: in Mexico, where Pizarro was welcomed as the "White Savior"; in Africa, and even in North America among

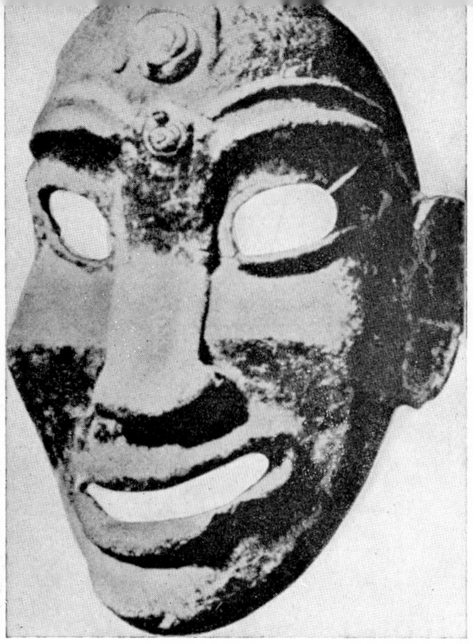

Two male masks, caricatures in clay of typical Phoenician faces, which were discovered in Carthaginian graves.

Phoenician deity in bronze. This statuette probably belongs to the period 1200 B.C.

This bull adorned the capital of a pillar in the great hall of Darius' palace. Dating from the 5th century B.C., it is made of gray marble, and was found at Susa. The beast's back supported massive wooden ceiling beams.

A Persian of about 2,500 years ago. The head is from a bas-relief at Persepolis. The hair is artistically curled. The Persians overthrew the might of Babylon and Assyria, then mingled with these races, and adopted their customs.

Tomb of King Artaxerxes II, in Persepolis. He reigned from 405 to 359 B.C. when the Persian empire was already in decline. Not only the king but also the members of his family were buried here. ▶

Through the upper window, now walled up, of this gatehouse in Damascus St. Paul escaped. In the Second Epistle to the Corinthians, Paul himself wrote: "In Damascus the governor under Aretas the King kept the city of the Damascenes with a garrison, desirous to apprehend me: and through a window in a basket was I let down by the wall, and escaped his hands." ▶

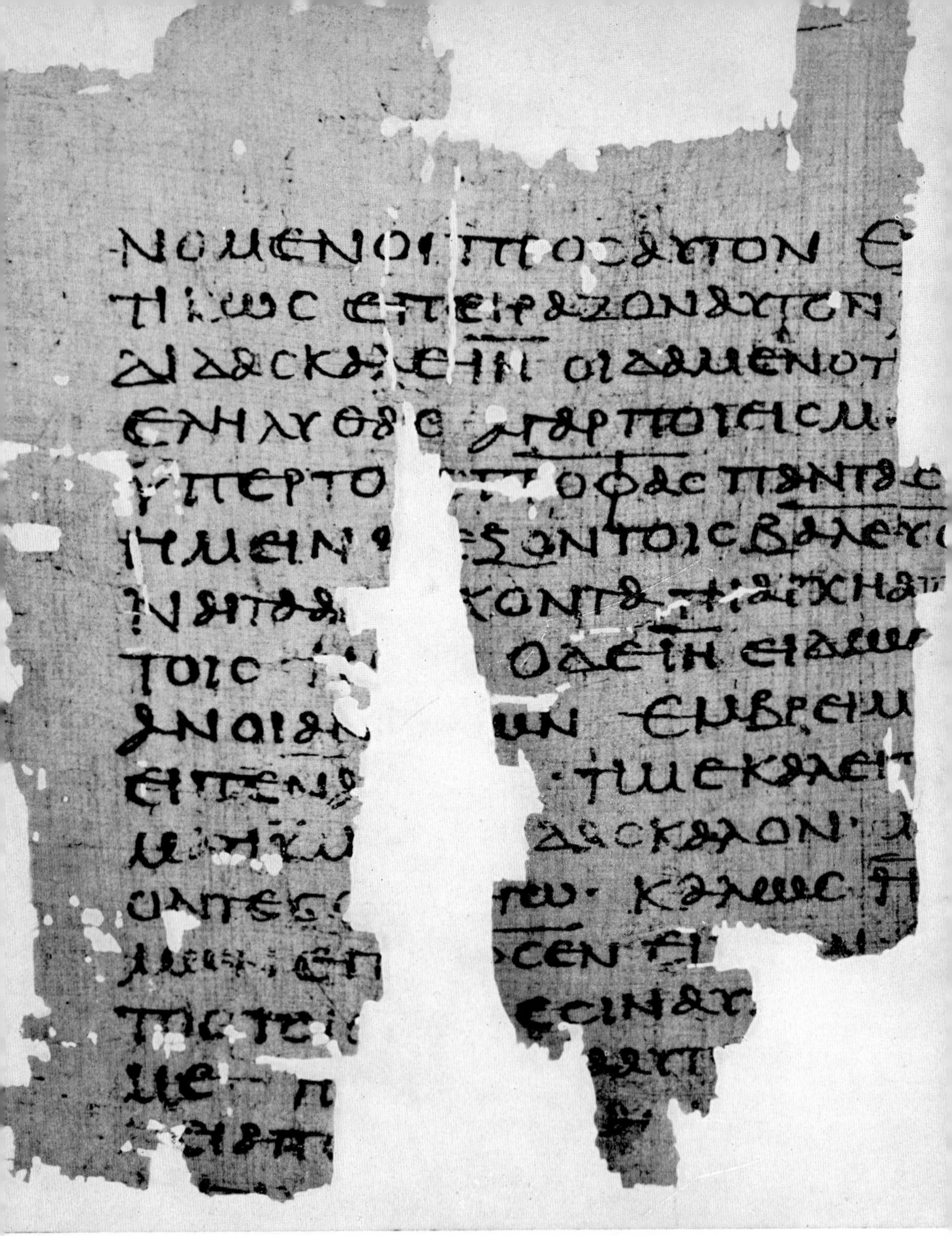

The "Egerton Papyrus," written only 70 to 120 years after the Crucifixion. It is based on and is an early confirmation of the four Gospels. Perhaps the writer was himself a contemporary of Christ. The fragment was first brought to the attention of the public in 1931 by H. I. Bell and T. C. Skeat and is one of the most valuable evidences that Jesus lived.

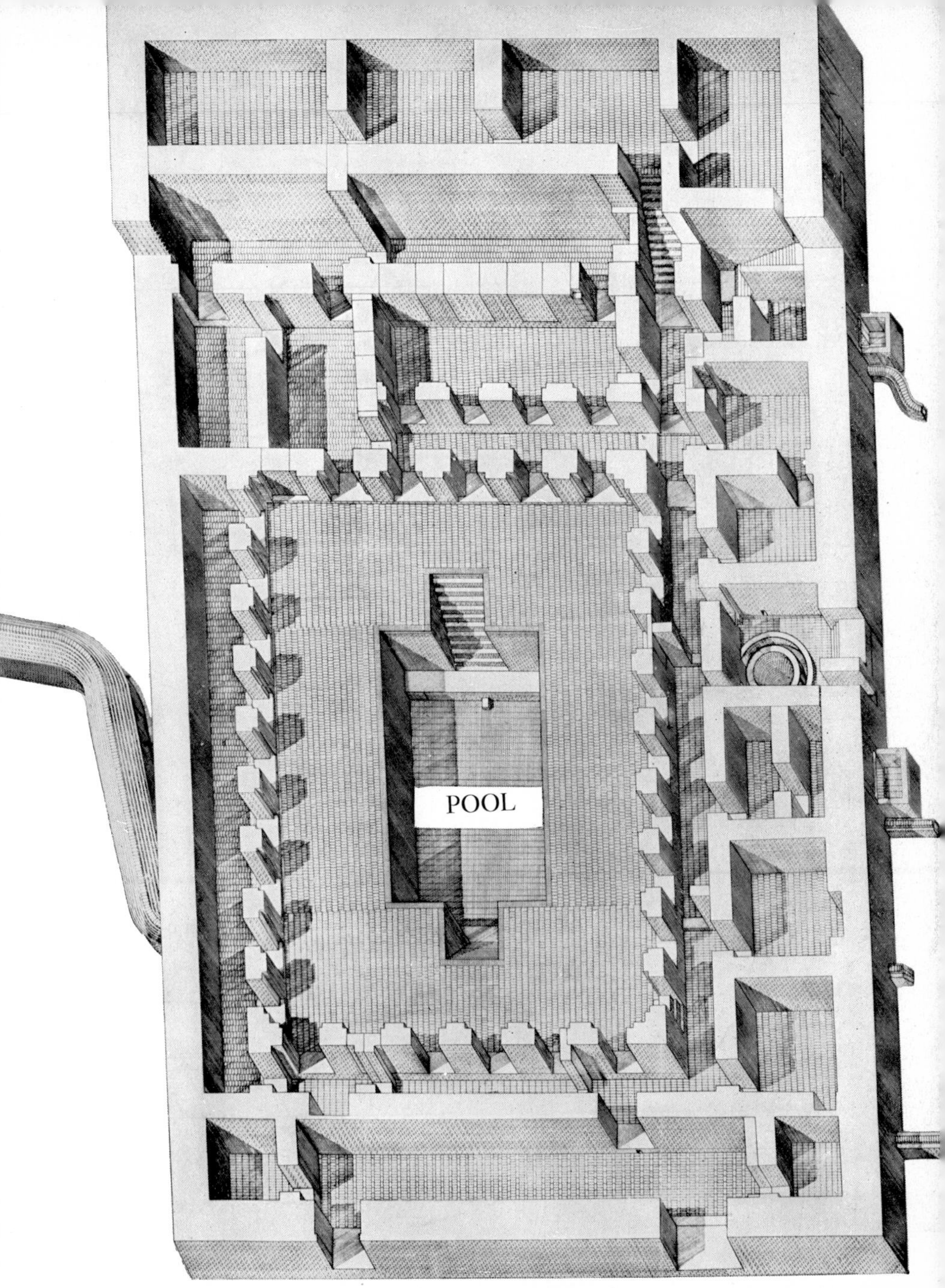

Reconstruction of the Great Bath at Mohenjo-Daro. The swimming-pool is still virtually intact after 5,000 years. The water was changed by means of an outlet drain (left) and a subterranean conduit. Steam baths and cold showers, dressing rooms, and all the comforts of a modern bathing establishment were to be found here long before the dawn of history as it is known to us.

Bronze statuette of a dancing-girl
from Mohenjo-Daro.

Statue of Buddha from the Gupta period, the golden age of Indian art which began in 320 A.D., with the accession of King Chandragupta. The writing on the pedestal belongs to the 5th century. The statue clearly exhibits the influence of Greek art, which allied itself to the indigenous art of north-west India.

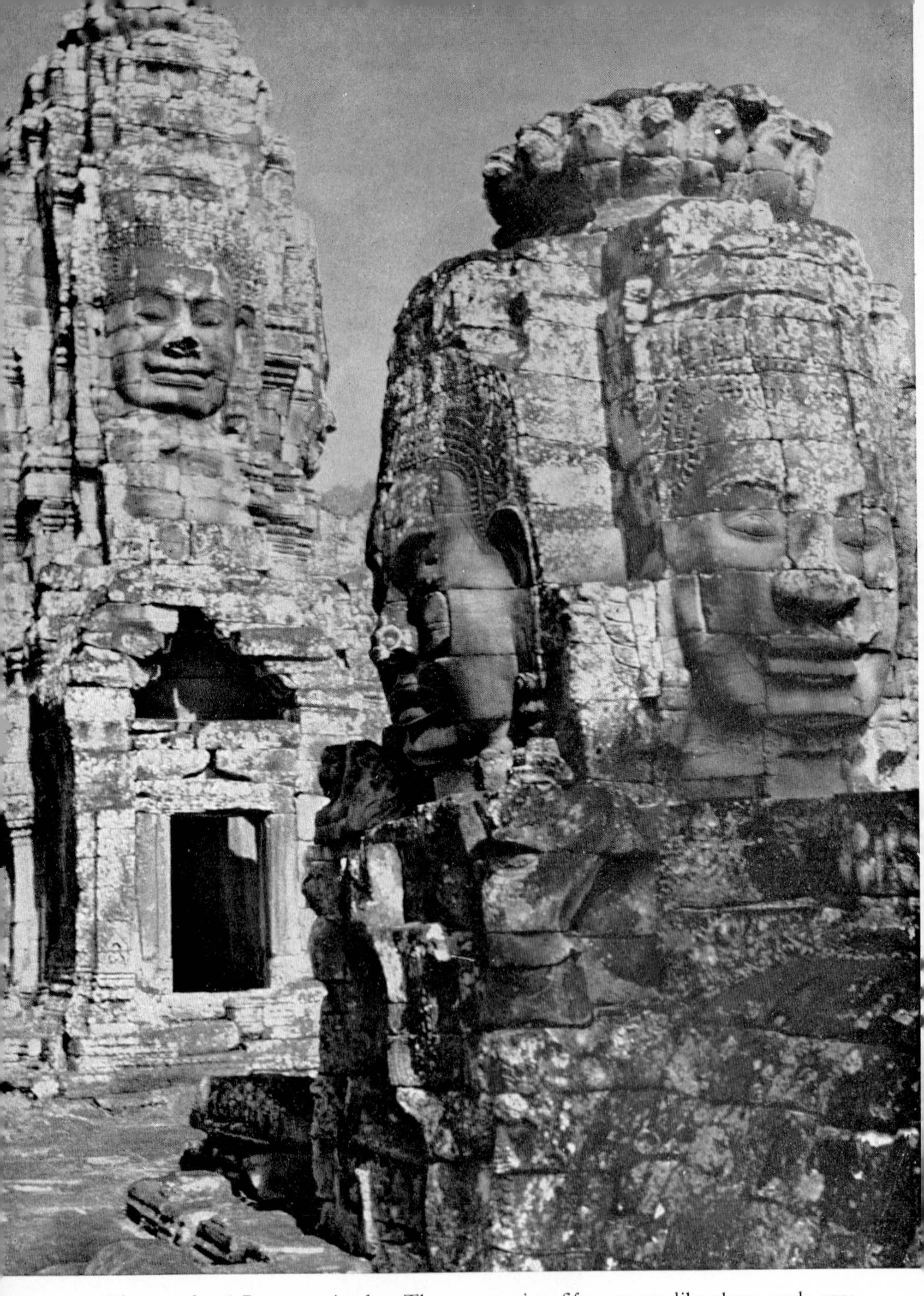

The temple of Bayon at Angkor Thom comprises fifty towers like these, each ornamented with four faces of Brahma. Angkor Thom became the capital of the Khmer nation in 890 A.D. [*Photograph:* Meissner.

the "white Indians." The book of Mormon is a reflection of the latter theory.

The modern Jews are descended from the smaller kingdom of Judea. They in turn were borne off to Babylon by King Nebuchadnezzar in 586 B.C. for the duration of what is known as the "Babylonian Captivity," but in 538 B.C., Cyrus of Persia allowed them to return to Palestine and rebuild the Temple; a task they finally completed in 516 B.C. Jews from all over Judea poured into Jerusalem to pray to Yahweh and look at the building which they regarded as one of the wonders of the world.

At the core of Judaism was the conception of sin. The flesh was weak, the laws were all-embracing: therefore sin was unavoidable. In times of drought, or when plagues raged and cities were destroyed, the Jews invariably felt that their sinfulness was the cause. And while they did not believe in Hell, they had a subterranean kingdom of darkness, Sheol, which the good and the bad alike must enter. Only the chosen –like Moses, Enoch and Elijah–were exempt.

Nor did the Jews believe at first in the immortality of the soul: both punishment and reward were found right here on earth. It was only after they lost their faith in their ultimate triumph as a nation that there awoke in them–influenced by their contact with Persia and, possibly, Egypt–a belief in resurrection. Devastation and hopelessness, endless suffering and the fate of millions of people who sought consolation–this was the soil from which Christianity could grow.

THEY FOUGHT AGAINST MANY GODS

SIXTEEN PROPHETS

They recognized something deep and fundamental: they knew what lies hidden in man, and beyond that they knew that there is One Who transcends human insight and Who orders the Universe. They lived, they suffered and died for the sake of a better world.

TODAY almost anyone can define what a prophet is: a prophet is a man who foretells the future. The prophets of the Old Testament, however, were not solely concerned with the future. They did not merely claim to know the future by divine inspiration; they did not merely predict the coming of the Messiah—their essential significance was something altogether different.

We should remember that *prophetes* is a Greek word, for the concept of prophecy cannot be expressed in the Hebrew tongue by one simple word. *Nabi* is the Hebrew term for prophet, and *Nebiim* was what the Hebrews called the prophetic books of the Bible. But the word *nabi* was not indigenous to Israel, and it is worth pursuing its origins since they cast light on its basic meaning. We find the word *nabaa* both in the Assyrian-Babylonian languages and in Arabic. In Assyrian, it means: to talk, speak, proclaim, or designate. There was a Babylonian god called Nabu, or Nebu, and we find the same word in the names of such kings as *Nabo*polassar and *Nebu*chadnezzar.

But Arabic is perhaps the most rewarding source for any scientific investigation of the Semitic languages, since it is even closer to Old Semitic than Sanskrit is to Old Indo-European. In Arabic, *naba'a* means "to announce," and here we find that the speaker is not expressing ideas of his own but passing on someone else's message. The *nabi* is therefore a spokesman who has a message to deliver or a specific communication to make. Thus we reach the heart of the matter: the Prophets were not conscious of speaking on their own authority but, rather, as the instruments of a superior will. They felt that they were "the mouth of God."

Incidentally, the Greek word *prophetes* is not identical with prediction either: the prefix *pro* does not mean "beforehand," but "forth."

The Prophets were unshakably convinced that their thoughts issued from Yahweh. "Thus saith the Lord" is a frequent preface to their discourses.

If the word *nabi* comes from Arabia, then perhaps Arabia was the original home of these early seers with their powers of ecstatic divination. There is unquestionably an aura of the desert about them. Elijah, the first Prophet mentioned in the Old Testament, came from East Jordan, a region where Jews and Arabs were racially intermingled, and Samuel was still known as a seer. For like everything else in the evolution of mankind, prophecy also has its history. At first the Prophets were seers; then they became the verbal transmitters of religious thought and mood; and finally, they put their prophetic utterances in writing.

When we speak of the Prophets of the Old Testament, we are thinking mainly of the "literary Prophets," the first being Amos. They numbered sixteen in all—men whose names we learned in Sunday School and have since forgotten. The body of written prophecy extends from Amos, who lived about 750 B.C., to the unknown author who wrote Zechariah (chapters 9-14) about 275 B.C. And as time went by, the authentic Prophets lost the desert aura that characterized their earliest predecessors.

We can easily recognize the difference between the Prophets' religious ideas and other oriental conceptions of the deity if we read the Koran. Mohammed (569-632 A.D.) was at such pains to emphasize God's omnipotence that he often painted him as a self-centered despot. In fact, if God were really as unpredictable and capricious as Mohammed suggests, it is difficult to see how the universe could function at all. To the Prophets, God's omnipotence never clashes with nature. God's essence is absolute, but we can rely on it as surely as we can rely on the course of the stars above. If nothing else, this particular conception of Yahweh often enabled the Prophets to predict the sort of destiny He had in store, and no amount of scientific argumentation can refute the nature of such a God.

The Prophets regarded God as the Lord of Nature, a concept which they had unconsciously realized by the eighth century B.C., and perhaps even earlier. This feeling found expression in the story of the Creation, for Yahweh was also the Lord of the Universe. This is natural, for anyone who tries to search for first causes and identify the unfathomable forces that motivate humanity must eventually come close to the laws of nature and the universe and, ultimately, to their creator.

Nevertheless, there were things that were not within the scope of Yahweh's design. If an individual or a nation violated the law of nature, and thus the law of God, this individual introduced the element of evil —self-perpetuating and deadly—into the world. Somewhere, sometime, this was bound to have consequences—namely, retribution.

And this was the true greatness of the Prophets: they were not mere dreamers or clairvoyants, they did not foretell the future and, above all, they claimed no magical powers. Yet at a time when the world was still governed by sorcery, black magic and evil spirits, they discovered a new heaven and a new world, unshakable ideals for mankind, and the way to the One God. Taking a lone stand against the convictions of their contemporary world, these men evolved ideals for countless future generations, ideals which still govern our life. Jonah and the whale, and Daniel in the lion's den are ancient fables that admittedly have a deeper meaning, but they have nothing to do with prophecy. Israel's Prophets despised charlatans and magicians. Spiritually, they stood head and shoulders above their country's neighbors. Spiritually, they remained undefeated either by natural catastrophes or foreign subjection. Spiritually, they were superior to the rest of the world—and this for thousands of years to come.

The great religious teachers whom we call the Prophets never pretended that they could perform miracles. The lives of Elijah and Elisha were full of miracles, but they departed without leaving posterity a single written word, even though Elijah lived only fifty years before Amos. And with Amos, the first literary Prophet, all miracles ceased.

The Prophets were the stormy petrels of history. They saw God's hand in the destiny of mankind. They embodied the people's conscience, they regarded all temporal things under the aspect of eternity, and discerned in everything the universal will of God. If we wanted to explain it rationally, as it were, we might say that they led mankind for the first time to the borders of that vast realm which can no longer be measured by any known criterion, physical or chemical, and which cannot be perceived through the finest telescopes of modern astronomy. This immeasurable and eternal realm knows neither witchcraft nor idolatry—its essence is God Himself.

The Prophets were a remarkable group of men. Ezekiel suffered from periodic spells of muteness: it was as though his tongue cleaved to his palate until he suddenly became articulate again. For a while he was also paralyzed. Isaiah went about naked for three years, to the consternation of his fellow men. Jeremiah occasionally appeared with a yoke on his neck, like an ox. Hosea named his daughter "The Hag" and had a wife who was notorious for her promiscuity.

Such strange behavior was characteristic of the Prophets. Did they wish to attract attention? Did they act in a state of ecstacy? Who can judge the ways of genius or sit in judgment on men who described the thoughts of God and were filled with passion and burning exaltation—men whose spirit transported them to spheres beyond the range of ordinary mortal thought?

Certainly all sixteen Prophets are historical personalities. The concrete details that are recorded in the Books of the Prophets cannot be mere invention, and the comparative study of their texts is producing more and more evidence for the historicity of these men.

Amos was a shepherd from Tekoa, and grew mulberry trees. He had a sharp eye for the thoughtless luxury of the mighty and for the oppression of the poor. It was probably some violent thunderstorm or earthquake which first caused him to put his discourses down in writing, and his verses still re-echo this experience (Amos 3,8). His style is very poetic and original, and he was a master of graphic description.

Hosea had a tragic life. He loved his wife as dearly as any man could, but she left him for a series of lovers and was finally sold into slavery. Nevertheless he took her back. From this experience he learned the meaning of great and divine love, and for the first time in human history put this love into words.

Isaiah, who lived in Jerusalem, was married and had two sons. Teaching between 740 and 700 B.C., he stands out like a giant among the historical Prophets and he is the classical genius of Judaism. In him, speech and thought reached their consummation. He was a great statesman, mingled freely with kings and politicians, and was perhaps the most brilliant theological teacher in Israel before Christ. Of all the Prophets, he probably wielded the greatest influence. Yet actually the probability is that at least one and perhaps several other men from later periods wrote the last half of the book attributed to Isaiah.

Micah (750-685 B.C.) lived near the great international highway between Egypt and Assyria. He was familiar with the peoples and political currents of western Asia, and he knew the historical future that his own people might expect. At times, the prophetic power of his language reaches great heights of dramatic expression: "But thou, Bethlehem Ephratah, though thou be little among the thousands of Judah, yet out of thee shall come forth unto me that is to be ruler in Israel; whose goings forth have been from of old, from everlasting."

Jeremiah was still a young man when he received the call to become a Prophet. He came from a family of priests. For forty-one years he prophesied and admonished, and even worried about the composition of his speeches. His public career lasted from about 626 to 584 B.C., and no other Prophet made such a deep impression on his contemporaries or on posterity by the sheer force of his personality as did Jeremiah. He bared his own inner struggle with unique candor; he could not remain silent because his inner voice left him no peace. But as soon as he opened his mouth he made nothing but enemies. He suffered unspeakably under the burden of his vocation, and in this respect he was probably nearer to Christ than any other Prophet. No one before Christ was so insistent in demanding the intensification of individual religious experience, and no one before Christ except Jeremiah battled against rigid laws and superficial dogma with such single-mindedness. Unmarried and lonely, he suffered, endured and prayed—like the Sufferer of Gethsemane.

Ezekiel was borne off into the Babylonian captivity in 598 B.C., together with many other Jews. Perhaps this is why his discourses combine a passionate vehemence with wisdom and circumspection. He was an erudite and cultured man of unwavering courage and faith.

Haggai was born in Babylon. He called upon the great of his country to resume and complete the building of the Temple. We can visualize all the cathedrals in the world when we read in Haggai: " 'The latter glory of this house shall be greater than that of the former, and in this place will I give peace,' saith Jehovah of hosts."

In the year 275 B.C., prophethood ceased. All Prophets were uncommunicative about their personal lives, but they all revealed their thoughts—a characteristic shared by both Homer and Shakespeare. The sixteen men present an almost unbroken succession of great minds all fighting against polytheism and foreign religious cults. Always before their eyes was an all-encompassing vision of the future, the work of Yahweh's creative powers. Some day, they declared, the greatest of all the Prophets would come; a man who would meekly submit to death, and about whom his disciples would say: "He is risen again." In the end, there would be a new Creation and a new golden age.

The Prophets recognized something deep and fundamental: they knew what lies hidden in man, and beyond that they knew that there is One Who transcends human insight and Who orders the Universe. They lived, they suffered and they died for the sake of a better world.

MAN'S DAYS ARE FEW AND FULL OF WOE

THE BOOK OF JOB

All the world agrees that the Bible deserves to be entitled the greatest book of mankind. It is the book in which our whole civilization has learnt to read, from which we have conceived all our moral, artistic and literary ideas, and out of which there has come, like a stream of fructifying water, an inexhaustible store of sanctity and spirituality.

Paul Claudel, December, 1940

ALMOST all great civilizations possess their own store of legends, but epic poetry among the Jews seems to have been virtually nonexistent. Such heroic narratives as exist were mostly taken over from ancient foreign sources and elaborated by prophets and priests for instructional purposes. Nor did Israel have a theatre; the drama could not develop because a live performance on the stage would have violated the law against human representation.

It was only in the field of lyric poetry that the Hebrews achieved true greatness. The word "lyric" comes from the Greek *lyra*, meaning lyre, and lyric poetry was once sung to the accompaniment of that instrument. Lyric poetry differs from epic and dramatic poetry in its closeness to music. Thus thirty of the hundred and fifty psalms in the Old Testament contain musical annotations, for the psalms were songs as well as poems. We find a parallel development in the epigrammatic poetry of the Proverbs and Ecclesiastes, while the Book of Job is a beautiful combination of song and proverb.

The poetic, or didactic, books of the Old Testament consist of Job, Psalms, Proverbs, Ecclesiastes, and the Song of Songs—five in all. The Bible of the Roman Catholic Church, in the Latin translation of St. Jerome, contains, in addition, the Book of Wisdom and the Book of Jesus Sirach, or a total of seven. In the Hebrew Bible, these books belong to the *Ketubim*, or Holy Writings.

We do not know who wrote the Book of Job. We can only surmise that the author was an Israelite although even that is open to question. He may have been an Arab who was ignorant of the Hebrew law. It has even been suggested that the story of Job came from Babylon for fragments of a song about the sufferings of a righteous man were found in King Ashurbanipal's library at Nineveh and at Sippar. In this story, a devout king is crippled by disease and is therefore regarded as a great sinner. He has to suffer every kind of abuse until, in his distress, he discovers his sin: he has considered himself the equal of his god. In the end he is restored to health and happiness and the god Marduk appears to him in a dream. Nevertheless, there is a considerable difference between the Babylonian and the Biblical stories: Job was innocent, while the Babylonian king was a sinner.

It is possible that Job lived about 1700 B.C. at the time of the patriarchs—Abraham, Isaac and Jacob—near the Arabian Desert on the eastern border of Palestine. In fact, we find the name of Job as early as 2000 B.C. in Egyptian documents, as well as in the *Amarna Tablets* (about 1400 B.C.). However, by the time the Book of Job was written, its protagonist was already a legendary figure. But exactly when was the book written?

Many erudite works have been published on this subject, and as so often happens, the scholars cannot agree. The book must have appeared somewhere between 600 and 200 B.C., but the only point of universal agreement is that this sacred work is the greatest masterpiece of Hebrew literature. Goethe, Victor Hugo and Tolstoy concurred in describing the Book of Job as the most important poetic work produced by mankind—an all-encompassing epic of spiritual life.

Using what was apparently an ancient folk tale for his theme, the poet has woven into the body of Job's story a spiritual drama in the form of discourses. Somewhere in the book, a certain Elihu makes his appearance. His discourses appear to be interpolations, since they are written in a language much closer to Aramaic, and they were probably added later.

There was a man in the land of Uz, whose name was Job; and that man was perfect and upright, and one that feared God, and eschewed evil. And there were born unto him seven sons and three daughters. His substance also was seven thousand sheep, and three thousand camels, and five hundred yoke of oxen, and five hundred she asses, and a very great household; so that this man was the greatest of all the men of the east....

Now there was a day when the sons of God came to present themselves before the Lord, and Satan came also among them. And the Lord said unto Satan, Whence comest thou? Then Satan answered the Lord, and said, From going to and fro in the earth, and from walking up and down in it. And the

Lord said unto Satan, Hast thou considered my servant Job, that there is none like him in the earth, a perfect and an upright man, one that feareth God, and escheweth evil? Then Satan answered the Lord, and said, Doth Job fear God for nought? Hast thou not made an hedge about him, and about his house, and about all that he hath on every side? Thou hast blessed the work of his hands, and his substance is increased in the land. But put forth thine hand now, and touch all that he hath, and he will curse thee to thy face. And the Lord said unto Satan, Behold, all that he hath is in thy power; only upon himself put not forth thine hand. So Satan went forth from the presence of the Lord.

That is the plot within the plot—God's wager with the Devil, the object of the wager being Job's faith.

From then on there comes a procession of messengers, each bearing "Job's tidings": an armed raid was taken place; Job's herds have been driven off and his servants massacred; lightning has struck and burned his sheep and his servants; the Chaldeans have fallen upon his camels; a great wind has killed his sons and daughters. "Then Job arose, and rent his mantle and shaved his head, and fell down upon the ground, and worshipped, and said, Naked came I out of my mother's womb, and naked shall I return thither: the Lord gave, and the Lord hath taken away; blessed be the name of the Lord."

Unable to bring about Job's downfall by these methods, Satan goes to the Lord once more, and says: "Skin for skin, yea, all that a man hath will he give for his life. But put forth thine hand now, and touch his bone and his flesh, and he will curse thee to thy face." Thus God puts Job entirely into Satan's hands, with the sole reservation that he must spare his life. Satan afflicts Job with virulent boils from the soles of his feet to the crown of his head, and Job sits among the ashes and scrapes himself with a potsherd. "Dost thou still retain thine integrity?" asks his wife, but Job is unshaken, and answers: "Thou speakest as one of the foolish women speaketh. What? Shall we receive good at the hand of God, and shall we not receive evil?" Job's friends Eliphaz, Bildad and Zophar visit him to express their sympathy, and, no longer recognizing him, they weep and tear their garments. Then Job breaks his silence, and curses the day he was born.

There follows an exposition of the unsolved problem of retribution. In three sets of discourses—Job counters each of his friends' arguments in turn—they search for the cause of Job's afflictions. Is it the unwarranted wrath of God? Is it an act of kindness on God's part, intended to convert Job from his errors? In general: how do justice, wisdom and power operate in this world? Conscious of his innocence and from the depths of his misery, Job launches into a vehement attack on God. Even so, he remains true to Him deep in his heart, hoping against hope that he will be vindicated and reinstated in God's grace. Eventually, with a plea that God should send him a judge, he reduces his friends to silence. Whereupon an arbitrator arrives on the scene, in the person of Elihu. "Why dost thous strive against Him?" he asks. "For God speaketh once, yea twice, yet man perceiveth it not. . . . In a dream, in a vision of the night, when deep sleep falleth upon men, in slumberings upon the bed. . . . He is chastened also with pain upon his bed." Elihu reproves Job for his presumptuous attitude. Suffering is not only a form of punishment, but also serves to ennoble and chasten the innocent and devout.

Finally Yahweh himself speaks. He opens Job's eyes to something greater than great. He shows him the nature, the omnipotence, the wisdom, the justice and the love of the Creator within the infinity of creation and the structure of the universe. All the apparent enigmas, secrets and contradictions of nature are only part of a well-considered if incalculable plan. Job is reduced to silence. Eventually he speaks: "I know that thou canst do everything, and that no thought can be withholden from thee. . . . I uttered that I understood not; things too wonderful for me, which I knew not."

The Lord thereupon restores Job's good fortune; indeed, he increases his possessions so that they number double of what he had before. Job lives on for another hundred and forty years, finally to die old and contented. Satan had lost his wager.

The Book of Job is so novel, unique and even revolutionary in character because it casts the age-old theory of retribution to the winds. Happiness and misery are not dispensed according to merit or demerit. God's plan embraces the whole world and the whole cosmos, and transcends human comprehension. All divine action is ultimately directed not at the individual or the nation, but at the world in its entirety. The innocent sufferer can thus hold on to his clear conscience. But he should not believe in God merely because he looks for recompense in the world to come, for that would be just another selfish motive. The idea of the beyond rises only once in the Book of Job, when Job cries out: "O that thou wouldest hide me in the grave. . . . If a man die, shall he live again? All the days of my appointed time will I wait, till my change come." But the hope which only Christ would eventually bring dies at once, and Job goes on: "Thou prevailest for ever against him [man], and he passeth: thou changest his countenance, and sendest him away." The Book of Job is the most moving testimony to man's poignant struggle with his God.

To live up to the ultimate truth contained in this book would be beyond man's capacity. For this he would have to free himself from the limitations imposed by his very humanity: from his human conception of God and godliness, and from his earthly appraisal of life's values.

This, then, is the spiritual drama of Job: it is the eternal floundering and struggling of humanity faced with the mystery of creation; it is the essential futility of all science and knowledge; it is the intimation of another, greater, all-encompassing truth which we do not know. And the only certainty we have is that nothing and no one in the universe is ever lost, and that a pure heart is the only key to this infinite problem.

CHRIST LIVED

It is precisely the fury with which so many people attack Christ which proclaims that He is not yet dead.
Giovanni Papini in his *Storia di Cristo*

IN THE fourth year before the beginning of our chronology, during the reign of King Herod, there was born at Bethlehem the Christian Saviour, Jesus, the son of Mary. The surname "Christ" comes from the Greek word *christos,* meaning "the anointed." Jesus was crucified in the 29th or 30th year of our era. He *did* live, and he *was* nailed to the Cross.

For 1,900 years, people have been trying to murder him a second time. They have tried to prove that Jesus was a fictional character; that he never did exist. Story writers and intellectual sophisters have attempted to reduce the Gospel to a myth.

Giovanni Papini, the Florentine author who wrote a life of Christ, asks one question of all these skeptics: "Who would take the place of the great man you reject? His grave is dug ever deeper, yet no one has ever managed conclusively to bury him." No amount of refutation, falsification, criticism, erasure and destruction has yet succeeded in driving Christ from the world. We are still living in the Christian era —it has still not ended.

From where do we derive our knowledge of Jesus, his life and his works, and what historical sources do we have? Our sources are the writings of the New Testament, a small library of books, differing in content, written by different people at different times, and assembled by the Church in the course of the first few centuries.

The earliest testimony about Jesus by a Christian is contained in Paul's Epistles—in particular those to the Romans and Galatians, and the two Epistles to the Corinthians. Paul—or Saul, as he was originally called—was born at Tarsus, the capital of Cilicia. And while he was a Jew, he was also a Roman citizen. While still an adolescent, he was sent to Jerusalem, where he sat at the feet of Gamaliel and learned the Law, as well as the trade of a tent and carpet maker. And always Saul strove with uncompromising fervor for justice and strict observance of the Jewish law.

Later he put men and women who professed the new Christian faith in chains and sent them to jail, persecuting them because they worshiped their crucified Christ as the Messiah and because Jesus' doctrine of God's love suspended the ancient Hebrew law. He even asked the high priest for special authority to work in Damascus, where he intended to arrest other heretics and bring them back to Jerusalem for punishment. On his way to Damascus, however, a great light suddenly shone down on him from the sky, and he heard a voice saying: "Saul, Saul, why persecutest thou me?" When he reached Damascus he asked to be baptized, probably in 35 A.D. Paul was the first to carry word about the Redeemer into the world of the gentiles. His life was one of the most heroic of all time, and his watchword was: "Not I, He in me!" Ancient tradition has it that Paul met death at the hand of the executioner in Rome on July 29, 67 A.D.

The New Testament contains thirteen of Paul's Epistles—or fourteen, if we include the Epistle to the Hebrews, which differs from the others in form, style and line of thought. These letters are the earliest evidence of the life of Christ to come from a Christian source. All other Epistles in the New Testament are of later origin.

Paul and the twelve disciples of Jesus were the chief missionaries of Christianity—the "ones sent forth," which is the Greek meaning of the word "apostle." About 60 A.D., when these men died one after the other, there was an urgent need to commit the Gospel of Jesus to writing. The word Gospel (derived from Old English) and its less common equivalent, the Evangel (derived from the Greek), are both compounds meaning "good tidings." We possess four different accounts of the Gospel of Christ: Matthew, Mark, Luke and John. Of these the first three constitute a group distinct from the fourth. They are similar in structure, choice of material and verbal detail—"seen together"—which is why they became known as the Synoptic Gospels.

In Jerusalem there lived a much respected Christian woman; she was a friend of Peter, and at her house the Apostles often met. Her name was Mary and she had a son, Mark, whom Peter converted and baptized. Mark became acquainted with the teachings of Christ through Peter's accounts of them, and between 65 and 67 A.D. he wrote them down "accurately, though not in chronological order." Justin the Martyr, a historical figure who was born in the year 100 and put to death at Rome in 165 A.D., called Mark's book the "Gospel of Peter." Papias, who lived about 100 A.D., held that Mark had never known Christ or followed him. Nevertheless Mark may have been the young man who was present when Christ was arrested, and who fled naked, leaving his garment in the hands of those who tried to seize him. If this is correct, the passage 14: 51, 52 in St. Mark would be autobiographical.

Matthews, one of the twelve disciples, earned his living as a customs official at the Roman custom house on Lake Tiberias. Between 70 and 80 A.D., he wrote down the story of Jesus with a remarkable sense of historical perspective.

Luke came from Antioch in Syria as we know from the evidence left by a historical figure, Eusebius. Luke was a doctor by profession, and wrote his Gospel about the year 70 A.D.

John was a fisherman's son from Lake Galilee. His mother Salome, the sister of Jesus' mother, was among those who mourned the Saviour at the Cross, and it was John to whom Jesus entrusted his mother Mary before he died. John himself died at a ripe old age about 79 A.D. He wrote his Gospel at the request of friends, probably in Ephesus.

All parts of the New Gospel were written in Greek. But what Matthew, Mark and Luke tell us in writing had been handed down by word of mouth in the Aramaic language; hence these three Synoptic Gospels were based on a verbal tradition in Aramaic. Christ's native language was no doubt Aramaic. But in the first century of the Christian era the language of literature was Greek, and since the Gospel was to be carried into the world, it had to be composed in a universal language.

Jesus was born in Galilee, the border land between the Jewish and the Hellenistic worlds, and it is quite possible—as Martin Dibelius belives—that Jesus and his disciples understood and perhaps even spoke Greek. Undoubtedly the Evangelists could speak and write this language in addition to their own.

What we know about Jesus is therefore neither myth, nor legend nor primitive magic; it is based on the texts written down in black on white only thirty to seventy years after the Crucifixion. Even if so far we have not found the Evangelists' original manuscripts, we do have fragments of very old copies of them, the most ancient among them being papyrus manuscripts. In the times of the Roman Emperors, when the writings of the New Testament were composed, there were large factories and export houses for this paper made from papyrus reeds. Great quantities of such papyri have been discovered and are now housed in the vaults of large museums the world over. Many have never been deciphered or read, and it is anyone's guess what discoveries still remain to be made.

However, what we have today is amazing enough. In 1931, one hundred and twenty-six papyrus sheets of the Chester-Beatty collection were published; they contained fragments of New Testament books written between 200 and 300 A.D. In 1935, C. H. Roberts published papyrus fragments of St. John's Gospel dating from the time of Hadrian, who died in 135 A.D. These documents relating to Christ therefore must have been written only about a hundred years after the Crucifixion. In the same year, H. I. Bell and T. C. Skeat published a large papyrus fragment from the British Museum containing a partial account of the life of Christ. This text is based on the four Gospels and is therefore called "Harmony." Scholars have established that the fragment originated between 100 and 150 A.D. This *Egerton Papyrus* can scarcely fail to inspire us with awe if we reflect how immediately it attests to the life of Christ.

Almost all papyrus fragments of New Testament books were discovered within the past forty years, and nearly all were found at Oxyrhynchus in Upper Egypt. The ground there is so dry that it preserves perishable materials remarkably well, which is why this ruined town, less than a hundred miles from Cairo, has become a research center for New Testament scholars.

The other important carrier of ancient literary tradition is parchment, a material which preceded papyrus. Parchment is the carefully prepared hide of goats, donkeys, sheep, calves or antelope. The process by which it was manufactured was improved in the second century B.C. at Pergamum, the city from which parchment takes its name.

The four most famous New Testament manuscripts are designated by scholars as B, X, A and C. B is the *Codex Vaticanus* of the fourth century, the oldest extant parchment manuscript of antiquity. X is the *Sinaiticus*, discovered by Tischendorf on his visit to Sinai in 1844 and also dating back to the fourth century. A is the *Alexandrinus*, and C the so-called *Codex rescriptus*, both dating from the fifth century. These are the four earliest and best-known complete manuscripts of the New Testament.

The books of the New Testament are probably better authenticated than any other documents in the literary heritage of mankind. By 1874, science had gathered 120,000 New Testament manuscripts of an early or very early date, with only minor divergences. Today we have almost as many versions of the New Testament as there are words in it, and even though these texts show certain deviations, their substance remains unchanged.

From this stream of early Christian literature the Church has isolated the oldest texts which were also regarded as the most reliable in the time immediately following Christ's Crucifixion. However much mankind may destroy; however many churches may be bombed or burned; however great the desecration—the spirit of the life of Jesus will continue to pervade our world.

THE GREATEST ENIGMA IN HUMAN HISTORY

MOHENJO-DARO AND HARAPPA

Everything a modern swimming pool has to offer existed here in Mohenjo-Daro long before the beginning of our history.
Sir John Marshall

IN 1856, during the reign of Queen Victoria, the British were engaged in building the East India Railway between Karachi and Lahore. The project was directed by two brothers, John and William Brunton. John was laying the southern section of the track, and William the northern section up to the Punjab.

In order to build a solid embankment one needs a firm foundation and plenty of stone, and John Brunton was perpetually racking his brains for a suitable source of supply. Not far from his route stood the ruined medieval town of Braminbad—a regular mountain of bricks—and the resourceful engineer made use of them. He informed his brother William how he had solved the problem of stone supply, and William began to reconnoiter the country on either side of his own stretch of track between Multan and Lahore. Soon he, too, discovered an ancient ruined city, and on its rubble the modern township of Harappa. The bricks there were exactly what he needed, and so the ruins at Harappa were speedily cleared away. Today the trains traveling between Lahore and Karachi thunder along over nearly a hundred miles of track laid on bricks made 3,600 years ago. Produced by one of the earliest advanced civilizations in the world, they are still so solid and indestructible that even modern locomotives cannot pulverize them.

In 1922, when the Indian archaeologist R. D. Banerji was excavating an old Buddhist monastery dating from about 300 A.D.—on the lower Indus at Mohenjo-Daro, the "Hill of the Dead"—he found that the bricks used by the early Buddhists dated from much earlier times, and that beneath the monastery and the "Hill of the Dead" a very ancient city lay buried. About the same time, the director of the Indian Archaeological Service, Sir John Marshall, began to carry out extensive excavations at Harappa. It was soon established that the territory of this prehistoric Indus civilization stretched as far as Baluchistan, and that long before the so-called Aryans migrated to India from the Caspian Sea region about 1500 B.C., a much more ancient civilization must have existed in northwest India; it flourished between 1700 and 1500 B.C. How did the scholars arrive at this date for Harappa and Mohenjo-Daro?

Scarcely any written evidence has been found in the Indus valley, only seals with unidentified and undeciphered characters. Thus, this line of investigation yielded no answer. However, the archaeologists who excavated Sumerian towns in the Euphrates and Tigris valley had found very similar seals and some pieces of broken pottery which unmistakably originated in the ancient cities on the Indus. Since Sumerian cuneiforms were deciphered together with their precise dates, the layers of earth which the Indus seals shared with datable Sumerian objects established the date of Harappa and Mohenjo-Daro. And it was found that the people of Mohenjo-Daro and Harappa were contemporaneous with a Sumerian period fixed between 1700 and 1500 B.C.

Where did these ancient city builders come from? Very little is known, except that their cities flourished long before the Aryan immigrants arrived in northern India. Perhaps the inhabitants of Harappa were themselves intruders who had come from somewhere beyond the northwestern frontiers of India. They certainly had an advanced civilization when they began to build their cities. The fact that their writing has been found only on seals (which are probably amulets), some pottery fragments and tools, and that the symbols found at different excavation levels at Harappa and Mohenjo-Daro scarcely changed through the different periods, would indicate that there was only a modicum of intellectual development among these people after they arrived in India—perhaps due to the climate. There may be another reason for the absence of larger documents: such writings were probably executed on bark, cotton, leather, palm leaves or wood, all of which obviously would long ago have disintegrated in the damp and saline soil of India.

Several groups of skeletons were found during the excavations at Mohenjo-Daro: one, fifteen strong, in a large room; and another, consisting of six, in a street. The contorted postures of the dead indicate that they died a violent death. Archaeologists believe that the people of Mohenjo-Daro and Harappa abandoned their cities simultaneously, although no one knows why they did so.

Both cities appear to have been built according to a careful plan.

The streets of Harappa run parallel and are crossed at right angles by other parallel streets. These ancient habitations on the Indus had no winding lanes, like the cities of medieval Europe, and town planning seems to have been in competent hands. In fact, Mohenjo-Daro and Harappa represent the oldest examples of city planning in the world.

It is equally remarkable that hardly any of the houses encroached upon the street, their frontages forming fairly straight lines. The main streets ran from east to west and from north to south, probably so that the northerly winds could keep them well ventilated. "Street No. 1," as it is called, is about a thousand yards long and runs in a straight line from north to south, dividing the city into two sections. Several of Mohenjo-Daro's streets were quite broad, some of them ten yards wide, so that carts and chariots could easily pass in two-way traffic. The walls of the houses along the main streets excavated so far go down to twenty feet, and will reach even further once they are fully cleared. Some house fronts have been bared to a depth of twenty-six feet, but the foundations have not yet been reached.

The houses at street intersections were rounded off so that beasts of burden and pedestrians would not hurt themselves at the corners. Almost every building in Harappa and Mohenjo-Daro is constructed of burned bricks whose shape more or less resembles our own. But the most remarkable feature of Mohenjo-Daro's houses is their simplicity. There is scarcely any ornamentation; no pillars, balconies, sculpture or windows—only narrow doorways and flat roofs; windows were impractical in the hot Indus valley. Many of the houses are regular labyrinths: perhaps their owners sought safety in the depths of their dwellings. It is of course possible that the ornamentation of the houses was carved out of wood, as is still done in India. In that case, it is not surprising that none of it survives after 3,500 years.

Anyone strolling through the ruins of Mohenjo-Daro and Harappa will see that these ancient houses had every "modern" convenience. There were baths, toilets, drainage and fresh-water tanks, handsome interior courtyards—similar to those that still exist throughout the modern Orient—comfortable bedrooms, guest rooms, dining rooms and janitor's quarters. And all of this is "prehistoric." It all existed at a time when Central Europe's only housing accommodation was the cave!

The most important building so far excavated at Mohenjo-Daro is the great bathhouse. It was equipped with hot air, steam and water, a fine swimming pool, dressing rooms, small bathrooms, running water, cold showers and the like. No one who examines the layout of these premises can fail to be astounded by the ultra-modern building technique which these people had mastered more than 3,000 years ago.

West of the great bathhouse was a huge granary, excavated in 1950, whose individual grain bins were so constructed that constant ventilation kept the stores moisture-free. The building originally must have measured 164 by 82 feet, but at some period it was enlarged on the south side. Sir Mortimer Wheeler describes how this commodity—the single most important factor of public prosperity—was at one time administered and distributed, and how government tithes must have filled and refilled the grain bins. He points out that, in a moneyless period of history, this granary, for all practical purposes, was the state treasury.

However, the mightiest building has not yet been unearthed, because a Buddhist shrine, or stupa, stands above it and would have to be demolished before the secrets beneath it could be explored. And since the Indians do not want their stupa damaged, this subterranean miracle, which may be a 4,000-year-old temple, remains inaccessible.

Many female statuettes have been found at Mohenjo-Daro and Harappa. They probably represent a goddess, but her name is not known, although the greatest authority on the Indus civilization, Sir John Marshall, believes her to be the mother goddess who is still worshiped by Indians today and obviously goes back to prehistoric times. On some of the amulet-seals there is a seated figure, surrounded by animals, who is rightly regarded as a forerunner of Siva, one of the two major deities of modern Hinduism. There were also animal gods, sacred fig trees and a whole menagerie of idols. Judging by the mother goddess' clothing, the women of Mohenjo-Daro wore nothing but a skirt that barely reached to their knees and was held up by a belt, but perhaps there also was a cloak that covered the arms but left the breasts bare. We also have a nude bronze statuette of a dancing girl. The men probably wore a kind of loincloth, and over it a robe draped across the left shoulder and tied under the right arm.

Many jewels have been found in silver, copper and bronze vessels: necklaces and ornaments of gold, electrum (an alloy of silver and gold), silver, copper and bronze. Great quantities of other objects were also unearthed: rings, bracelets and nose ornaments; examples of almost all the precious and semiprecious stones we know; bronze mirrors with wooden handles; cosmetics, razors and even a saw with serrated teeth,

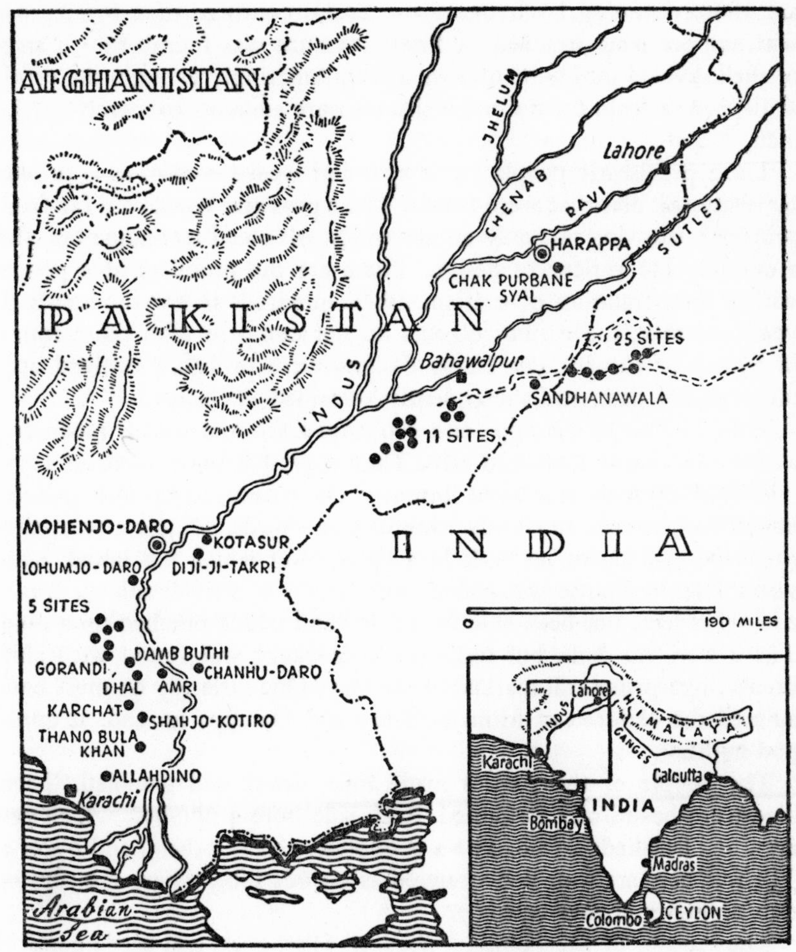

Excavated sites of Indus civilization.

the first of its kind. The large number of fishhooks would point to angling, and some of them still showed remnants of cotton threads.

Many of the tools and weapons have small inscriptions—perhaps names, perhaps numbers. There were weights made of alabaster, quartz, jasper and limestone, with a unit weight of .0302 ounces and increasing in the following ratio: 1, 2, 4, 8, 16, 32, 64, 160, 200, 320, 640, 1,600, 3,200, 6,400, 8,000 and 12,800. The people of Mohenjo-Daro were apparently honest, because there were scarcely any dishonest weights, *i.e.*, those deviating from the norm. Scales consisted of a bronze bar with copper pans attached. A linear measure was found, too: a strip of shell divided into units of 2.1999 feet. Amazingly enough, the error, or departure from the norm, on this measure amounts to merely .00299 inch.

These prehistoric people could spin and weave cotton, as is proven by many spindles that were found. Their pots and vessels are far from primitive, showing not only an extremely advanced technique but also a considerable variety of design. These are the products of a people with a long tradition of craftsmanship, hundreds if not thousands of years old. Yet, the various objects do not compare with those found in Sumer or Egypt. The Indus designs were probably evolved at a much earlier date, and subsequently remained unchanged.

The children of Harappa and Mohenjo-Daro had just as much fun as the children of a modern city. They played with all kinds of toys: miniature oxen pulling carts, brightly decorated rattles with pebbles inside, toy animals and birds. One of these birds, complete with tiny toy cage, still opens its beak in a silent song which has lasted 3,500 years. Even a whistle was found, and there was a small animal, which zoologists have not been able to classify and which climbed up a pole. There were no dolls, but some doll's crockery was found with children's fingerprints still marked in the clay. One little toy ox must have amused the children of Mohenjo-Daro and Harappa no end: it could nod its head.

The people of these cities made love, drank and gambled. Their dice were beautifully fashioned. Each side bore a number, which can even be identified: 1 to 6. The 2 is opposite the 1, 4 the 3, and 6 the 5. The numbers are thus not arranged as on our dice, where the sum of two opposites always equals 7.

The remains of deer, buffalo, hogs, tortoise, goats and cattle confirm that the people of the Indus valley were meat-eaters. They took their meals sitting on mats, but they probably used tables and chairs as well, as certain pictographics seem to indicate. The many sets of antlers and horns found at Mohenjo-Daro make it seem likely that they were used in powdered form for medicinal purposes, a custom which still prevails in India and China.

The excavations at Mohenjo-Daro and Harappa have shown that we will forever be rewriting history for India's prehistoric age had been presumed to be a dark and uncivilized period of barbarity. Now it is recognized that long before the "beginning of all civilization" mankind had known an extremely high level of culture. It is nothing short of fabulous when we hear such a meticulous scholar as Sir John Marshall declare that the jewels of these Indus people were cut with such consummate skill that they might better have come from London's Bond Street than from a prehistoric household more than 3,000 years ago.

Thus at a time when Queen Nefertiti and her husband, Pharaoh Ikhnaton, lived in Egypt, a highly advanced civilization also flourished on the Indus, in modern cities whose origins are hidden in the mists of prehistoric times. And most amazing of all: it is always the oldest examples of the Indus civilization that show the greatest finesse and the highest cultural perfection.

Therefore, what was unearthed here was already marked by decadence, and the glorious beginnings remain to this hour one of the greatest mysteries of human history.

AN ATOM CAN NEVER COMPREHEND THE UNIVERSE

Never in the world has hate ceased through hate. Hate can be displaced only by love.

Gautama Buddha

OUT of the darkness of an age long past—3,000 years ago or perhaps much earlier—India sends us these words: "Learning and teaching bring joy, strength of mind and freedom. We benefit from them day by day, sleep in peace, and become our soul's best doctor. Mastery of the senses, pleasure in solitude, growth of knowledge, authority and maturity will be the result."

Whose was the mind that shaped these words? Where lived the people who had such complex minds? Where can we read more of such words?

The origins of India's history are hidden in impenetrable darkness. We do not know which people first inhabited the subcontinent of India. We do not know what happened to them.

The earliest advanced civilization we have unearthed from India's soil, as has been mentioned, is that of Mohenjo-Daro and Harappa, a civilization which goes back 3,500 to 4,000 years, and is prehistoric.

Somewhat later—perhaps about 1500 B.C., the Aryans invaded northern India. But they left no mementos in stone or metal, no writings, no tangible evidence of their existence. Instead, they left a startling heritage of ideas that have been handed down by word of mouth from century to century. These thoughts were neither written down nor chiseled in stone. Like the oldest epics of mankind—the *Iliad*, the *Odyssey* and the Germanic sagas—the Indian *Vedas*, too, were passed on verbally from generation to generation.

It was only in the seventh or eighth century B.C. that Hindu merchants imported from western Asia a Semitic script—the so-called Brahmi script—from which all subsequent Indian alphabets are derived. In the centuries that followed, the *Vedas* were recorded in writing. Sacred hymns, sacrificial rituals, liturgical formulas, ceremonial precepts, theological-*cum*-philosophical discources: all these things are laid down in the *Vedas*—the amazing spiritual monument which these Indo-European immigrants built for themselves and which continued to grow through the centuries. The oldest collection in this great Vedic literature is the *Rig-Veda*, comprising about a thousand hymns containing some ten thousand verses. The other sections of Vedic literature are the *Sama-Veda*, the *Yajur-Veda*, the *Atharva-Veda*, the *Brahmanas*, the *Aryanas*, the *Upanishads* and the *Sutras*.

The most important works of later periods are the *Mahabharata* and the *Ramayana*. The *Mahabharata* alone consists of 100,000 couplets, and is thus about eight times as long as the *Iliad* and the *Odyssey* combined. Apart from being the great heroic epic of India, it is also an enormous reservoir of sagas, legends, myths and didactic treatises of every kind.

The *Ramayana*, consisting of 24,000 couplets, describes the strange heroic adventures of King Rama, and we know that the man who composed this epos was called Valmiki.

We can now understand that the only people capable of memorizing such immense works and passing them on through the centuries were those to whom "learning and teaching bring joy." (This particular sentence is found in the *Brahmanas*.)

The immemorial ideas contained in the *Vedas* embrace every thought, dream and vision that man has ever had. There is Indra, the god who embodies Adam, Noah and Siegfried in one. "He slew the serpent, made an outlet for the waters, and clave the groins of the mountains. He slew the dragon which stretched itself out on the mountain.... Just as a tree-trunk is felled by the axe, so the dragon lay felled flat upon the earth." There is a Pilate washing his hands in innocence: "Take away all that is sinful in me, ye waters; if I was faithless or have cursed; and every lie." And there is a beautiful passage about the night: "O Night, you have filled the earthly space according to the commandments of the Father of All. You spread in the height to the heavenly abodes. Star-sparkling darkness draws nigh."

And how clearly did the author of the following precept perceive the impermanence of all earthly possessions: "The prosperous man should give to him who has fallen upon evil days and consider the long road ahead; for riches turn like wagon-wheels, forever coming to a different man in turn."

Here is some advice on the choice of a wife: "A man should marry a woman who is intelligent, beautiful, virtuous, lucky–and healthy. Of course, the signs of luck are hard to recognize...."

A word about the virtue of rising early: "Like Indrani, an early riser, you should wakefully await the dawn which precedes the glow of the fire." On sleep and dreams: "In that you are neither alive or dead, O Sleep, you are the heavenly child of the gods. You set an end to things, you are death; thus we know you for what you are, O Sleep. Keep us, O Sleep, from evil dreams."

And here is an example of a woman's jealous love for a man, dating from a time when people knew how to sing but not how to write: "I am in command, not you. You can be spokesman in the assembly, for aught I care. You shall belong to me alone. You shall never once even speak of other women." And what woman could have resisted the man who made these demands: "As the liana holds the tree entwined, so cling to me that you may fall in love with me and may never be untrue to me." He wanted not only her body, but her soul as well: "As the griffin flying upward with both wings holds fast to the ground, so do I hold fast to your soul."

A story of the Creation: "In the beginning was darkness veiled in darkness. This whole world was a chaos past recognition. The seed of life which was surrounded by the void, the One, was born by virtue of its urgent heat. To it was added, from the beginning, the craving for love.

"In the beginning this world was neither being nor yet non-being. It was, and it was not. It was but thought.

"This world, and everything in it, in the last analysis is rooted only in thought. This thought is the Brahma. . . ."

Some words on the effect of time: "Through time the purifying wind blows, through time the earth is great. The great heavens repose in time."

A lonely man's fear: "He was afraid, as a man is afraid who is all alone. But he reflected: if there is nothing here except myself, of whom should I be afraid? Then his fear abated."

It is truly amazing that even in the darkness of India's earliest history mortal man was striving for the deepest insights. His efforts were often poignant in their human frailty, and yet how daringly his intellect soared up to the immeasurable realms of time and space, in search of his gods and his guiding principles. Nothing had as yet hardened into rigid formulas. Man was still wrestling, free and unprejudiced, with all his problems.

Schopenhauer says of one section of the *Vedas*, the *Upanishad:* "It makes the most rewarding and uplifting reading in the world: it has been the solace of my life and will be that of my death."

But what was at first pulsing with blood and life gradually degenerated into a hodgepodge of false doctrines, witchcraft, magical beliefs, delusions and superstitions—and inevitably many people became nihilists, despising the priests and doubting all gods. One teacher named Sanjaya discarded all knowledge as useless and demanded that philosophy should strive solely for peace. Another, Purana Kashyapa, taught that the soul was merely an ungovernable slave of chance. Maskarin Gosala believed that fate decided everything, regardless of human merit. Ajita Kesakambalin declared that once their bodies had perished, wise men and fools alike were destroyed, and that after death they would be nothing. It was a time of quibblers and slippery orators who were preaching the absurdity of all virtue.

It was about this time, roughly 560 B.C., that a son, Siddhartha, was born to the wealthy prince Shuddhodana and his wife Maya who lived near Kapilavastu in what is now Nepal. Close by, the Himalayas soar from the plain of the Ganges into the sky, and about 250 miles from Buddha's birthplace Mount Everest rises in its majestic solitude.

The name Buddha is a theological title meaning "the Enlightened," but the man who was to bear this title was known to his contemporaries by his family name, Gautama. Gautama spent his early years in luxury and self-indulgence, but at the age of twenty-nine, when he realized that the ultimate fate of man is old age, sickness and death, that living means suffering, and that all things are transitory, he left his wife and child and became a wandering ascetic. He subjected himself to the most rigorous physical privations, until he was so thin and weak that death loomed before his very eyes. Only then did he abandon this self-torture, although he persevered in his profound meditation on life and its meaning. Enlightenment finally came to him after a wakeful night spent beneath a pipal tree at Uruvela in what is now Bengal.

Gautama had become Buddha, the Enlightened, and he resolved to make his spiritual experience known to the world. He converted five ascetics who were his companions and set up housekeeping near Benares, but before long he had sixty more disciples whom he sent forth as missionaries. He personally converted a thousand people in Uruvela and won a supporter in King Bimbisara, who presented him with a park where he and his followers were to live.

Little is known of Buddha's preaching and teaching in the forty-five years that followed these events. In all probability he traveled through the eastern regions of the Ganges valley, spending only the rainy season in houses or caves.

Unfortunately, neither Socrates nor Christ nor Buddha ever thought of writing down their doctrines, and thus their teachings were passed on by their disciples. Buddha was a man of iron will and tremendous powers of persuasion. Proud, but of great charm in speech and manner, he never asserted that he was acting as the instrument of a god. He meditated day and night on ways of preventing the destruction of life; he tried to reconcile enemies, and brought peace wherever he went. Like Christ, he strove to requite evil with good, and listened quietly to anyone who attacked him. But in contrast to most of the heroic figures of this world, Buddha had a sense of humor: he realized that metaphysical insight must be tempered by a smile lest it become arrogant.

He wandered tirelessly from one village to the next, accompanied by 1,200 devoted followers, caring little for his physical well-being and never worrying about the morrow. He even shocked his disciples on one occasion by taking a meal in the house of a courtesan.

Buddha was convinced that suffering and misfortune overshadow the good side of life so decisively that it would be better if man were never born. "More tears have flowed upon this earth than there is water in the four oceans." And he regarded all earthly pleasures as dubious because they were so fleeting. He laid down five moral precepts: "No one should kill a living creature. No one should take what is not given him. No one should lie. No one should get drunk. No one should be unchaste."

Buddha was ill at ease in the company of women. "What should we do when women speak to us?" asked one disciple. "Be very circumspect," replied Buddha.

"Never in the world has hate ceased through hate. Hate can be displaced only by love." Buddha's one and only concern was with human conduct: he never demanded any worship or doctrinaire theology. But the most interesting thing about this holy man of Asia is that he founded a world-wide religion without ever discussing the concepts of eternity, immortality or God.

"An atom can never comprehend the universe." Therefore Buddha refused to be drawn into tenuous speculations about the beginning and end of the world, the identity of body and soul, or the chances of a holy man entering some kind of heaven. He dismissed all such questions as idle, spurious and sterile. The only people of whom Buddha was sharply critical were the priests. He denied that the Vedas were divinely inspired, and he attacked the caste system. "Rich and poor, young and old, we are all one," he said.

And if Buddha established a religion without a god, he took reincarnation for granted—probably the only idea he accepted without reservation. All his thoughts and energies were directed toward attaining nirvana, the Buddhist idea of perfect happiness reached by complete absorption of one's self into the supreme universal spirit. But we shall not attempt to explain the essence of nirvana in detail, for whole libraries have been written on the subject.

At the end of his life, Buddha's followers were beginning to worship him. He was now eighty years old and very weak and emaciated, yet he wandered on and on, forever teaching and preaching. Then, while on his way to the ancient town of Kusinara, he was taken ill after eating some bad pork. His last admonition to his disciples was that they should henceforth make his doctrine their supreme guide, and earnestly strive to live up to it. He died about 480 B.C.

"Now then, O Monks, I speak to you. All material things are destined to perish. Strive ye in earnest." These were his last words.

As the centuries passed, however, Buddha's doctrine, overwhelmed by the sheer weight of India's age-old native religions, began to die out. It foundered on Hinduism, its ancient rival, and on the Indians' traditional susceptibility to polytheism, miracles, mythology and witchcraft. Eventually, Buddhism adopted numerous legends from the Hindu religion and took over its rituals and gods, until scarcely anything of the original Buddhist doctrine remained. About 750 A.D., Buddhism in India was at an end. Outside India, however, Buddhism lived on. It took root in every country in the Far East, conquering almost the whole continent of Asia—from the Siberian borders to the steaming islands of Indonesia, from the lamaseries of Tibet to the tinkling gongs and incense candles of the Zen priests of Japan.

WHO CREATED THE IMAGE OF BUDDHA?

The more I ponder on Buddha's philosophy, the more convinced I become that death is the true mother of all religions.

BUDDHA was undoubtedly the greatest, wisest and most brilliant man India ever produced. But the Buddhism which has become a world-wide religion is quite alien to its founder's original conception. A mere two hundred years after the death of this genius from Nepal there already existed eighteen variations of the Buddhist doctrine, and the main forms of Buddhism—Mahayana and Hinayana—have divided the Buddhist world in two. China and Japan (as well as Tibet, Bhutan, Sikkim, Nepal and Mongolia, which adhere to it in the form of Lamaism) follow Mahayana, the "Great Vehicle." Ceylon and Indo-China follow Hinayana, the "Little Vehicle." Mahayana is the endeavor, born of universal compassion, to be reincarnated as a future Buddha (Bodhisattva), for the welfare and happiness of all. The adherents of Hinayana seek only their personal salvation.

Did Siddhartha, the man who today is worshiped by one half of all humanity—even if people often pay no more than lip service to him—really exist?

Statues of Buddha are found all over Asia, but do these effigies bear any resemblance to the features of the man who once taught the people by the Ganges to "overcome rage with kindness"?

The historicity of Gautama Buddha's life is attested by many detailed accounts which have been handed down from the past. We know his birthplace and parentage, we know his name and the towns he visited. Buddha supposedly was cremated after his death and his ashes, being sacred relics, were distributed among numerous princes and aristocratic families. His own family, the Sakya, also received a share, which they interred in a stupa at Kapilavastu. (A stupa, or Buddhist shrine, is a conical doorless structure, a sealed tumulus with a sort of protrusion at its summit.)

In 1898 this stupa was discovered near Piprava in Tarai. An inscription records that the urn containing Buddha's ashes was "consecrated by the brothers, sisters, children and womenfolk of the Exalted one." We may safely assume that the stupa was not opened from the date it was built to the year 1898, which is further proof for Siddhartha Buddha's historicity.

Everything must have some origin. Buddha's philosophy, or at least the basis of it, must have been evolved by *someone*. Detailed accounts, stories and legends grow only around persons who have really existed. As we shall see later, modern archaeology has proved that numerous Greek legendary figures were actually historical personalities.

However, if there is a lack of concrete information about the man who became Buddha and if no one knows exactly what he looked like, how can we explain the fact that Buddha's statues, which are found throughout India, China, Japan and Eastern Asia, all somehow resemble each other? Why is it that the more Buddha effigies we study, the more convinced we become that the same flesh-and-blood personality inspired all of them?

Buddha was born in Nepal, but his earliest images came from what is now Afghanistan, from the region once known as Gandhara. But when we speak of Gandhara as the birthplace of Buddhist sculpture, we are thinking less in terms of a geographical location than of a cultural area which extended far beyond ancient Gandhara itself. It was this general area that produced the first portrayal of Buddha which served as a model for all subsequent representations.

Now we might ask: why should the spirit and countenance of Buddha have been immortalized in stone somewhere outside of India, in Afghanistan, of all places? The mystery is solved if we consider that there had to be two factors: the idea of Buddha, and the people who could give this idea artistic expression. The idea came from India, but the only artists then capable of dramatizing it in stone lived in Gandhara—and they were not Indians.

The man who spread Buddhism far beyond the frontiers of India was King Asoka, who reigned roughly between 260 and 232 B.C. This was the time when Buddhist missionaries reached Gandhara, and we know that the Buddhist apostle Madhyantika visited Kashmir and Gandhara in 242 B.C. What sort of civilization did these missionaries find there?

When Alexander the Great died in 323 B.C., his dominions were divided among his generals and the kingdoms of the Diadochi, or Successors, were established. Alexander's Indian possessions fell to Seleucus Nicator, the ruler of Syria. During the reign of his grandson Antiochus II (261-246 B.C), the governor of Bactria, a Greek named Diodotus, gradually established his independence and proclaimed himself king, thus creating the Greco-Bactrian kingdom.

Before long, this realm split up into numerous small states ruled by Greek kings. But that by no means was the end of it. Added to this racial melting pot, in 140 B.C., were the Yue-Chi, a Scythian tribe chased out of eastern China by the Huns. In 50 A.D., 190 years later, they founded the Indo-Scythian kingdom under the Kushan Dynasty. This dynasty produced a ruler who is almost unknown in Europe, but who became one of the greatest figures in world history: his name was Kanishka. He came to the throne in 144 A.D. and adopted the Buddhist faith, expanding his domain from the Aral Sea in the north to Chotan in the east, and in the Ganges plain down to Benares in the south. His influence on Gandhara art must have been extremely important, for as a king and Buddhist convert he focused all state subsidized artistic activity on the Great Exalted One from Nepal. It was during Kanishka's reign that Gandhara art had its greatest flowering.

In Gandhara, then, Buddhism encountered a Hellenistic civilization, a culture compounded of Greek and oriental elements. And when the sculptors in Gandhara began to make statues of Buddha, they were guided by their idea of Buddha as he emerged from his life and doctrine. From the start, therefore, the Buddha image was an idealized conception and not an accurate representation of the prince called Siddhartha.

Since the artists of Gandhara were either of Greek origin or the descendants of the racial mélange that characterized this Hellenistic civilization, they thought in terms of Greek art forms. Thus when they decided to create an idealized image of the man whose doctrines they had accepted, they clothed him in Greek garb. And since that time, wherever Buddhism has gained a hold, Buddha has often been portrayed in Greek attire. Of course, the styles have varied, but the heavy folds that lend dignity to the human figure have always been in evidence.

The seated Buddha, however, is purely Indian in conception, for this posture is typical of Indian ascetics of all periods. The standing Buddha, on the other hand, belongs to the classical Greek realm of ideas. Thus the artist of Gandhara expressed an Indian ideal by using the artistic techniques of ancient Greece.

Buddha is supposed to have had physical attributes that distinguished him from other mortals—the thirty-two major and the eighty minor "bodily features of the great man." The Indians thought that Buddha must have been different from other men, not only spiritually but physically. It is interesting to note that several of these features point to effeminacy or hermaphroditism. It is as if nature had blurred the sexes in Buddha, thereby expressing something suprasexual; something divine.

People are inclined to describe the art of Gandhara as Greco-Buddhistic. This is not quite accurate, because its Greek components are no longer related to classical Greece but to Hellenism, by definition a blend of Greek and oriental elements. Gandhara, for that matter, shows traces of Roman art, and the latest research tends to the belief that Gandhara art was the easternmost outpost of Roman civilization, with the oasis of Palmyra as a possible intermediate link.

Gandhara's conception of Buddha's physical appearance became the pattern on which all later portrayals of him were modeled–in Java, Siam, China, or Japan. By the same token, Gandhara's representation of the *mudras* were adopted throughout eastern Asia. The *mudras* are the symbolic positions of the fingers during religious meditation, and there are various constantly recurring gestures, each of which has a different significance. One gesture symbolizes "turning the wheel of the law." Another, in which the hands lie in the lap, one on the other, means meditation. Yet another signifies "calling the earth to witness," and is expressed by touching the ground.

No paintings have been found in Gandhara proper, but it is fairly certain that paintings–and probably a school of painting–did exist there. The glorious frescoes in the cave temples at Ajanta, dating from the second century A.D., show us likenesses of Buddha which were obviously influenced by far earlier paintings in Gandhara.

The Buddha sculptures of India could not have been made without the Gandhara originals. The Indians did not simply copy those prototypes, however, but merely adopted the basic styles and then applied their own artistic imagination.

Even in the first century A.D. there were Buddhist monasteries in China, but the earliest Chinese stone sculptures of Buddha date from the period of 400 A.D. Buddhism was introduced into Korea in 372 A.D., in 552 A.D. it reached Japan, and in 632 A.D., Tibet.

Curiously enough, the most beautiful statues of Buddha are to be found in Japan. The Japanese have always collected fine Chinese originals, but they have also evolved their own magnificent school of Buddhist art. And in many of their sculptures the Gandhara style has survived with astonishing purity.

The Chinese, on the other hand, have endowed the figure of the religious founder with far stronger, specifically Chinese, characteristics.

The famous Daibutsu statue at Kamakura in Japan may have a Japanese cast of features, but the rich folds of its draped robe are much closer to Gandhara art than many Indian or Chinese sculptures of Buddha.

No one who stands before the Daibutsu Buddha and surrenders to the enormous figure's sublime tranquillity, no one who absorbs the quality of its absolute composure, can fail to understand something of the spirit of this genius from Nepal: the suspension of all pain, the quenching of all desire, the cessation of self-torment and the end of personal identity that is extinguished like a candle flame—all of which is nirvana, the condition of non-suffering.

MAHAVIRA AND REBIRTH

Man is entirely composed of desire; just as his desires are, so is his intelligence; just as his intelligence is, so are his actions; just as his actions are, so it fares with him.

Upanishad 4, 4, 5

THE Hindu religion is based on age-old Indo-Aryan traditions. And all the earliest sacred Indian traditions are summed up in the word *Veda*, meaning "knowledge." Hence a *Veda* is a book of knowledge or, more precisely, a whole literature of knowledge and insight.

In Sanskrit, *upa* means "near," and *sat* means "to sit." It was from the "sitting near," or the proximity of, the Hindu teacher that the word *Upanishad* derived its meaning of the religious doctrines the teacher imparted to his most promising pupils. Thus the *Upanishads* are the thoughts and teachings of numerous wise men to whom religion and philosophy were one. Conceived between 700 and 500 B.C., these works strike to embrace all the secrets of life on earth and after death, and mark the impressive beginning of philosophical thought. Here we find the belief in transmigration, in the eternal cycle of existence (*samsara*), and in reincarnation, in human or animal form, as the consequence of good or evil conduct—an inexorable process the Sanskrit calls *karma*. Yajnavalkya, one of the greatest Upanishad philosophers, expresses it in these words (Brhadaranayaka, Upanishad 4, 4, 5):

"Just as a man acts, just as he changes, so will he be born; he who does good will be born good; he who does evil will be born evil; he will become holy through holy works and evil through evil. Wherefore is it truly said: man is entirely composed of desire; just as his desires are, so is his intelligence; just as his intelligence is, so are his actions; just as his actions are, so it fares with him."

No matter how sublime a religion starts out to be, it is always in danger of being corrupted by human inadequacy. We shall never know how many anonymous religious founders sacrificed their lives in prehistoric times for noble ideals which were later distorted by acquisitive priests. Thus by 600 or 500 B.C., Brahmanism had already degenerated into a vast, rigid system of intricate rituals, whose punctilious performance by the priests, or Brahmans, was man's only way to salvation. Superstition, a continual emphasis on magic, the abuse of sacrificial offerings, self-torture as a means of achieving supernatural powers, and a lifeless formalism led finally to a revolt against the Brahmans and their religion. They had strayed very far indeed from the former ideals of Indo-Aryan priesthood. Claiming that they alone were entitled to interpret the sacred *Vedas*, they tyrannically abused their religious monopoly and attended to people's spiritual needs according to their own arbitrary and often unfair standards. Hence a crop of skeptics, fatalitists, materialists and new religious founders rose, attacking the Brahmans for their lack of spirituality, and invented new ways of human salvation. And since secular power is always jealous of spiritual power, the Brahmans' opponents were effectively supported by the warrior caste, or Kshatriya.

It was during this period of "great spiritual upheaval," as the Indologist Waldschmidt puts it, that the mysterious heavens bestowed on India two of the greatest religious founders that ever lived. One of them was Buddha, of whom we have already spoken. The name of the other is relatively unfamiliar to Western civilization.

Mahavira Vardhamana was born in 540 B.C., about the same time as Buddha, and like him, he was the son of a rich nobleman. His birthplace was on the outskirts of Vaishali, in modern Bihar. His parents belonged to a sect which, in common with all Indian religions, wrestled with the problem of reincarnation and its attendant suffering. They worshiped an itinerant ascetic called Parsva, who two hundred and fifty years earlier had probably laid the foundation for their son's religious ideas. The parents believed that suicide would accelerate the cycle of reincarnation and therefore was a sacred right, and when Mahavira was thirty-one years old they voluntarily starved themselves to death. It may well have been this experience which turned the young genius into an ascetic, wandering completely naked through the whole province of Bihar. In any case, after thirteen years of this purification, Mahavira experienced the light of infinite knowledge. His disciples proclaimed their master as a *jina*, or victor, invested him with the title of "Great Hero," and called themselves Jains.

Mahavira's doctrine, known as Jainism, is one of the most remarkable religions in the spiritual history of mankind. All earthly truth is limited, for each man sees only his immediate environment and judges the phenomena from his own standpoint: hence his perceptions are invariably distorted. The ultimate truth is revealed only to the *jinas*, the redeemers who appear on earth at rare intervals. Jainism is fundamentally atheistic: it assumes neither a creator nor a first cause. Since a cause must in turn have a cause, the Jains say, there cannot have been an original creator–the world has existed from all eternity, without a beginning or a god. And in place of a god the Jains worship their twenty-four *jinas*, or Tirthankaras–men who in earlier stages attained absolute perfection.

How is this absolute perfection to be attained? The ordinary mortal can never hope to qualify. A monk may possibly succeed, but even that is doubtful. The path to redemption is open only to those who by continual ascetic penance and abstention from any and all violence reach complete *ahimsa*, or non-violation, which is similar to Gandhi's preachings of non-violence, or passive resistance. No man should injure another and, above all, no man should take another creature's life. No man should lie or take what has not been given to him. Everyone should be chaste, renounce all worldly desires, and become completely detached from external influences.

All this is, of course, easier said than done: indeed it is scarcely possible to observe even the first of these prohibitions, the one against taking life. The orthodox Jain monk covers his mouth with a veil lest he inhale a fly and kill it. He must also cover his lamps lest their light attract moths; nor is he allowed to use artificial lighting. He must sweep the ground before him while walking in case his naked foot should crush some small creature to death.

Like all Indian religions, Jainism consists of numerous sects. There are, for example, the Swetambaras who dress in white robes, and the Digambaras who wear celestial robes (namely, no robes at all). But even the Digambaras wear clothes nowadays, despite the fact that by rights they should not; for clothing means comfort, and comfort means the indulging of bodily desires. However, only very few holy men still wander around unclothed. There are 1,618,000 Jains among India's 340 million inhabitants, and of these 80,000 live in Greater Bombay. Their influence is greater than their numbers would imply, however, for Jainism includes India's richest merchants among its adherents. Countryfolk can never make good Jains anyway, for they cannot help but kill worms and, if they are cattle breeders, animals as well. Hence the Jain peasants are (should be) constantly worried about their spiritual welfare.

There are many similarities between Buddha and Mahavira. Both men rebelled against the rigidity of Hinduism, both came from aristocratic families in eastern India, and both abhorred a life of self-indulgence and luxury. And, like all other religious founders in history, both went into retreat—Mahavira when he was twenty-eight, and Buddha at the age of thirty. Both experienced enlightenment beneath a tree, both believed in a sincere morality and in a high standard of ethics as the minimum prerequisite on the long, steep and arduous road to salvation. Both men founded monastic and lay orders. Neither acknowledged a deity, neither believed that the world had any beginning, and neither preached in Sanskrit—the ancient classical tongue of the *Vedas* and *Upanishads*—but in the idiom of their respective regions.

But there were differences between them, too. For Buddha, rebirth had nothing whatever to do with the transmigration of souls. The Jains, on the other hand, place great emphasis on the soul. All things have souls. By nature the individual souls are pure and unclouded, but the material world intrudes into everything and only by strict asceticism can a man prevent this intrusion and suppress all craving, desire and activity. Buddha set no great store by mortification of the flesh, teaching instead a "middle path." But the Jains firmly believe in the complete renunciation of the body, of all things physical and material, which logically leads to self-mortification.

Like most religious founders, neither Buddha nor Mahavira left any written works behind: the teachings of both these great geniuses were not committed to writing until long after their death.

The most beautiful Jain shrines in India are found on Mount Abu in Rajputana: they are the five celebrated Dilwara temples, two of which deserve to be reckoned among the wonders of the world. One of them was built in 1032 A.D. by a minister and general called Vimala, and the other by two brothers, Vastupala and Tejpala, orthodox Jain merchants who meant to honor their religion by vast financial sacrifices. Each of these temples is dedicated to one of the twenty-four *jinas*, the earliest adherents of Jainism who attained true perfection. The temples are built entirely of white marble; they are miracles of architecture because their wealth of sculptures is scarcely rivaled anywhere else in the world. The famous Indologist Ananda Coomaraswamy describes this rich relief work as one of the rare instances where "superabundance becomes beauty."

The temples are not deserted. Day by day the faithful come to pray before the twenty-four statues, bringing sacrificial flowers and sandalwood. The chief figure of the cult—the *jina* to whom the temple is dedicated—is enthroned in the near-darkness of his inner sanctum.

Otherwise the temples are wide open, like a forest of pillars surmounted by a roof, for neither Hindu nor Jain architecture knows a real vault. In this respect Indian architecture is completely different from our own, its whole roof structure exerting only a one-dimensional vertical pressure.

If you stand among these pillars and ceilings with their unexcelled ornamentation, you feel that all the traditional laws of architecture have been suspended. It is as if you were in some fabulous submarine world, surrounded by pearls and coral reefs and dazzled by a perfection of beauty bestowed by the heavens only on the *jinas* themselves.

It is here, at the still-pulsing heart of this dying religion, that one can still feel something of the lofty ideals that once proclaimed the grandeur of Jainism to ancient India.

Why do the good suffer? Why must a man who commits no sin, who lives righteously and never transgresses the commandments, suffer sickness, misfortune, death and doom? Like Job, the Christian religion wrestles everlastingly with this vast and unanswered problem, but the ancient religions of India–Hinduism, Buddhism and Jainism–solved it long ago. They all believe in cyclical rebirth: we are reborn either as human beings or as animals. Hence the problem of apparently undeserved suffering holds no further mysteries. Anyone who suffers without due cause must have incurred his unhappy lot in a previous life. By the same token, people readily accept the fact of being born into a particular caste, because this, too, is something that was determined in a previous life. But since suffering predominates in all reincarnations, the Indian has only one desire: to extricate himself from the eternal cycle of rebirth. And the only way to do this is to attain perfection.

It is this act of conquering and transcending one's self, this escape from the eternal cycle, this final cessation of rebirth, which is the sole aim of Jainism. And to the Jains, the only men who traveled the road to perfection and showed others the goal of ultimate peace are the twenty-four true *jinas* who are worshiped in their temples. Symbols of harmony, composure, victory and gentleness, they alone rest in timeless tranquillity, their faces rapt and withdrawn, proving to the faithful that there is something above and beyond mankind's eternal round of petty cares–something higher than the preoccupation with earthly affairs.

ANGKOR LIES ABANDONED IN THE JUNGLE

All roads of Asia start in India.
Ananda Coomaraswamy

"FIVE pineapples on a hill." Thus the French novelist Paul Claudel described the most magnificent temple ruins in Asia. He was referring to the towers of the temple city of Angkor Wat which glow red in the setting sun and shimmer gray-green in the pale light of dawn; and which at night, when the moonlight bathes the virgin forest, take on an unearthly shade of blue.

Temples, cities and shrines lay forgotten here for centuries, hidden by the luxuriant jungle foliage. Forgotten, that is, until the arrival of some Jesuit Fathers in 1815. Until Abel Rémusat translated old Chinese accounts of some cities that were believed to have disappeared. Until a French explorer, in 1858, on his arduous trek along the valley of the upper Mekong peered through the undergrowth and saw the vast temples overgrown with lianas, undisturbed like some Sleeping Beauty of the jungle, some of their massive stone blocks burst asunder by jungle trees in the eternal triumph of nature over man's handiwork. Until, in 1863, Henri Mouhot published the story of his voyage around the world and mentioned the ruins. Until, in fact, it was finally realized that the ruins of Angkor had been rediscovered.

Then ponderous scholars attired in frock coats and wing collars began to plod their way through the jungle. Then de la Porte brought the first sculptures back to Paris, and the Guimet Museum was crammed with admiring top-hatted gentlemen and skirt-swinging ladies genteelly peering through their *lorgnons*. And on December 15, 1898, Paul Doumer, then Governor-General of Indo-China, founded the Far East School at Hanoi, primarily for the study of Indo-China's history, architecture and language.

Even today one temple and one city after another are being wrested from the jungle, their ancient splendor reconstructed, and the measuring, deciphering, translating and exploring goes on uninterruptedly.

"All roads of Asia start in India," says Ananda Coomaraswamy, the famous Indian archaeologist, and it is true that India's art accompanied her religion to Ceylon, Java, Cambodia, Siam, Burma, Tibet, Turkestan,

China, Korea and Japan. The ruins of Angkor Wat reflect the spirit of India, and the temple ruins at Borobudur in Java mirror India's cosmic vision, immortalized in stone.

The main tower of Angkor Wat soars 230 feet above the floor of the jungle, and with its three terraces and nine towers, the temple covers an area of roughly 48,000 square yards. The protective moat surrounding the precincts is nearly 360 feet wide and twelve and one-half miles in circumference. Angkor Wat is a gigantic rectangular edifice; a hymn in stone to gods who nevertheless were not strong enough to preserve their temples. Angkor Wat is a microcosm—a four-cornered surface surrounded by water—the earth surrounded by the oceans. The deity was embodied by the king, and the world's highest mountain was the highest temple tower from which the power of the god radiated in all directions.

Actually Angkor Wat as a geographical term is misleading, for the *wat* (temple), though one of the largest of the ruins, is only one of several hundred structures all dating from the ninth to the fourteenth century A.D.

Who were the builders of these prayers in stone? At the time Christ was born in Bethlehem, Cambodia was inhabited by a people known as the Khmers. Their racial and linguistic characteristics seem to have come from different worlds. The Khmers were taller, darker and slimmer than their neighbors, and their eyes resembled those of the Indo-European races. Linguistically, they were related to the peoples of Indonesia and the South Seas, as well as to the Melanesians and Polynesians. But whereas the Polynesians, Mongols, Chinese and Japanese all have straight black hair, the hair of the Khmers tended to be curly. They were probably the product of continuous interbreeding with the many races they came into contact with. Above all it was China which, with its human masses incessantly streaming north and south, added to Indo-China's population pressure that may have launched the daring voyages of the Polynesians who eventually reached Easter Island at the eastern end of the Pacific. It is even quite possible that racially related peoples from northeast Asia migrated as far as the tablelands of South America where, since the time of Columbus, they have been known to us as Indians.

Angkor Thom, the ninth-century capital of the Khmer nation, supposedly received tribute from more than a hundred subject kings and purportedly had the fantastic number of fifteen million soldiers under its over-all command. When Kublai Khan's ambassadorial secretary

Khuta-Kuan visited Angkor Thom about 1290 A.D., he found the Khmers to be a strange people toiling endlessly in the rice fields and building temples for their gods. The king of the Khmers had five wives: one principal consort and four morganatic wives—one for each of the cardinal points of the compass. He also kept four thousand concubines and virtually waded in gold and jewels. Pleasure boats drifted on the lakes and royal elephants swayed through the streets of the capital. More than a million people lived in Angkor Thom alone.

The temple of Angkor Wat was built for King Suryavarman II between 1113 and 1150 A.D. by slaves and prisoners of war, at an enormous cost in human lives. As an architectural accomplishment, it is as impressive as anything built by the Egyptians and Greeks, and as massive as the cathedrals of Europe. Thousands of slaves cleared the jungle; then, from the hills forty to sixty miles away, they hauled the great sandstone blocks into position. Millions of bricks were baked and bound by an unidentifiable vegetable matter and acres of laterite, a coarse red sandstone forming the substrata of the surrounding countryside, were cut to build the foundations, walls and high towers of the structures. And all the while, artists sculpted and priests kept the evil spirits away. To have a steady supply of slaves, the king conducted several wars, but the outcome of wars is a matter of chance and so the temples and cities were eventually overrun by the Siamese—until nothing remained of them but ruins.

Most of the peoples who ruled the area while the vast building program was in progress were either Hindus or Buddhists, as is apparent from the style of architecture and ornamentation. Massive towers rise above the sanctuaries, and huge statues of emperors, Buddhas, mystical birds and animals as well as details of religious ritual characterize new generations of architects and new dynasties. Sanskrit-inscribed tablets identify many of the buildings as temples, others as libraries or courts of justice, and still others as hospitals, of which more than a hundred are credited to one ruler alone.

Stone columns, doors and walls are elaborately carved in both high and low relief. Brick walls covered with heavy plaster coating are decorated with low reliefs representing battle scenes, historical episodes, the phases of man's life on earth, everyday communal activities, as well as many Hindu and Buddhist deities. Ornamentations include innumerable temple apsarases, the celestial water nymphs and dancers of Indra's heaven.

Along the roads and jungle paths of modern Cambodia the natives still use as their principal tool a razor-sharp blade about twelve inches long, attached to a foot-long curved wooden handle. The same tool is pictured on several murals on the long walls of Angkor Wat. And the narrow, two-wheeled bullock carts with protruding "fenders" on both sides to ward off jungle obstructions, which are the modern peasants' chief mode of transportation, are also pictured in thousand-year-old scenes of battles and supply trains on the walls of Angkor Thom. The same jungle, the same tools, the same conveyances, the same people—living and working as of old among the ruins of their former greatness.

It was between 2000 and 500 B.C. that India's sacred Vedic literature came into being. The god Vishnu is the central figure in the Sanskrit texts of the *Mahabharata* and *Ramayana*. Siva and Brahma, the two other gods, also originate in ancient Indian literature. And here on the Mekong River these Indian gods again found their shrines and cities. The spirit of Buddha, who lived from about 560 to 480 B.C., also joined them, and everywhere in Khmer art we meet the fan-shaped head of Naga, the sacred snake. And thus all the gods of India found a common home in Cambodia.

It is always the same story: men will never relinquish anything that comes from heaven. The Romans often allowed the gods of the conquered to have their own temples; Mohammed adopted all the Prophets for Islam, Abraham, Moses and even Christ himself; the Christians adopted the pagan festival of Christmas, and so the Khmers appropriated every god in the Indian pantheon.

The natives of modern Cambodia are descended from the Khmers. But whereas their ancestors once built for eternity, on a scale which is still the object of admiration of modern archaeologists, the latter-day Khmers live fearfully in flimsy huts built on stilts and reached by ladders. At night they pull these ladders up, but leave the topmost rung for the spirit to perch on, so that it may guard the sleepers against the demons.

CHINA'S ANCESTORS LIVED 500,000 YEARS AGO

All the peoples about whom we know anything at all possess at least the beginning of a civilization. Even Peking man (Sinanthropus pekinensis) *manufactured implements and knew the use of fire.*
Kaj Birket-Smith

IT ALL began with some chicken bones.

Not so long ago the bones and skeletons of many birds were dug up on a hill some thirty miles southwest of Peking. The local Chinese, taking them for chicken bones, called the small mound "Chicken Bone Hill," and thought no more about it. But archaeologists, examining the bones under the microscope, established that they were in fact the fossilized bones of birds, rodents and even beasts of prey. Chicken Bone Hill became the object of fresh interest and the entire neighborhood, known as Choukoutien, was soon a favorite haunt of European archaeologists.

It is significant that Europeans are far more interested in archaeology than Orientals. Europeans want to *know;* Orientals want to *live.* Europeans explore things, destroy and recreate them. Orientals let them go the way of all flesh.

Among the many things discovered beneath Chicken Bone Hill was the molar of a manlike creature. Ultimately, more than a thousand crates of fossilized bones were shipped to Peking, where they were examined and sorted. Human jawbones and fragments of skulls were identified, and when everything was reviewed it was established that the bones belonged to twenty-five different individuals.

Then came the year 1929, and a truly sensational find. A complete skull was unearthed—the skull of the so-called *Sinanthropus pekinensis.* This gentleman is not the Adam of mankind, his early forerunner being the apeman of Java, who walked upright. Nevertheless, the Peking man had been buried beneath Chicken Bone Hill for a considerable length of time—about 500,000 years. We do know that he could think, for the capacity of his skull was 58.8 cubic inches, only slightly less than modern man's 61 cubic inches. His speech center was also studied and it was found that he could talk. Furthermore, his teeth and jawbones showed that he was related to the Mongols, Eskimos, Chinese or Japanese. If that is any indication, then the Chinese, whom we regard as belonging to the Mongolian race, have lived in northern China from time immemorial.

But in spite of these astonishing discoveries the archaeologists would not rest. They determined from traces of yellow ashes that the Peking man was familiar with fire. Three thousand bones modeled into identical forms by human hands proved that a small "industrial center" once existed there. Thousands of quartz stones had been shaped by powerful hammer blows and the remains of buffalo, deer and other forest animals indicated that the area at one time had possessed a warm, damp climate and been dotted with marshes, lakes and forests. Today this region around Peking is treeless, dry and extremely cold in winter.

Near Chicken Bone Hill, but still in the same Choukoutien district, a second site was discovered—the so-called "Upper Cave." Here these aborigines displayed a degree of artistic talent. Thousands of years ago, some pretty woman already wore a necklace, as is shown by twenty-eight animal teeth strung together, and bone utensils were painted red.

Another archaeological site sheds further light on this Stone-Age civilization. This was found at the Ordos Bend, where the people were even more advanced. Traces of charcoal mark the former site of their campfires and fragments of rhinoceros, hyena, antelope, cow and buffalo bones, together with egg shells belonging to an extinct species of giant ostrich, indicate their bill of fare. Have we come across a highly developed species of apes? Not in the least! Here, too, *homo sapiens*, man himself, left his traces—only a single tooth, but enough to cast a little light on the unfathomable darkness of the past.

Between the Paleolithic Age—about 500,000 B.C.—and 2500 B.C. lies an immeasurable span of time about which we know little or nothing. What had happened? Had the Chinese Noah of some deluge taken refuge on some mountain top? We do not know.

The next message from ancient man comes from Yang-shao, where, in 1921, a whole village was discovered. Here existed an advanced civilization 4,000 or 5,000 years old, whose beginnings remain shrouded in mystery. It is exactly like Mohenjo-Daro in India: not a trace of anything—and then abruptly a completely civilized, fairly sizable population. Clay discs forming some kind of spinning wheel would indicate the cultivation of certain fibrous plants, and earthenware vessels are decorated with woven patterns. There are tools made of bone and horn;

sewing needles with finely cut eyes; pots with necks and handles; fragile vases with slender necks; large urns adorned with human figures, dogs, horses and other ornaments. A cat, barely over a tenth of an inch high, suggests that even in those days this animal was a household pet. Perhaps this period, which is called the Stone-Bronze Age, even had a form of writing, for the earliest signs of hieroglyphics have been found in graves in the province of Kansu. The skeletal remains of some hundred and twenty men and women found at Kansu prove that they belonged to the Mongolian race. However, we do not know whether these ancient "Chinese" of the Stone-Bronze Age were descended from the 500,000-year-old Peking man.

The earth had revolved around the sun another thousand times or so when man already buried his dead, as is evidenced by the graves of the Shang—also known as the graves of the Yin—which were opened only in very recent times. They lie in the modern town of Anyang in Honan province, some seventy-five miles north of the Yellow River. The Shang Dynasty is the first period of Chinese history about which we have really reliable information. This imperial line was founded about 1450 B.C. and lasted until 1050 B.C. The heavens themselves lent a helping hand in their discovery, for in 1079 A.D. a mighty storm ripped up the ground and disclosed the grave of a Shang emperor.

The Chinese of this region found a number of bronze vessels, and —practical-minded as they are—speedily sold them at the nearest market. Later, a village was built on the site, and human feet continued to trample unconcernedly on the relics of past millennia. At the turn of the century, some plowing peasants turned up animal bones and tortoise shells covered with symbols.

Unfortunately the Chinese invariably regard anything that is mysterious and even halfway edible as medicine. The 4,000-year-old-bones and tortoise shells were therefore pulverized and sold to apothecaries as an elexir guaranteed to prolong life. The human stomach can stand more than is commonly supposed, but archaeology suffers greatly from such practices. The new medicine sold well until the arrival of inquisitive white men, who quickly bought up the bones and tortoise shells and sent them to museums all over the world. Soon still more "white barbarians" arrived, and the Chinese peasantry looked on in astonishment as these dull old bones were bought by the thousands.

These finds bore China's oldest written characters, and such messages, 4,000 or more years old, are a treasure trove of inestimable value for the study of human history. The tortoise shells and bones from the graves of the Shang emperors not only reveal the questions people used to put to their local oracle, but also provide the answers. There are questions addressed to gods and ancestors; questions about journeys, fishing and hunting; questions about harvests, illnesses and the interpretation of dreams. The bone and tortoise-shell documents answer them all. And a picture of Chinese civilization is conjured up from the mists of the past.

Here is an example: "Tonight it will rain; an elephant must be caught." So there were elephants in Central China in those days.

Or: "Pray to grandmother Yi for rain." So there was ancestor worship almost 4,000 years ago.

The pictographs for fishing show us that the Shang people used lines, rods, nets and bait, while the symbols for hunting prove that they were familiar with arrow and spear. The script reveals that horses were used for pulling carts. The word "man" was expressed by combining the symbols for "strength" and "field." The symbols for grain show millet and rice. Mulberry trees were cultivated and silk was manufactured at a time when most of mankind went around naked or clothed in animal hides and only the civilizations of the Mediterranean and Central America had any woven fabrics.

The graves of the Shang yielded articles of bronze, but the people of that period also knew how to smelt copper, tin, iron, silver and lead. The scholars marveled at the sacrificial vessels, the beautiful bronze vases with animal designs, the bronze mirrors and incense burners produced by this extremely refined civilization.

But the scholars were not the only ones who marveled. Any visitor to northern China could go into a curio shop and buy genuine bronze bowls of the Shang period. It should be remembered, however, that this era of consummate craftsmanship was also marked by excessive cruelty. Thousands of people were sacrificed to the god of the soil, and their blood poured into sacrificial urns. Ultimately the Shang Dynasty grew degenerate amidst high living and debauchery. Just as Rome had her Nero, so the Shang period ended with the monstrous Chou Hsin. He was as strong as Samson and reputedly could slay wild beasts with a single blow of his fist. "He used his eloquence to refute all good counsel, and his wit to cover up his mistakes."

But inevitably the day of reckoning came. Abandoned by his warriors, Emperor Chou Hsin was at the end of his wits. Donning his most gorgeous robes and jewels, he set fire to his palace and perished in a sea of flames.

His concubines, who had been his companions in debauchery, were taken over by the victorious invaders.

CONFUCIUS AND LAO-TSE

If you do not know life, how shall you know death?
Confucius

Never be the first in the world.
Lao-tse

EVERY age believes that it has achieved wisdom. Men invariably refer to "our progressive age," despise the past, never envy the future. But, after reviewing the history of the past millennia, if one wished to award one particular epoch a prize for the greatest intellectual achievements, he would, in my opinion, have to select the sixth and fifth centuries B.C. For the period between 600 and 400 B.C. witnessed a dazzling outburst of religious, philosophical and literary genius in almost every quarter of the world.

About this time, Buddha was teaching in India, and Zoroaster in Persia. In Palestine, Jeremiah, Ezekiel and Isaiah were preaching the coming of the Messiah, and the Old Testament was taking shape. In Greece, democracy was lifted from its cradle by Solon and Cleisthenes, and it was between 480 and 430 B.C. that Athens enjoyed her golden age of power and culture. And these centuries also witnessed the birth of China's two greatest philosophers: Lao-tse and Confucius.

Greece, Judea, Persia, India and China still had little mutual contact at that time, and we are almost tempted to believe in an astrological miracle if we consider that mankind's greatest ideas were evolved so simultaneously among such different races and in such different and far-flung corners of the world.

China's greatest philosopher, Confucius—in Chinese, K'ung Fu-tzu—was born in 551 B.C. in what is today Shantung province. We know little about his childhood except that he was a serious, thoughtful boy who, after his father's death, had to work in order to support his mother. As a boy he quickly mastered the arts of bowmanship and music. He married when he was nineteen and was divorced at the age of twenty-three—for a moral philosopher should remain celibate, as Socrates' marriage to Xanthippe would indicate. Confucius soon became known as a teacher, because he did not attack other philosophers or waste any time in refuting their arguments. He was strict with his disciples, yet he loved them dearly, and it is recorded that when one of them—Yen Hwui—died, he wept and said: "He loved to learn. I never had a pupil who learned as willingly as he. His time was short, and there is not another like him." Evidently Yen Hwui must have been a sort of St. John to his master.

Confucius lived at a time we refer to as China's feudal period, when feudal lords ruled in walled cities surrounded by arable land and hunting preserves. Those feudal cities were located in modern Honan and in parts of Shansi, Shensi and Shantung. Two cities, Ch'i and Ch'in, became the most important of these city-states, and Ch'in finally gained mastery over all its neighbors, to found the empire from which China probably derives its name. It may be here noted that the whole world knows "the Kingdom of the Center" as "China"—except the Chinese.

In Confucius' day, however, the feudal states had not yet been united, and the master wandered from one to another. He observed the universally low standards of governing, expressed his annoyance and suggested methods for improving them. One or two princes even gave him the opportunity of holding office in their administrations, but it was probably never long before Confucius grew tired of battling with officials and princes. Perhaps he was also a nuisance to them, for he was a man of wisdom and integrity.

"When I was fifteen," he said, "my mind was occupied with learning. When I was thirty I held firm views. At forty I was free from doubts. At fifty I knew the laws of heaven. At sixty my ear was an obedient recipient of truths. At seventy I could apprehend whatsoever my heart desired without abandoning the path of righteousness." Confucius died at the age of seventy-two. There came a morning when one of his disciples heard him moan softly: "The greatest mountain must crumble, the strong beam must break, the wise man must wither away like a flower." Then another disciple hurried along, and Confucius called out: "No intelligent ruler arises. No one in the entire land will make me his counselor. It is time for me to die." So saying, he lay down, and after seven days he expired. But Tze Kung, the disciple who had loved his master best, sat by the great teacher's grave for three years, mourning him in solitude.

What exactly did this genius of practical morality teach?

He left behind five volumes, known in China as the five *King*. Actually Confucius was probably not the author of these writings, but merely passed on the unsurpassed wisdom of the past, dedicating himself to the publication of the ancient classical texts which have influenced Chinese thought and culture up to the twentieth century. But he undoubtedly left the imprint of his own mind upon the age-old doctrines he edited, although solely in an effort to gain acceptance not for his own ideas, but for the knowledge and ethics of the ancients.

Mesopotamia, Judea, Arabia and India are the lands that have produced the great religions of mankind. China on the other hand has always been the land of the great philosophers, the land of practical moral doctrine. The Chinese have never worried about God or the world to come or any systems of theology, but they love life—life as it really is. They accept life for what it contains: the rich and the poor, good and evil, bandits, generals and kings, the bright rainbow and the pale moon. They love arched bridges and their mirrored images in the ponds, lotus blossoms and tea, silk and incense, fine-boned women and good food, cicadas in cages and sails in the evening breeze. China's novelists write about the things of everyday life: good fellowship, holiday banquets, the tittering of young girls, dark clouds over the moon, wild ducks making for the water, family celebrations, marriage, childbirth, dutiful sons and obedient daughters-in-law—the whole poignant beauty of life with all its joys and tragedies. But for immortality, for a life after death, for thoughts that do not spring from the good earth, for what happens in heaven or what lies beneath the ground, the Chinese have neither the time nor the inclination. That is why Confucius never created a philosophical system but founded a school of clear thinking. That is why he never held any theological discourses but concentrated upon setting up rules for the conduct of individuals and governments. That is why he never established a theocracy, but strove to strengthen and improve the rigidly aristocratic state of his day. When someone questioned him about the admittedly important problem of death, he answered: "If you do not know life, how shall you know death?"

All of Confucius' teachings may perhaps best be summed up in the following sentences: "The ancients, wishing to set an example of supreme virtue in the land, first put their country in order. In putting their country in order, they first worked on themselves. In working on themselves, they purified their hearts. In purifying their hearts, they endeavored to be sincere in their thoughts. In being sincere in their thoughts, they extended their knowledge. In extending their knowledge, they explored matters. When these matters had been explored, their knowledge became comprehensive. When their knowledge was comprehensive, their thoughts became sincere. When their thoughts were sincere, they themselves became decorous. When they themselves were decorous, their families became orderly. When their families were orderly, their country became well governed. And when their country was well governed, the whole world lived in peace and contentment."

Wisdom, therefore, like charity, necessarily begins at home. Thus Confucius is one with all the geniuses of this world in holding that a man should first set his own soul in order before he begins to organize the outside world. Confucius was indeed a very wise man, for he was convinced that the decent behavior of the individual was the key to an orderly world and a peaceful life. But he went far beyond this demand on the individual. He was perhaps the greatest teacher of sociology. He strove to regulate the relations of men toward one another, and of the people toward their government. When he was asked: "Is there any one word which can serve as a practical guide throughout one's life?" he answered: "Reciprocity," meaning the interdependence of all things, all actions, all doctrines and all people. He meant forgiveness. He meant the harmonious relationship among all men on earth. As Dostoyevski put it: "Each man is responsible for the other."

Above all else, Confucius disliked obscure allusions and muddled thinking. He regarded ambiguity as a national catastrophe. "Act before you speak, and then speak as you have acted." This was a safe enough policy. "The 'superior' person so acts that his actions blaze a common trail for all generations. He so conducts himself that his conduct becomes a law for all generations. He so speaks that his words are a valid precept for all generations." Confucius was probably the most persuasive advocate of the golden rule: "Do unto others as you would be done by." But he went even further, for when someone asked him: "What is your comment on the statement that evil should be repaid with good?" he replied: "In that case, with what should one repay good? Repay evil with justice, and good with good."

Confucius' teachings constitute a vast kaleidoscope of practical instructions. If we were to follow them, we might have neither a god nor a religion, but we would certainly have a tolerable life on earth. Nor have the Chinese ever regarded Confucius as a god or religious founder. All that can be found in his temples is the tablet with his name and the smaller tablets bearing his teachings; and at that it was only several centuries after he died that his rules of conduct became the accepted moral code of aristocratic Chinese society. "Only two sorts of people can never change," he said, "the very wise and the very foolish." Confucius was one of the very wise, and he hated fools.

His contemporary Lao-tse was also a very wise man, but he loved simple folk. We know even less about Lao-tse than we do about Confucius. He probably did live, although even that is open to question. The story goes that Confucius once met Lao-tse and spoke with him. Be that as it may, they most certainly did not get along because they were too dissimilar in character.

Confucius belongs to the city, Lao-tse to the country.

Lao-tse, in Chinese, means "the old master," but the philosopher's family name is said to have been Li, or "plum." His work is a compilation of individual experiences and insights called *Tao-te-king* or, roughly, "Book of the Way and of Virtue." Whereas Confucius attempted to organize human relations, Lao-tse's teachings were the most far-reaching (and humorously mischievous) ever devised by the mind of man. He did not take the easy way out, like Confucius, for it was precisely the meek in spirit to whom he addressed his teachings, which were as comforting as they were effective. Basically "the way" means "the way to think." Thinking, we are told, is only good for quarreling, while a dearth of thought guarantees peace. We should therefore live modestly, always efface ourselves, love the land, be content in the tranquil contemplation of nature, and do what Voltaire says is the wisest thing left for man to do: cultivate our gardens. Knowledge has nothing to do with wisdom, and the "intellectual" is as far removed from happiness and wisdom as the moon is from the earth. To have a philosopher at the head of the state would be the horror to end all horrors: Lao-tse's ideal ruler is a kindly, simple man. The more people think, build, discover and achieve, the nearer catastrophe looms. (Lao-tse may have a point there if we look at the latest product of human knowledge and ingenuity: the planned exploitation of the atom.)

Like Rousseau after him, Lao-tse called for a return to nature. He is much closer to the true spirit of the Chinese people than Confucius, and his doctrine is presumably very old, springing from China's primeval consciousness: man is free only so long as he remains simple, and a good government is a government which does nothing. "Never be the first in the world," taught Lao-tse, and "The wisest thing in life is never to become involved in anything." Chwang-tse, his greatest adherent and a brilliant and graphic writer, assessed Lao-tse's teachings quite correctly when he summed them up: "To follow the stream as a drop of water does, and not conduct oneself arbitrarily therein."

It is this attitude toward life—this patience, this quiet resignation and submissiveness, this strength derived from a passive wait-and-see outlook—which has determined the rhythm of life in all civilizations of the

Far East. Lao-tse's genius lies in conceiving the most successful philosophy of self-preservation. It is the philosophy of hiding, avoiding violence, shunning argument and therefore never coming to harm. It is the theory of strength through ignorance and stupidity as the safest defense against the tyrants of this world. Like Solomon, Lao-tse recognized the futility of all striving, and with it the advantages of the simpletons, the strength of the weak, and the genius inherent in the game of blindman's buff. Anyone in China who became a great, and perhaps even a good and just, statesman almost certainly had read Confucius. But the ruler who fled the world, plucked apples from the trees as if he were in the Garden of Eden, and stayed alive, belonged to the school of Lao-tse.

"It is only because everyone beneath the heavens recognizes beauty as beauty that there is such a thing as ugliness."—"He rules wisely who makes hearts light, fills bellies, destroys intelligence, braces himself and endeavors to protect his people from knowledge and keep them free from desire."—"The force of words is soon expended. It is far better to keep what is in one's heart to oneself."—"In ancient times," Lao-tse tells us, "nature made men straightforward and peaceable, and the whole world was happy. But then man acquired knowledge, and life became complicated. Mankind made discoveries and lost its innocence. Mankind moved from the fields into the towns and began to write books. Then misery was born, and tears welled in the eyes of philosophers. The wise man will avoid towns and the corrupting and enervating influence of laws and civilization. He will hide in the lap of nature, far from towns and books, from spiteful officials and frustrated social reformers. The secret of enduring happiness lies in obeying nature and wandering quietly along the tranquil paths of the earth."

And for sheer wisdom and insight it would be hard to surpass the following description of nature's workings:

All things in nature do their work quietly; they are created and they possess nothing. They fulfill their purpose and crave nothing. All things accomplish their ends; then we see them recede again. When they have reached their prime, they return to their source. This withdrawal is peace and the fulfillment of destiny. This ebb and flow is an eternal law. To know that law is wisdom.

THE EIGHTH WONDER OF THE WORLD

If a son be born to you, beware and do not take him up; if a daughter be born to you, feed her and rear her; she need not mark how corpses and bones lie heaped together at the foot of the Wall.

Shui-ching-ch'u, Chap. 3

IT IS the largest structure man has ever built, a gigantic monument to human will power. More than 2,000 years old, even today its lonely grandeur mocks all modern techniques we know. The Chinese call it Wan Li Ch'ang Ch'eng, or "Wall of the 10,000 Li," a *li* being about 550 yards. Does this mean that the Great Wall of China is more than 3,000 miles long?

We cannot really be sure because we do not know very much about China in general: it takes more than the mere fifty, sixty, seventy years of a human lifetime to understand this country with its 400 million people and its 5,000 years of history. All we can say is that the largest nation in the world built the largest wall in the world, for the dimensions of this serpent in stone are so staggering, its ramifications so labyrinthine, that no explorer, cartographer or traveler has proved equal to the task of measuring them.

Perhaps the Wall itself is "only" about 1,500 miles long but the Chinese built smaller branch walls on a scale that could encircle countries the size of Belgium—double and triple sets of wall which, if laid end to end, would reach across the Atlantic from England to America. The Wall runs along all of China's northern frontier, separating agricultural land from steppe, China from Mongolia, peasants from nomads.

Forty thousand towers project from the Wall; for the most part they were built first and only later linked by the Wall, which was originally an earthwork of immense length. Today it is made of brick.

I have wandered along this wall, and can say it is truly quite an experience. One can walk westward for days, weeks and months, and yet with every step the whole structure seems to become more incomprehensible. It crosses mountains at their highest point, invariably winding its way along the loftiest ridges. It towers steeply into the sky and then falls precipitously from the dizzy heights into the depths beneath. The scenery is one of infinite loneliness, with barren brown mountains and deserted steppes forever lashed and stung by the wind.

The Wall is a vast defensive work; whole regiments could march on it and carts could conveniently pass one another wherever the road was not too steep. It could accommodate troop units; it had forts, signal stations, food depots, embrasures, shelters and dungeons.

The press recently announced that the Chinese government was permitting its citizens to dismantle the Wall and use the bricks for building houses. The government bemoaned this cultural loss, but the Wall—if it could—would merely laugh at such nonsense. People have been "dismantling" it for 2,000 years, purloining its stones and masonry with about as much effect as a bird might have by sharpening its beak on the Himalayas.

The Wall is an authentically Chinese work. No other race could have had the perseverance and energy to assemble the vast quantity of stone that must have been required. And the Chinese loves seclusion: walls surround his house; and walls surround his towns. If the Great Wall and all the town walls in north China were laid end to end, they would encircle the world at the equator.

In 214 B.C., when the building of the Wall began, the peoples of the distant Mediterranean marveled at the seven wonders of the ancient world:

1. The Hanging Gardens of Babylon, which towered 430 feet into the air welcoming the traveler from a distance. Bold arches supported terraces with exotic flowers, ponds gleamed in the sun, trees thrust into the blue sky, and lianas gracefully snaked their way through all this vegetation. Pumps worked day and night to water this celestial garden, built by the king of Assyria as a pleasure seat for Shammuramat, the queen whom the Greeks called Semiramis.

2. Pharaoh Khufu's pyramid at Giza, the only one of the ancient seven wonders which can still be admired today.

3. The Temple of Diana at Ephesus, begun in 772 B.C. Thousands of people labored for two hundred years to build this miracle. On the night Alexander the Great was born, a man called Herostratus set fire to it. His motive: a desire for everlasting fame.

4. The Olympian Zeus by Phidias, a statue in gold and ivory completed at Elis in 435 B.C. It was a work of such perfection and beauty that it was believed nothing would ever surpass it. Chiseled on its plinth were the words: "Phidias the Athenian made me."

5. The tomb of King Mausolus—to whom we owe the term of mausoleum—a fabulous structure enclosed by Ionic pillars and built in 354 B.C. at Halicarnassus in Caria. Mausolus never did rest in this tomb, however, for according to one legend, his widow poured her husband's ashes into a goblet of rare wine and drained the appalling concoction to the dregs.

6. The lighthouse at Pharos, near Alexandria, whose beam was visible nearly a hundred miles out to sea. The tower was completed in 283 B.C., and a fire burned continuously on its upper platform for fully 1,500 years.

7. The Colossus of Rhodes, big enough for a large sailing ship to pass between its legs. It was completed in 280 B.C., after twelve years of work. The metal casting was so enormous that the statue's thumb was too big for a man's arms to encircle. Glass lenses suspended from the giant's neck were used as an early sort of telescope enabling the viewer to look twenty-five miles out to sea.

These, then, were the seven wonders of the ancient world. The Great Wall of China, the greatest of them all, was not among them. China was too far away, but—something we find difficult to grasp nowadays—it was also regarded as something of a fairy tale if any news about China reached the Mediterranean at all at that time.

In 218 B.C., the one-eyed Hannibal's elephants lumbered laboriously across the Alps as the Carthaginians marched on Rome during the second Punic war. It was at that time, at the close of antiquity's greatest architectural attainments, that the mind of a half-crazed genius conceived the idea of building the Great Wall. The man who initiated this vast project was Ch'in Shih-huang-ti, the first emperor of the Ch'in Dynasty. He intended his dynasty to last forever, with all emperors after him to be known as "the second," "the third," and so on, for his empire to endure for all time; and work on the Wall should never cease. He was a man with a pronounced hooked nose, narrow eyes set close together, the chest of a bird of prey, and the voice of a jackal. He vowed that all Chinese history before him, and the memory of the states that had fought him for supremacy, should be erased.

So the bamboo archives and scientific records began to crackle and blaze; Confucius' Book of Songs went up in smoke, the words of the intellectuals burned away. The spirit of tradition was to be eliminated once and for all.

When the scholars protested this wholesale destruction of the past to Emperor Shih-huang-ti, he had them thrown into a pit and silenced them by stoning them. Other carping critics and malcontents followed, and a crop of plump melons grew over the place of their summary burial.

Shih-huang-ti did not believe in half measures. He had the vast earthwork which later became the Great Wall thrown up as a rampart against the ancestors of the Mongols, the nomadic Huns (then known as "the demons") who constantly threatened China's northern frontier. Hundreds of thousands of people were sent off to work in the barren mountains: soldiers, prisoners of war, criminals, corrupt dignitaries, scholars who had not surrendered black-listed books for burning, embarrassing intellectuals and complacent bureaucrats. Fortresses and watchtowers sprang up like mushrooms on the craggy heights, and garrisons were established in the valleys. In winter, the winds from Siberia howled about the teeming army of laborers without respite, while in summer a scorching breeze filled the luckless men's eyes and ears with fine dust. The Wall was responsible for many nostalgic poems, homesick letters and melancholy songs. And the plaintive chant of men watering their horses in the puddles beneath the Great Wall rang out over the desolate countryside.

No words can convey how much blood, tears and suffering went into the building of this Calvary in stone. Yet even this was not enough for the First Ruler of the World. To safeguard his craze for power, he called all the rich and powerful men in the country to his capital Hsien Yang, not far from the modern Hsianfu, where he could keep a sharp eye on them, while their presence lent his capital prestige and glamour. He divided his empire into forty-one provinces, established a new system of weights and measures, standardized the system of writing, and built canals and a vast network of roads. His armies overran all the lands as far south as Canton, and his influence extended all the way to modern Tonking in Indo-China. He was perhaps one of the most powerful emperors in history.

The emperor built several palaces near his capital Hsien Yang, and even today, about three miles northwest of the city, there is an earth wall with still recognizable openings for gates. His summer residence stood in an imperial park known as "His Majesty's Forest." Some 700,000 prisoners helped to construct this Ah Fang Palace, as it is called, and the emperor built another hundred and seventy palaces within a radius of sixty miles. He appropriated works of art, precious stones and rare woods from all the countries he had conquered, and the most exquisite women of China lived in these palaces.

The emperor's main palace is said to have contained so many rooms that it would have taken him thirty-six years to live in a different one each day. This brings us closer to the heart of this tyrant's secret: like all other Asiatic dictators, he suffered from persecution mania. People knew his weakness and warned him never to sleep in the same room for two nights in succession. Thus he changed his bedroom every night, and at dusk a mute procession of eunuchs and ladies of the harem carrying pillows and silken sheets would parade through the interminable corridors of his palace.

Shih-huang-ti with inexhaustible, almost obsessive energy, traveled back and forth across his dominions, supervising building projects and governmental administration. Whenever people ridiculed him the emperor would suddenly appear like a specter, which was the signal to dig a pit to bury the irreverent citizen. All who disobeyed him had to die.

But the emperor wanted to live forever, and the magicians—the chemists of those times—worked night and day to manufacture "elixirs of life." When the emperor heard that there were geni on the islands of P'eng Lai (probably Japan) who tended the Herb of Life, he sent 3,000 young men and women across the sea to gather some of it. It was said that all animals there were snow-white, and all palaces and gates made of gold and silver, and people who lived there were always happy. However, contrary winds prevented the youthful pilgrims from landing, and the emperor had to die after all, which he did in 210 B.C.

"But he *must* not die!" whispered the palace eunuchs and councilors. So they placed the lifeless emperor in his sedan chair and carried him through the country, where he gave worldess audiences from behind a curtain and, in a manner of speaking, lived on after his death. His corpse eventually began to give off an unpleasant smell, and huge barrels of salted fish were stacked near the emperor's sedan chair so that the smell of fish would cancel out the imperial odor. (Chinese history is so wonderful because of its unique blend of humor, poetry and grandeur.) Finally—after nine months—even the fish would no longer do, and the emperor had to be buried.

He was interred beneath a hill called the Mountain of the Black Horses. His last resting place, which he began to build when he first came to the throne, was just as magnificent as his palaces, which shows that he did not entirely trust the elixir of life prepared by his magicians. Hundreds of thousands of laborers worked on this tomb. Its interior flooring was encased in bronze and the vault furnished with splendid works of art, replicas of his palaces and administrative buildings; gold, silver and jewels were added and, finally, his sarcophagus. Rivers of quicksilver were pumped noiselessly into the depths of the tomb, and automatic crossbows were installed to insure that anyone who desecrated the sanctuary would meet with certain death. Artificial torches were intended to keep the darkness away, and all the women of the emperor's palace who were unfortunate enough never to have borne him any sons were buried alive with their master. And when the workmen who knew the tomb's secrets were making their way back up into the light of day, their labor completed, a trap door sealed them off for all time. Finally, the entire magnificent structure was covered with trees and flowers and the emperor slept. . . .

But the Wall lived on. Like every other fortification, it was an effective bastion against attacks when its troops were in a fighting spirit. When their morale was low, however, the Wall lost its purpose. And indeed, during most of the past 2,000 years it has proved to be the most useless piece of construction in human history.

Wandering along the Wall, with Mongolia on one side and China on the other, one is tempted to dream about China's vast history. Soon after Shih-huang-ti's death, his palaces vanished from the face of the earth in the flames of revolutions. Then came the flourishing age of the Han emperors, who reigned from 206 B.C. to 220 A.D. and founded the new metropolis of Ch'ang An, "the city of the long peace," near the ruins of Hsien Yang. This dynasty produced some truly great rulers, like Emperor Wen, "the Cultured One," and his son Ching, "the Radiant One." "The Cultured One" was a thrifty man who wore simple black silk robes. He was ashamed of the great fortune he had inherited from his father.

Emperor Wen did not build any palaces or summer residences, and kept his favorite wife at a safe distance from expensive couturiers. And the people became so rich and contented that even today the Chinese like to be regarded as the "sons of Han." Another Han emperor was Wu Ti, "the Warrior," who between 141 and 86 B.C. transformed China into a great Far Eastern power. He was also a brilliant diplomat, who tried to form an East-West alliance against the Huns, or Hsiung Nu. To this end he sent a certain Chang Ch'ien on a journey across half the world, as far as Bactria and Sogdiana, until news about China eventually reached Rome, where it aroused great curiosity about Serica, or the Land of Silk. The silk would travel along the interminable caravan routes to Rome and Greece, and Ptolemy spoke of a silk capital he called "metropolis of Sera." Now the first peaches and apricots, "Chinese fruits," began to reach Europe.

The Wall crawls endlessly across the mountain ranges and deserts, much as China's history crawls through the centuries. We can still hear the wild battle cries of the Tartars scrambling over the Wall between 200 and 400 A.D., with the weak dynasties retreating before them. Between 618 and 906, the T'ang emperors mounted the Chinese throne: it was an era of the highest culture—but also of luxury, frivolity and dalliance.

This was the great age of Chinese poetry. China had reached her cultural zenith, one of the most dazzling periods the world had ever known. Among her literary achievements were a large annotated edition of Confucius' works, 48,900 poems, and an imperial library of 54,000 volumes. The country had 12,300 major poets. Buddhist monks arrived from India, missionaries from Persia, Nestorian Christians from central Asia. The emperor, T'ai Tsung, attracted all these different theologians and scholars to his court, while he himself remained loyal to Confucius. This was the time of China's most brilliant poet, Li T'ai-po. It was the time of the cruel Empress Wu Hu, who chopped off the arms and legs of her rival and turned her into a "human swine." It was the time of Yang Kuei-fei, the emperor's mistress, who eventually ordered a eunuch to strangle her, and who to this day plays her frightful role in the great Chinese dramas. It was the time when the dead were buried in beds filled with pearls, when statuettes were carved out of rubies and bowls out of jade, when masterpieces of the most refined culinary art were served on tables inlaid with green precious stones. It was the time when thousands of workers filled the silk factories with the humming of spinning wheels. It was the golden age of China's sculpture and painting.

Incidentally, had the ancient Chinese developed their writing with stylos or quills instead of brush, it is unlikely that Chinese painting would have attained the magnificence it did. But for more than 3,000 years the arts of painting and calligraphy developed parallel, producing such disciplined brushwork that for centuries Chinese artists worked on the finest of silks which allowed no erasures. The most beautiful paintings were handed down through the generations, with each collector adding a red seal of ownership and his own appraisal of the work, often in poetical form, in his own hand, at the top of the silk. Indeed, eventually the pleasure with which the Chinese viewed their paintings was enhanced by the calligraphy added by later generations and by deciphering the seals. But, as might be expected of the nation that produced Confucius and Lao-tse, the primary concern of the

Chinese poets of antiquity was not the works of man but the works of nature—and their greatest success traditionally was with landscapes.

Thereafter came centuries of chaos, poverty and disunity, followed by the important three hundred years of Sung rule, which saw a renascence of literature, art and Confucianism, and produced beautiful paintings and porcelain.

New conquerors arrived, ushering in the age of the Mongols. Genghis Khan raced westward and Kublai Khan to the east. Once again the Great Wall proved no obstacle, and the Kublai sat proudly on the dragon throne at Peking when Marco Polo, setting out from Venice and traveling through all of Asia, paid homage to the Mongol emperor.

Fresh armies of laborers were sent to the Great Wall; hundreds of thousands. Not far from Peking and Nanking the Ming emperors (1368-1644) built themselves magnificent tombs flanked by massive animal sculpture. This proved a wise precaution, for they, too, were destined to go the way of all flesh.

For out of the northern forests—modern Manchuria—came other ambitious princes, who fought their way slowly down to Peking. They were the Tungus, foreign overlords who abandoned their native forests for the silken comforts of the south.

But what has survived all these changes is the grace and charm of China's women. Each dynasty succumbed to them in turn, and the rugged princes from the Manchurian north were no exception. In the arms of their Chinese sweethearts they became more and more Chinese, and while the people of China cheerfully adopted the Tungus pigtail, the Tungus themselves were gradually assimilated. Under these Manchus, who reigned from 1644 to 1912, Peking became probably the most beautiful city in the world. And even at this writing, as the north wind continues to gnaw at the stones of the eternal Great Wall, the last descendant of the Manchus, Emperor P'u Yi—still alive but a political prisoner—is still wondering why this fabulous past ever perished.

And, indeed, it does seem incomprehensible.

LI T'AI-PO IS IMMORTAL ONLY WHEN HE IS DRUNK

Your Majesty, this genius unfortunately has one failing: he drinks.
Ho Chih-chang

THE darkness of the early Middle Ages still hung over Europe. In Arabia, the prophet Mohammed was beginning to expound his religious teachings.

Meanwhile, China stood on the threshold of her golden age, the T'ang Dynasty (618-906 A.D.). Emperor T'ai Tsung (627-650), Empress Wu Hu (684-704) and Emperor Hsüan Tsung (713-755)—these are the resounding names which dominate the three centuries of the T'ang period. The fertile valleys of the Yellow River and the Yangtze glowed under the pale green mantle of their rice fields. Peasants plowed their fields contentedly between sparkling canals and gleaming lakes. Ch'ang An, the capital—now the city of Hsianfu in Shensi province—was the wonder of its day. Apart from the main palace with its nine gates, thirty-six other palaces towered above the city, their pillars made of gold, and the villas of the various princes surpassed one another in splendor. The streets swarmed with people, with noblemen on horseback and mandarin coaches drawn by black oxen. Lovely girls, their faces pale as the moon, danced in the many places of entertainment. The life of China was suffused with the spirit of Buddha, Confucius and Lao-tse. Ch'ang An, a true metropolis, attracted within its walls Syrians, Arabs, Persians, Tartars, Tibetans, Koreans, Japanese and Tonkinese. Calligraphy, mathematics and music were taught there; the shelves of the imperial library held more than 200,000 volumes; the city had drama schools, and there were sculptors, painters and musicians. And of the 3,000 palace maidens, one, the famous Yang Kuei-fei, possessed greater beauty than all the others.

Poetry held first place among the arts during the T'ang period, and everyone who had any name at all was a poet. This is no exaggeration, for the *Anthology of the T'ang Dynasty* comprises 900 books and contains more than 48,900 poems by over 12,300 poets. Since the collection was assembled as late as the eighteenth century, it contains only such works as have not been destroyed by the ravages of time. It is almost impossible to conceive the enchanted forest of poetry which sprang up from the fertile soil of the T'ang period.

Under these circumstances we can imagine what it means when the Chinese unanimously declare that of this vast host of immortals Li T'ai-po was the greatest. To them, he is not only the greatest poet of the T'ang period, but the greatest poet of all time. One prominent Chinese wrote of him: "Li Po is T'ai, the titanic peak which soars above ten thousand mountains and hills. He is the sun in whose light millions of stars lose their flickering brightness."

Perhaps Li T'ai-po happened to live at a period that was ideal for a poet. Certainly he witnessed an age of peace and prosperity, a great epoch of cultural universality. He encountered hospitality and an understanding for literature. He heard the tales of distant wars, observed the court intrigues of his day, and in the end lived through revolution, Tartar invasion, and saw the fall of Emperor Hsüan Tsung —a drama of unimaginable grandeur.

China's greatest poet also had a tremendous capacity for enjoying life. He drank continually, traveled and wandered about a great deal, and loved beautiful women. One of his aristocratic patrons even built him a wine-tasting room. Li T'ai-po used to go on pleasure trips with this gentleman, whose name was Tung Tsa-chiu, but he never forgot to take several pretty young singing girls along.

At the age of thirty-seven, the poet came to Shantung, and it was there that he met his greatest rival and China's second immortal poet, Tu Fu. Like two comets which drift in the universe and only come into contact every few million years, the two men were irresistibly drawn to each other, became great friends and kept exchanging poems to the end of their lives. They lived in the same house, slept beneath the same coverlet, and went about hand in hand like brothers.

Li T'ai-po used to stand in drunken reverie on arched bridges and among the ruins of ancient palaces and conjure up the past before his mind's eye. He sat by lakes and admired the lotus blossoms. Yearning to embrace the whole world, he strode along, up hill and down dale, on the wings of wine. At last, in the year 742, he stood before the gates of Ch'ang An, the capital. Ho Chih-chang, a guest of the emperor, was enchanted when he met Li T'ai-po; and, quickly grasping the poet's need for wine, he traded a piece of golden jewelry for a barrel of wine for him. He commended the poet to the emperor with the words: "I have in my house the greatest poet who ever lived. Your Majesty, this genius unfortunately has one failing which can scarcely be cured.

He drinks, and sometimes he drinks too much. But his verses are magnificent. Sire, judge for yourself!"

Thus it was that Li T'ai-po declaimed his verses before the Son of Heaven in the Hall of the Golden Bells. The emperor was perfectly sober, but he soon became intoxicated by what he heard; a banquet was spread in Li Po's honor on the Table of the Seven Jewels. The poet was granted a chair at the Han Lin Academy, where he had nothing to do save write poetry—whenever the spirit moved him. He dined with princes and ladies of the court, made solitary excursions to the taverns of the city, got drunk to his heart's content, and immortalized his boon companions in verse.

Li T'ai-po died in the town which is now called T'ai P'ing, in the province of Anhwei. And how did this extraordinary man face death? He calmly let it come up to him, and even went a little way to meet it. He was sitting in a boat. It was a beautiful night, and the moonbeams were dancing on the water. Draining his last goblet of wine, Li T'ai-po decided to do what only China's greatest poet could have done: he leaned over the gunwale, put his arms about the moon's reflection, and sank from sight. So even his death became a poem.

Li T'ai-po wanted to be buried in the green hills near T'ai P'ing: he had spent the better part of his life in the open air, walking the roads beneath blossoming trees and the stars, and nature herself had guided the brush that penned his eternal poems. He knew even then that he would live on in another world. "Why am I now beneath the green hills?" he wrote. "I laugh, yet I cannot answer. My soul is now quite pure. It tarries in another heaven. And the earth belongs to no one. The peach trees blossom, the waters flow and flow."

He wanted his poems never to fade—that was his will. That is why he still speaks to us today, after 1,200 years:

I paint letters, attended by solitude
The bamboo surges like a sea. From bushes
The dew falls like strings of pearls.
I cast verses onto the gleaming paper
As peach blossoms are scattered in the snow
How long does the scent of the mandarin fruit endure
If a woman carries it beneath her arm?
How long does snow thrive in the sunshine?
But may this poem which I write down now
Last forever, and forever, and forever!

Neck of a burial urn with human features, from the Stone-Bronze Age civilization of Yang Shao. It is 4,000 to 5,000 years old. The eyes betray a distinct Mongoloid slant.

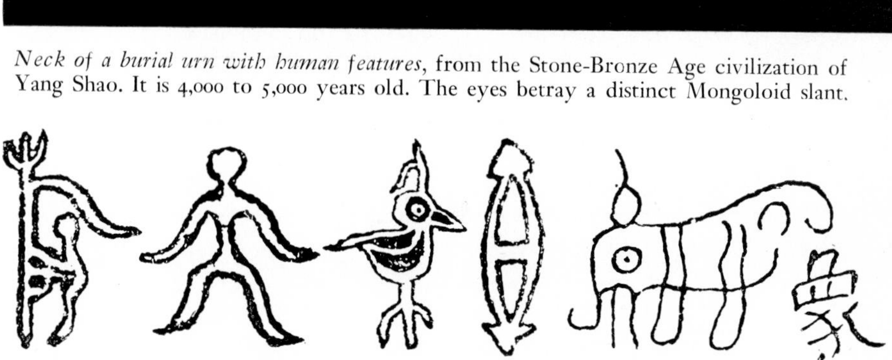

China's earliest written characters. Read from left to right, they signify: son, grandson, cockerel, cart, elephant, and on the extreme right, the modern equivalent of elephant.

Buddhist saint in glazed clay from the T'ang Dynasty (618-906 A.D.).

Confucius (551-479 B.C.), teacher, philosopher, statesman, sociologist, and upholder of ancient morality.

Clay statuette of the T'ang period (*c.* 600-900 A.D.). This Taoist goddess was found in a grave.

The Great Wall ends at Chia Yu Kwan, not far from Soochow, more than 2,000 miles from the sea. Only caravan trails lead to this "last station" of China, then wander on to the oases of the Gobi desert.

Genghis Khan.

Kublai Khan.

The Great Wall of China. Originally built of earth, it was reconstructed in its present form in the 15th century.

Tamerlane provided himself with this durable mausoleum during his lifetime. It is in Samarkand, which is now in the Soviet Republic of Uzbekhistan.

►

The weeping rakan. This remarkably lifelike sculpture is preserved in the Horyuji, the celebrated monastery which is reputed to be Japan's oldest wooden building. It stands in the sacred temple grove at Nara.

The Ainu bear festival, which ends with a feast over the slaughtered animal's body. The dead creature's soul floats up to the constellation of the Lesser Bear. [*Photograph:* Hecht.

PEKING, THE MOST BEAUTIFUL CITY IN THE WORLD

On coming to the Gate of the Eternal Order, one can see in the distance the five pavilions on Coal Hill, towering high into the air, and the maze of galleries in the palace buildings, shrouded by mist and rain.
The Palaces of Peking by Hsieh Chu, 1938

PEKING has been everything in its time. In 1121 B.C. a village stood on its site. In 936 A.D., 2,000 years later, the Tartars attacked and took the city. In 1151 the Chinese reconquered it. Another hundred years, and the Mongols were encamped beneath the city's mighty walls—led by Genghis Khan, the most feared man of his day. When all the metal inside the city had been used up for cannon balls, the defenders started melting down silver and eventually gold, and their ancient muzzle-loaders poured golden shot into the Mongols' camp! But in the end the city was taken and destroyed, later to be rebuilt by Kublai Khan. Each new conqueror undertook his own building program: the Ming emperors, the Manchu emperors, and finally even the Europeans, who established the small garden city known as the legation quarter. Between 1421 and 1928, Peking was the capital of China. Today there are new masters within the walls of the ancient fortress and Peking is once more the capital of this nation of four hundred million people: they patiently accept their new regime as they have all the others.

Nearly twenty miles of stone wall surround the two large quadrilateral sections of Peking. The northern part is the Tartar city, and the southern part the Chinese. Nine gates lead into the latter and six into the former, inside which stands the rectangular walled enclosure which contains the forbidden quarter of the imperial palaces.

The third ruler of the Ming Dynasty, Emperor Yung Lo, first made Peking his capital in 1421, and erected palaces which surpassed in magnificence all the buildings of his age. Even Versailles must pale beside the bold and grandiose design of these palatial structures. Yung Lo built temples and altars and laid out gardens, he built bridges and ponds apart from the imperial buildings, another fifteen palaces for the various princely families sprang up. The walls of Yung Lo's city were sixty-five feet thick at their foundations.

In 1643, 225 years later, the last Ming emperor stood on his tower with a telescope, watching his enemies marching to the attack. In despair, he stabbed his daughter and then hanged himself from a tree, which can be seen to this day, closed off by an iron chain.

It is almost impossible to express in so many words just what *is* the magic charm of this most beautiful city in the world. Perhaps it is the symmetry of the sloping roofs, stone replicas of the tents of ancient nomadic tribes. Perhaps it is the red and yellow colors of the glazed bricks that gleam in the sunlight. Perhaps it is the splendid vistas that stretch from gate to gate, from palace to palace. Perhaps it is the wide, straight streets. Perhaps it is the artificial lakes, or the arched marble bridges, or the venerable old trees. Perhaps it is simply the courageous spirit that caused these bold visions in stone and wood to materialize.

As long ago as 1279, ancient China established the earliest modern astronomical observatory in the world in Peking, where scholars studied the movements of the sun, moon and stars. Not far from the observatory are the examination halls where civil servants were obliged to undergo their written tests—the final examinations being so difficult that they drove many candidates literally out of their minds.

The huge columns inside the palaces, the filigree work of their ceilings, the massive beams towering above the visitor, the dark green walls hung with silk, the works of art, bronzes, porcelains and idols—all this is so overwhelming that the study of this civilization makes a human lifetime seem like the second hand on some eternal clock. Green jade is a very valuable semiprecious stone, especially if it is almost transparent. Even a piece of opaque green jade the size of a man's fist is worth a good deal. In the forbidden city there is a sacrificial basin too heavy for three strong men to lift, and it is carved from a single block of green jade!

The Ming period, particularly in the fifteenth century, produced the finest porcelain the world has ever known. Under the Manchus, Emperor K'ang-hsi and his successor Yung-cheng had the best porcelain manufactured in the ancient imperial factory at Ching-te-Chen. The Chinese porcelain factories always tried to produce everything in pairs: i.e., two specimens of each vase, vessel or large bowl they made. These pairs from the Ch'ien Lung period (1736-1796) are only rarely found in the great museums of the world, and their value runs into thousands of dollars, especially if they belong to the black, green or rose-colored "families"—namely, if these colors predominate. Yet there are thousands upon thousands of such pairs in the palaces of Peking, ranging from tiny, almost transparent, bowls to vases taller than a man.

Peking clearly confirms the truth of Gautama Buddha's dictum: "He who sits still, wins." China's revolution was not initiated by Mao Tse-tung, nor even by Sun Yat-sen. It is fifty centuries old, and a miraculous example of one race surviving in one place. Babylon and Egyptian supremacy, and the golden ages of Greece and Rome, flared up and died on the funeral pyre of history. China survived them all intact. She never brooded on the past or doted on the future. Unlike any other country in the world, she lived for the present, with a shrewdness that overcame all her difficulties, and with an inexhaustible patience that preserved her from rash action. Her only weapon was time. She never tried to conquer or die in the attempt. She lost thousands of battles without ever fighting "to the bitter end," knowing that a decisive war spells danger and that it is better to delay than to decide, for delaying means staying alive. Lao-tse, the sage of China, said: "Who can clear muddy water? If it keeps still, it clears of its own accord."

At a time when the whole world was on the move and hungry for progress, the "Kingdom of the Center" remained aloof and at rest. In the long run every foreign visitor found himself weaken when he contemplated the greatness, timelessness and earth-bound quality of Chinese life. China's immense vitality, her great powers of endurance, her instinct for compromise, her skepticism and her adaptability are all tried and sterling qualities. Her whole civilization is based on the principle that it is better to survive than to fight to the death. Under duress the Chinese have on occasion died for unattainable ideals, but not even coercion could make them die a mere hero's death.

That is how it was.

And how will it be in the future?

GENGHIS KHAN AND TAMERLANE—HATED, CURSED, LOVED, AND ADMIRED

The conquered never become their conquerors' friends. The destruction of the conquered is the conquerors' best guarantee of safety.

Genghis Khan

FROM the Hungarian puszta across the Ukraine, the Caspian lowlands and western Turkestan to Iran, and from the Kirgiz steppes across Czungaria and Mongolia to Manchuria, a huge belt of steppe land stretches from eastern Europe almost to the Pacific. From time immemorial these regions have been inhabited by nomadic races.

Roy Chapman Andrews, who has undertaken numerous expeditions on behalf of the American Museum of Natural History, and Henry Fairfield Osborne have established that central Asia represents a vast reservoir of human history. In fact, they regard the Gobi desert as the original birthplace of mankind. Two or three million years ago human beings lived in a great forest paradise, where barren, lonely Mongolia now lies. Andrews found forests of petrified trees which had died millions of years ago when dinosaurs were feeding on their foliage. The bed of a dried-up river produced the remains of early mammals and fresh-water mussels. Furthermore, the skeleton of a pre-Mongolian man was unearthed; he was more than 6 feet 6 inches tall and must have hunted in those parts whole eras before King Tutankhamen ruled in Egypt.

Attila, Genghis Khan and Tamerlane—these are the three great names that ring in our ears whenever we think of the Huns' and Mongols' magnificent conquests. Attila was beaten on the Marne in 451. Genghis Khan and Tamerlane were never defeated. The quest to discover just how far these people with their high cheekbones and narrow eyes penetrated into Europe from the eastern end of Asia across the Urals—and precisely to what extent Tartars, Turkestanis, Mongols, Kalmucks and Buriats are ethnologically related—leads us into a scientific jungle that would be pointless to explore. It must not be forgotten, however, that Finnish, Estonian and Hungarian are closer to Torki than to any language of Western Europe.

Only 700 years ago, a single man conquered almost all Eurasia. Genghis Khan and his horsemen covered nearly a hundred degrees of latitude, trampling into the dust such cities as did not submit voluntarily. Genghis altered the course of rivers and peopled the deserts with fugitives and the dying, leaving them for the wolves and vultures. He was only a nomad, a hunter and a herdsman king, yet he managed to confound the strategy of three world empires. He had never seen a city nor learned to write, yet he laid down the laws for many peoples. He ruled the world from Korea to Hungary and from China to Iran. Even Moscow was captured ten years after Genghis Khan's death.

The land between the sources of the Kerulen, the Onon and the Tula is an immeasurable vastness of grassland and high, wind-swept plateaus, lit during the icy winter nights by the mysterious glow of the aurora borealis—a country which knows only freedom and the open air. Here was the home of the Huns, Turks and Mongols, and here Genghis Khan was born. The children in this corner of the northern Gobi were born tough! Their baby foods were mother's and mare's milk. As they grew up, they had to sit farthest from the tent fire, reflecting on the toughness of a young life and on the futility of perishing by cold and hunger. In the spring, when the mares and cows yielded abundant milk, life was bearable, and wolf and antelope were added to the native diet. But in winter the strongest men always ate first, followed by the women and old people, while the children battled for the leftovers and bones, with the dogs joining in the fray. Toward the end of winter, when the community's stock of cattle had dwindled down and no more animals could be slaughtered, one and all learned to live with hunger. So long as the world was conquered not by superior machines but by greater human endurance, it is easier to understand why the campaigns of Islam, the Arabs and the Mongols were so successful.

Genghis Khan was born in a felt tent or *yurt*, a mobile dwelling transported on carts drawn by dozens of oxen. One day while Temuchin, as young Ghengis Khan was called, was still a youth, he and his father were entertained in the tent of a foreign warrior, and Temuchin noticed a little girl sitting in one corner. She was very pretty, and he asked his father whether he might marry her. The girl's father said that although his daughter Bortai was only nine years old Temuchin was welcome to open negotiations for her. The next day the transaction was completed and the young couple were betrothed. A few days later, however, Temuchin's father was poisoned, and from then on the boy was always on the run, constantly pursued by enemies who sought to prevent the young prince from assuming his father's place. Once he was captured and tied to a wooden yoke, but managed to escape although his hands and arms were still lashed to it. All this was perfect training for the future commander and conqueror. And he did marry Bortai eight years after he first saw her.

After interminable battles against numerous Tartar tribes, Genghis was finally proclaimed Khan of his united peoples.

It was at this juncture that the Khan declared he had been called upon by heaven to conquer the world. This implicit belief in his divine vocation communicated itself to his troops, and he led them on from one victory to another. First the land of the Uigurs in central Asia submitted to him voluntarily, and Genghis Khan became overlord of all the Tartars. Then in 1211, when he was probably forty-nine years old, Genghis Khan led hundreds of thousands of Mongols against the Great Wall, stormed the gate forts, and conquered China in five years of campaigning. In 1215 the capital, Yen-King, the modern Peking, was itself overrun and pillaged.

Now Genghis Khan sent ambassadors to Turkestan, only to have them murdered by the commander of a frontier fortress who mistrusted them. A Mongol army 700,000 strong set out to wreak revenge. Bukhara and Samarkand were stormed, plundered and burned. Samarkand, a royal capital and one of the largest trading centers in the world, was enclosed by walls and fortifications two and one-half miles in circumference, and garrisoned by 110,000 men; they even had twenty elephants trained for warfare. Whenever the insatiable Khan had taken such a city he would single out the artisans and present them as slaves to his sons and generals. Samarkand supplied no less than 30,000 such prisoners, and a similar number of able-bodied men were earmarked for military chores, transport, and so forth. The most beautiful girls were of course taken to the Khan's personal chambers, while the rest of the inhabitants were beheaded. If any enemy escaped conquest–as the Kankalis, for instance–they were defeated by cunning. Genghis Khan generously permitted the Kankalis to don Mongolian uniforms, ostensibly to join his forces. They happily complied, marched into his camp, and were collectively liquidated.

After the conquest of Merval-Shahidshan, one of the oldest cities in the world, Genghis Khan is reputed to have massacred 1,300,000 people. Indeed the city was so thoroughly razed to the ground that practically nothing was left of it. Now Genghis Khan dispatched his victorious armies all the way to the Dnieper River, and later, in 1226, when he was some sixty-four years old, he marched once again at the head of his warriors against northwest China. But after several successful battles, he left it to his sons to crush the enemy's armies.

Genghis Khan lived by the motto: "The conquered never become their conquerors' friends. The destruction of the conquered is the conquerors' best guarantee of safety."

In the summer of 1227, Genghis Khan retired to the mountains of Liu-pang, west of Peking. Restless, and perhaps divining that death was near, he went to Shan-si, where he was struck down by a severe fever. As he lay dying, he turned to his friend Kiluken Bahadur and said: "Be a true friend to my wife, Bortai, and be a friend to my sons Ogotai and Tule. A man's body is not imperishable; it passes away without a house or resting place. What you must do, do with all your strength. Do not be influenced by the wishes of others, and you will win the support of many. I must take leave of you and depart. The boy Kublai will some day sit upon my throne, and he will guard the people's welfare as I have done."

Just as he had always been not merely a ruthless conqueror but also a brilliant statesman, organizer and planner, so now Genghis Khan attended to the most important affairs of state from his deathbed. He ordered his youngest son Ottshigin to start another campaign against China, this time according to a plan prepared in every detail. As for his empire, he divided it among his five sons.

Genghis Khan had some 500 morganatic wives and concubines, among them the most beautiful captives from every race in Asia and Europe. He had a much more efficient method of choosing "beauty queens" than the judges of our modern contests. Every captain in his army turned the most beautiful girls of a defeated city over to his colonel; the colonel, after some intermediate screening, turned them over to his general, who, after further careful selection, passed them on to the army commander. The army commander then sent this handpicked international elite to the Khan. In this manner every land was systematically combed for the benefit of the Khan's personal chambers. Besides his first and dearest wife Bortai, he had four other legitimate wives. They wept loudly by his grave, but Bortai grieved in silence for the world conqueror whom she had first enchanted when he was still known at Temuchin.

In the history of Asia, 110 years are as a single day, and the year 1336 saw the birth of Timur, the fabulous Tamerlane, at Kesh in western Turkestan. Genghis Khan was a Mongol; Timur was of Mongolian extraction, but he spoke Turkish. While not a direct descendant of

Genghis Khan, he was a true son of the steppes who became chieftain of his tribe at the age of thirty-four, after a brief joint rule with his brother-in-law, Hussein. One day he became tired of sharing authority, so he murdered his rival, put his small kingdom in order, and set out to conquer the world. During one battle he was wounded in the foot and limped for the rest of his life. Hence the Persians called him Timur Lenk, or Timur the Lame.

The "Lame One" subjugated Persia, then central Asia from the Great Wall to Moscow, and in 1398 he penetrated deep into India. He took Syria away from the Mamelukes, overran the sultan's empire with his immense army, and in 1402 defeated Bayezid the Ottoman on the plain of Angora. In 1405 he was preparing an expedition against China when death overtook him.

Like Genghis Khan, this dictator and conqueror was also a brilliant statesman. He required his political officials to combine severity with justice, to take care of the peasantry and to protect trade. He insisted that his officers keep their troops well-fed and well-equipped. Each horseman had to have two mounts, a bow and a well-filled quiver, a sword, a battle axe, a saw, some twine and ten sewing needles. Moreover, one tent had to be provided for every eighteen men.

Timur sponsored the arts and sciences, and even developed a talent for writing. He was a Napoleon with the disposition of a Himmler. He was serious, gloomy and a foe of all gaiety, a strange mixture of cold calculation, incredible hardness and generosity. But he knew how to defer to others and efface himself when prudence demanded it.

In later years Timur time and again sought to recuperate from the great hardships of his military campaigns at his residential city of Samarkand, where he had assembled enormous quantities of booty: the finest works of art from every country in Asia, many princesses complete with dowries, slaves, servants, artists, musicians and scholars. Here he held fabulous banquets, with thousands of guests eating from golden plates and drinking wine from golden beakers. Here entire roasted horses were served, and ladies of the court paraded in gowns of silk, velvet and satin, or in red silken robes trimmed with gold lace and furnished with trains of such length that it frequently took fifteen maidservants to carry them. Here the women wore charming helmet-like hats set with pearls, rubies, emeralds and long white feathers hanging down to their eyes and gracefully moving with every step they took.

Timur had great personal courage. After his fourth campaign against Khwarizm, one of his enemies hit upon the bizarre idea of substituting for the wholesale slaughter of pitched battle a hand-to-hand combat between himself and Timur. He proposed to Timur what even today might be an interesting suggestion. "How much longer must the world suffer pain and misery for the sake of two men? The welfare of mankind and the nations demands that they should enter the lists alone and try their fortune."

Timur was delighted with the challenge, and was the first to arrive on the scene. But when he called for his opponent in a loud voice, the man was nowhere to be found!

Human life, whether his own or others', meant as little to Timur as the life of an insect. Yet he was capable of mourning deeply for relatives or friends who had died. If necessary, he could play the Islamic fanatic, and he was as adept at changing his political posture as any versatile actor who plays different characters.

Genghis Khan wanted to unite all nomadic peoples in order to subjugate the settled civilization. Timur had no such fixed goal. Still a nomad himself, he was hopelessly in love with the culture of the settled races, and luxuriated at Samarkand while his armies camped in tents.

Hated and cursed, loved and admired, Timur died at last at the age of seventy-one. No other figure in history is so rich in contradictions. For what other tyrant or ruler has caused so much destruction and devastation, been such a brilliant administrator, been at once so dreaded and so admired? This admiration kept increasing with time, and the kings of Europe and the tsars of Russia alike marveled at his accomplishments for centuries after his death. The people of Asia still sing Timur's praises and the peasants of modern Pamir point proudly to the miles of drainage installations he had hewn into the rock. Showing the foreign visitor the roads and canals, the rivers diverted from their courses, the wells and dams, they will say: "Timur did all this." And to this day, when Mongol mothers suckle their babies during the stops on their endless wanderings, they still sing them lullabies about Timur Lenk and the great Genghis Khan.

SOME DAY THE BEAR WILL RETURN: THE LAST OF THE AINU

I have reached the age of retirement, but I am still on the spot to go on helping the Ainu.
Dr. John Batchelor

IT SEEMS fantastic that amidst all the Mongoloid peoples of eastern Asia there should still survive one isolated racial group of Caucasian stock, a little band of primeval Siberians related to West Europeans in physique, skull formation and color of skin. The last descendants of a dying race, some 15,000 of these Ainu are still living on the large island of Sakhalin at the northern extremity of Japan. The Ainu have presented ethnologists with a number of problems; the most difficult of which, namely their origin, remains more or less unanswered. This question becomes even more mysterious when we consider that this ancient Caucasian (Indo-European) race once inhabited all the Japanese islands long before Polynesian and Mongoloid peoples ever set foot there. The Ainu had long been established by the time Japan's first emperor, Jimmu Tenno, crossed the waters from the southern island of Kyushu to the main island of Yamato in 660 B.C.

Indeed the names of many mountains and places throughout Japan derive from the Ainu language. Hokkaido's capital, Sapporo; Mauka on Sakhalin; Tarato in Siberia—all are Ainu names. Even the extinct volcano Fuji, one of the most beautiful mountains in the world, owes its name to the Ainu. The Ainu's ancient household god and father of their race is called Skisei koro Ekashi, and his wife—the divine grandmother of the fire, whose throne floats invisibly in the flames on the hearth—is called Fuji. Fuji must have been a sacred mountain long before there was a country known as Japan and long before the men who were to make Nippon a world power arrived on her shores.

The period following the ice age, when the earth already enjoyed a warm, dry climate, is known to science as the Neolithic Age. Late in this period man learned to chip or flake stone to make tools and weapons. He had a permanent abode and grew wheat, barley, millet and leguminous plants, storing his supplies, domesticating animals (among them dogs), and using wood for building dwellings. But before man thought of building shelters he lived in caves, and the Japanese originally called the Ainu *Tsuchi-gumo*, which means "earth spiders." In the Ainu language that would have meant "cave dwellers," and the Ainu did, indeed, at one time live in caves.

This puzzling creature, the Caucasian Ainu, apparently already lived in Japan during the neolithic period. For two different kinds of earthenware have been found in the graves dating from neolithic times—the Jomon and the Yayoi types. The Jomon types are more common in the north and east and are considered to be of earlier origin. While technically inferior to the Yayoi, they are artistically more beautiful. A thorough examination of the fossils taken from neolithic graves has led scholars to conclude that the Jomon people were of the same physique as the Ainu still surviving today. These particular Ainu must have spread their Jomon culture throughout Japan before another race, or races, came after them and introduced the Yayoi style.

These different races must have waged terrible wars; the new arrivals having finally driven a wedge between the Ainu, forcing them to withdraw farther and farther to the north and south. In the south the last Ainu was ultimately killed off, leaving a remnant of these Indo-Europeans or primeval Siberians to hold out on Hokkaido and Sakhalin in the far north. Even in 720 A.D. they still put up such fierce resistance that the Japanese had to muster soldiers from nine different provinces to defeat them. However, eventually the Ainu expended so much of their strength in internecine struggles that they became exhausted and were left to await their final extinction on Hokkaido and Sakhalin.

About 1600 there were still 50,000 Ainu on Hokkaido as compared with 12,000 Japanese; in 1700 there were 30,000 Ainu and 20,000 Japanese. By 1800 the scales had tipped in favor of the Japanese, with 20,000 Ainu and 30,000 Japanese, and today a mere 15,000 Ainu are eking out a poor existence there while the 3,000,000 Japanese exhibit them to the tourist trade as an "ethnological curiosity." The inexorable mathematics of the Ainu's steadily declining population almost enables us to forecast the date when the last of them will return to dust.

It is as if history has given every race on earth its one big opportunity, its golden age, its span of life, its "season." Humanity's time clock ticks on inaudibly, until suddenly death is at hand. One is tempted to ponder what might have been the course of history had the Ainu maintained their hold on the islands of Japan.

The question is a difficult one to answer, for races not only replace one another but also invariably intermingle. Thus the Ainu and the Japanese mingled since the dawn of history, and just as Ainu blood flows in the veins of the Japanese, the Ainu have some blood of the Mongols and the South Seas races.

In 1877 a young and industrious theologian went to visit the Ainu. His name was John Batchelor, and he was a scientist and missionary. He got to know the Ainu well, studied their language and customs, won their affection, and remained their staunch friend until the end of his days. It is to Batchelor that we owe our deepest insight into the nature, language and grammar of this dying race, for almost all information we possess about the Ainu is the result of his painstaking research.

Anyone wandering through the squat gray Ainu villages on Hokkaido today will see only a feeble reflection of an ancient life which was close to nature and on intimate terms with departed spirits and ancestors.

The spirits are still there however, perching and lurking everywhere, hovering on the breezes. Even now the old Ainu men hear their voices, struggle with them, feel themselves persecuted by them and are reminded of the inevitable annhilation of their race. The clothes chests of the Ainu still contain ancient and beautifully ornamented robes of elm bark. The call of the mountains still echoes alluringly from primeval eras when the mountains of northern Asia were still sacred. And many an Ainu will climb the volcanoes, yet if you ask him why, he will not know. The Ainu still wear fine furs—bear, seal, dog, fox and reindeer—for Hokkaido has always been cold in winter when an icy wind blows across from the Okhotsk Sea. They still have their totems—a bird, a fish, a wolf or a fox carved from wood—those animistic clan symbols which mysteriously link all the civilizations of the Pacific.

The Ainu seem to have been inspired from earliest times by the belief illustrated in the Old Testament story of Samson: namely, that physical strength rests in a man's hair. Thus they take great care to lose none. The men wear long beards and regard this adornment as sacred. Only a woman who has lost her husband may tear out her hair—and probably she has good reason, for authorities unanimously agree that Ainu men treat their womenfolk well. Indeed, women were once so highly esteemed that polyandry, or the custom of several husbands having the same one wife, was the rule. Later, however, polygamy became customary, and one man could marry several women.

In early times Ainu women were tattooed. Their hands, arms and foreheads were ornamented in this fashion and their mouths were enlarged by blue-black tattoo marks. This operation was carried out in early childhood by a series of knife incisions which could never be effaced. The cuts were then cauterized with juices extracted from tree bark, an extremely painful procedure. The origin of the custom is unknown, but it may once have been a method of branding women who had been captured in battle, so that they could not escape.

One is so easily tempted to dismiss any dying race as "primitive." On the verge of extinction, at the end of a cultural evolution that lasted thousands of years, little survives of the Ainu's world, yet it once had great vitality. Their gods were as numerous as the phenomena of nature, for the Ainu religion was a form of nature worship. Amorphous and invisible beings dwelt everywhere. Rocks, fish, trees, the sun, and, in particular, fire were all worshiped as sacred. Witchcraft and magic dominated the Ainu's life, and the invisible link between man and superhuman powers was maintained by their witch doctor, or *shaman*.

There is something of the Tungus in the Ainu, something of the Siberian forest peoples, with their unshakable belief in the animation of inanimate objects, or animism, something of the demonic spirits haunting the forests, mountains and marshes of the taiga of northeast Asia.

All the Tungus tribes believed that the bear, the most similar to man of all the creatures they knew, was the mediator between this world and the next, and northeast Asia is full of strange fairy tales and legends about the bear. The bear speaks, acts and intervenes in the destiny of man. He has compassion with man and suffers like man. He is the "exalted being that lives in the mountains." And this last is exactly what the Ainu call him: *kim-un-kamui*. And the word *kamui* is probably the original form of the Japanese word *kami*, meaning godhead.

All peoples on earth have pondered on man's communication with the dead. We are born, we live, we toil, we laugh a little, we cry, we die. Each generation contributes new experiences and yet would be so much wiser if only the spirits of the departed could help out. A man's lifetime is so short that he cannot achieve or learn very much. To the Ainu, if there were no means of communicating with one's forefathers and the spiritual world of the departed, life would be unbearable. But how is this liaison with the spiritual realm, this freedom from all physical and carnal bonds, to be effected?

That is precisely what the bear is there for, the Ainu tell us. When a bear is stripped of his hide he looks alarmingly like a man. Thus, to them, he is a man disguised in fur and they see in the bear a mediator between their own harsh world and the world of disembodied souls. Exactly when they came to this conclusion, no amount of research will ever explain, but the Ainu just *know*, and that is that. That is why their most important festival is the *iyomande*, or home-coming of the soul. A bear is killed, but his still living soul is sent forth to visit his bear ancestors. Someday the bear will return, only to be sent forth once more. His flesh is eaten, his blood is drunk, and his soul performs its mission. To the Ainu, this is the divine order of things, the eternal cycle, the be-all and end-all, and thousands of years of evolution have been unable to shake their belief.

A bear cub is carefully reared, fed and fondled. He has a nurse, an Ainu woman who even suckles him at her breasts—until the young bear's claws become too sharp and he is locked up in a cage.

The villagers regularly visit the bear in his abode, greeting him in friendly fashion. Master Bruin lives in this fashion for two years, and then comes the big festival with its preparations and invitations. "I, so-and-so, living at such-and-such a place, am going to send my dear little bear cub back to his home in the mountains. Come, masters and friends, to the feast. We wish to celebrate the joyful departure of the exalted one, come!"

The guests arrive, a few of the women coming earlier to help with the preparations. The bear is led around the huts for the last time to receive the friendly salutations of all the villagers; then he is taken to the place of "transformation," where he is addressed as follows: "We greet you. We have nourished you with great care because we love you so much. Now that you are fully grown, we are sending you off to your father and mother. When you arrive, speak well of us, and tell them how good we have been to you. Come back to us again, and we will hold a new festival and send you off once more."

After that the bear is tied up, tormented by all the guests, shot full of arrows that are not intended to kill him, and then beaten. As the animal's frenzy grows, the pleasure of the guests increases. When he is finally too weak to move, he is "dispatched homeward" by strangulation, or, less commonly, by being tied to two stakes and killed by an arrow through the heart. After part of the meat has been eaten raw and the blood drunk, the remainder of the animal is boiled. The meal is enhanced by the invisible presence of Fuji, the goddess of fire, and her daughter, "the maiden of the cooking pot." The men anoint themselves with the bear's blood, an effective means of insuring success in hunting, and the bear's skull is exhibited outside the house, facing east, to be worshiped. Then, as the unfortunate beast's soul leaves its body to rise to heaven, the men shoot off a few more arrows to the northeast.

We now come to the most mysterious feature of the bear cult. After his death, the bear is known as *chinukara-guru*, which means, "prophet" or "guardian." The Ainu use the same word to describe the North Star in the constellation of the Little Bear. So it seems that from primeval times the civilizations both of the Mediterranean and the Ainu have associated this constellation with the bear. And up there the soul of the creature, which the Ainu believe to be their redeemer and mediator, has its final destination.

A PEOPLE IN LOVE WITH ART

Hanawa Hokiichi, the famous blind scholar, was reading the Genji Monogatari *with his pupils. Suddenly the wind blew their lamp out. Hanawa quietly went on 'reading.' His pupils started to fidget. 'The light has gone out,' they said. 'That only shows you,' answered Hanawa, 'what a nuisance it is, to have to rely on your eyes.'*

FOUR large islands, six hundred smaller ones, and eight thousand minute islets which are often little more than mountain peaks sticking out of the sea—that is Japan.

Eleven ranges comprising one hundred and ninety-two volcanoes extend over the whole length of the islands, from Kyushu in the south to Hokkaido in the north. Fifty-eight of these volcanoes are still active. Fuji-no-Yama is Japan's highest as well as her most beautiful mountain. This king among mountains, 12,395 feet high, is a volcano which has been extinct since 1707.

However, to see the biggest crater in the world you must climb Aso-take, whose rim measures nearly a hundred miles in circumference. But it is a dangerous walk, for Aso still sends the smoke from its subterranean furnaces into the skies, and occasional large fragments of magma still come hurtling from its depths.

There are hot springs, beautiful natural parks and rugged mountains all over Japan. Indeed, only one-fifth of her surface is arable land. The Japanese experience a slight earth tremor every third day. As recently as September 1, 1923, an earthquake killed 120,000 people, and since then there have been 12,000 noticeable tremors.

Fuji-no-Yama is said to have sprung blazing from the ground one dreadful, haunted night in 286 B.C., and now offers one of the most beautiful vistas in the world. No one who stands on the summit of the mountain to watch the red disc of the sun leaping over the Pacific horizon can fail to understand why Japan is called the "land of the rising sun."

To say that these islands are close to the gods is not to quote mere legend or myth dreamed up by the ancients. Every morning and evening the mountain peaks seem to float above the clouds, swathed in mists, just as they did when Ninigi, the forefather of Jimmu, Japan's first emperor, climbed down them from heaven.

Japan's official history begins in 660 B.C., but Japanese historians explicitly state that this year marks only the *earthly* beginning of the world's oldest imperial dynasty. The emperors' ancestors lived in heaven long before that, and history and legend alike link their origins directly with the story of Creation! The primeval god Izanagi and his consort Izanami created the first island where they settled down and created more islands and gods. Izanami died giving birth to her son, the fire god, and, like Eurydice, went down to the underworld, only to have Izanagi follow her, Orpheus fashion, with the intention of bringing her back. But as he was leading her out of the underworld he turned to look at her, which he had been forbidden to do. Izanami immediately vanished, and Izanagi escaped from the realm of the dead, alone.

The Greek legend of Orpheus and the Izanagi myth of Japan show marked similarity. Separated by a hemisphere, these two ancient works nevertheless agree in detail after detail. Why? We do not know, and never shall. All we can say is that in the beginning was the word, and the word then was apparently valid all around the globe.

But why did Japan's first emperor climb down from heaven?

The Japanese have an explanation.

Izanagi gave the sovereignty of the sky to the sun goddess Amaterasu-Omikami. However, her brother the storm god, Susa-no-o, was a lout who devastated rice fields and irrigation ditches and performed all kinds of mischief; so the sun goddess Amaterasu took refuge from her brother in a cave, and the world darkened. All the other gods (the Milky Way, perhaps) gathered outside and debated how to lure the offended lady out of her hiding place. Meanwhile Amano-Uzume, the celestial ballerina, performed a highly suggestive dance which brought roars of laughter from her divine audience. (The Japanese gods were no prudes!) Out of curiosity, the sun goddess pushed the stone that blocked her cave a little to one side, just to have a peep—and again the earth was bathed in sunlight.

Shortly afterward, the sun goddess sent her grandson Ninigi-no-Mikoto down to earth. He landed on the island of Kyushu, carrying a flawed jewel, a sword and a mirror. And one of Ninigi-no-Mikoto's great-grandchildren was Jimmu Tenno, the first emperor of Japan.

If there really is a nation of artists in the world, a people which has fused life and art into one, a people whose houses look like extensions of nature itself, whose painting, lacquer work and woodcuts have scaled the heights of human achievement, it is the Japanese. They are so in love with art that it would never occur to them to question if the story of Tenno's heavenly origin is true or only a fairy tale. The legend of the sun goddess was so beautiful that in this scattered chain of islands, it became both history and religion. After all, Ninigi-no-Mikoto did bring with him the circumstantial evidence of his heavenly origin in the shape of the jewel, the sword and the mirror.

How can the Japanese question the divine origin of their emperor when the state insignia are preserved to this day: the jewel in the imperial palace at Tokyo, the sword at Atsuta Jingu, and the mirror at the great shrine of Ise? This Shinto shrine, the most sacred in all Japan, stands by the banks of the Isuzu near the town of Uji-Yamada in the district of Mie, in the care of a high priest who has seventy-four priests under him. The three royal insignia have been passed on from emperor to emperor down to the present day. Every Japanese citizen is obligated to pray before the Ise shrine at least once in his life, and until 1945 every Japanese prime minister visited it on taking office. The shrine itself is the abode of the sun goddess.

This belief in an imperial dynasty which began with the Creation and has lasted to the present day; this belief in the Tenno who, as we have seen, to the Japanese is really a son of heaven; this belief in Japanese history—this is the essence of Shintoism. Up to the end of World War II, Japan had 306 national Shinto shrines, 49,579 shrines in the various prefectures and villages, more than 60,000 private shrines, and 129 soldiers' shrines.

To insure the continuance of the imperial line, the emperor was permitted to take as many wives and concubines as he pleased. The right of succession did not, however, always fall to the eldest son, but rather to the most suitable. Sometimes this most suitable son happened to be the strongest and wisest, but sometimes the wirepullers at court arranged it so that he was the weakest. Japan has had 124 emperors—many were kind and honest, some were great and influential, some eccentric, and some downright evil. One of them became a monk and entered a Buddhist monastery, while another forbade the starving people of his island realm to eat fish. Emperor Yozei, who died in 949, was cruel even as a child. When he came to the throne it is recorded that he would on occasion order some of his subjects to climb trees, and then shoot them down like so many sparrows. Such spectators as did not laugh at this brutal sport were severely punished. He also used to seize young girls in the street, tie them up with lute strings and throw them into ponds. Emperor Yozei loved riding: when he was in particular high spirits he would gallop his horse through the streets of his capital lashing the humble population with his horsewhip. This by no means exhausted His Imperial Majesty's list of "entertainments." Japan's Nero had a good many other hobbies which are frankly unmentionable. In the end, a true miracle occurred: he was dethroned.

In 794 A.D. the seat of Japan's government was transferred from Nara with its rustling trees to Kyoto; and a golden age was ushered in which lasted for 400 years. In 1190, a half million people lived in Kyoto, more than in any European city of the same period, with the possible exceptions of Constantinople and Cordoba. Here influential aristocratic families like the Fujiwara, the Taira and the Minamoto enthroned and dethroned emperors at will. During the reign of the Emperor Daigo (898-930), Japan's culture and way of life came close to rivaling China's, and at that time China was at its height under the T'ang Dynasty.

From its beginning to the present day, Japan's history has been filled with dramatic tension, vitality, grandeur and unpredictable impulses—a great Shakespearian theater complete with kings, executioners, generals and slaves, and propelled by love, hatred, suicide and murder. Nor did it become this reluctantly, but was created so by a people who always retained their individuality and endowed everything they adopted with their highly unusual style. The Buddhism they took over from China became something essentially Japanese, and the same happened with Chinese writing, poetry, administration, music, art and architecture. The Japanese assimilated Chinese culture over a thousand years ago, just as they are now assimilating the culture of Europe and America. They have always been inquisitive and quick to absorb foreign elements. Then they invariably Nipponize these foreign imports to suit their own style.

There is one particular fascinating figure in Japanese history: this is Yorimoto, who lived from 1147 to 1199. He was a very handsome man and a great favorite with the ladies. He often fell in love and he was faithful, in his fashion. But he had one failing: he could never bring himself to remain faithful when he saw a woman more beautiful than his current mistress. On one occasion, when a certain Hojo Tokimasa's daughter was about to wed a powerful governor, the bridegroom turned up at his wedding—but alone. Like Ibsen's Peer Gynt, Yorimoto had borne the bride off into the mountains—and the young lady enjoyed every minute of the escapade.

Yorimoto was constantly on the run, constantly harried by pursuers, but in the end he settled in Kamakura in beautiful Sagami Bay, and turned it into the most powerful city in Japan. He became Japan's first *shogun*. (The *shogun* were military governors who for centuries greatly cut down the emperor's power.)

Kamakura remained the heart of the empire for 150 years. The metropolis then had a population of some 800,000; today it is merely a fishing village. However, Yorimoto's tomb is still there, a small stone pagoda on the slopes of a hill behind the local grammar school on the way to the Kamakura shrine. It is a lonely spot; moss is growing over the pagoda behind its stone fence and Yorimoto's tomb lies forgotten —an ideal place in which to meditate on the transitory glories of this world.

Emperors in the north—emperors in the south—and behind them ruled the increasingly powerful *shogun*. While splendid buildings sprang up in the imperial capital of Kyoto, Kamakura was twice burned to the ground. It was an age of warring princes, warring knights, highwaymen and lawlessness. And into this turmoil the Portuguese came, bringing firearms. But gradually a semblance of order was brought into this chaos as three powerful personalities ruled Japan in succession.

"The first made the cake, the second baked it, and the third ate it," the Japanese say, referring to Nobunaga, Hideyoshi and Tokugawa-Iyeyasu, the soldier-king.

English scholars have fiercely debated the underlying motives of Hideyoshi's attempted conquest of China in 1592. Almost as an afterthought, they mention that he wanted to marry a Chinese princess. Be that as it may, he did write a letter to the king of Korea, asking him to march with him against China. But the king of Korea, Lien Koku O, replied: "So you want to conquer China. Then you are like the mussel that wants to drain the sea dry, or like the tiny bee that exhausts itself in trying to sting the giant tortoise through its armor." Hideyoshi was furious, so he invaded Korea instead with an army equipped with foreign cannons. His campaign ultimately failed, however, and his life's work crumbled just as Napoleon's did later.

When Tokugawa-Iyeyasu came to power, he abandoned the Korean adventure. It was he who made Edo, the modern Tokyo, his capital, and he and the great Hideyoshi are regarded as the founders of Tokyo. This Tokugawa "Shogun" Dynasty lasted for 265 years, until 1868; all this time the emperors played second fiddle to the *shogun* while Japan remained isolated from the rest of the world. The system brought the country 250 years of peace, but it could be maintained only so long as no foreign interference or emigration was tolerated.

Since the islands of Japan were then no longer than they are now, this isolationist policy had murderous results, and within Japan's over-populated territory mass slaughter became the normal method of birth control. With the increase of the Japanese population the rice fields shrank and so did the rice crops. The day came when the *daimio* (the feudal lords who once employed the samurai warriors to fight for them) could pay them no longer. A leaderless band of men now known as *ronin*, the samurai roamed through Japan. They were warriors no more—just so many bellies to fill. They knew nothing about domestic or foreign policy, they had no outlet for their abilities. They could not hold any civilian office because the officials sat entrenched behind the barriers of a caste system modeled on the Chinese, where promotions were based on nepotism rather than competence. The officials controlled the administration, the priests beat their gongs, and the mercenaries yawned at their posts. The brush strokes in the official ledgers dried and grew dusty, the dull booming of the gongs rang emptily across the weary paradise, the sentries fell asleep. And the *shogun* had to finance this whole useless apparatus, for that was his cross to bear.

Outside Japan, however, the world advanced at a terrific pace. Whole continents were seized, distributed or partitioned at the whim of the empire-building nations, and merchant ships plowed through the seven seas. It was a time of awakening, when any nation loitering at home would regret it for centuries to come. At last the gates of Japan were thrown open. But not from within: from without—and by foreign hands.

It was in 1853 that Commodore Matthew C. Perry of the United States Navy broke open the gates of Japan's fairy-tale castle. It must have been a remarkable moment when Perry, commanding the frigate *Mississippi*, met the governor of Uraga in Edo Bay—two creatures from different planets. And it must have been even stranger five years later when the American consul-general expounded the basic principles of international law to the astonished *daimio* of Bichu and his officials—men accustomed to ancient ceremonial, who had governed according to their own ideas and the even more ancient tradition of China.

It is a truism—but how history does repeat itself.

STARVE IF NEED BE . . . BUT PAINT!

It is good that life seems unending. . .
Hokusai

NO OTHER race on earth can fashion the little things of this world with such perfection as the Japanese: tiny bowls, or little curved colored platters for serving fish, lacquered boxes, small containers for writing materials, the fine arts of floral arrangement, the controlled growth of dwarf trees, miniature gardens, miniature bridges, miniature pavilions. The Japanese are unrivaled masters of the small and delicate.

These island people of the northeast Pacific have always been strangers to the massive, the spacious, the superdimensional. Yet they have a bold genius for painting, the combination of colors and the choice of silk patterns; for dancing and acting; and, above all, for the art of making life on their cramped, scattered islands as pleasant and enjoyable as possible. The Japanese have often been victimized by the very characteristics that have made them such great artists: by their naïve and childlike qualities. Yet they have always realized man's insignificance in the face of nature's vastness.

The Japanese have always, for better or worse, been at the mercy of their cramped island home with its perilous earthquakes and its smoking volcanoes. Always close to the sea, they have forever been prisoners of their natural environment. And because they know so much about nature they have never bothered to tame it; they have never framed their pictures nor barricaded their houses against the elements; they have never wept when an earthquake or a tidal wave engulfed their mothers, wives and children.

Eternally submissive toward nature, the Japanese have always bowed to the sun and revered the chief product of their fields: the precious rice that feeds them and supplies the straw for the mats upon which they sleep at night. They have always been obedient and disciplined, and have known how to die without lamentations. For the Japanese are deeply convinced that beauty is invested only in nature, or in an extension of nature. And death itself is a part of nature.

The Japanese undertook an incredibly bold task when, with Polynesia on the wane, they became the only race to preserve the culture of Oceanis and the Pacific. They have willingly taken over everything of value from Asia, just as eagerly adopted the civilizations of Europe and America, and yet have remained true to their own character—the character of their island home. Even today the Japanese weep with emotion when they see their emperor. Even today they sing: "May the imperial house flourish until a little stone grows into a moss-covered rock."

Incredible as it may seem, Hokusai, the Japanese genius born in the mid-eighteenth century, passed on to posterity not only an impressive series of novels and hundreds of glorious poems, but more than 500 illustrated books and over 35,000 pictures. He was a fanatical worker, and the scope and grandeur of his output have seldom if ever been exceeded. They surpass ordinary human standards. Hokusai used countless pseudonyms, among others the significant "maniac painter." So rich and inexhaustible were his talents that he generously gave his pseudonyms to pupils who, thanks to them, made a brilliant start in their careers. He is the culmination of all that is best in centuries of Japanese art.

Hokusai's father was a mirror cutter by trade, and when Hokusai was a little boy he would gaze into his father's stock of mirrors and see enchanted worlds which seemed to lie beyond the frontiers of reality. Wishing to become an artisan like his father, he decided to learn the art of wood engraving.

An apprentice had to follow his master's instructions to the letter, for the Japanese have always been sticklers for obedience and held that before anyone could "freely develop" his talent he must first master technique. Every day new drawings and pictures in color arrived in the workshop. The apprentice was given delicate cutting knives and had to adapt himself to the varying styles of the many different artists. He had to cut his blocks of wood so that their imprint accurately reproduced the original brush drawing. It was a difficult job: one wrong cut and a brand-new drawing had to be furnished, for the original drawing was pasted on the wood and thus was destroyed in the process of engraving. The artist merely did his drawing on transparent paper, and then the apprentice had to copy it several times over. A five-color picture required five wooden blocks for reproduction, and a ten-color picture, ten. The apprentice also mixed the paints according to the artist's exact specifications.

Hokusai was fifteen years old when he prepared his first drawing for subsequent printing. At the same age he wrote his first poem, and by the time he was sixteen he had written his first novel. Then, at the age of eighteen, he entered the atelier of Shunsho, at that time the most famous painter of actors. Shunsho's studio was a beehive of feverish activity, for the master had to keep pace with the latest productions at the Kabuki Theatre. The public wanted to see their favorite stage personalities. And the actors? They were just as hungry for fame as they are now, and Shunsho's establishment was frequented by all the renowned mimes. The atmosphere was conducive to song and poetry, and Hokusai later wrote some very famous short poems. He worked day and night at his poetry and painting. Time and again he was able to give simultaneous fame to two different pseudonyms he happened to use, so that the people of Yedo—as Tokyo was then called—could not grasp that they both belonged to one and the same painter, novelist or poet.

Hokusai was an eternal wanderer, changing his studio and lodgings more than a hundred times during his life. He was always poor and often hungry as he roamed through the country, buffeted by the autumn winds. At one time he peddled his own drawings on street corners; on another occasion he sold red pepper in a market. But the force that drove him grew with each passing year, spurring him on to ever greater achievements. On the one hand he attained great successes, and on the other, he lived in poverty. Poverty dogged him throughout his life, for that matter, for he had such contempt for money and fame that he tried to throw both away.

Thousands of pictures took shape under Hokusai's brush. He painted Fuji at least a hundred times, depicting the sacred volcano in an amazing diversity of moods. Hokusai's vistas are so grandiose that he might almost have seen the mountain from an airplane many miles up. Nothing seemed beyond the reach of his brilliant observation of nature.

Hokusai strove to evolve entirely novel techniques. He painted with his fingers, with his left hand, now working from the bottom upward, now from left to right, now the other way around, sometimes using a bottle, and sometimes an egg. He painted marvelous seascapes with cliffs and pounding breakers. Looking at prints of his woodcuts, one is apt to forget the engraving technique that produced them—so bold are their colors and designs.

Hokusai mingled with the people, and no Japanese painter has ever portrayed the faces of common folk with such perception and obvious delight. Here Hokusai was in his element. He ridiculed people, he caricatured them, he showed up their grotesque little idiosyncrasies. He rarely painted a beautiful woman, because the subject did not interest him.

The public marveled, then laughed, as they always do when they cannot understand genius. "So you laugh, do you?" cried Hokusai. "Am I too small for you then?" And he began to paint a picture of gigantic dimensions such as the world had never seen. He ordered a sheet of paper no less than 635 feet square. To keep it taut, thick layers of rice straw and wooden blocks were spread over it as ballast; otherwise the wind might tear the paper and blow it away. A vast scaffold was erected along the wall of a temple to support rollers on which the picture could be raised by means of pulleys. Dozens of barrels held the paints that were transported to the site in huge pails. An enormous throng of spectators crowded the scene.

At midday Hokusai appeared followed by a procession of pupils carrying bronze pails. Hokusai's brush was an immense broom, and dipping it into one of the pails of paint he drew a nose, then an eye, then the second eye. Gradually a *daruma*, or wizard, took shape under his strokes. Running at top speed along the width of the paper, Hokusai drew the mouth, ears, neck, hair and beard. Then his pupils dragged up a huge bronze basin, and this time Hokusai's brush turned out to be a bundle of rice sacks tied together. Pulling it after him by a cord tied around his neck and taking small steps backward, he painted the *daruma's* clothes, scooping the red paint out of a bucket with a ladle.

Night had fallen over Tokyo, but no one noticed. There was no sound; the crowd held its breath. The *daruma's* picture was finished. It was pulled up and now it hung there, in the sky.

The people were entranced, terrified, dumbfounded. A few women wept. Hokusai's huge painting was a revelation. The painter's name was on everyone's lips, and he had to endure public acclaim. Then, to demonstrate his skill once more, he painted a giant horse.

Now the emperor himself summoned the darling of the people into his presence. Hokusai bowed low; then he lifted one of the great temple doors faced with paper off its hinges. Plunging his hand into a paint pot, he threw some indigo onto the paper and smeared it over its surface. Then he opened a basket he had brought along and took out a live rooster. Dipping the bird's feet in red ink, he let it walk all over the paper. Again he bowed to the emperor. The whole court knew immediately what Hokusai had painted: it was Tasuta, the River of the Poets, with red maple leaves floating upon its surface.

Hokusai was enthusiastically acclaimed: he was the only commoner ever to be received by a Japanese emperor of the Tokugawa period. For months his house was besieged by mobs of people, all wanting a personal drawing bearing the illustrious signature. But Hokusai soon tired of success and adulation. He withdrew and went to live under an assumed name. But still he worked like a man possessed, and it was now that he painted his terrifying ghost pictures. In a symphony of intoxicating colors he painted the most grandiose waterfall ever sketched by an artist—the cataract of Yoshino, its huge spidery fingers groping their way into the depths. He painted glorious azaleas, with a cuckoo swooping down on them from the blue sky; a dragonfly hovering over kikyo flowers, and—over and over again—Mount Fuji, the clouds and the sea. What other painter has ever attempted such bold and magnificent pictures?

Hokusai also wrote an educational work—a fifteen-volume pictorial encyclopedia, in which he touched on every aspect of the life of the common people. And no matter where he sought refuge, no matter what pseudonym he used, the people always recognized him. Yet he remained a pauper, and he had his personal troubles.

Hokusai married twice, but his only son turned out to be a ne'er-do-well, as often happens with the sons of geniuses. Ragged, vermin-ridden and destitute, Hokusai lived for five years in an unheated garret, begging for money to buy brushes and paints. He did not mind starving, but he had to paint. It was good that life seemed unending. Hokusai was seventy-three years old before he thought he understood nature; at eighty he said he was making some progress; at ninety he meant to explore the mysteries of the material world, and he prophesied that at a hundred and ten he would reach the stage when his works would throb with real life.

This giant among men was a cosmos in himself. He had an inexhaustible power of observation, and his genius allowed him to capture the essence of a subject without sacrificing it for mere detail. His energy bordered on the miraculous, and all his works reveal that in spite of his dire poverty, this genius never lost his sense of humor.

Hokusai was not always popular with the Japanese, because this giant did not take his compatriots seriously, but the Western world regards him as one of the greatest artists of all time. He died on May 10, 1849, in his ninetieth year, and his last words were: "Had heaven granted me another five years, I might have become a painter."

THEY PAINTED THE RHYTHM OF THE WORLD

HARUNOBU–SHARAKU–HIROSHIGE

To rob the moment of its impermanence—that is art.

JAPANESE colored woodcuts are a fairyland of their own; an art form which inspires admiration, infatuation and consternation, in that order. For the artistic vision and the craftsmanship that went into the making of a Japanese colored woodcut borders on the phenomenal.

The Japanese woodcut was probably the most refined and mature artistic product of eastern Asia. Its masters did not strive to achieve mere replicas of nature: they had absorbed the atmosphere, the spirit, the sound and the whole tumultuous rhythm of life itself. The artist did not just sit down and paint a picture. He first had to have a painting clearly in his mind, down to its last detail; then he broke this image down into its component colors. Only then did he paint several pictures, one for each color occurring in the whole conception. Pasting them on a woodcut block, he cropped the unpainted areas until only the colored portions remained, and sent the individual color-tone pictures one by one to the wood engraver's workshop. The reproduction of a picture with fifteen colors thus necessitated fifteen individual one-color pictures. As soon as the printer received the fifteen blocks, he wet each of them with the necessary paint and impressed them on paper, one by one. It was only then that the artist saw his work for the first time. Making a colored woodcut might be likened to composing a symphony.

The individual color prints had to register with the utmost precision: an infinitesimal discrepancy between one block and another might mean an altered facial expression. And every line had to be in place—not only once, but as many times as there were colors. When we realize that the Japanese used no tracings but cut each separate block from memory, accurately to a fraction of an inch, the true wonder of this art is revealed. Only those artists whose memories had mastered the totality of such a work could be truly creative.

Once, three years after delivering the blocks for one of his pictures, Hokusai decided that additional colors might improve it. Without any guide whatsoever he made the one-tone paintings for the additional colors: they registered down to the last detail. In such an art slipshod work, indistinct outlines or blurred colors were unthinkable. There was no way of correcting a cut once it was made, and the advance selection of the colors was a creative act of the first magnitude. The masters of the Japanese polychrome woodcut who gained a world-wide reputation therefore had real genius. They had to have an unerring sense of composition, they had to be practiced mathematicians, they had to have a sense of perspective and an ability to visualize the interplay of colors without first seeing them. In addition, they had to be brilliant craftsmen. But, most important of all, when they were doing the portrait of a graceful girl, for instance, they had to portray the *essence* of grace, not merely its form. Their art was called "the moving world" —in Japanese, *ukiyo*. And the man who gave the Japanese colored woodcut its name was Ukiyo-Matabei, and the school of painting he founded is called the Ukiyo-e school. The masters of the woodcut who followed his lead in painting the rhythm of the world never concerned themselves with pure fantasy, but painted the world around them. And the timeless quality they achieved with their work lies in the secret of all great art—to rob the moment of its impermanence.

Anyone who knows Japan will also know what a great role is played there by a small article which we Occidentals rather disdain: the toothpick.

About two hundred years ago there stood near the Kwannon temple in the Asakusa quarter of Tokyo the shop of a tooth-brush and toothpick merchant named Niheiji-Yanagi-ya. His small establishment went by the name of "The House of Willows." Tokyo may have been called Yedo in those days, but her cherry trees blossomed just as gloriously, her gold-fish ponds sparkled as brightly, and her gingko trees flaunted their foliage as bravely, silver-green and as glossy as patent leather. And then, just as now, there were some very pretty girls in Japan.

There was also, just as there is now, a great demand for toothpicks. There was something about Niheiji's shop, however, which particularly attracted the masculine portion of his clientele. It was his beautiful daughter Ofuji. Ofuji was just sixteen years old, and so beautiful that dramatists were already—in 1769—naming their heroines after her, and children singing little songs about her in the streets. One day, a gentleman in a dark robe walked into the shop. Ofuji inclined her head. After the gentleman had paid several visits to the shop, she put a few cherry blossoms into the bowl of saké which it was usual to offer every good customer. The stranger was Harunobu the painter, and he had fallen in love with the girl. She began to figure in many of his pictures. In one of them she is seen kneeling in her shop smoking "tobacco," with Harunobu himself sitting beside her. The look passing between the two sensitive faces is not easy to define, but it has a tenderness, a yearning and timeless quality which scarcely any other artist has ever achieved.

Harunobu could never paint unless he was in love, and he only fell in love with very young girls who still had the charm of naïveté. He painted sweet, flower-like creatures with tiny faces and hands and arms of incredible delicacy and childish grace. For all that, his style is never mawkish. It remains a mystery how Harunobu managed to imbue his young creatures with so much life, quite apart from their tranquil grace. In his eternal craving for beauty, the artist had discovered another sixteen-year-old girl even before he found Ofuji. Her name was Osen, and she was employed by the Kagiya tea-house at Kasamori, the site of the Inari shrine which contemporary Japanese records inform us pilgrims visited less from a desire to pray than to be served by charming Osen in the Kagiya teahouse! Osen was really a peasant girl, and wore a long comb in her hair and humble clogs on her feet. No rouge or powder adorned her fresh face, yet if ten men passed her by, ten men turned to stare.

Osen had the humility proper to all well-brought-up Japanese girls, and loved her parents. She was also conscious of her beauty and made a patient artist's model. She is perhaps the only girl in history who sang the praises of her own beauty in classical verse and not only failed to irritate anyone by doing so, but gave all who heard her song (which she composed herself) a brief moment in heaven.

> Out of violet-colored clouds of steam
> she steps, as if
> lacquered all over in gold and silver....
> She sits by the tea-filled kettle
> musing, musing all alone,
> thinking, ever thinking of this and that
> and stroking her little head with a silver pin.
> —He who would rest his legs a while
> should do so at Kasamori
> in the shade of a tree.

Harunobu idealized his enchanting models after his own fashion. He wanted to stir the beholder's tenderest emotions, and was less concerned for effect than to express the absolutely timeless concepts of love and grace in an absolutely timeless way. In one of his pictures a frail and lovely girl is seen crossing a bridge in a snowstorm. Another delightful child is blowing soap bubbles for her brother in the garden. Another is listening to a cuckoo, and another to the evening bell tolling from a temple near by. Another is seen buying a fan, another taking leave of her lover, and yet another entrusting a love letter to a little girl.

Two of Harunobu's models were so beautiful that they were engaged to dance at a ceremonial consecration of the effigy of the god Shoshi at the Yushima temple in Yedo. We also hear of another beautiful girl who came from the Tsuta-ya teahouse in the Asakusa quarter.

Harunobu had the profoundest contempt for everything coarse and vulgar for he was an aristocrat, both by brush and by birth. The theatre was a particular *bête noire* of his, because actors had such unsavory reputations. Harunobu wanted to raise the level of Ukiyo-e art, and even when he painted Hinatsuru, the famous courtesan from the "House of Cloves" in Yoshiwara, he made her so innocent and fine, so lily-like and unselfconscious that any hint of the ephemeral nature of his model's real everyday life was quite absent, and all that remained was the artist's own conception delicately expressed in line and color. Harunobu painted Hinatsuru many times, but if he had only painted the courtesan once, as he did in "Pictures with Contourless White Robes," it would have been enough to set her on the throne of immortality.

On the other hand the masters of Japanese wood engraving did not slavishly copy nature. The engravers gathered mental impressions until they had formed a clear perception and were ready to paint the essence of their subject. And if they were familiar with oil paints, they were wise enough not to use them.

Long before the invention of woodcuts, the Japanese had painted in water colors on silk and paper, and the resultant *makemono* or *kakemono* could be rolled up. And Ukiyo-e is also above all a style of painting. The long list of brilliant Ukiyo-e exponents proves that no genuine artist has ever suffered by starting out as a faithful imitator of his master, that this does not necessarily lead to a lifelong career of mere copying, and that individual style and originality can develop only after imitative craftsmanship has been mastered.

Four people had to co-operate in the making of a colored print: the publisher, the artist, the wood engraver and the printer. And perhaps this group should also include the paper manufacturer, the man who supplied the beautiful handmade mulberry-bark paper on which the colors showed to their best advantage.

The Japanese were always aware that art should be more than a mere imitation of Nature. As draftsmen, the Ukiyo-e artists have never been rivaled by any others in the world, the masters of Japanese wood engraving concentrating above all upon bringing out the essentials of their subject in line and color. Nothing ever intimidated them, and it can be said that Hokusai, for instance, turned the disorder in Nature into order–though it may be added that his kind of order was an uncommonly dramatic one.

The Paris exhibition of prints by Hokusai, Utamaro and Hiroshige in 1867 made a great sensation, and the most celebrated French impressionist, Manet, saw in their works quite novel methods of achieving realism, while from them his contemporary Monet realized that color was not inherent in an object, but depended on its lighting. Europeans began to buy and collect Japanese woodcuts, and museums all over the world followed their example.

It is far too often forgotten that the masters of Japanese wood engraving exerted a very considerable influence upon modern European painting. It was the works of the Japanese which helped the French impressionists to recognize the essence of a subject–its *impression;* which helped them to observe atmospheric influences, the play of light and the color tones, not as they appear under close scrutiny, but rather as they are affected by light and the reflections of nature.

Of all the Japanese masters, however, it is now Sharaku whose works command the highest prices. He is really a European discovery, for the Japanese themselves did not begin to be interested in him until European and American art dealers had turned his prints into "best sellers." All too belatedly, the Japanese began to investigate his life, but the only thing they found out was how very little they knew about him. His real name has been forgotten, and the date of his death is unknown. All that is known is that he was a gentleman and the vassal of a princely house, received a regular income from his prince, knew neither poverty nor hunger, and never worked for money.

Japan has always been a land of the theater. The Kabuki Theatre owed its origins to the Nō dramas of the aristocracy, Japanese dancing, and the puppet theater. Even princes took part in stage productions, and Sharaku was also a performer.

Actors need publicity, a fact which is not just a Hollywood discovery, for Yedo was well aware of the fact, and her theaters used portraits of actors as advertising posters. It was in the spring of 1793, during Yedo's theatrical "silly season," that Sharaku suddenly appeared on the scene. Under the magic of his dancing brush there appeared a whole series of heads and full-length portraits of the mimic actors of the day, with their large pale faces. Sharaku painted in a most arresting way, producing such bizarre, terrifying and repulsive compositions that the viewer's attention could not fail to be caught and held. But Sharaku offended the public, and it was probably their hatred which drove him back into obscurity.

Glaring pupils, grimaces, extremely slanting, piercing eyes, dark mica backgrounds—all these things were symptoms of his diabolical struggle with the invisible souls which remained, for all his audacity, beyond his powers of expression. Sharaku wrestled eternally with Fate and with the limitations which the material world imposed upon him. He was like some giant fighting with an invisible force stronger than himself. It seems almost uncanny that everything we have by Sharaku was painted within the space of a single year—between 1793 and 1794. None of the Nō dancers or actors had ever been painted before.

Sharaku vanished as suddenly as he had appeared: perhaps his prince forbade him to give "the despised race of actors" a chance of immortality. So much mystery surrounds this great master of the woodcut that today he might almost be a ghost, despite his neglected grave at Tokushima. Yet the man about whose life we know so little presented the humble actors of his day to an audience larger than they ever dreamed of—the whole world.

Utamaro was Japan's most brilliant painter of women. Hokusai was her prodigy, her Leonardo da Vinci. Harunobu was her amorous painter of naïve feminine grace. Sharaku was the comet which illuminated the Japanese theater in its darkness. Finally there was Hiroshige, Japan's most truly national painter in that he painted the Japanese landscape, showing helpless little mortals caught in the toils of their menacing natural surroundings.

All the wonders of the Japanese islands are captured in Hiroshige's colored woodcuts: the thirty-six views of sacred Fuji-no-Yama; the eight faces of Lake Biwa; the countryside around Yedo; snowy

A young courtesan from Yoshiwara, a colored woodcut by the great Utamaro (1753-1806). Yoshiwara, now the red-light district of Tokyo, was in Utamaro's day a town in its own right devoted almost entirely to prostitution, and the girl wears the sign of her establishment on her purple dress.

►

Portrait by Sharaku of the actor Ichikawa Ibitso IV, playing at the Kajiri Theatre in Yedo (now Tokyo) in January 1794. All Sharaku's brilliant paintings were produced within the space of a single year.

A young girl at her morning toilet, colored woodcut by Toyokuni (1768-1825).

Two lovers under an umbrella, by Utamaro.

Torii Kiyonaga's favorite subject was the unsophisticated charm of beautiful women of the people. He lived in Yedo (now Tokyo) from 1752 to 1804. ►

Early Australian aborigines' cave drawings found on cave walls near the Humbert River, Northern Territory.

The ancestors of the Worora tribe are buried in a cave near Port George IV. From time immemorial, each descendant to visit the sinister place has left his hand print on the rock wall. Hence the ghost picture.

Wooden shield surmounted by the head of an ancestor, from New Guinea which offered both physical and magical protection against enemies. [Völkerkunde-Museum, Munich. *Photograph:* Herbert List.

◄

Wooden figure from the volcanic island Nukuhiva, in the Marquesas group, carved with primitive stone implements. Once 75,000 Polynesians lived here; today there are fewer than 2,500 left. [Völkerkunde-Museum, Munich. *Photograph:* Herbert List.

Wooden statuette from Easter Island, carved from driftwood. Statuettes like this serve as totems and soothsayers and are of considerable value.

Melanesian ancestor figures from New Ireland in the Bismarck Archipelago. Ancestor worship has existed there from time immemorial. [Völkerkunde-Museum, Munich. *Photograph:* Herbert List.

A Melanesian from New Caledonia. 30,000 aborigines still inhabit the island.

Scene on a door-post from Yaxchilan, Chiapas, Mexico, in the British Museum, London. The penitent on the right is pulling a rope of thorns through his tongue, and the blood runs down into a sacrificial basin. The standing priest wields a stylized maize plant.

mountains peopled with stooping figures, so lifelike in their cold that you shiver looking at them; the racing rapids at Naruto; snowflakes; a slanting downpour of torrential rain; tardy raftsmen punting upstream against the current; lonely moonlit landscapes; stormy, dangerous seas.

Before Hiroshige, the artists regarded the human being as their most important subject, and landscapes were merely background. Hiroshige, however, ventured to lay a bold hand upon nature itself. His pictures are boldly conceived, and always express a mood. If they often seem unrealistic to our eyes, it is only because we do not know Japan, for it really looks the way Hiroshige painted it. Mountains soar into the air out of their banks of mist, and nature is always ready to pounce as man, its slave, scurries through life. In his works Hiroshige came uncannily close to capturing the ephemeral creature that is man, and to the timelessness and omnipotence of nature.

WHERE THE DEAD LIVE ON

The continent of Gondwana was engulfed, but men were living in Australia a million years ago.

A GREAT Dutchman died in 1941, in the middle of the second World War. And although he left behind many erudite works, he took a great proportion of his knowledge to the grave. He was Eugene Dubois, who discovered the oldest human skull the earth has ever surrendered.

Dubois, a professor of anatomy, did not make his discovery (incidentally, it was only the roof of a skull) by chance. Before leaving Holland for Java, he announced that he would probably find there the remains of a primitive creature related to man. And in Java, digging in the neighborhood of Trinil, Dubois unearthed Pithecanthropus erectus, the Adam of anthropology. The age of this creature is estimated at 500,000 years. His brain capacity was 54.9 cubic inches, as compared with a gorilla's (33.55 cubic inches), and a modern man's (73 to 79 cubic inches). Most authorities assign Pithecanthropus to an extinct branch of the hominoids (cf. Boule-Vallois, *Les Hommes Fossiles*, Paris, 1952, p. 127). The structure of his bones places him halfway between modern man and his earliest *human* ancestor, and thus the term Pithecanthropus—from the Greek *pithekos* (ape) and *anthropos* (man)—is slightly misleading.

Because Pithecanthropus erectus resembled a man, he must have been preceded by hundreds of thousands of years of evolution. And neither he nor his forefathers would have recognized the earth as it is today, for the continents, mountains, islands, oceans, and even the positions of the poles have altered more markedly than has man's own appearance. Some portions of the earth's crust have been swallowed up by the oceans, while others have risen from the water.

Australia was not always an island continent—at one time it was connected with southeast Asia by a land bridge. It is even possible that South Africa, India and Australia were all linked together by that now submerged portion of the earth which zoologists call Lemuria, and geologists, Gondwana. However, since man existed long before the continents were severed, Australia today is regarded as mankind's anthropological museum. It cannot be mere coincidence that Man No. 1 was found on the neighboring island of Java.

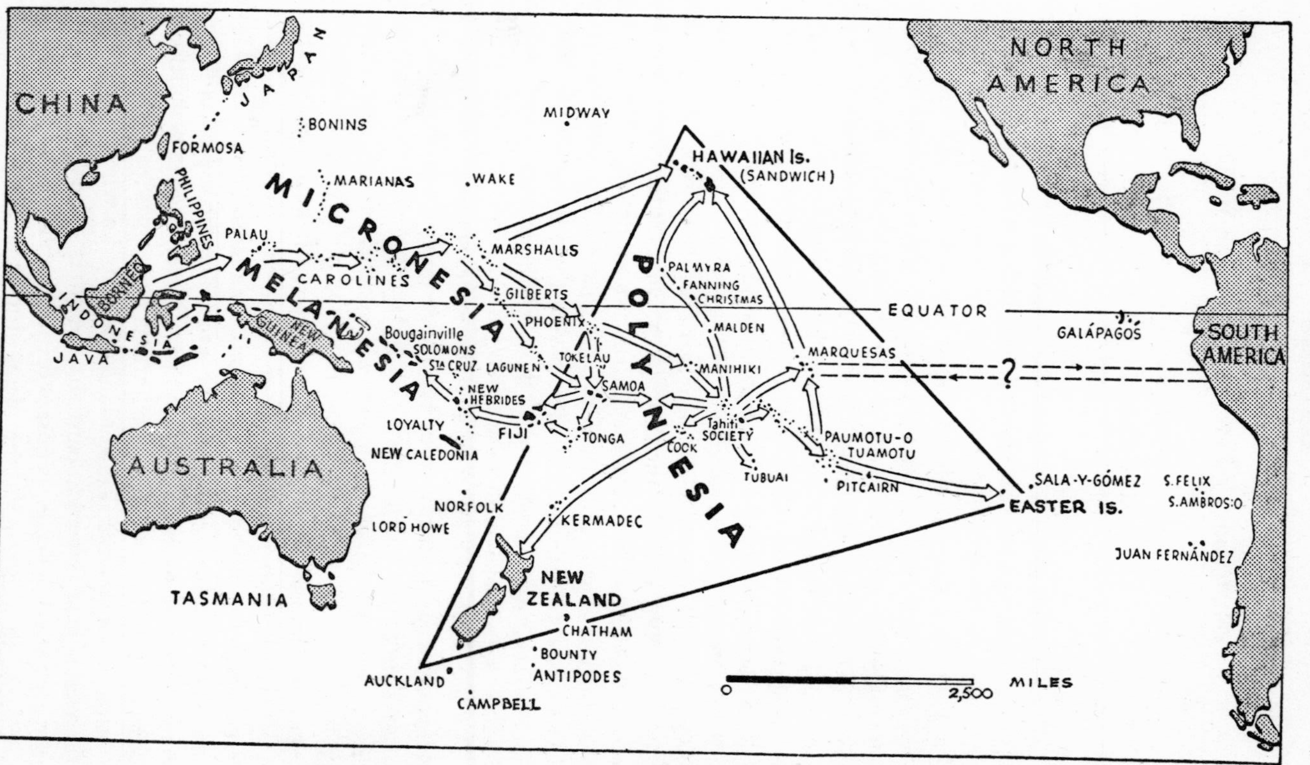

CHINA
JAPAN
FORMOSA
BONINS
MIDWAY
MARIANAS
WAKE
MICRONESIA
PHILIPPINES
PALAU
MARSHALLS
MELANESIA
CAROLINES
GILBERTS
BORNEO
INDONESIA
JAVA
NEW GUINEA
Bougainville
SOLOMONS
STa CRUZ
LAGUNEN
PHOENIX
TOKELAU
SAMOA
NEW HEBRIDES
LOYALTY
NEW CALEDONIA
FIJI
TONGA
AUSTRALIA
NORFOLK
LORD HOWE
KERMADEC
TASMANIA
NEW ZEALAND
CHATHAM
BOUNTY
ANTIPODES
AUCKLAND
CAMPBELL
HAWAIIAN Is.
(SANDWICH)
POLYNESIA
PALMYRA
FANNING
CHRISTMAS
MALDEN
MANIHIKI
MARQUESAS
Tahiti
SOCIETY
COOK
TUBUAI
PAUMOTU-O
TUAMOTU
PITCAIRN
EQUATOR
GALÁPAGOS
NORTH AMERICA
SOUTH AMERICA
SALA-Y-GÓMEZ
EASTER IS.
S. FELIX
S. AMBROS:O
JUAN FERNÁNDEZ
0
2,500
MILES

The most important discovery relating to Australia's aborigines was made at Talga, southeast Queensland, in 1884, when a fairly well-preserved skull was brought to light. Although no other human bones were found nearby, the remains of extinct animals were unearthed, including bones belonging to the diprotodon (an early kangaroo), the nototherium and certain horned reptiles. After a recent study of this proto-Australian skull, Dr. S. A. Smith concluded that it resembles that of the modern Australian aborigine. Considering that Australia's aborigines have not yet discovered their national consciousness, and with it their national pride, we may safely add that the characteristics Dr. Smith saw in the proto-Australian are closer to the ape than to any human race, living or extinct. Further finds of human bones were made in the Wellington Caves, and the fossilized footprints of an early Australian aborigine were discovered in the tertiary rock at Warrnambool, one hundred and twenty-five miles southwest of Melbourne. All this indicates that men were living in Australia during the tertiary period at least a million years ago and probably much earlier.

Then came the catastrophe.

We do not know precisely when the water masses split Australia from Asia. We only know that when Gondwanaland drowned—an event considerably less mythical than the story of Atlantis—a vast continent was submerged, and Australia remained.

And so did the inhabitants. Time passed them by. Australia had few dangerous animals, there was good hunting; and it took many thousands of years before the sun's heat dried up the endless tracts of fertile land. Completely cut off, the early aborigines squatted on their lonely and isolated continent surrounded by a watery waste. There, over 9,000 miles from the shores of South America and 5,000 miles from Africa, man and beast developed independently from the rest of the world.

Australia remained undisturbed until 1605, when the Dutch navigator W. Janszoon landed at the Gulf of Carpentaria. Then the Dutchman Dirck Hartog reached western Australia in 1616, and Captain James Cook discovered *Terra Australis* in 1770. But the explorers had more or less expected to find some continent there, since it was held to be "indispensable to terrestrial equilibrium."

In discovering Australia, mankind had found a whole continent that was virtually a living museum for the study of an early species of man which had scarcely progressed for thousands, if not hundreds of thousands, of years. Also, the plants that grew there could be found nowhere else on earth. Nine-tenths of all Australian plants flourish *only* on that continent, which alone is enough to prove the length of Australia's insular existence. At long last a "land of living fossils" had been discovered. The animals that lived there were of a kind found only in early geological periods. There were more than a hundred and fifty kinds of marsupials in Australia, from the opposum to the giant kangaroo; mammals that laid eggs covered with skinlike shells, like the duck-billed platypus; birds like the cassowary and the emu that had lost their ability to fly because they were no longer pursued by natural enemies. The vast eucalyptus forests were populated by nature's toys—the koalas which clambered around like animated teddy bears.

It was in this lost and isolated world that the tribes of mankind's oldest race hunted and roamed, men who were still directly linked to primeval humanity. Trapped in immemorial cults handed down from generation to generation, rigidly upholding their ancient customs and rites, split into five hundred different tribes and alienated by as many different languages and dialects, living more and more frugally on a continent that was gradually drying out, always searching for water, these ancient Robinson Crusoes were forced into a life that was nothing but a struggle for survival. Their needs constantly lessened, and their skulls grew thicker to withstand the scorching heat of the sun.

As late as 1914, there were still aborigines in Australia who had never met a white man. And it is estimated that at the time of the white man's first appearance in Australia—putting the date at 1788—there were approximately 300,000 aborigines living on the continent.

Slowly, like some malignant disease, the Europeans pushed into Australia's interior, and everywhere the life of the black people degenerated under the impact of this white invasion. No sooner had the white tide rolled over their young men—bringing them into contact with that most destructive and unsettling of all influences which we call Western civilization—than they no longer obeyed the ancients who had defended their tribal customs and their totems—the symbols of ancestor worship—for so many thousands of years. The black men began to die off. They became indifferent huntsmen. They forgot the thousand little skills that were essential to the preservation of life on their continent. For the first time they had enough water, yet they withered away in their new clothes and corrugated iron huts like so many flowers in a dank cellar. The 300,000 dwindled to 60,000 and then to 50,000, and today only 25,000 lead the nomadic life of their forefathers.

Eventually those Australians who were still able to cope with their rugged continent were found only in the hot central regions of the country, in an arid wasteland where they still hunted kangaroo and emu while their women caught edible snakes, rats, frogs, lizards and grubs; where they still gathered lily bulbs, acacia and grass seeds for food; where they still conquered thirst (in a desert where in years of extreme drought literally not one drop of rain fell) by extracting water from roots—an art not even the ablest white explorers ever learned to master. The aborigines never had vessels of any kind for boiling water or food, but cooked their meat in hot ashes, earth, clay or mud. When they caught a kangaroo they immediately cut off its hindquarters—to their way of thinking a much better way of holding onto it than merely killing it.

All the tribes had their own living and hunting areas, and very seldom infringed upon each other's boundaries. In fact, we may generally say that nomads are far better at keeping within their frontiers than settled races, for the nomad is far more familiar with the farthest limits of his country than the settled river-valley dwellers.

The Australian aborigines rarely waged war on neighboring tribes. On the inter-tribal level they were invariably peaceable, and the fact that some explorers claim to have heard the distant sound of wooden clubs thudding dully on heads at night does not prove the contrary. In Australia thwacking one's wife on the head with a piece of wood has from time immemorial been regarded as a useful disciplinary measure. Duels in which male or female opponents beat each other on the head with wooden clubs were always conducted in a fair and sportsmanlike manner. If the contestants were women, the men usually sat quietly by and watched, interrupting the proceedings only if they became too rough. When men were fighting, the women would interfere only to the extent of shielding the men with their own heads.

No civilization can be judged by comparing it with another that is completely alien, nor can any civilization be assessed by the criteria of another. The Australian corroborees, performed under the stars, with much stamping and rhythmical leaping around red fires to the accompaniment of guttural male voices, is one of the most impressive communal dances in the world. These dances tell complete stories in pantomime, portraying birds catching fish, or relating the history of the totem, or tribal ancestor. The designs on the aborigines' shields, bodies and cave walls may be primitive, but the imaginative conception behind them was marvelous.

The drawings that were discovered in the caves along the Humber, Glenelg and Forrest Rivers, as well as in the Musgrave range, are extremely old. Among them is the sketch of a diprotodon's paw—the artist must have been a contemporary of this extinct species of kangaroo. The hand imprints of the Worora tribe in the cave at Port George IV are like ghostly nocturnal conspiracies. The animals pictured are at once naïve and compelling, and the fish swim along the rocky walls as if in a petrified aquarium.

Civilization has neither beginning nor end. Just as the discovery of the wheel was an epoch-making cultural achievement, so the invention of the Australian spear marked a step on the road to civilization. The *woomera*, or boomerang—the "long arm" of the aboriginal, which would enable any expert to out-distance the world javelin-throwing record without trouble—is a masterpiece of human ingenuity. Truly it was a life of great vitality that perished here, with its countless skills in mastering nature at its harshest and most inimical.

Forever guarding the northern coast of Queensland is the Great Barrier Reef, a gigantic coral rampart—the largest coral formation in the world—which forms a barren and uninhabitable natural breakwater 1,250 miles long, shaken by the everlasting thunder of the surf.

Between the Great Barrier Reef and the mainland, less than fifty miles north of Townsville, lie the Palm Islands. It was here that I saw ancient Australia's last terrible awakening from the dream which has endured for so many thousands of years. For these islands are a reservation for aborigines who came into contact with white civilization. There these great hunters of old are now living, in clothes that do not fit them, in huts they managed to do without for 100,000 years, and under modern hygienic conditions that are sapping their resistance to disease. They go on living, yet they died long ago. They go on dancing, and the ocean sings their requiem.

EXPERTS IN THE ART OF DOING NOTHING

Without doubt the Pacific Ocean is aeons older than the Atlantic or the Indian Ocean. When we say older, we mean it has not come to any modern consciousness. Strange convulsions have convulsed the Atlantic and Mediterranean peoples into phase after phase of consciousness, while the Pacific and the Pacific peoples have slept. To sleep is to dream: you can't stay unconscious. And oh heaven, for how many thousands of years has the true Pacific been dreaming, turning over in its sleep and dreaming again: idylls: nightmares.

D. H. Lawrence

"BEFORE us lies the horizon; the horizon which is forever vanishing, the horizon which always seems close at hand, which arouses dread, doubt and oppresses us with fear—the horizon, with its unsuspected and primeval power, which no ship's prow has ever yet cut asunder. The unfathomable skies hang over us, the wild seas roar beneath. The untrodden path lies before us—our ship must away!"

That is a Polynesian song, a song of the great seafarers who, centuries before the Vikings or Columbus, conquered a maritime area three times the size of North America.

These Polynesians discovered hundreds of enchanting islands, towering volcanoes and thousands of palm-fringed coral reefs. They became masters of an ocean as studded with islands as the sky is with stars; they ruled over the triangle formed by Hawaii, New Zealand and Easter Island. It is most probable that they reached the shores of South America long before Cabral, Amerigo Vespucci, da Gama or Magellan, and modern scientific research is continually finding fresh parallels between the Polynesian and American Indian civilizations. The Polynesians were always a race of seamen, and needed no Pacific version of Atlantis to help them reach the west coast of America dry-shod. Thus the many books written by geologists, biologists and archaeologists about the "Pacific Atlantis," or the continent Mu seem to rest on rather shaky foundations.

No other race on earth has ever inhabited as large a geographical area as the Polynesians. Their world extended over 69 degrees of latitude and 70 degrees of longitude, covering 4,700 miles between Hawaii and New Zealand and 3,700 between Tonga and Easter Island. It was a world of outriggers and huge war canoes manned by crews of up to three hundred men, of voyages lasting months or years, of interminable wars and migrations. These seafarers had neither compasses nor iron. They have left us no written history. The Easter Island inscriptions have never been deciphered, and as for the waters—who knows how much evidence they have engulfed?

But the Polynesians have always been a people of poetry and song, passing on their legends from one generation to the next, storing up the stories of their origins in their minds and repeating them to their children. They firmly believed that anyone who recited an important tradition incorrectly would perish before the wrath of the gods.

The Maoris of New Zealand relate that it was a chieftain from Tahiti named Kupe who discovered New Zealand, forty generations before the arrival of the Europeans. Another Maori legend tells of a land called Uru which had at one time been the cradle of their forefathers, and people have tried to identify Uru with the Ur of the Chaldeans in Mesopotamia, although in the Maori dialect of the Polynesian language *Uru* simply means "West." The Polynesians also know of a land called Irihia, and some enterprising scholars decided that Irihia was a corruption of Yrihia, an old Sanskrit name for India. The Polynesian word for sun is *ra*, and it was not long before certain so-called authorities claimed that the Polynesians must at one time have lived in Egypt, because Amon Ra was ancient Egypt's sun god.

Another mythological link between Polynesia and the Asiatic "homeland" is the widespread Hawaiki saga. The Hawaiki version of the story of Creation is told everywhere in Polynesia (except in Samoa and Tonga), admittedly with many variations, but always basically the same: "We come from the great Hawaiki, from far Hawaiki, from the distant Hawaiki," the Maoris sing. Hawaiki was the Polynesians' former Paradise, the place they left behind when they set off across the seas, sailing on and on into the rising sun, to discover and colonize their island world. And the souls of their dead wander westward into the land of the setting sun, back to Hawaiki.

But where was Hawaiki?

In general, experts now believe that the ancient Polynesians probably came from Indo-China via Indonesia, though the evidence is not altogether conclusive. There are numerous cultural similarities between the Polynesian and Indonesian races. Like the Indonesians, the Polynesians kept dogs, pigs and chickens, and in both Indonesia and Polynesia (and among the American Indians) fire was produced by rotating a vertical stick in a hollowed piece of wood placed on the ground. Thousands of Polynesian words are related to Indonesian words both in sound and meaning. The Indonesians are Malays, and the Polynesian and Indonesian languages have so much in common that, together with the Micronesian and Melanesian languages, they are included in the Malayo-Polynesian family. It is quite possible therefore that the Polynesians were driven across the sea from that part of the world which we call Southeast Asia or Indonesia.

What we do not know is their reason for undertaking these dangerous voyages across the vast and treacherous expanse of the Pacific.

A whole literature containing thousands of volumes has grown up on the subject of the route the Polynesians followed in their leapfrogging journey across the ocean. Although it was long believed that they passed through the Melanesian archipelago, modern theory holds that they actually chose a route through Micronesia, the group of islands that belonged to Germany before the first World War.

These migrations did not all take place at once. They continued through the centuries, caused sometimes by necessity, but more often inspired by a spontaneous desire to explore the Pacific. About 650 A.D. the Tonga chieftain Hui-te-Rangiora even pushed as far as Antarctica. A race of land-hungry master-mariners driven by a craving for freedom, the Polynesians discovered and colonized island after island, and Polynesian history is a dramatic record of expulsion, exile, tragic explorations, shipwrecks, inter-island wars, internecine strife, elephantiasis, abortions to stem overpopulation, starvation, countless human sacrifices and even cannibalism.

To this day it remains a mystery how the Polynesians managed to cross such immense distances and find tiny islands in the vast stretches of sea without the aid of navigational instruments. However, they have always been experts on winds and weather: they could apparently tell in advance how long a wind would hold, they recognized the first signs of storm and tide, and they knew what currents prevailed in the various parts of their ocean. They were also good astronomers and knew the position of the planets at any given hour of any given day. They could "see" the remotest atolls, long before the curvature of the earth revealed them, by their greenish reflection in the clouds. They noted minuscule plants floating on the waves and deduced from them the exact position of a given island. They could estimate the depth of the sea, and had an infallible instinct for gauging the nearness of their destination by observing the flight of birds.

American, French, English and German scholars have carefully studied the Polynesians' past, their voyages, their culture, languages and anthropology. When Captain Cook visited Tahiti and the Sandwich Islands (Hawaii), he estimated their populations at 300,000 and 400,000 respectively. Today there are only 30,000 natives in Tahiti, 21,000 in the Sandwich Islands, and about 300,000 in all Polynesia. Here in the ocean, as elsewhere, the white man's civilization proved to be fatal to the indigenous population. Missionaries and colonial officials tried to wean the Polynesians from everything belonging to their ancient civilization, drenched in sun and swept by salty winds. They tried to accustom the Polynesians to clothes, soap, religion and schools, and wherever their civilizing attempts succeeded, the true Polynesia ended for all time. A modern version of it lives on in Hawaii, but what with modern songs and dance rhythms and the admixture of Japanese, Chinese, Portuguese and American elements, it is no longer the ancient ocean culture it once was.

Polynesia's ancient civilization was something altogether different: free love until the time of marriage; the liberal adoption of children; the prohibition of any kind of communication between brother and sister (in western Polynesia); a contempt for virginity and an equally deep contempt for excessive sexuality; marital fidelity but divorce freely granted whenever desired; strict segregation of the sexes during meals and even during the preparation of food. As soon as King Kamehameha did away with these customs in Hawaii, the old civilization there was finished.

The Polynesians possessed one virtue which they still have not lost: they are the world's greatest experts in the art of doing nothing. From the cultural standpoint, their way of life is surely the most satisfactory for which man could wish: a naïve enjoyment in living for the moment; a complete indifference to material possessions; a wise limitation to indispensable necessities; a serenity unclouded by worries–in other words, paradise. Ever since the Stone Age, Polynesia has preserved her leisure and freedom, her instinctive simplicity, without demands or ambitions.

Western planation owners, colonial administrators, missionaries, scholars–all those people we call the bearers of civilization–have foundered on the Polynesians' inveterate indifference to work. Yet it would be quite wrong to call them lazy. Any work that *must* be done is done collectively, but only until what *must* be done has been accomplished. After that, they return to their timeless tranquillity, their pleasures and games, their hospitality, their radiant smile, their generosity, and their indifference to material possessions. Because the Polynesian is firmly convinced that the accumulation of money, which he does not immediately need and which merely spoils his permanent holiday, actually lowers his standard of living, he works in order to live: it never occurs to him to live in order to work.

In 130 years of painstaking cultural education the West has not succeeded in altering the Polynesians' way of life, except perhaps in a few seaports. Far from getting down to the work we consider so essential, the Polynesians devote their time to aesthetic pleasures, village festivals, music, dancing, wood carving for their gods rather than for the furniture industry, painting on tapa cloth, and free love undimmed by moral scruples.

In spite of all the catastrophes of the past, the Polynesian islands remain the last surviving paradise on earth. They are a world of carefree tranquillity and pleasure, a world that lives for the day, a world that is as indifferent to the future as it is to the past—a fairy-tale world we have forfeited long ago.

THE UNSOLVED MYSTERY OF THE EASTER ISLAND SCRIPT

Twenty-five hundred miles west of Valparaiso a small and lonely basalt island, the easternmost island in the Polynesian world, protrudes from the waves. Massive stone statues, some of them colossuses up to 46 feet high, stand or sprawl on the island's beaches, hillsides and volcanic slopes. They represent the greatest prehistoric enigma of the South Seas, for the Easter Islanders' script is yet to be deciphered.

EASTER ISLAND was discovered by a Dutchman, Admiral Jakob Roggeveen, on Easter Sunday in 1722. But with his departure the island lapsed into oblivion until Captain Felipe Gonzales y Haedo rediscovered it in 1770. Captain Cook visited it in 1774, La Pérouse in 1786, and Otto von Kotzebue in 1816. Then, in 1862, a band of Peruvian pirates appeared on the scene. Finding that there were 3,000 or 4,000 natives, they summarily carried off 900 of them to the Guano group of islands. A year later the survivors of these 900—a mere fifteen—were brought back suffering from smallpox. The disease quickly spread, and before long the indigenous population of Easter Island had dwindled to 650.

Such was the promising start of Western colonization among the members of the only small Polynesian race which still commanded the ability to read and write a script of their own. It is now extinct.

Eugène Eyraud was a pious lay brother who came to this small triangular island and tried to acquaint its brown-skinned people with the blessings of Christianity. One and a half centuries after the island's original discovery, this first missionary made a singular discovery: long wooden tablets—the largest were over six feet long—bearing neat lines of hieroglyphics and outlining human beings, animals, plants, stars, harpoons, paddles and other objects not readily identifiable. The tablets were made of toromiro, or driftwood, and the inscriptions had been scratched in with pointed stones, obsidian knives or sharks' teeth.

Thus did Eugène Eyraud discover Polynesian writing. But the pious brother was not an erudite man, and he had no inkling of the immense significance of his pieces of wood. Those among the natives who adopted the Christian faith used the tablets as firewood. No sooner had they been baptized than they set about burning their "books," although they did so with mixed emotions. On the one hand, they were not quite sure that the old gods would tolerate the destruction of the sacred tablets; on the other hand, they finally had some fuel on their treeless island.

It was a colleague of Brother Eyraud, Father Zumbohm, who took a fragment of a tablet to Tepano Jaussen, the bishop of Tahiti, while a certain Father Roussel dragged along another five tablets, better preserved than the first. We are also told that the natives sent the bishop a gift, a long cord spun from human hair and wound around a piece of wood—one of the writing tablets. At all events, it is to Bishop Jaussen that we owe the recognition of Easter Island writing as well as the preservation of the last remaining tablets. The most important collection of them is to be found in the *Congrégation des Sacrés-Coeurs de Picpus*, the religious order of which Bishop Jaussen was a member.

Troubled by a bad conscience about both the old and the new god, one of the islanders made a fishing boat from the "speaking timber." Later when the boat fell apart, he carefully saved the pieces and eventually built a canoe out of them. It was this two-way heretic whom Thomson, the American expert on Polynesia, had to thank for one of the last surviving tablets.

When Thomson visited the island in 1886 he found an old man named Ure-vaeiko who had some knowledge of reading and was familiar with some of the tablets' contents. Unfortunately, Ure-vaeiko had become a good Christian. Using the missionaries' prohibition as an excuse, he refused to read the tablets and hid in his house, quaking under the twin threats of purgatory and inquisitive science. It was only on the eve of Thomson's departure that he manage to surprise the old man in his hut.

Shrewdly he plied the native with alcohol until at last, late at night, the old man consented to look at some photographs of the tablets and read them. Thomson soon found out, however, that Ure-vaeiko was not so much reading the individual symbols as reciting something from memory. When he was caught red-handed the old man excused himself by saying that while the meaning of the individual symbols was lost, he could recognize the contents of the tablets by certain unmistakable details—and that his interpretation was substantially correct. The interpreter during these proceedings was a French-Tahitian half-caste known as Paea Salmon, and it was his translation of the so-called texts of the five tablets that Thomson later published. The Austrian ethnologist Michael Haberlandt has said that these texts are incomplete—to

Not yet deciphered. Obverse of one of the writing tablets peculiar to Easter Island. This tablet was inscribed to mark the occasion of a festival which lasted for weeks. Even after 1914 there were still natives on the island who could recite parts of this text from memory, but today its real significance is unknown. Many such tablets have been found and certain of the symbols can be identified, since a proportion of them clearly refer to the objects they represent: the moon, a star, a fish, a crab, a fishing hook. An examination of the swarm of characters reveals that some of them recur frequently. Looked at from the bottom, only the characters in the 1st, 3rd, 5th and 7th rows are in an upright position, while those in the 2nd, 4th, 6th and 8th are upside-down. Reader and writer alike began at the right of the bottom line and on reaching the extreme left, turned the tablet round and retraced his steps along the line immediately above, rather like an ox ploughing a field. Hence *boustrophedon*, the term applied to this method of writing, from the Greek *bous*, meaning ox, and *strophe*, turn.

use understatement—since the number of symbols far exceeds the number of words the texts contain. But what casts the gravest doubts on Ure-vaeika's accuracy is that although Thomson switched some of the photographs in mid-translation, the old fellow went right on reciting the text he had already begun!

The two tablets Thomson managed to obtain on the island are now at the Smithsonian Institution at Washington, D.C.

Between March, 1914, and August, 1915, Easter Island had a woman visitor, a competent ethnologist who devoted her time to finding out all there was left to know about the script. Mrs. Routledge showed the natives photographs of various tablets which the good-natured islanders were only too happy to read for her. But unfortunately they usually read the same text, regardless of the symbols Mrs. Routledge designated.

Eventually, Mrs. Routledge found an old man who knew how to write a second kind of script which had once been used for keeping historical records, and she set out to question this man, whose name was Tomenika, on the meaning of the individual symbols. Her investigations were attended by considerable risks, since he was a leper. Alas, the old man had forgotten a good deal, and what little his sick mind vaguely remembered he could not express in words. His brain grew more and more befogged, his replies became more and more muddled and hesitant until, in the end, in the middle of spelling a word, he died under the very eyes of his plucky interrogator. But through him, Mrs. Routledge has left us a vivid picture of the old priest-king who still held power at the time of the Peruvians' raid.

This ruler's name was Ariki Ngaara, he ruled over the Miru tribe which lived on the island's northern coast, and he could trace his ancestry all the way back to Hotu Matua, the first immigrant ruler of Polynesia. No one was permitted to watch Ngaara eat, and only a few special servants were allowed to enter his quarters. And tribal magic forbade him to partake of Easter Island's most prized delicacy—roasted rat! Ngaara's chief responsibility was to coax the island chickens into laying as many eggs as possible, and since rats are by nature hostile toward chickens and their eggs, it was felt that the chieftain might absorb some of this hostility if he ate any rat meat.

It is interesting to reconstruct a picture of Easter Island as it used to be. Chief Ngaara would be enthroned on top of one of the famous colossal stone statues whose construction and transportation still puzzles modern scholars. Then the newly tattooed natives would parade before him. As they passed, he sorted out those who were well tattooed from those whose decorations displayed slipshod workmanship. This act was the signal for a shout of derision by the assembled tribe and the Chief abandoned the unfortunates to ridicule by the throng.

Ngaara was also, in a manner of speaking, president of the island's literary society: he supervised the great art of reading the tablets. The mastery of the hieroglyphics was the prerogative of a small, select circle of learned *rongo-rongo*. These men lived in separate huts away from their wives, had pupils and gave lessons. Beginners would write on banana leaves, while advanced students used sharks' teeth on toromiro tablets. Ngaara was himself an assiduous calligrapher and school inspector who held regular *rongo-rongo* conventions at which the island's most erudite men could gather while the general public sat around to watch.

There were also tribal banquets and important examinations, which Ngaara had to preside over, sitting on piles of writing tablets. If one of the young men bungled his reading he was merely reproved, but if an old man showed that he was not letter-perfect, a youngster took him by the ear and led him away from the assembly. The conference and its accompanying celebrations were rounded off by presenting a chicken to each of the members of the *rongo-rongo*. Some of the numerous tablets Ngaara left behind are still supposed to lie hidden in one of Easter Island's many caves.

According to Easter Island tradition, Chief Hotu Matua, the first arrival, brought sixty-seven tablets with him from his original homeland. Hence it is possible that the inscriptions of the tablets we still have are the end product of a far earlier and far more complex script. There are many indications that these hieroglyphics are extremely ancient and that the *rongo-rongo* men in the end used no more than a meager kind of shorthand. Anyway, in 1770 when the Spaniards officially took over the island, the native chiefs and dignitaries signed the treaty in hieroglyphics resembling the script on the tablets.

The Easter Island script consists of ideograms—pictographs expressing certain ideas. Each character was designed to portray the intended object as faithfully as possible, but although we can interpret a symbol here and there the full meaning of the script remains hidden from us.

There are other mysteries. Is Easter Island a part of some archipelago now submerged, or has it survived through the millennia in its present shape?

The archipelago theory is contradicted by the *ahu*, or stone images, still standing erect on the island's shores. With their West Mediterranean headdresses and facial features so unlike those of the native inhabitants, the history of these giant sculptures present a complete mystery to modern science. They were obviously dragged over great distances to their present sites from the quarries where they were carved. In fact, many of them are only half-finished as if the work was abandoned abruptly—stopped by some natural catastrophe or foreign invasion. But the identity of the workmen who carved the statues, when and why this was done—these riddles are still to be solved.

Neither the beginning nor the end of Easter Island civilization can be explained by geological changes. Easter Island is neither a portion of a submerged continent or archipelago, nor was its culture destroyed by volcanic eruptions. Some scientists even think that this culture is so markedly different that it should not be lumped together with the rest of Polynesia, even though the natives there were Polynesians when the island was discovered.

Alfred Metraux, of the Bernice P. Bishop Museum at Honolulu, argues quite convincingly that Easter Island belongs in Polynesia's cultural orbit, but doubts remain. Also, the parallels between the civilizations of Easter Island and the Indians of South America—a theory eloquently defended by Thor Heyerdahl, author of *Kon-Tiki*—seem based on wishful thinking, although the discovery of two Easter Island spearheads in a grave in Chile is indisputable.

Probably the natives of Easter Island left the insular world of central Polynesia before the various Polynesian civilizations had reached their peak; and, since there was no wood of any quantity on Easter Island, the natives could no longer build boats and their seafaring skill died out. Wood on Easter Island was as rare as jade in New Zealand, which is why Easter Islanders made all their precious ornaments from wood.

The only native inventions of Easter Island seem to have been the wooden tablets and the giant statues. But the "speaking timber" has lost its voice and the giant heads stand mute and immobile. And the waves breaking against the shores of the lonely island have no memories, and thus guard its secrets well.

COCONUT AND SHELLFISH CIVILIZATION

Scarcely any other race in the world has posed as many problems for scholars as the Melanesians. The origins of the natives of this island world have never been definitely ascertained: it may even be that they hold the key to the mystery of the totem. This much is certain: Melanesia is a veritable anthropologist's El Dorado.

THE Pacific is not the vast, empty expanse of water it often seems in our school atlases. Actually it contains over 10,000 islands—perhaps as many as 30,000, for they are virtually uncountable. For example, the name of the Tuamotu group in the language of its inhabitants means "cloud of islands," for it is made up of some eighty major islands and innumerable small islands. There are a great many such island clusters in the Pacific, the Philippine group alone comprising 7,000 islets. Even a single atoll, or ring of coral surrounding a central lagoon, actually may be composed of a multitude of small islands dotting the sea.

The Pacific is larger in expanse than all the continents in the world put together, and its island archipelagos are myriad. The culture and history of its peoples—Indonesians, Melanesians, Micronesians or Polynesians—are as unfathomable as the ocean surrounding their insular homes.

A hundred million years ago the west coast of the Pacific basin may have stretched from Japan to New Zealand via the Carolines and the Fiji Islands. If so, epoch after epoch has been swallowed by the waters of the Pacific. The known history of Oceania goes back many thousands of years.

Oceania's first inhabitants were the Pygmoids; a short, dark-skinned, kinky-haired race that was driven out of Asia perhaps during the last ice age. At that time the waters separating the world's land masses were much narrower than today, for vast layers of polar ice kept the oceans small and the land masses large. When the ice age ended about 14,000 years ago, low-lying lands were inundated and mountain-tops turned into islands on which human beings probably took refuge. But we know little or nothing about what actually happened; and the

Pygmoid migrations into what is now Oceania might have taken several thousand years.

Later, from the region of Malaya, a second tide of humanity swept down to New Guinea and Australia. These Oceanic forerunners were unlike the Pygmoids: their skin was lighter, their hair was straight instead of kinky, and their bodies were hairy. They belonged to a very ancient white stock, the Ainoids, similar to the racial type still found on Hokkaido, Japan's most northerly island. These white people spread across western Oceania and intermingled with the Pygmoids, but the latter must have been much more vigorous, prolific and hardy than the Ainoids, for the light-skinned race was absorbed by the dark people.

The Ainoids were followed by other peoples, known as Veddids: hunters and food gatherers of the pre-agricultural period who had a physical resemblance to the Veddas, or aborigines of southern India. It is possible that Mongoloid peoples also joined them. But in the island world we call Melanesia the Negroid element is far more pronounced than that of the other three races. In fact, Melanesia derives its name from the Greek, meaning "black islands."

At least three races (probably many more), three or more civilizations, and at least three or more languages mingled here, only to split up into a variety of different dialects, customs and social organizations. For while the huge maritime area of Polynesia shows considerable cultural and racial uniformity—its natives looking almost like brown-skinned Europeans—the far more ancient Melanesian realm is a composite of hundreds of different civilizations. There is nothing that can be called typical about the world bounded by New Caledonia, New Guinea and the Fiji Islands; indeed there is no other ancient cultural region so heterogeneous as Melanesia, whose dark-skinned, woolly-headed, mysterious inhabitants have defied all scientific attempts to classify them.

Even today the islands of Melanesia show clear traces of the many migrations. In the course of centuries, later arrivals settled along the coasts and drove the earlier aborigines, the Negroid peoples, into the forests, mountains and marshes of the interior. Water is often a better link than land, and while the coastal peoples of the various islands developed cultural ties, the communities in the interior became more and more isolated, with the result that, today, we can clearly distinguish between the coastal native and the bush native. Papuan languages are spoken almost exclusively in the interior of certain large islands, notably New Guinea and New Britain. But the numerous Papuan dialects are so different that very often the inhabitants of one village can scarcely communicate with their immediate neighbors.

The coastal inhabitants, on the other hand, speak Melanesian. Bougainville in the Solomons, for instance, has about 35,000 native inhabitants. Eight different linguistic Papuan groups are spoken in the interior and in the south, while Melanesian-speaking peoples—representing seven linguistic groups—live in the coastal and northern regions. This island illustrates perfectly the difficulty of classifying the various races in the area—linguistic and cultural assimiliation. Not too long ago, Melanesian-speaking natives from the Shortland Islands landed on the east coast of Bougainville, and are now "Melanesianizing" the Papuan communities of the interior. Conversely, the coastal Melanesians of the southwest are gradually abandoning their unhealthy seaside villages and migrating inland, where they are becoming thoroughly "Papuanized," not only linguistically but culturally as well. To complicate Bougainville's picture still further: the inhabitants of the southern coastal part of the island are tall, while those of the mountainous interior are almost pygmylike. Yet, all natives of Bougainville—whether they speak Melanesian or Papuan, whether they live on the coast or inland, whether they are tall or short—are coal-black, blacker even than the Papuan-speaking peoples in the most inaccessible parts of New Guinea. As for New Guinea, a part of its native population is predominantly Melanesian, and the remainder belongs to the Negroid, Papuan race.

There are only five island groups that are indisputably Melanesian: 1) parts of the Solomons, 2) the Santa Cruz group, 3) the New Hebrides and the Banks Islands, 4) New Caledonia and the Loyalty Islands, and 5) the Fiji Islands.

Melanesia may be the ethnologist's nightmare, but it is also a living museum for the study of primitive forms of civilization, for no other region in the world contains so many diverse cultures within so small a radius. Many features are common to all of them: chipped stone tools, the bow and arrow, spears, pig-raising, domesticated dogs, chickens, fishing, agriculture and the gathering of wild plants, animism, secret male societies with their initiation rites, the importance of masks and, finally, exogamy.

Here we come to the most interesting aspect of Melanesian civilization. Exogamy, which means marriage to someone outside of one's own strictly defined community, is the most interesting aspect of Melanesian civilization. There is no more important law among Melanesians than the division of all people into two or more clans; and the fact that no marriage may ever take place within the same clan. A person who belongs to clan A must marry someone belonging to clan B or C. It is not clear how or when these clans were formed, but they exist and that is the law.

Membership in a particular clan is passed on to children by their mothers so that sons and daughters thus belong to the same clan. Neither geographical location nor tribal custom have any bearing on the consummation of a marriage—only the mother's membership in a particular clan. Nor do these clans have any political or tribal significance. An identical system prevails in Australia. To a Melanesian, all the women of his generation are either taboo, like sisters, or are potential brides; to a Melanesian woman, all men are either taboo, like brothers, or are potential suitors.

In Melanesia, as in Australia, this type of individual marriage probably originated in some ancient system of collective marriage, where all women of one group were the communal wives of all men in the other. Scholars have tried to base this assumption on the fact that in certain Melanesian languages the words for "mother," "spouse," "wife," and "child" exist only in the plural. From this they have deduced that there must have been a time when all life was dominated by group relationships and individual relationships were unknown. Except for New Caledonia, marriage within one's own clan among Melanesians has always been inconceivable, and punishable by death. The same penalty applies to a man who seduces a girl of his own clan.

Another custom that is common to all Melanesians is totemism. This extremely complex phenomenon is also found in the civilizations of Australia and America. The word "totem" derives from *ototeman*, which in the related Ojibway and Algonquin languages of the American Indian literally means "one's brother-sister-relative." Totemism is a person's belief in his blood relationship to some animal, plant, star, or flash of lightning, and the totem is the common link between a related group of people. Especially in Melanesia this active belief in totemism has produced artistic creations of haunting grandeur, tribal rites, taboos (sacred prohibitions), and important festivals at which the totemistic union is renewed. Entire families and clans are named after specific animals and plants. Some clans in New Caledonia, for instance, regard the large gecko as sacrosanct and inviolable, while others believe the same of the sparrow hawk, lizard or shark.

In complete contrast to the brighter and light-hearted world of Polynesia, Melanesia was always a gloomy place governed by witchcraft and magic. Not too long ago head-hunting and cannibalism existed on certain Melanesian islands, and it was common practice to kill off the aged and infirm. It has also been established that the natives of many Melanesian islands exterminated the seriously ill. When questioned about their motives, the natives invariably replied that they did it because they felt "sorry" for them.

Related languages were spoken on the various Melanesian islands, but on the whole there was an utter linguistic confusion. For example, there are about twenty different languages and dialects in New Caledonia alone. The native languages had no written grammar, yet the Melanesians seldom make grammatical errors in their speech. This meticulous use of the language is based on their deep realization that words have power: every Melanesian knows that the spoken word possesses a dangerous magic that must not be annoyed, a force that takes vengeance if it is abused.

The Melanesian world is remarkable. The long breakers of the Pacific beat forever against the beaches, and coral reefs gleam where race after race has dreamed away the millennia. Volcanoes erupt from small islets, myriads of tiny marine creatures labor to build reefs and atolls, tidal waves rear up and engulf entire islands, moonbeams glitter at night upon the water, and the Milky Way, 700,000 light-years distant, is reflected in the ocean below.

Frenchmen, Englishmen and Americans are now arousing the South Sea Islands from their slumber. Western scholars are laboriously investigating these coconut and shellfish civilizations and their ancient taboos, trying to discover why these Oceanians found so much happiness in a life of unending tranquillity.

THE ARRIVAL OF THE INDIANS

They left Asia and wandered across the Bering Strait, reaching North America 37,000, or more, years ago.

SOME four million years ago a strange creature stood up and walked on only two of his limbs instead of the four he had. After a while, seeing that he no longer needed the extra two limbs for locomotion, he gradually developed them for keeping himself alive and supplied with food. Later—we do not know when—something entirely new happened in the creature's head, something totally unknown before—the development of a mind and a will, and the concept of work. The two limbs were now free for other things, but they could accomplish so much more if they gripped a stone—a tool. *Homo sapiens* discovered the use of fire and learned how to speak. He also learned how to use his eyes differently from any other creature in the world.

There is scarcely a more interesting science than the one investigating the traces of the first humans on earth, the traces of that mysterious creature called man. A fragment of chipped stone, the remains of a slaughtered animal, or just the ashes of a fire—those are the clues that give anthropology its endless fascination.

The oldest human remains anthropologists have so far brought to light—protected by layers of stone and earth for all of 500,000 years—were found in Europe, Asia, Africa and Java. "I was here. I lived here"—this is man's eerie greetings across hundreds of thousands of years from Java (Pithecanthropus), Peking (Sinanthropus), Rhodesia or Germany's Neanderthal. Yet in America no human bones, skulls, tools or, for that matter, no traces of any human habitation have been found which are definitely more than 37,000 years old by radio-carbon dating (these were discovered in Texas)—although one or two recent "finds" may be somewhat more ancient and are still being investigated.

The advanced culture of the Mayas and Aztecs in Central America, and of the Incas in Peru, might point to the assumption that such peaks of human cultural achievement could only have been the culmination of a very long time, and that men must have lived in the same area for many thousand years before they attained such heights. But this is a fallacy, for we have seen that the advanced civilizations of Mesopotamia and the Nile and Indus valleys took only a few thousand years to reach their greatest heights, and then lapsed into oblivion. The earliest known advance culture in South America, the Chavin civilization, flourished in northern Peru roughly from 100 A.D. to 500 A.D. The oldest Mayan city, Uaxactun in Guatemala, was founded in the first quarter-century after Christ. There is nothing so far found in North, Central or South America that would point to an advanced civilization prior to 700 ± 200 B.C., as shown by present radio-carbon dating. But when did the Indians, as we have called them since Columbus—when did the people we now regard as the aborigines of the two Americas—arrive there?

North America has yielded many arrowheads and spear points obviously made by human hands and discovered near the fossils of animals now extinct; such as camels, early species of bison, giant sloths and forerunners of the American horse. The dates of the finds were deduced by means of radioactivity and from the age of the geological deposit containing these fossils and objects.

The oldest finds belong to the Folsom, Sandia and Cochise cultures, although the latter word is misleading and should perhaps read "industries" or "crafts." The Folsom industry derives its name from the site of its initial discovery in 1926, in the northeast of New Mexico, but Folsom articles were also found on the eastern slopes of the Rocky Mountains in Alberta, Canada, and scattered over almost all North America east of the Rockies. The Sandia objects were discovered in a cave in the Sandia Mountains of New Mexico, and the Cochise articles were found in southern Arizona together with fossils of bisons, mammoths, camels and early species of horses. These industries are 10,000, 15,000 or, at most, 20,000 years old. Indigenous to North America, they were established by people who knew fire, as traces of charcoal prove, and were nomads and hunters.

We know that human beings have probably lived in North America for approximately 37,000 years, and that they did not develop any advanced civilizations in Central America, and later in Peru, until many thousand years later. We do not know what these people did following their arrival in North America, although excavations in the Ventana Cave in southern Arizona throw some light on the matter. The lowest layer contained tools of the Folsom type (7932 ± 350 B.C., radio-carbon); the next, articles of the Cochise type; this was followed by vessels made as late as 1400 A.D., and the top layer contained fragments of almost modern Indian manufacture. Can it be that the Ventana Cave was continuously occupied for over 10,000 years?

Whole libraries are devoted to the origins of the American Indians. There is the Atlantis theory; the legend of Mu, the submerged Pacific continent; there is the resemblance between Indians and Egyptians, and the theories about the Phoenician or Sumerian ancestry of the Indians. There are people who place their origin in Polynesia, and others who think the Indians came from Melanesia; there is Heyerdahl and his *Kon-Tiki*, and there are a thousand other speculations. Whenever a Polynesian boat is dug up on the South American coast, or an Inca god resembles one of the stone colossi on Easter Island, or a tool is found both in Polynesia and the Americas, all it means is that at one time a man, or a group of men, were stranded on American shores. But anthropology cannot work with such flimsy evidence, for only a comprehensive picture made up of many cultural and anthropological similarities can be at all conclusive.

Which leaves us with the question: where did the Indians, the first inhabitants of North and South America, come from?

All groups of North and South American Indians have certain physical characteristics in common: blue-black hair either curly or straight, skin ranging from yellow-brown to red-brown tones, dark eyes, prominent cheekbones, large features. Other characteristics tend to vary enormously between one tribe and another: flat and aquiline noses, thick and thin lips, small and tall bodies.

As for their color of skin, eyes and hair, the Indians resemble the Mongolian race, and their cheekbones also point to an Asiatic origin. Hence we may say that the American Indians are more closely related to the Mongoloid than to the white or Negroid races. But this does not mean that they are Chinese. They, and other east Asiatic peoples, are probably descended from a pre-Mongolian type that branched off into several races.

Nobody who has seen Indians in North and South America can fail to recognize that the skull formation and build of the various tribes are so diverse that it is almost impossible to describe them in terms of a single Indian race. America has probably experienced many migrations across the Bering Strait, separated by thousands of years. Totally different Asiatic peoples wandered into North America, and turned into equally different American Indian peoples. And all the tools and hunting weapons would indicate that North America was the first to be settled, for here is where the earliest finds—belonging to the Folsom, Sandia and Cochise types—were made.

Since the continents of America and Asia almost meet at the Bering

Strait in the far north, it must be assumed that the first crossing from Asia into America was made right here. We know that a land bridge did exist between the Tchuktchen Peninsula and Alaska for thousands of years, so that mammals wandered back and forth between northern Asia and North America.

Further proof for subsequent migrations from Asia to America is offered by the various products of Asiatic culture which America adopted: ceramics with ornamental bands, the crossbow, moccasins, clothes cut from a pattern rather than draped, ivory carving and countless legends. Everything else—agriculture and architecture, pottery, the art of writing, the calendar and, above all, a numerical system—the Indians invented themselves. In fact the Mayan numerical system of Central America was a masterpiece of native ingenuity never matched by Central Europe. The Europeans inherited a clumsy system from the Romans, superseded only in comparatively recent times by the Arabic numerals now in use.

Europe's gifts to the American Indians include Christianity, alcohol, Cortez and Pizarro, smallpox and the Indian reservation. In return, the Indians have given us potatoes, chocolate, rubber, tobacco, peanuts, pineapples, tomatoes, corn, manioc, quinine and cocaine.

When Columbus discovered America he truly lifted our world from its hinges—the ancient hinges of the Mediterranean.

WE SHALL NEVER KNOW

TIAHUANACU

Professor Posnansky's theories about Tiahuanacu seem in the realm of fantasy. He regarded these ruins as "the cradle of American man."

FOR nearly 3,600 miles along the western length of South America run the Andes, a continental system of mountain ranges 100 to 400 miles wide and containing fifty-seven peaks over 17,000 feet in height.

It was in these highlands that the greatest South American Indian civilizations flourished, and it is here that the largest surviving Indian populations are found. It is here—especially in the mountainous highlands of Bolivia and Peru and in the deserts on the west coast of Peru—that the civilizations of the American Indian races lie buried, cities of the dead that even in another 1,000 years will not be fully unearthed.

While in North America man left traces of his life that are about 37,000 radio-carbon years old, in South America there is very little evidence of prehistoric man any older than approximately 5,000 years. While a type of nomadic huntsman roamed in southern Patagonia before that time, all we know about him is that he was a landlubber who did not know the canoe. But in 1921 a human skull, which certainly appeared to be much older than 5,000 years, was discovered at Punin, Ecuador, and the Peruvian coast has yielded large mounds of shells, left there by some unidentified race of fisherfolk who lived at a time when agriculture was not practiced in that region.

Our knowledge of human *history* in South America only goes back to the Inca dynasty. Our knowledge of *man*, however, goes back to the primitive hunters near the Straits of Magellan (6688 ± 450 B.C., radio carbon). In Peru, after early undated lithic cultures, we have an economy based on seafood gathering and a few domesticated plants of about 2348 ± 330 B.C., radio carbon. Maize, cotton, pottery, and complex weaving came in around 1200-1000 B.C.

Peru and Bolivia are a single archaeological realm made up of civilizations superimposed upon each other many times over. Race after race has lived and built here, only to vanish in the end. Nevertheless, certain characteristics are common to them all. The archaeological past of the people of Peru and Bolivia knew neither the wheel

COLOMBIA
Quito
Manta
ECUADOR
Salinas
Is. PINA
Tumbes
P
AMAZON
Cajamarca
E
BRAZIL
Trujillo
Chavin de Huantar
RIMAC
R
Lima
Pachacamac
Macchu Picchu
Huari
BOLIVIA
Ica
Cuzco
ICA
Nasca
U
LAKE
TITICACA
La Paz
Tiahuanacu
PACIFIC
0
550 MILES
CHILE

nor the bow, and they had no script in the sense that we know it. They had no burial urns. They worked the land and planted corn, beans, potatoes, cassava, quinoa, tobacco and oca. They chewed a mixture of coca leaves and lime. They bred llamas and alpacas, wove cloth from wool and cotton, carved wood and made baskets.

Over the centuries, these Peruvian and Bolivian civilizations developed almost independently from other regions in the two Americas. Both Peru and Bolivia were so highly organized that they could counter major foreign influences and invasions—until the Spaniards arrived. What the first Spanish conquistadors learned from the Incas who were still living was a rather sketchy history of thirteen generations of royal dynasty. Apparently the Inca empire's greatest expansion began one hundred and twenty-three years prior to the Spanish conquest.

It was not until 1936 that scholars started to form an idea of the most important pre-Inca civilizations or, rather, art forms, which flourished roughly between 700 B.C. and 500 A.D. Notable among these is the Chavin style, named after a site known as Chavin de Huantár in Peru. Products of this Chavin culture have been found everywhere in the northern mountains and coastal regions of Peru.

This culture should be more accurately called a world of the imagination, because the centuries spanning this whole civilization and its people are, archaeologically speaking, still hidden from us. The art works of the Chavin style express a fanatical religious belief. The men who wielded the wooden molds and chisels were filled with a passionate strength and fanaticism bordering on an almost frightening grandeur. Although it belongs to the earliest advanced American civilization we know—the earliest period within reach of current archaeological research—at its very beginning this style attained amazing heights which were never surpassed and could only lead to decline. One of the ruins at Chavin de Huantár—the so-called *castillo*, or fortress—not only contained halls, galleries, ramps, stairways and corridors, but also had a system of ventilation which to this day supplies its deepest chambers with fresh air. The castillo was probably the seat of a religious cult.

Between 200 and 300 years after the Chavin period came the Nasca style, which flowered in the Inca and Nasca valleys on the south Peruvian coast and ended around 750 A.D. Burial places found in these valleys contained grave shafts varying in depth from 20 inches to 14½ feet. Some of the skulls displayed artificial deformities: an elongated head was apparently fashionable during the Nasca period. Pots decorated with painted birds, mice, llamas, bats, fishes, human heads, fruits and unidentified monsters exhibit a range of up to eleven colors. Cloth was woven from wool and cotton, and often dyed in a variety of colors. In fact, L. M. O'Neale announced in 1939 that she had distinguished no less than a hundred and ninety different shades. But the only metal known in the Nasca period seems to have been gold.

One of the least explored, though relatively late, civilizations belongs to Tiahuanacu, even though its ruins speak an eloquent language. During the centuries the Tiahuanacu people apparently expanded their rule northward over the whole of Peru, dominating the coast as far as Trujillo and perhaps even reaching Ecuador. But now all that remains is the ruins of Tiahuanacu in the Bolivian mountains, some thirteen miles south of Lake Titicaca. They cover an area measuring about 1,100 by 500 yards, and their building materials—sandstone and basalt—must have been brought to the site from at least three miles away. The transportation of stone blocks weighing up to 100 tons cannot be done without organized mass labor, and the dressing and placing of the massive blocks must have required great technical ability and armies of laborers.

According to the findings of archaeologists, the Tiahuanacu civilization is divided into four periods: an early period, a second period, a classical period, and finally a period of decline. Its largest building, the Acapana, resembles a natural hill which at one time must have looked like a step pyramid. A water reservoir and several buildings probably were on its summit, and the whole edifice may have been a kind of fortress or place of refuge. Northwest of the Acapana are the ruins of another massive construction known as the Calasasaya. Exactly what this building was used for remains a mystery, but it contains the famous Gate of the Sun and many stone statutes. West of the Calasasaya stand the ruins of the *palacio*, which was at one time enclosed by a double ring of earthwork; east of it is a semi-subterranean building. In addition to the main group of ruins there is the platform of Puma Puncu, constructed out of sandstone and lava blocks, all of them smashed and shifted from their original positions.

Wendel C. Bennett, Professor of Anthropology at Yale University, warns us against assuming that every building, stone and relief at Tiahuanacu, symbolically speaking, reveals an early knowledge of astronomy. The harsh climate of the mountains makes him conclude that ancient life was about the same as it is today. Llamas and alpacas were bred here 1,400 years ago (and still are), as the finds of bones would indicate. Nor was the expanse of arable land any larger or more fertile than it is in our own day. During its classical period Tiahuanacu may have been a sort of Mecca visited by pilgrims, but Professor Bennett does not believe that any great civilization could have subsisted up there—nature simply would not have permitted it.

Bennett's view is important, for just as Troy found its Schliemann, so another scholar, Arthur Posnansky, devoted his whole life to the ruins of Tiahuanacu. In 1914 he completed his monumental work on early Andean civilization, *Tiahuanacu, the Cradle of American Man.* Professor Posnansky was an engineer and anthropologist, and held many academic degrees, and his work is so diverse and romantic, so imaginative and breath-taking in its theories and conclusions, that Bennett's more recent and cautiously conservative verdict is rather saddening, in spite of the fact that Bennett is probably right.

Posnansky literally appropriated Tiahuanacu about fifty years ago, and in his ardent zeal for his subject enlisted the services of astronomy, geology, meteorology, archaeology—in short, every conceivable science—to prove his theory that Tiahuanacu was the cradle of American man. Dig in the plateaus of Tibet, the Andes and Mexico, he claimed, and you will trace the story of man, from his earliest beginnings to the splendor of his advanced civilizations in an almost uninterrupted chain of evolution. And it was such an evolutionary scale, ranging from primitive cave dweller to astronomer, which Posnansky thought he had discovered in Tiahuanacu. He even disputes Eurasia's claim to the site of the Garden of Eden and man's first appearance. He believed that American man existed earlier—a theory which is demonstrably wrong.

The cultural development of a large race would have never been possible in the High Andes under today's climatic conditions. So, after extensive studies of geomorphology (the science of geological evolution), Posnansky concluded that the plateaus of the Andes were at one time neither as high nor as cold as they are now. He pointed out that even during the Pliocene age (ten million years before the beginning of our chronology), and from then on time and again, the earth has undergone structural changes. Posnansky quoted many geological examples for such changes in altitude before he finally got around to Tiahuanacu and Titicaca, the lake that deserted the Pacific and landed in the clouds. Look at its fauna, he says, and you will see that Lake Titicaca is merely an elevated oceanic trough. Here in the waters of Lake Titicaca we find the Pacific hippocampus, or sea horse, as well as various species of ocean shellfish, but many of the ocean creatures died off after exchanging their tropical environment for the much colder temperatures prevailing at 12,000 feet.

According to Posnansky, Tiahuanacu was once a vast political and religious metropolis whose influence extended over the whole South American continent, a center of death cults and vast burial grounds. Then a terrible catastrophe happened, a tremendous earthquake that caused the waters of Lake Titicaca to overflow and volcanoes to erupt. Thirty miles from Calasasaya there is indeed a volcano called Cayappia, and Posnansky established that the ruined site was covered with layers of lava. He attributes the downfall of this cradle of American civilization to a combination of natural catastrophes and civil wars. The early Tiahuanacu people, he says, apparently suffered their first great disaster about 500 A.D., and in 900 A.D. Tiahuanacu perished for the second time, but by now its civilization extended across all of Peru, and an epoch marked by many small and flourishing principalities was followed by the age of the Incas. The Incas' name for the ruins of Tiahuanacu was "City of the Dead," and Tiahuanacu had indeed been dead and ruined for hundreds of years when the Inca Empire was at the height of its power.

Cieza de León, who visited the ruins of Tiahuanacu in 1540, saw large portions of its magnificent buildings still in their original form. Since then the unique sun temple has been gradually demolished and its stones have been carried off for building houses and bridges in La Paz and other places. Whole carloads of such stones were shipped to La Paz, and only a few years ago modern architects were helping nature and her catastrophes to eradicate the ancient glories of Tiahuanacu. In 1904, an archaeologist introduced still another element of confusion into these ruins by pointlessly removing stones and walls for the sole purpose of finding gold.

There are many theories as to the identity of the people who built Tiahuanacu. The site is now in a part of Bolivia inhabited by the Aymara or Colla Indians, and the present Colla race is undoubtedly descended from the people who lived up in the Andes 1,500 or 2,000 years ago. They lived there when the Incas first arrived, and archaeological research reveals that Tiahuanacu's civilization flourished until almost that time. The Colla priests and rulers must certainly have belonged to a special caste, for they were excellent astronomers who had preserved the experiences and traditions of many centuries. The sun temple of Calasasaya proves that they must have had a wide knowledge of astronomy: they knew how to determine the seasons, dates and equinoxes, and were familiar with "the sun's revolving around the earth." They evidently believed that the earth was the center of the universe and that Tiahuanacu was the center of the world.

When they reached the peak of their knowledge, they set about building the sun temple. Completely ignorant of theodolites, sextants or astronomical calendars, they achieved remarkable results with the most primitive methods. They devised a stone calendar which divided the year accurately into twelve months, and the months into thirty days. September marked not only the beginning of spring (we are in the southern hemisphere, of course), but also the beginning of the year.

Posnansky went so far as to classify the various ornamental symbols decorating the sculptures and ceramics found at the ruined site, as well as on the frieze of the Gate of the Sun. The Tiahuanacu people had no script, but they had obviously evolved certain religious and astronomical ideograms. There was a stairway symbol signifying earth or sky, and there were ideograms representing fish, snakes, winged eyes, mouths, ears, quarters of the moon, arms, legs, tails, wings, crowns, scepters, human faces and many other things.

The Gate of the Sun is the most remarkable among all the buildings of the splendid third Tiahuanacu period. It remains an unsolved mystery, however, why virtually none of the buildings around Lake Titicaca were ever completed. Even today archaeologists confirm that every one of them was abandoned at one stage or another. The trouble with Posnansky's theories is that, even at the site of Tiahuanacu, the style of architecture is not very old, and older, but by no means primitive, remains have been found repeatedly under Tiahuanacu itself. Furthermore, as far as present research can tell, Tiahuanacu did not "fall" between 800-900 A.D. At about 700 A.D., the art of Tiahuanacu started to spread so rapidly and with such obliteration of older art forms that military conquest is implied, at least for Peru. At about 1200 A.D. the Tiahuanacu styles disappeared, at least on the Peruvian coast, completely and suddenly. Older styles were revived or new ones were evolved. There can be no scientifically acceptable basis for the fascinating but impossible theories of Posnansky.

At 12,000 feet the air is thin, and fast walking, mountain climbing or any form of physical exertion becomes difficult. One wonders how the Colla people or their slaves managed to transport the massive stone blocks which they used as building materials. How could this Gate of the Sun, which consists of a single stone, ever have been transported to its site? And yet it is formed from a rock which is unobtainable anywhere within a wide radius of Tiahuanacu: a hard trachytic stone not used for any other idol or sculpture of that period.

The most sacred place in the sun temple had been set aside for this gate, and although the monolith was not discovered on this particular site, everything had been prepared to erect it there. In fact, the gate was found lying overturned a short distance away. It was not until 1908 that the gate was erected again on the spot where it was found.

In view of its sacred character, the priests of Tiahuanacu presumably arranged that the huge stone block for their Gate of the Sun should be brought from far away, from some remote place which played an important role in their mythology. But if Tiahuanacu then stood at its present altitude of 12,000 feet, we are left to wonder how the immense monolith could have been trundled across hundreds of miles and up into the soaring heights of the Andes when even with our latest techniques such a task would present almost insuperable difficulties.

We shall never know the answer.

IN RAREFIED AIR—12,000 FEET UP

THE INCAS

The Inca kings knew that a people with too much leisure may start to criticize its government.

WE do not know the reason for Tiahuanacu's downfall. We only know that this civilization, with its most magnificent buildings centered around Lake Titicaca, enjoyed a second great period of great brilliancy between 900 and 1200 A.D., and then sank into oblivion. Tiahuanacu's many uncompleted buildings may indicate that its end was sudden and unexpected. As for the pre-Tiahuanacu civilizations of Peru and Bolivia—Chavin, Nasca, Mochica and the rest—they had long since passed their prime and relapsed into the dust. The short duration of all these civilizations is in sharp contrast to the splendor of their artistic and architectural achievements. The artists and craftsmen of Peru and Bolivia lived as wretchedly as though they expected to die on the morrow, yet they built for eternity.

The history of art in ancient Peru impresses us as having regressed from its earliest and brilliant beginnings. Chavin, Nasca and Mochica are a magnificent start, Tiahuanacu an indifferent intermediate stage, and the Inca period, artistically speaking, mediocre. But in the field of architecture Tiahuanacu represents only a modest level of attainment when compared with the vast drainage installations, fair-sized towns and almost unique road systems of the Incas.

Who were the Incas and precisely what was Inca civilization?

The Incas and their civilization appeared suddenly out of nowhere about 1000 A.D. By the time Pizarro landed at Tumbez in 1532, by the time Atahualpa had been taken prisoner and Cuzco conquered, the Incas were finished. Inca civilization thus lasted only about 300 years.

The word "Inca" was actually the king's title. These Inca rulers were of Quechua stock and spoke the Quechua language. About 1000 A.D. they lived somewhere near Cuzco, which we may call the cradle of the Incas. From there they proceeded, in the course of five centuries, to carve out a mighty empire which ultimately extended for well over 2,000 miles from northern Ecuador through Peru and Bolivia to central Chile.

Before these conquests started, the whole Andes area had been split into countless political entities, and almost every valley and range of hills had its own language. In order to eliminate this confusion, the Incas declared that Quechua, their own tongue, was now the official language of the empire, and when the Spaniards landed they soon found that Quechua was the only language which could get them anywhere. They therefore did not trouble to learn the numerous local languages and dialects, and dealt with the natives exclusively in Quechua. For this reason, dozens of ancient Indian languages have died out.

This, then, was the over-all picture: the Incas were a small elite, the rulers, governors and military leaders of an immense region inhabited by native Indians. They were foreign overlords, aristocrats, men with paler skins than their Indian subjects, men with greater knowledge and wisdom, men with their own language not always understood by their subjects. Since the people of the Andes had no script, all we know about Inca history is what Spanish authors of the sixteenth century tell us. These Spaniards learned something of the Incas' ancient traditions by word of mouth, obtaining such information from narrative poems and statistical entries which were preserved in the form of knotted strings. Apart from these records, the Incas had professional "history memorizers," learned men who carried their "reference libraries" in their heads.

In this fashion the Incas handed down legends about their gods and heroes, the origin of mankind and the adventures of their ancestors. Their dynasty began with Manco Capac and ended with the third ruler after the luckless Atahualpa. This dynasty, which comprised thirteen kings, was founded about 1200 A.D., but its members are all somewhat shadowy figures, until the year 1438 saw the coronation of a man called Pachacutec. Thus our real knowledge of Inca history boils down to about 100 years. Like all other histories it is a very human tale, a chronicle of wars, conquests, the enslavement of prisoners, subjugation, tribute, tyranny and disputes over the right of succession. But it is also the story of brilliant colonization and competent government.

The genius of the Incas lay less in the arts than in political organization. In a sense, they were the Romans of South America. They built a magnificent network of roads running through the rugged highlands and coastal deserts of their empire—roads which Alexander von Humboldt described as being among the most remarkable and useful projects ever conceived by human ingenuity. And, as a matter of fact, their total road network was more impressive and enduring than that of any other ancient people, including the Romans. For 400 years—that is to say, until Napoleon repaired the Roman roads of Europe—the royal highways of the Incas were the only really good road system in the world. While the cultural communications of Europe were bogged down for centuries in mud and sand, Inca couriers were trotting comfortably across the ridges of the Andes carrying dispatches between Tiahuanacu and Cuzco, almost 1,250 miles apart. Such a postal service took only a week to cover this distance, even though the Incas lacked one of the most important devices known to man: the wheel. That is why they built the longest footpaths in the world, although the word "paths" is an understatement. These were straight roads built on solid foundations, designed for mass traffic and traversed by llama caravans, columns of troops, messengers, and royalty borne in sedan chairs on the sturdy shoulders of porters as they swayed over plaited suspension bridges and through tunnels from one range of hills to the next.

The Incas built a coastal road from 23 to 26 feet wide and running for some 750 miles through deserts which rarely saw a real downpour—only once every seven to twenty-five years. This road was bordered by a waist-high wall, a smaller South American version of the Great Wall of China. In constructing this desert road as well as their mountain roads, the Inca engineers followed a simple plan: they were never deterred by any natural obstacle, but kept on building as the crow flies. If a marsh lay in their path, they built interminable stone causeways across it—so solid that they are still in use today. They spanned lakes with pontoons and precipices with daringly constructed bridges. One such bridge survived until July 20, 1714, when it collapsed, hurling a group of travelers down into the waters of the Apurimac. When they reached cliffs, the Incas either tunneled beneath them or cut flights of steps leading conveniently over their ridges.

These phenomenal results were achieved at heights of 12,000 feet, where breathing is difficult, the sun beats down mercilessly and the snow-capped peaks reflect a blinding glare. Here were the Incas' suspension bridges, supported by fiber cables nearly six inches thick. Halfway between heaven and earth these swinging miracles, plaited structures paved with matting, made excellent walking.

At intervals varying between four and eleven miles along this road system (nearly 2,000 miles in all) stood rest houses, where meals could be obtained. There were also post stations for the royal express messengers, who were conditioned to traveling rapidly in the rarefied atmosphere. The messengers operated in relays, each of which could cover a hundred and fifty miles a day.

It is a truism that where there's a will, there's a way. But where there's a way, it may also inspire a will: it was the very convenience of the Incas' magnificent road system which tempted the Spaniards to conquer the whole country. Thus the Incas' greatest achievement also determined the speed of their own destruction. And Spanish ox carts, horses' hoofs and lack of maintenance eventually led to the deterioration of the roads.

The Incas were not only brilliant road builders, but also created the most important horticultural center of their time. They cultivated over forty different kinds of plants and grains, and made use of and expanded the remarkable pre-Inca irrigation systems. Their principal source of meat was the guinea pig. These small creatures were kept right in the kitchen, and reared on scraps and greens. They were clean, and their meat was tender and contained enough fat. The Incas abominated dog meat, but regarded duck as a great delicacy.

The Incas built their dwellings from stone, usually in groups of six, with a central courtyard and a surrounding wall. Their armies, however, lived in tents. Only high officials appointed by the king sat on chairs, while the king himself sat on a throne.

Ruins of massive stone palaces and sun temples are found throughout the former Inca empire. And while Inca cities were seldom fortified, they usually possessed a place of refuge on some nearby hill. The chief city of Cuzco, for example, consisted of a center of worship—where noblemen, priests and government officials lived with their servants—and a ring of small villages surrounding this center.

The average Inca's wardrobe consisted of a sleeveless shirt, a second, larger poncho-shirt for cold weather, a cloth apron and leather sandals with woolen laces. Women wore a long gown tied about the waist with a sash, and a cape of the kind worn by the men. Their skirts reached down to their ankles, and their hair was held back by a headband. All Inca aristocrats wore huge cylindrical ear-pegs frequently made of gold and about two inches in diameter, and the ears of the boys were pierced when they were only fourteen years old. Women, on the other hand, never wore ear ornaments. The Incas, like most other Indians, used to paint their faces for war, mourning and religious ceremonies.

The Incas worked with many metals, including copper, gold, silver, tin and lead. All gold, which was panned, belonged to the state. But rather than gold, it was the number of wives that served as an indication of a man's wealth and authority. Indeed, the king often rewarded deserving subjects by giving them several wives.

The king of the Incas was an absolute ruler by divine right. He traced his ancestry back to the sun, and was worshiped as a deity throughout his lifetime. He demanded slavish obedience from his subjects, and his power was limited only by the dangers of revolution.

There was little private property in the empire, the nation being organized along collectivist lines. All agricultural land was owned by various clans whose heads parceled it out among the individual members. These latter farmed their allotments for a year, at the end of which time the land was distributed afresh. The whole system was a form of state communism ruled by an autocratic god-king. There were various government departments: for public highways, game and hunting, forestry and the like. The design and construction of towns, temples and bridges was handled by a corps of engineers, while official statisticians kept track of crops, births and able-bodied laborers. A certain number of children were trained by the state to become soldiers, another group was earmarked for the priesthood, and yet another for the civil service.

In addition to his principal wife, every ruler had a large harem. From the time of Topa Inca, however, the king's principal wife was invariably his own sister. The morganatic wives won special privileges according to the number of children they bore, and these children were responsible for the upkeep of the royal palace and tended to the ruler's personal needs. (There were about 40,000 persons of direct royal descent still living at the time of the conquest.) The perpetuation of the "royal ideology" was in the hands of a group of learned men, who might be described as state propagandists and from whose ranks the highest administrative officials were drawn. The king usually selected the most able of his principal wife's sons to succeed him, and trained him for his future task.

The royal throne took the form of a low chair only eight inches high, carved from redwood and covered with fine rugs. Here sat the man whose titles were: "Only Inca," "Son of the Sun," "Friend of the Poor." His principal wife was known not only as "Queen" but also as "Mother." Each king built a new palace at Cuzco during his reign (his predecessor's palace automatically became a temple of remembrance) where anyone who wished to see the king had to take off his sandals and place a burden on his back before entering the royal presence. Normally the king sat behind a folding screen, and it was regarded as a great honor if he showed a visitor his face.

The empire was continuously combed for talented men to fill the many thousands of state offices in the royal dictatorship. Anyone with the slightest talent for leadership or administrative ability might suddenly find himself transplanted to a remote village where he had to govern according to official ideology.

All taxes were paid either in work or in kind, for there was no money. Taxpayers had to cultivate lands whose yield went into the treasuries of the Inca government and priesthood. A certain part of their lives was spent in compulsory military service, public works, or personal attendance on the king and the nobility. The building of the fortress of Sacsahuaman, a unique undertaking and probably the most impressive of all the Inca's structures, required a labor force of 30,000 men. In the mines, the usual term of compulsory labor was only one month.

One of the king's greatest worries was to find enough work to keep his labor corps continually occupied. Huayna Capac, for instance, ordered a hill to be moved from one site to another merely because temporarily he could think of nothing better, and he knew that a people with too much leisure may start to criticize its government. Revolutions broke out even when the subjects were well occupied, so the kings shuddered to think what would happen if they allowed their people any prolonged spells of idleness.

Inca women were just as strictly supervised as men, all girls being classified at the age of ten by royal officials who visited each village in turn. Girls of striking beauty were raised by the government, while the rest had to stay home and marry taxpayers.

Marriages were organized on a communal basis under the auspices of the state. On a given day all the young men and girls of marriageable age were lined up in two rows, and in the name of the king some official allotted one girl to each young man. The girls who were selected for government service entered state schools where they learned spinning, weaving, cooking and other domestic duties. When they were released, some of them served in the sun temples (which entailed perpetual chastity as "Virgins of the Sun"), and others became the wives of deserving noblemen and warriors. Still others became royal concubines who also prepared the king's meals and made his clothes.

LAW, ORDER AND POETRY

I blossomed, my season came, I withered, and I died.
From an Inca poem translated by
Sarmiento de Gamboa

NO matter how great the power of the Inca kings, no matter how vast their empire, stretching from the highland plateaus of the Andes down to the Pacific, no matter how absolute their authority—they still lived in constant dread of revolution. After all, there has never yet been a tyrant or dictator who could sleep peacefully at night.

The Inca kings did not consider the conquest of new territories as a great achievement. Universal military conscription combined with the feeling of the individual that he was merely the king's property and without a will of his own, convinced these kings that they could lead their armies to the ends of the earth, if need be. Conquering new lands was easy, but holding them was quite another matter.

So the Incas adopted a policy which has only recently been revived. The seething unrest prevailing in each newly conquered country was rendered impotent by mass deportations. No sooner had a new province been occupied than it was depopulated. Thousands upon thousands of Indians, burdened with their most treasured possessions and accompanied by their wives and children, trudged along the magnificent straight roads. And as these displaced persons of the Inca period trudged along in endless columns, they met the future occupants of their former homes headed in the opposite direction unhappy, also, that they had to leave their own land.

These settlers were called *mitimaes*, and as the new owners of the foreign villages and fields they never did get along with the few original inhabitants who were allowed to stay behind. This antagonism was understandable because hereditary rights were regarded as superior to the royal edict on which the new colonizers based their claims. The new arrivals were expected by the state to set the defeated peoples a good example. They spread the Quechua language and established Inca garrisons. And as a mark of royal gratitude, they were permitted to appropriate as many local girls as they wished.

By the time the Spaniards conquered Peru, the colonists in many provinces outnumbered the original inhabitants, and a large proportion of them originally came from the royal capital, Cuzco. By sending out his own people, the Inca ruler provided himself with a reliable source of inside information on all these foreign elements; by ordering innumerable deportees to come to his own realm, he was able to study their languages, customs and character as it were in his own back yard.

The Inca empire was the New World's first authentic melting pot, a vast, whirling vortex of many different nationalities. And if the Spaniards—the "white gods"—had not arrived on the scene when they did, the Inca people would undoubtedly have been fused into one homogeneous nation, with Quechua as its universal language.

In the empire, work and leisure were apportioned by the state, which saw to it that no one starved, no one froze and also that no one had too good a time. There was no such thing as unemployment, and even women between fifty and eighty had to continue working. Men who were so old that their teeth fell out were still considered fit for feeding and breeding guinea pigs. These men were known as "old sleepers," or *puñucrucus*, probably because they went about their duties in a perpetual doze.

The Indian author Felipe Huaman Poma de Ayala reports that the Incas allowed absolutely no one to be idle, not even the infirm, the blind, the deaf, or the feeble-minded. As the state was constantly concerned with increasing its manpower, not even men with serious disabilities were allowed to remain celibate. However, since a healthy young woman would probably not want to marry an aged cripple, the state decreed that the lame should marry the lame, the blind man the blind woman, an aged stutterer or deaf-mute a woman with the same affliction.

Trade was a state monopoly, but taxpayers held village markets where they bartered their surplus goods and such articles from the state workshops as the government had allotted them. Money did not exist, but since the government demanded taxes only in the form of manual labor and some produce, a hard-working family could amass a considerable quantity of goods and chattels. Precious metals and objects of artistic or ornamental value, however, belonged exclusively to the king and the aristocracy. These magnificent roads were reserved for government traffic only and taxpayers were not permitted to use them, both to avoid traffic congestion and because travel would interrupt their labors.

Law enforcement in the Inca empire was "strict but just," with every misdemeanor regarded as a crime against the state or the king. Punishments included public reprimand, removal from office, banishment to the coca plantations, torture and death. One method of torture—a sort of divine ordeal—was the *hiwaya*, a punishment which involved dropping a very heavy stone onto the condemned man's back—which usually killed him. Capital punishment took the form of hanging by the feet, stoning, hurling from a cliff, or beatings on the head. Cruel as these methods may seem, it must be remembered that the death sentence could be passed only by government officials of the highest rank or by the Inca himself. There was, however, no right of appeal. In Cuzco, the capital, there existed a subterranean cave inhabited by jaguars, pumas, bears, foxes, poisonous snakes and scorpions; and reserved for those guilty of high treason. But despite the manifest dangers of staying in that cave, these men still had a slender chance of escape, and if they managed to stay alive for two days they were released and even honored as the protégés of the gods.

The Inca penal code distinguished between nobles and commoners, for the dignity of the aristocracy had to be upheld at all costs. A convicted nobleman might merely lose his office, for instance, whereas a commoner would be subjected to torture for the same offense. In cases of adultery, however, the positions were reversed. A commoner was merely whipped, but if the adulterous wife belonged to the nobility, both guilty parties were executed. All in all the incidence of crime seems to have been low in the Inca empire, partly no doubt because the penalties were so severe, and partly because the state provided for all material needs, thus eliminating the necessity for many offenses.

The Inca army had neither cavalry nor siege engines, and its soldiers were dressed in heavy woolen shirts and quilted cotton armor. They carried shields, slings for hurling stones, clubs and spears, and marched into battle with their helmets on, shouting abuse at their foes, beating drums, and blowing clay trumpets and bone flutes. The king had his personal bodyguard known as the "Big Ears" (no doubt so named because of their big ear pegs), all of whom were recruited from the aristocracy.

Prisoners of war were ordinarily brought to Cuzco, where some of them were sacrificed to the gods in gratitude. In the sun temple the king strode across the prisoners' necks. Particularly dangerous enemies, however, were thrown into the snake pit. Noblemen who distinguished themselves in battle were granted the right to carry an umbrella or sit on a chair.

If there is much that seems harsh or inhuman about the Incas, we must remember that most men who lived in the past five thousand years shared about the same degree of good and evil. They all had their troubles, they all wept, laughed and made love. Garcilaso de la Vega remembers a little poem he heard from Indians of the Inca period: "This is the place where you shall sleep. At midnight . . . I shall come to you." Sarmiento de Gamboa translated this dramatic little song: "I was born like a lily in the garden. Like a lily I was reared. I blossomed, my season came, I withered, and I died." The little love message and the observations on the impermanence of life both prove that the Incas were capable of deep and tender feelings. And they believed in one supreme god—Viracocha, the creator of all supernatural beings. He was portrayed as a man, and his statues were worshiped in the Inca temples. One such statue stood in Cuzco, made of solid gold. Viracocha commanded all divine power, but he delegated the administration of his cosmos to numerous supernatural beings. Tradition has it that when Viracocha saw what he had created, he traveled through the land and taught the people many good things. He performed miracles, eventually reached Manta in Ecuador, and there found his own Sea of Galilee, in the Pacific Ocean, walking dryshod out on its waves.

The creator's most important assistants were the sun, moon, thunder, stars, earth and sea, but the Incas also worshiped various places and objects. The Spaniards found *huacas*, or shrines wherever they went.

The state made regular sacrifices to Viracocha the creator, the holy ceremony being conducted by priests. Human sacrifice was very rare, and then only in times of greatest crisis such as plague, famine, or when the Inca king was ill. The usual sacrifices were animals.

After death people either lived together with the sun in the higher world—where there was plenty of food and drink—or they went as sinners to a place of hell in the center of the earth—where it was cold, and stones took the place of bread. It was only the nobles who had no alternative: they always went to heaven, even if they had been the greatest scoundrels on earth. The dead were buried either in natural rock graves or in man-made stone graves with their entrances blocked by boulders.

So there the departed Incas sat, their knees drawn up, waiting for their souls to go to heaven—or for their tombs to be ransacked by Spanish conquistadors. The nobles attained both ends; they were guaranteed to go to heaven, but the same heaven sent them the Spaniards—who plundered their graves.

ATAHUALPA TUMBLED INTO THE DUST

It was the will of Heaven.

Pizarro to Inca Atahualpa after the massacre at Cajamarca on November 16, 1532

IT was a great moment in a great year—the year when Emperor Charles V was born—a pinnacle in the history of Western civilization 1,500 years after the birth of Christ. It was the golden age of the renaissance, the rebirth of classical antiquity. Michelangelo built St. Peter's, Albrecht Dürer carved his great Passion, Copernicus realized that the world was only one planet among other planets, Raphael joyously painted his most beautiful Madonnas. Luther, Calvin and Zwingli reformed the Church. Leonardo da Vinci's genius seemed to embrace in its elemental greatness all the artistic and creative impulses of his age. Paracelsus was physician to the people of those times, Hans Sachs their shoemaker and poet. Jakob Fugger financed papal elections, wars and the largest merchant fleet of his world. But the greatest explorers and conquerors of the day were three sons of Spain and a Genoese; men who added to the wealth of the Western world a whole new continent and the largest of all the oceans.

It is inspiring to visualize the world as it was at the turn of the sixteenth century. Columbus was then forty-five, his hair snow-white. He had suffered interminable hardships, and now the discoverer of America was lying in chains at Cadiz, hearing again and again in his dreams the voice of Rodrigo de Triana who cried: "Land, land!" Cortez, destined to conquer Mexico, was fifteen at that time; Balboa, who later discovered the Pacific, was but twenty-five. And Pizarro, who was to seize Peru, the gold mine of the world, and who saw the legendary Inca brought before him in chains, was as yet poor and unknown.

Pizarro was born in Trujillo, a town in the Spanish province of Estremadura. He was an illegitimate child whose mother was too poor to raise him. Not knowing where to turn, she laid him down outside the door of a church. But no one took him inside, and he should have died right there and then. But in an age of so many marvels, when the Madonna's portraits looked down on suffering humanity and occasionally worked miracles, the child survived—nourished, so the Spaniards used to say, by nature. No one taught him to read or write, and he grew up to be a swineherd.

Pizarro was thirty-nine before he reached America, in the service of a bold *caballero* named Morales who founded a New World settlement. When next we meet him, he is at Balboa's side in Darien, south of the isthmus of Panama, after an arduous trek over the mountains. One of the first Europeans to set eyes on the Pacific Ocean, Pizarro feverishly set about gathering gold and pearls from the islands off the coast of Panama. It was loot, loot, and more loot—not for his own benefit, but for Morales, his knight and master.

Pizarro recognized early that the New World spelled hardship, danger and privation, and that his plans and dreams could materialize only by dint of incredible energy and foresight. And age was creeping up on him. He was fifty years old; soon it would be too late. He owned an unhealthy strip of land, but he had no gold. He had become renowned for his courage but he was still dogged by his past; the stigma of his illegitimacy. In despair, he offered a little golden shoe to the Madonna, and wept.

Cortez had just conquered all Mexico. Had Pizarro not seen with his own eyes how Balboa waded into the surf and claimed the vast Pacific for the king of Castile? Had not Magellan imperiously given the ocean its name, "el Mar Pacifico"? Was not Andagoya continually talking about his journey south, about a fabulous Inca empire and the gold which lay beyond the slopes of the Cordilleras? And all this was happening while he, Pizarro, was sitting wretchedly on the isthmus of Panama, devoured by mosquitoes! All he needed was money, ships, a royal charter and some stout hearts, and there might still be a chance of making a name for himself—a name that would resound in the streets of Seville and be spoken with awe.

Finally Pizarro found the men he needed. Diego de Almagro was a foundling like himself, a career soldier sprung from nowhere, with no noble family to back him up. The third member of the party was Hernando de Luque, a curious blend of schoolmaster and priest who also administered the public funds in the small settlement of Darien, in eastern Panama. The three men first financed the conquest of Nicaragua and then reinvested their gains in the conquest of Peru.

By a quirk of history, one of his ships was built by Balboa, who had died five years before. The caravel was still lying unrigged in Panama harbor. Pizarro weighed anchor in the middle of November, 1524, and sailing southward, eventually steered his small ship into the mouth of the Biru, the river from which, according to Zarate's reports in his *Conquista del Peru,* the Spaniards derived the name of Peru. Pizarro and his companions undertook repeated marches into the unknown Inca empire. Sailing on and on down the coast, they landed at several points and pushed into the Peruvian interior, armed only with swords, for they were not yet equipped with muskets. They returned to Panama, only to sail southward again, solemnly pledging their lives to their bold undertaking and swearing to kill one another if they ever became disloyal. Before their departure Father Luque administered Holy Communion to his companions, dividing the consecrated bread into three pieces so that each received a third of it. Standing before an altar in Panama, the three men divided an unknown empire among themselves, an empire of which they virtually knew nothing.

Whenever the conquistadors entered a Peruvian village the Indians fled, leaving their gold behind in their homes. The Spaniards' appetite for gold kept growing, while the Peruvians, as if driven by some instinct of self-destruction, time and again received the dangerous white visitors in a submissive and friendly fashion, showing them remarkable courtesy and hospitality. In one place, which they named Santa Cruz, the Spaniards were met by an Indian princess who came on board their ship of her own free will. Pizarro gave her a few worthless presents, and she begged him and his companions to return the visit, which they did. Once ashore, they found that the princess had erected arcades of sweeping branches intertwined with scented flowers and sweet-smelling shrubs. For the first time Pizarro enjoyed Peruvian cooking and tasted unfamiliar fruits of strange and exotic colors. He heard strange music and watched graceful young girls performing dances which no European had ever seen before. He showed his gratitude by presenting the princess with a Castilian flag, and asking her to fly it as a token of submission to the ruler of his country—and she obeyed him!

In the summer of 1528 Pizarro, now a man of about fifty-eight, returned to Seville, only to be thrown into prison on a charge of debt lodged by a scholar named Enciso. Pizarro had been away from his native land for twenty years. He left it as a poor and unknown adventurer; now he had returned triumphant, only to be clapped into jail.

Pizarro's name, however, soon came to the ears of the emperor, who summoned him to his court and inspected the astonishing exhibits which Pizarro had brought back with him. He saw the first llama ever to be brought to Europe, and examined various articles made of gold and silver—and before their metallic luster his interest grew by leaps and bounds.

Unfortunately for Pizarro, the court received another visit at this time, also from a man returned from the New World: Hernando Cortez, the conqueror of Mexico, who, with a whole new empire to lay at His Imperial Majesty's feet, put Pizarro's achievements in the shade. Cortez had reached the end of his career, Pizarro was just at the beginning of his own. Still, Pizarro enjoyed a measure of success. He was granted the rank and title of governor and commander-in-chief of the new country, with a salary for life of 725,000 maravedis. In his capacity as a kind of viceroy he had to maintain a civil service and an army, and was empowered to erect fortifications. Meanwhile, Pizarro's associate Almagro was appointed as commander of a fortress, with the rank of hidalgo and a salary of 300,000 maravedis. The Reverend Father Luque got the bishopric of Tumbez and the title "Protector of the Peruvian Indians." One of Pizarro's navigators was made "Grand Pilot of the South Sea," and one of his cannoneers became commander-in-chief of the artillery. The rest of his men became hidalgos and caballeros. When it came to titles and offices, Emperor Charles was not stingy with the Spanish conquerors of a land that did not belong to him. Money, however, was another matter, and it is said that Pizarro had considerable difficulty in raising enough funds to put out to sea again, and that he was helped in his predicament by Cortez, who was enormously wealthy.

So, in 1532, Pizarro returned to the land of the Incas once more, this time equipped with muskets, the miraculous new weapons against which the South American continent proved to be powerless.

At the head of his small band of adventurers, Pizarro thrust far inland toward the Incas' main encampment. Ordering his men to treat the natives well, he led his little troop on a daring and successful march into the heart of the country. Then Inca Atahualpa sent them an envoy, who welcomed them in the name of his master and invited them to visit the king in his mountain camp. Pizarro asked the courier to inform his master that he, Pizarro, had been sent by a mighty prince who lived across the sea. Furthermore, he wished to pay his respects to the Inca and would shortly present himself in person. The natives offered no resistance, and immediately took to their heels whenever Pizarro appeared. Then Pizarro's brother Hernando caught a Peruvian, stretched him on the rack, and forced from his prisoner the confession that the Inca's invitation had been merely a ruse to trap the foreigners.

Pizarro's column wound its way up steep roads, along the crest of the

Andes, meeting on the way several more messengers from Inca Atahualpa who brought their master's greetings and the information that he was near the town of Cajamarca, famous for its warm springs. The Spaniards marched on, gazing in surprise at the carefully tended fields of a country inhabited by civilized, cleanly dressed people, among them many graceful women. At last the conquistadors made out a large number of white tents, unlike anything they had seen in Indian country before.

Pizarro marched into Cajamarca on November 15, 1532. Between the town and the royal encampment was a meadow which alone now separated Pizarro from the legendary Inca.

After a period of anxious waiting, Atahualpa informed the Spanish commander that he would visit him accompanied by his armed warriors. When he was about half a mile from the town, however, he came to a halt, then pitched camp while he hesitated. Could he trust Pizarro?

Shortly before sundown, borne in a sedan chair on the shoulders of his vassals, Atahualpa entered the town on a throne made of solid gold, his throat adorned by a necklace of huge emeralds. When the king finally swayed into the main square, there was not a Spaniard in sight. Then Father Vicente de Valverde, a Dominican monk, appeared. Stepping up to the Inca with a Bible in one hand and a crucifix in the other, he announced that he was there on the orders of his commander, to convert the Inca to the true faith. The monk gave a detailed account of the Creation, the Fall, the Redemption by Jesus Christ, the Crucifixion, the Ascension, and the Trinity. Furthermore, he called upon Atahualpa to pay tribute to Emperor Charles V.

The Inca's reply, as translated by Felipillo the interpreter, was short and to the point: "The Christians believe in three gods and one god. That makes four. I will pay tribute to no man for I am greater than any other prince in the world. The Pope must be a madman if he gives away countries that do not belong to him. I shall not change my faith. You say yourselves that your god was killed by the very people he created. My god is alive. He lives in heaven. He looks down on his children below. What gives you the right to put forward all these claims?"

The monk pointed silently to the Bible in his hand. Atahualpa snatched it, leafed through it for a moment, and then threw it into the dust. "Tell your companions that I call them to account. I demand satisfaction for all the injustices they have committed in my country."

The monk picked up the Bible and went off to tell Pizarro what had happened. "I give you absolution," he cried to the assembled Spaniards. "Strike now!" At a signal from Pizarro, the Spaniards poured out of their places of concealment into the square, hurling themselves into the midst of the Indian ranks and firing their guns. A dreadful carnage ensued.

Atahualpa stared in horror as most of the Indians were cut down, and blood flowed like water. Strange weapons flashed before his eyes like lightning, and their thunder rolled about him. His sedan chair swayed on the shoulders of his loyal men like a ship about to founder. Some of the nobles who were supporting it dropped down, and Atahualpa was thrown clear. He tumbled into the dust, and his badge of royalty, the *borla*, was immediately torn from his forehead.

The greatest ruler in South America, the most mighty Inca, the god-king, was Pizarro's prisoner. Not one Spanish life had been lost.

"Such are the fortunes of war," the Inca said. Pizarro told the king to be of good cheer, and lodged him in a large building where he was closely guarded but allowed to retain some of his Indian servants.

"It was the will of heaven," Pizarro told Atahualpa, "because you insulted the Holy Book. Take courage and trust me. We Spaniards are a magnanimous people. We have come to this land to spread the religion of Jesus Christ. No wonder we are victorious."

All courage left the Peruvians once their king had been captured. Men, women, many servants, and the wives of the Inca all gathered around the prison which housed their king. They seemed to be under a spell, and gazed in wonder at the "white gods." The Inca's power had been smashed, and with it his people's belief in miracles. Pizarro would be murdered, but right now victory had dropped into the Spaniards' laps like a ripe fruit. It was as if some sinister power had chained the Inca and his people and driven them inexorably to their own destruction.

THEIR GODS WERE ALWAYS HUNGRY

THE MAYAS

The Mayas were the "Greeks" of Central America, just as the Aztecs may be compared with the Romans. At the time of Cortez's conquest of Mexico there were scholars who could read the Mayan script. But today no one can decipher it.

MEXICO forms the northern half of the most interesting land bridge in the world, the bridge connecting the two Americas. Deserts and mountains account for two thirds of Mexico's area, and the few clouds that occasionally drift across the blue Mexican sky bring very little rain—scarcely enough for a mere tenth of the thirsty land.

When Cortez, the conqueror of Mexico, stood before Charles V, the Spanish king asked him: "What is this Mexico of yours like?" Without speaking, Cortez gave his king the best description anyone could give. He crumpled up a piece of paper and threw it onto the king's desk.

Today, Mexico is both poor and rich, happy and unhappy. It is the greatest silver-producing country in the world, but the Mexicans know only too well that what fate gives them with one hand it takes away with the other. This is how it has always been in this country, and the Mexicans are a race with several thousand years of practice in the art of patience.

Ignorance, superstition and cruelty have ruled over Mexico for thousands of years, and her highlands have always been at the mercy of chance that never gave them any real security. Nothing is certain in Mexico. "Who knows?" the Mexicans say. "*Quién sabe?*" Anyone who seeks to fathom the culture, civilization or spirit of this country will find himself in ever-increasing darkness the deeper he probes. Even the American historian Prescott, who studied the history of ancient Mexico as thoroughly as that of the Incas in Peru, had to admit that he found it extremely difficult to deal with a territory where fact and fiction were so inextricably interwoven. Anyone trying to establish cultural or historical facts about Mexico will be confronted at every turn by the aura of myth, legend and poetry that emanates from

all her ruins, picture writings and archaeological sites. And, indeed, Mexico provides no sure guide for her history, culture or the origins of her peoples, and no solid frame of reference for her past.

There were documents here, to be sure, but we can no longer decipher them. When Cortez landed, the peoples of Mexico had already developed an advanced civilization, and several thousand years of history and culture were behind them.

Several thousand years of history and culture! What does that mean? We recognize the first clear outlines of a fully developed civilization in southern and eastern Mexico about 300 A.D.: that of the Mayas. We know that most of their culture developed outside of Mexico, but of this evolutionary period we know little save that it must have lasted for several hundred, if not a thousand, years.

The Mayan civilization reached its zenith roughly about 600 A.D. Then something extraordinary happened: sometime after 800 A.D. this amazing civilization simply dissolved. The master-builders stopped building, the sculptors stopped modeling, the painters laid down their brushes, and one by one all the great ceremonial centers were abandoned.

The reason remains a mystery to this day. Perhaps the Mayas collapsed as a result of pressure from the barbarians, such as the Aztecs; perhaps the proletariat rose against the priests and rulers; perhaps most of the population died off in epidemics; perhaps famine broke out. Perhaps, perhaps . . .

At all events, Mayan civilization collapsed to the level of the formative period within the span of a century. The large towns lay deserted, abandoned by their inhabitants.

Their inhabitants? This question, too, cannot be answered clearly. All we know is that the ruling caste vanished, never to return, leaving behind their massive temples, palaces, everything they had laboriously built and created over the centuries. But there is always someone who stays behind. In this particular instance it may have been the peasants or the slaves. These remaining inhabitants probably supported themselves by agriculture and hunting in the local forests. But all planning and building ceased.

The very early Mayan settlements were in the highlands of Guatemala. Thence they spread to found such great cities as Uaxactun (Guatemala), Palenque (Chiapas), and Copán (Honduras). But these were abandoned, part of the people wandered back into the Guatemalan highlands, where they founded several small states, and later, the Quiché "empire," while others moved into the northern part of the Yucatan Peninsula where they established another Mayan "empire." However, this was only a pale reflection of the ancient glories of the past, and never achieved the splendor of the older culture.

Why is it that we know anything at all about Mayan history?

First, there are the Mayan manuscripts, texts which were written by Mayan priests long before the conquest of Mexico. Unfortunately the Spaniards regarded them as works of the devil, and the Spanish bishop Landa organized a great book burning in the plaza at Merida so that only three manuscripts survive. One of them is—or was—in Dresden; this is the most interesting since it dates from the best period of the new Mayan cities. The second, of later date, is in Paris, while the third is in Madrid. However, none of these three texts contains anything more than ritual or calendar entries. All religious, medical and mathematical treatises went up in smoke when the Spaniards decided to exorcise the devil. As it is, the hieroglyphs in the three surviving texts present us with more problems than information.

There are also some notes made shortly after the Spanish conquest. These suffer from the disadvantage that Mayan civilization was already on the decline when they were compiled. Then there are also a few historical dates taken down by the Mayas in hieroglyphics before the conquest, and later translated into Spanish.

Finally, we still have the stone pillars, the steles which the Mayas erected in their towns every five, ten and twenty years, and into which they carved records of the most important events. But the Mayas' chronological system differed from our own, so it is not easy to relate the individual events to our own chronology.

Among the first Spanish ecclesiastics in Yucatan were one or two erudite men who learned to read the Mayan script, and some of them could even write it. In the course of time, however, this art was lost, and today even the foremost experts of ancient Americana are groping in the dark. On the other hand, the Mayan numerical system, one of place-value notation, has been deciphered. It was vigesimal (counting by twenties) and numbers are placed in vertical, not horizontal, lines. Dots were used for numbers one to four, and a bar for five. Nine is a bar and five dots. There were two further symbols for 20 and 0, and the completion symbol commonly used was a shell. With great ingenuity, the Mayas used these simple devices to express figures up to several millions. The bottom figure was taken at its face value, while the second, fourth and all succeeding rows represented 20 times the value of the row immediately beneath. The third row, however, was only 18 times the value of the second. With this numerical system the Mayas were superior to every other race in America, and even to the Greeks and Romans.

The Mayas also must have been far advanced in the art of writing, as the delicate characters of their manuscripts prove. And even if we cannot decipher them, they do tell us what objects, buildings and sculptures belonged to the Mayan cultural orbit, for the Mayas adorned not only their buildings and sculptures with inscriptions but their pottery as well.

The Mayas had compact skulls and receding brows, a physical trait they greatly prized and even tried to produce artificially. Their skin was a pale cinnamon color, and they were of small stature, although sturdy and well-built. A squint was regarded as a mark of great beauty. Young girls and mature women alike adorned their faces with red, white and black paint.

From his birth to the hour of his death, the Maya was ruled by religious cults and a large and powerful priesthood. He worshiped everything that seemed powerful and mysterious in nature, and above the center of every city towered step pyramids with temples on their flat summits.

If one were to arrange the gods of all pagan races in the order of their performance, the Mayan gods would come very nearly last, followed only by the Aztec gods. The Mayan gods were always hungry and did so little to earn their keep that their worshipers finally came to grief, at a phenomenal cost in human lives. For a long time, scholars believed that human sacrifices were unknown in the ancient Mayan empire. But even a highly developed civilization needs food and drink, especially drink, and since the Mayas believed that they could humor their sun, earth and rain gods by offering them blood, they resorted to human sacrifices. The victims were stretched out on a sacrificial block high up on the pyramid's altar, and their hearts torn out. The lifeless bodies were thrown over the edge and tumbled all the way down the pyramid's steps to the ground, where the waiting multitude cut them up. Each individual took a piece home, where it was boiled and eaten.

There is a certain place at Piedras Negras where this procedure is illustrated in stone. Victims included captured warriors, children and young girls. Whenever harvest prospects looked bad or a prolonged drought set in, the Mayas hastily sacrificed a few virgins. Virgins were also used for placating wells and springs, and the Maya threw them in unceremoniously and with little regard for the insanitary consequences. It should not be forgotten that these races had only the most rudimentary notions of medicine and hygiene, even if they did know how to extract quinine from tree bark and were familiar with certain medicinal herbs. A thorn in the foot could lead to fatal blood poisoning, there was no way of fighting epidemic diseases, and Mayan babies were put on an adult diet after a short period of breast-feeding. It seems a miracle that these races survived for as many centuries as they did, and that their descendants are still living today.

The Mayas knew nothing about dairy farming or draught animals and they were probably even ignorant of the wheel, although there is some evidence to the contrary. All loads had to be carried on men's backs. At the same time, the Mayas were good at arithmetic and had an astonishingly accurate calendar, in which 405 lunar revolutions corresponded to 11,960 days. Modern astronomical computations put it at 11,959.888 days—or only 0.112 of a day less than the Mayan estimate. Mayan astronomers also worked out a Venusian calendar based on a remarkably accurate knowledge of the movement of the planet Venus. There are only very small discrepancies between their figures and our own, which is all the more impressive when we remember that the Mayas made their observations of Venus with the naked eye.

We know the Mayan hieroglyphics for sky, earth, sun, moon, Venus, Mars and Jupiter as we know the symbols for the 20 days of their month and the 18 months of their year. We also know the symbols for certain gods and ceremonies and for the four cardinal points of the compass. It is interesting to note in passing that modern astronomy has helped us decipher some of the hieroglyphs because Mayan calculations and modern science agree in this particular field.

The Mayas were brilliant craftsmen, wore clothes and sandals, manufactured cotton fabrics and even velvet, and were talented artists. Their architectural achievements—their temples and their town planning—were remarkable. Temples and houses, public square, ball courts, whole networks of streets, palaces with numerous rooms, corridors and open courtyards—all these can be identified in the ruins still standing today.

One of the riddles which has not yet been solved is the so-called Stele B at Copán. Above the head of the god portrayed upon it are the distinct outlines of elephants' heads complete with trunks. They are Indian elephants, with mahouts perched on their necks. Experts of ancient Americana have been racking their brains as to how the Maya got hold of them, since elephants had been extinct in America for thousands of years prior to Mayan culture.

Where did it all come from—the Mayas' urge to shape things the way they did, the inspiration that created ornamental and pictorial styles reminiscent of Egypt, India, and even of Buddhist art? Was it some cultural flotsam that drifted thousands of miles across the Indian Ocean and the Pacific?

We do not know—and we never shall.

THEY TOO BUILT PYRAMIDS

THE TEOTIHUACÁNS AND TOLTECS

Are you weary? It is only granted us to venture into the world for a short time, just long enough for us to become warm...

Translated from the Aztec by Sahagun

FATHER Bernhardino de Sahagun was a pious monk who looked like a Spanish aristocrat and had the energy that overcomes all obstacles. He came to Mexico as a missionary in 1529, arriving only eight years after the capture of Mexico City, a time when the history of the Aztecs was still vividly remembered, and also that of the Toltecs, though this regime broke up 350 years before the conquest.

Any attempt to convert the natives of a newly conquered land to the Christian faith required a knowledge of the very core of their nature, their thoughts, legends, religion and their gods. Realizing this, Father Sahagun spent years listening to everything the Aztec sages could tell him. To write it all down would have taken a hundred years, so Sahagun ordered his young pupils to take down the Aztec accounts in their native Ilahuatl and sometimes phonetically in Latin characters. They worked night and day, and it was their parchment transcripts which formed the basis of the famous historical work roughly translated into Spanish by Father Sahagun himself.

Anyone who turns the pages of this so-called first-hand source will feel closer to the vanished empires of the Aztecs and Toltecs. He will find descriptions of their gods, their attire and their peculiarities. He will find lists of annual festivals. He will meet Quetzalcoatl, king and god, the mysterious prince and prophet of the Toltecs. He will read about the abodes of the dead, the education of boys, about sorcerers, conjurers, soothsayers and, finally, about the conquest of Mexico City by the Spaniards.

Four advanced civilizations have existed in Mexico: Teotihuacán, Mayan, Toltec and Aztec.

The builders of Teotihuacán are an unknown people. We do not even know the original name of this metropolis belonging at one time to a great civilization. Teotihuacán is probably a late Aztec translation of the city's former name, but we have no idea what language it was translated from, for even the language of its inhabitants remains a closed book.

The beginnings of Teotihuacán civilization coincide roughly with the birth of Christ and its end with that of the Classic Maya period about 900 A.D. The ruins of their city, remarkable both in design and planning, are still visible today some twenty-two miles northeast of Mexico City.

Teotihuacán was laid out along both sides of a wide, straight avenue which had some religious significance, called today "The Road of the Dead." At the northern end of the road was the moon pyramid; to the east lay the much larger sun pyramid. Also to the east, but at the southern end, stood the temple of the god Quetzalcoatl, the so-called *ciudadela*, or fortress, although *ciudadela* may be a misnomer since there probably were no fortifications at that time.

This massive quadrangular complex is actually a pyramid city composed of the bases of two large pyramid temples and fifteen smaller temples. The whole sanctuary was erected in honor of the wind god, who controlled the rain clouds and, consequently, fertility. Magnificent stone sculptures were found here which included heads of snakes and other grotesque portrayals supposedly representing the rain god Tlaloc. All these sculptures were at one time painted in glowing colors. The massive friezes, galleries, flights of steps and platforms are the products of an art which, while it may not have achieved the greatest finesse, nevertheless has a powerful and dramatic impact. Here we find Quetzalcoatl himself, carved in stone: he is always represented as a plumed serpent, and the eyes staring out of his head were once carved from obsidian.

The sun pyramid has a ground plan of roughly the same area as that of the largest Egyptian pyramid: the pyramid of Cheops. On the other hand, it is only half as large in height and cubic content. The Teotihuacáns' sun pyramid is filled with earth (the smaller Mayan pyramids are filled with rubble) and covered with dressed stone. The sun pyramid shows that there were some unrivaled architects among the people of Teotihuacán. The most striking feature about it was its bulk and apparent height, for it conveyed an amazing impression of infinite height and space. The sun pyramid consisted of five steps, or terraces, linked by a series of very steep stairways. On the height was the sun god's shrine, where the communication between priests and gods took place.

Archaeologists have driven shafts into the heart of the sun pyramid, but they found no vaults or tunnels such as are common in the Egyptian pyramids. The whole construction is solid earth throughout. Nor was it erected one section at a time and then enlarged, like so many other pyramids, but built in one operation according to a preconceived plan. The grandeur of the Teotihuacáns' project proves that they were inspired by deep religious faith. The same is true for all ancient cultures, including the pyramid building of Egypt's III Dynasty: the most monumental and impressive structures were always the result of religious fanaticism.

The surface of the Teotihuacán pyramid was faced with stone, but the rubble of old mud bricks and earth in the interior proved a valuable source of information to archaeologists. It contained clay vessels, clay figurines and stone implements, all of which must have belonged to the ancient Teotihuacáns, or their predecessors, and indicate that the pyramid was built at a relatively early stage in Teotihuacán civilization. Exactly when this happened we shall never know. All we know is that this artificial mountain was erected for a god, and not as the tomb for some king.

The excavations at the moon pyramid are less extensive, although its location at the end of today's "Road of the Dead" points to its greater importance even if its cubic content is only one fourth as large.

Even today, many of the buildings in Teotihuacán have not been excavated. But several of the ruins have subterranean chambers with extremely fine frescoes. The walls of one group of buildings—called the Temple of Agriculture—are decorated with frescoes of various fruits and flowers which used to be sacrificed to the gods; but we do not know what they really looked like because all we have is drawings made at a later date. Excavation has also revealed fragments of walls which probably belonged to dwellings of priests. Such huts as may have stood on the outskirts of this religious metropolis would have fallen into ruin long ago during the past 1,400 years.

It is impossible to determine the exact beginning and end of Teotihuacán civilization, although it is thought that the sun pyramid was built in the second century A.D. and that Teotihuacán was destroyed in 856 A.D. We do know that the city mets its end in a terrible conflagration.

Why has the date been set at 856?

The year 856 A.D. is traditionally regarded in Central America as the date of the founding of a city which was excavated only in 1940, and whose discovery marks one of the greatest archaeological triumphs of our time. This was the city of Tollan, which succeeded Teotihuacán as a cultural metropolis. Its ruins are near modern Tula in the Mexican state of Hidalgo, some sixty miles north of Mexico City. Tollan was founded by people who stormed out of the northern deserts. These "barbarians," who spoke the Nahuatl language, were, like the Chichimeces, linguistically related to the Aztecs. These Toltecs received their name from Tollan, their capital, and their sole connection with the old city of Teotihuacán was that they conquered it. Excavations at Tollan soon showed that the legendary capital of the Toltecs, the metropolis whose former existence was still remembered all over Central America, had at last been discovered.

The ruins of Tollan have by no means been fully unearthed. So far we have found pyramids, palaces, stone colossi, portrayals of human beings in stone reliefs and murals, and friezes depicting jaguars and eagles devouring human hearts. An efficient drainage system was dug up here, but perhaps the most interesting finds were two arenas designed for ball games. Ball games in courts originated in South America and were used by the Maya of the Classic Period.

The principal importance of Tollan lay in the fact that it was the residence of the Toltecs' priest-king Quetzalcoatl. Quetzal is a species of bird and *coatl* means snake. This personage has caused tremendous confusion among historians and archaeologists. For the Teotihuacán civilization, Quetzalcoatl was a god; for the Mayas and Toltecs he was a priest-king; in Yucatan he was known by the name of Kukulcan, and during the Aztec period Quetzalcoatl became a title.

Many imaginative authors have tried to see in Quetzalcoatl the Christ of Mexico—a reincarnation of the Saviour, as it were. One particular writer, the Irish archaeologist Lord Kingsborough (1795-1837), devoted his whole life to this theory, collecting all available information about the ancient advanced civilizations of Mexico and then compiling a monumental work in nine volumes, *The Antiquities of Mexico*. Kingsborough wanted to prove that the ancient peoples of Mexico were the descendants of the ten lost tribes of Israel, and in his effort to document his theory he collected literary works of both the Old and the New Worlds, together with Mayan and Aztec accounts dating from pre-Columbian times. He also got hold of the volumes which the Spanish monks had so diligently compiled at the time of the conquest. In fact he spent so much money on collections, research and publication that he eventually went bankrupt and his printer had him thrown in the debtors' prison at Dublin. Even in prison, he still dreamed of demonstrating to the world that Christ had appeared among the Toltecs after all. But the prison was damp and teeming with vermin, and Kingsborough finally caught typhus and died.

Nevertheless, Kingsborough had many adherents who meant to prove that the ancient Mexicans knew the Book of Genesis. Mexico had its own tradition about a Flood. The last surviving Aztecs and their ancient sculptures were found to have "Semitic features." Like the Jews, the Itza Mayas worshiped one supreme god of whom they made no physical images; and, like the Jews, they said their prayers toward the east—could it be toward Jerusalem? The Toltecs revered the snake, like the heathen of the Old Testament. And, finally, a virgin named Chimalman from the Toltecs' capital, Tollan, gave birth to a son. This was Quetzalcoatl, who became the Toltecs' king, priest, astronomer, bearer of civilization, prophet and god.

Even without an overwrought imagination the parallels between the Christ of the West and the Toltecs' Quetzalcoatl are striking enough. Quetzalcoatl was supposedly a white man, and not dark-skinned like the Toltecs. Tradition has it that he was sent to mankind by the godhead, became a human being, taught all the arts, preached wisdom and goodness. He brought the Toltecs a golden age, and even nature shared in his good works. After visiting the Mayas, he supposedly presented the Toltecs with the Mayan calendar.

According to Toltec tradition, Quetzalcoatl eventually incurred the wrath of his divine superior. This spelled the end of the Toltecs and their destruction. Quetzalcoatl was forced to flee to the "eastern ocean" (*i.e.*, the Atlantic coast), interrupting his flight to spend twenty years in their city of Cholula, where the greatest pyramid in America was erected in his honor.

Today, this pyramid is little more than a shrub-covered hill. Nevertheless, it remains the largest building in the world in terms of cubic content.

When Quetzalcoatl arrived at the Atlantic, he built himself a boat out of snakeskin and sailed away across the ocean in the general direction of Europe, to the legendary country called Tlapallan. Nobody knows where this land was supposed to be.

Quetzalcoatl disappeared, but not the hope that he would return—not just any time but at a definite period. He never did come back, but in the same year for which his second coming was predicted someone else arrived—Hernando Cortez.

HE OVERTHREW LARGE AND POWERFUL NATIONS

HERNANDO CORTEZ

Perhaps it had been resolved that he should receive his reward in a better world. I firmly believe so, for he was a goodly knight, and most sincere in his prayers to the Virgin, Peter the Apostle, and all the other saints.

Bernal Diaz del Castillo in his *Historia Verdadera de la Conquista de la Nueva Espana*, 1568

IN 1518, the long, sweeping arc formed by Florida, Cuba, the Antilles and the coasts of Venezuela and Panama was known at least in its outlines. Only one country awaited discovery: Mexico and its large peninsula, Yucatan, the nearest land to the western tip of Cuba.

It was Hernando Cortez whom the governor of Cuba entrusted with an expedition into the country from which the first rumors of its golden treasures were just beginning to leak out to the world at large. Cortez was then a man of thirty-four, and an adventurer if ever there was one. The governor had scarcely commissioned Cortez to start preparations when he became envious and tried to cancel his orders. However, Cortez and his men were already on board their hastily assembled and ill-equipped ships and halfway out of the harbor when the disconcerted governor arrived at the water's edge. Three other Spaniards had reached Mexico before Cortez, but the Conquest was to be his.

Cortez and his fleet set sail for Yucatan in February, 1519. On arriving at the island of Cozumel, he immediately had the natives' idols destroyed and erected an altar in one of the Indian temples, complete with effigies of the Virgin and Child.

At Tabasco, Cortez and his small party had to battle a greatly superior force of Indians. But this was the first time the natives had ever seen horses or cavalry, and believing rider and steed to be one, they fled before these monsters. The next day, however, they came along and brought gifts. Among these gifts were twenty women, one of them an extremely beautiful Aztec slave from Tabasco called Malinche, whom the Spaniards renamed Marina.

Marina spoke Aztec and Mayan and, with a Spanish captive rescued from the Maya by Cortez, became one of the two links between the Spanish tongue and the Aztec. And Marina knew from the first moment that she was in love with Cortez, and since there is no finer teacher than love she quickly learned Castilian. Marina first acted as Cortez' secretary, but it was not long before she became his mistress. She had a beautiful body, she was young, she was clever, and she always remained unswervingly loyal to the Spaniards, several times rescuing them from dangerous situations, while frequently preserving her own people from disaster. Although she had a son by Cortez—Don Martín—Cortez never married her as he was already married to a Spanish woman.

Cortez sailed along the coast with his fleet, and on Good Friday, April 21, 1519, they landed at what is now Mexico's modern seaport of Vera Cruz.

The Spaniards had long since heard of the powerful Aztec king, Montezuma, and Montezuma, who was expecting the return of the white god Quetzalcoatl in that year, was already informed by his scouts that Quetzalcoatl's ambassadors had landed. Now the king's soothsayers declared that there were two possibilities: if the king met the strangers with hostility he would perish, and if he welcomed them with open arms he would lose his throne. After deliberating, the king decided to welcome the strangers, so he sent them gifts. And as soon as Cortez set eyes on them, he knew this was the land of which the Spanish conquistadors had dreamed, the land which must be won, whatever the cost. Solid gold was heaped before him: golden bowls as big as wagon wheels, golden plates representing the sun, silver dishes representing the moon, turquoises, feather cloaks, gold and silver animals, and a helmet filled with gold. There are accurate contemporary inventories of the treasure secured by Cortez. The gifts acted like a lodestone, drawing Cortez and his men deeper and deeper into the country's interior.

Cortez soon learned that the great Montezuma had many enemies—the same tribes against whom the Aztecs were continually waging war to obtain the prisoners they sacrificed to their gods on the lofty summits of their pyramids. Cortez defeated the Totonacs and Tlaxcalans, and others, in battle and then forced them to become his allies. Cortez realized that he would be advancing with only a small body of men into a country fraught with a thousand dangers. With his restless crew there would be the ever-present threat of war and

Burial accessory found on the northern coast of Peru, a product of the Mochica civilization (c. 500-800 A.D.).

Mexican stone mask from the 2nd century B.C. [*Photograph:* Susanne Schapowalow.

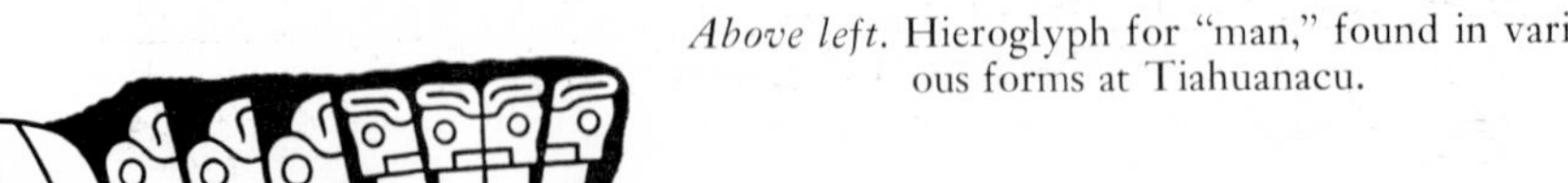

Above left. Hieroglyph for "man," found in various forms at Tiahuanacu.

Above right. Professor Posnansky claims this sign, found on Tiahuanacu urns, stands for a crown.

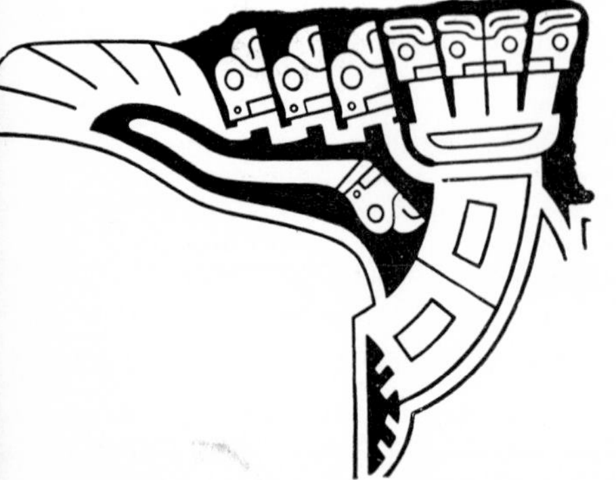

Left. A similar design, still according to Posnansky, appears as decoration on pots and stones. The sign shown here the Professor identifies as meaning "bird."

Female statuette from the coast of the Gulf of Mexico. The peculiar form of the teeth probably has some magic significance. The image comes from the region inhabited by the Totonecs, the first tribe with which the Spanish conquerors came in contact. The earrings are characteristic of pre-Colombian America. They were the sign of a privileged class, as with the Incas. Found in a tomb, the image is about 6 inches in height.

A clay figure from Oaxaca Museum reminiscent of ancient Egyptian sculptures. It was the work of the Zapotecs, who lived on the southern coast of Mexico at about the same time as the Maya.

This aerial photograph shows us what is really the most gigantic calendar in the world. Engineers of the Nasca civilization used this dry and infertile desert as a gigantic drawing-board, marking out a series of dead straight lines many miles long in the arid soil. Nasca astronomers then sighted along them and observed their relationship to particular stars as they rose above the horizon, using the results to fix dates.

The Incas' slaves and oppressed tributary peoples betrayed all their other secrets to the invaders, yet Machu Picchu, overgrown with tropical vegetation, eluded discovery. It remains a mystery why the Spanish conquistadors never heard about this town. It was not until 1911 that Hiram Bingham discovered these ruins.

Clay model of a head found on the coast of Vera Cruz. It dates from the Toltec period (c. 900 A.D.) and is assumed to represent Xipe Toltec, the God of Spring. The ears are adorned with pale blue knots.

A mask of high-carat gold, from the Chimu civilization of the 14th and 15th centuries, which was found on the northern coast of Peru. Masks like these were attached to mummies as a kind of artificial face. They were more commonly made of wood or cotton cloth than of gold or copper.

Inca knot writing. Principal strings had subordinate strings attached to them. Different colored strings signified different categories of articles. Countless combinations could be achieved by varying the colors and types of knot. The Incas had no other system of writing or of figures.

▲ *A face of classical Mayan style.* It dates from the 9th century A.D. and comes from a priest's grave recently discovered inside a pyramid at Palenque.

Figurine from the Yucatan Peninsula, probably of a pre-Mayan period. Nine inches high and carved in greenstone, it was probably made sometime during the first five centuries A.D. ▲

▼ *Tenochtitlan (now Mexico City) as it was in* 1519, when Cortez entered it. The large pyramid on the left was where Cortez and Marina stood with Montezuma. *Center:* an altar for human sacrifice.

mutiny, and death would be his constant companion. So he made a decision that has almost no parallel in world history. There, in a completely strange country, separated from his native land by a vast ocean, he made up his mind to convince his men that there could be no retreat, that they must fight and win—or die. Therefore he had every one of his ships destroyed except one small vessel for carrying dispatches.

The trek into the mountains began. The captive natives groaned as they dragged the cannons up the steep defiles, and the pack horses sweated under the weight of their loads. The Spaniards crossed a trackless desert and vast fields of maize. And although they met some initial resistance in the country of the Tlaxcalans, these people defeated ultimately became their allies.

At last they reached Cholula, the sacred city of the Toltecs. They settled down, but at night Marina slipped out of the temple courtyard where the Spaniards were encamped, and learned that Cholula was in league with Montezuma and that the Spaniards were to be ambushed on leaving the city. Cortez ordered a wholesale massacre. The temple on the great pyramid crashed down and a massive stone crucifix was immediately set up in its place. Soon afterward Montezuma sent envoys to Cortez inviting the Spaniards to visit him in his capital Tenochtitlan, the modern Mexico City.

It must have been a breath-taking moment when the Spaniards for the first time looked down from the mountain heights into the valley of Mexico with its sparkling lakes and houses and towns. Far in the distance towered the pyramids of Teotihuacán and then there was the capital itself—Tenochtitlan, the Venice of ancient Mexico. Montezuma welcomed the Spaniards in person, and at last Cortez saw before him the ruler of an empire that surpassed even his own wildest dreams. Montezuma, for his part, saw in Cortez the emissary of his god Quetzalcoatl, whose return the oracle had long foretold. He offered the Spaniards one of his own palaces. When the great king stepped back into his sedan chair the crowds prostrated themselves and lay motionless on the ground.

"I shall never forget this spectacle," wrote Bernal Diaz, the Spanish chronicler who had come to Tenochtitlan with Cortez. Crowds of people surged through the streets, and countless faces peered from every gateway and window. The inhabitants stood shoulder to shoulder on the rooftops and gazed at the Spaniards in wonder. The city had a huge market place, long rows of buildings, and streets which were cleaned daily by thousands of sweepers. Since the water of Tenochtitlan's lake was brackish, drinking water was brought into the city through earthenware pipes from a mountain reservoir. This clear water supplied the many fountains in Tenochtitlan.

Montezuma owned numerous spacious palaces, as well as an armory stocked with weapons and military accoutrements. Young Aztec noblemen fought duels and enacted warlike spectacles. There were granaries, vast warehouses and an aviary containing brightly feathered birds from all over the empire. In the molting season the multicolored feathers were gathered for making the feathered robes that were a specialty of Aztec art. There was a zoological garden containing wild beasts and snakes. Montezuma also kept a human menagerie of monstrosities, dwarfs and other unfortunate creatures. All these buildings were surrounded by vast gardens planted with flowers, shrubs, trees and medicinal herbs. Sparkling fountains shed their refreshing drops on the luxuriant gardens. Waterfowl and fish of every description swam in the king's ten large fish ponds.

Montezuma's palaces were equipped with every conceivable convenience, including special quarters for the ladies of his harem. These concubines had everything they needed for their comfort. They were experts at weaving and knitting, and produced elaborate feather garments. They were supervised by a number of old women who saw to it that their charges took plenty of baths. Montezuma himself changed his clothes four times a day, and garments he had worn once were immediately given away to his servants.

Even Henry VIII would have envied Montezuma, for the Aztec king used to dine sumptuously, sitting in solitary splendor with hundreds of dishes piled on mats in front of him. Servants of noble birth would carry in the food, which was served by girls selected for their special grace and beauty. The king sat on a cushion, his person concealed by a screen, while venerable councilors stood at a respectful distance, ready to answer his questions. Golden dishes were placed on a cotton tablecloth, and the dining hall was lit by torches fed by a special resin that gave off a sweet scent as it burned. After his meal, the king was handed finger bowls and then pipes, from which he inhaled the smoke of a soothing herb called tobacco. During this pleasant after-dinner interlude the ruler amused himself by watching jugglers, or his court jester. The dancers employed by the palace occupied a whole district of the city, and the expense of maintaining the court was enormous. Nevertheless, a strict account of income and expendi-

ture was kept, and the king's household was managed in an exemplary manner.

Meanwhile, a game of cat and mouse was going on. Montezuma showed Cortez one of his pyramids. They stood by the jasper slab reserved for human sacrifices. The air reeked with stale blood. Cortez saw the Aztec gods on the sacred towers, with human hearts lying in golden basins on the altars before them.

Cortez wanted to sweep all this idolatry aside without much ado and replace it with the cross of Christianity, but Montezuma was outraged. "These are the gods that have led the Aztecs to victory," he protested.

The Spaniards inspected Montezuma's private treasury. "It was to me," wrote Diaz, "as if all the riches in the world had found their way into one place." Montezuma visited the Spaniards in their palace. The Spaniards visited Montezuma. And at last Cortez decided to take Montezuma prisoner. Choosing five courageous knights, he called on

Montezuma who received the party amicably and even offered Cortez one of his daughters in marriage.

Cortez found it hard to drop this conversational banter for a more serious tone, but he eventually requested Montezuma to leave his own palace and move in with the Spaniards. And in the end, Montezuma consented to leave his palace—never to see it again.

The Aztecs started to mutter in discontent, and when they finally appeared outside the Spaniards' quarters, brandishing their weapons, Montezuma went out on the balcony to pacify them. They looked at their ruler as if he were some wild beast now tamed and submissively caged by its enemies.

"Woman, coward!" they shouted. "The white men have turned you into a woman, fit only for spinning and weaving!" Spears flew quivering through the air, and a volley of stones and arrows hurtled down on the emperor. The Spaniards hurriedly covered him with their shields, but it was too late—Montezuma had been mortally wounded.

Father Olmedo knelt at the dying man's side. "Embrace the cross," the priest said, "the symbol of man's redemption." Montezuma pushed it away: he wanted none of Christianity. He died on June 30, 1520, in the arms of the Aztec nobles whom the Spaniards had always allowed to stay with their rulers.

The rest of the story was uprising and rebellion, massacre and carnage. The Aztec temples toppled to the ground and churches and monasteries, built from their ancient stones, rose on their ruins. The great Aztec Empire had vanished.

A LABYRINTH 5,000 YEARS OLD

The palace put into the shade all that was known about European antiquity or had been supposed to exist there.
Sir Arthur Evans

OFF the southern coast of Greece, roughly equidistant from the coasts of Asia and Africa, lies the island home of the oldest advanced civilization in Europe: Crete, "a land set in a wine-dark sea," as Homer described it.

Crete is the first and oldest link in the splendid chain of European civilizations, and by the time Greece had reached her prime, Crete was almost submerged in a sea of legend and fable. When the war was raging around Troy (1194-1184 B.C.), Crete could already look back on 2,000 years of civilization. When Christ was born, the laughter of the elegant ladies-in-waiting and courtesans in the palace at Knossos had been silent for 1,400 years. The gorgeous clothes, the rustling skirts and petticoats that could have competed with the most modern Paris creations, the bodices, lace trimmings and puffed sleeves had all turned to dust. For almost 2,000 years, everything about Crete was regarded as a myth—and then fifty years ago it became clear that it was completely true.

In 1878, a Cretan merchant with the resounding name of Kalokairinos dug up several objects of great antiquity on a hill south of Candia. Eight years later, in 1886, a stranger visited the district. A gaunt, restless man, he had an uncannily sharp instinct for ruins which had lain forgotten under the ground for thousands of years. He was a German, and his name was Heinrich Schliemann. He had already rediscovered Mycenae and Troy, and now he stood there in Crete and insisted that the legendary palaces of Knossos must lie buried beneath his feet.

Schliemann was a careful reader of the Greek classics, and he always knew where to dig and what to look for. Now he opened negotiations with the proprietors of the land, wanting to start excavations without delay. The owner asked for too high a price, however, so Schliemann abandoned the project, and with it the chance of following up his success at Troy, for he died shortly after.

Then in 1893, the British archaeologist, Dr. Arthur Evans, found a number of small engraved stones in an antique shop in Athens. He was told they came from Crete where the peasant women wore them as amulets, but Evans was more interested in the undecipherable hieroglyphs which were scratched on them. Up till then it had been thought that unlike the Egyptians, Sumerians and Babylonians, Europe was illiterate until the Greeks borrowed an alphabet from the Phoenicians. But since a good archaeologist must also be something of a detective, Evans succeeded in establishing, by a method of comparison, that the hieroglyphic trail led to Crete. So he went to the island and traveled about collecting such objects as had accidentally come to light from time to time. Finally, he purchased the land beneath which Knossos lay buried, and hired 150 laborers to excavate it.

They dug for nine weeks, and then Evans brought to light one of the richest of all treasures of modern archaeology—the palace of Minos at Knossos.

"We were entering a completely undiscovered world," Evans wrote. "Each step forward was a step into the dark. There were no buildings which could serve as a pattern, and systematic digging was therefore impossible. The palace put into the shade all that was known about European antiquity or had been supposed to exist here. . . . The extraordinary phenomenon—nothing Greek, nothing Roman . . . its great period goes at least well back to the pre-Mycenean period."

Evans found thousands of bricks and clay tablets bearing the same hieroglyphics found on the amulet he had bought from the woman at Athens. The magnificent civilization of a race uncommonly gifted both in the intellectual and artistic sphere lay once again exposed to the Mediterranean sun.

We already know that cities grow and that past civilizations lie in layers one on top of another, with the top layer being the most recent and the lowest layer the oldest. Evans established that while the Minoan Bronze Age went back to 3000 B.C., the late Stone Age civilization lying beneath it embraced the fantastic span of 10,000 years. The palace at Knossos, and Minoan civilization therefore must have taken shape in a prehistoric era which makes us—trapped as we are within the confines of our own historical thinking—slightly dizzy when we contemplate it. Advanced Minoan civilization obviously did not suddenly appear out of nowhere 2,000 or 3,000 years before the birth of Christ. After all, wherever we go in the world we can nearly always be sure that we are treading upon a vast accumulation of debris left behind by man's exertions and his struggle for progress. Like many others, therefore,

CRETE
MYCENAE
ATHENS
TIRYNS
PYLOS
AEGEAN SEA
SMYRNA
ASIA MINOR
RHODES
CRETE
0
200 m.
DIKTYNNAION
PHALASARNA
MODION
KYDONIA
KISAMOS
CHANIA
KERAITAI
APTARA
POLYRRHENIA
PERGAMON ?
DIA
KYTAION
PANORMOS
APOLLONIA
HERAKLEION
RHETHYMNA
ELEUTHERNA
AMNISOS
CHERSONASOS
HYRTAKINA
LAPPA
PHALANNA
MILATOS
ELYROS
KANTANOS
OAXOS
TYLISSOS
KNOSSOS
OLUS
MOUNT-IDA
MALLIA
SYIA
LISSOS
POIKILOSSOS
ANOPOLIS
RHAUKOS
LYKTOS
DREROS
ITANOS
PHOINIX
ASOMATOS
HELEIA
KAMARA
ARKADIA
LYKASTOS
SETEIA
LATO
DIKTAION
MINOA
SULIA
RHIZENIA
ARKADES
PRAISOS
ISTRON
GORTYN
GOURNIA
DRAGMOS
PHAISTOS
AMPELOS
HIERAPYDNA
BIANNOS
HAG.TRIADA
PYLOROS
PRIANSOS
RHYTION
MATALA
LEBENA
GAUDUS
CHRYSEA
LEUCAE
0
50 miles

Minoan civilization must have gone through many thousands of years of slow and independent evolution.

It was only in 1936 that Evans—by that time Sir Arthur Evans and the possessor of many honors and academic awards—finally completed his monumental six-volume work *The Palace of Minos at Knossos.* It is a marvelous work, the result of a lifetime's endeavor, and it has a mysterious quality of drawing the reader deeper and deeper into a strange and fabulous world until he eventually finds himself at the very heart of this Mediterranean civilization, wandering in the legendary realm of the sea kings of Knossos.

Evans takes a great deal for granted, however, and his readers must have a sound background of knowledge before they can find their way about in his large volumes. It is, for instance, natural to inquire why any archaeologist should have hit upon Crete, and nowhere else, in his search for the palace at Knossos, and in particular for the palace where a king named Minos was reputed to have reigned.

We should not write off every ancient legend as mere fiction, but should have the courage to follow up the ancient narratives and epics as literally as we can. Our oldest legendary sources about Crete are Homer's *Iliad* and *Odyssey*. Homer, who lived about 800 B.C., mentions King Minos, the palace at Knossos, and many things relating to the Cretan king. Herodotus, the "father of history," who lived from 484 to 425 B.C., also gives an account of Minos, his fleets and a Cretan expedition against Sicily. Thucydides, an Athenian aristocrat and extremely objective student of history, who was born around 455 B.C., tells us about Minos' sea power. Aristotle, a Greek doctor's son born in a small Macedonian town in 384 B.C., wrote that Crete's geographical location was such that it enabled King Minos to dominate the whole Aegean realm, *i.e.*, the islands in the Aegean Sea and the countries bordering it.

Greek sagas and legends tell us a great deal more. Apparently Knossos was inhabited by a raging Minotaur—a monster, half man, half bull. Was this a mere figment of the imagination?

The word Minotaur is composed of King Minos' name and the Greek word *tauros,* meaning "bull." During the excavations at Knossos, many different representations of the bull were found, and it became obvious that the animal had a special significance. At the court of King Minos there were bullfights; young girls and men had to run and seize the bull by its horns and vault over the savage beast, and one mural shows a girl impaled on a bull's horns while jumping. It is possible that captured children were also trained in this sport. Thus if King Minos did at one time subjugate Athens and received tribute from her, it was easy to understand why the Athenians might have made of the king and the bull one terrifying creature.

King Minos, so the legend goes, confined the Minotaur in a building called a labryinth. Was this fiction? By no means!

The Cretans' most sacred deity was a mother goddess whom the Greeks called Rhea and who was almost invariably portrayed in the company of a male deity, possibly her son. Both god and goddess carried an auspicious symbol, a kind of fetish, into which they could vanish at will: this was the two-bladed ax. The Carian term for this double ax was *labrys*, and the symbol of the *labrys*, or double ax, was found everywhere in the excavated palace at Knossos; so it is no wonder that the palace itself came to be called *labyrinthos*. Our word "labyrinth" therefore originated at Knossos and is a good 5,000 years old, if not considerably older.

We do not know if the palace itself was the original labyrinth, or if the Minoans could remember another labyrinth which had disapppeared long before. On the seals found at Knossos and in the palace of Minos were the outlines of a building, sometimes round, sometimes square, which contained a single long passage twisting and turning at right angles. It must have required a long time to reach the heart of the building, and once inside one could never get out. These may have been ground plans of the celebrated labyrinth.

Far away in Italy on August 24, 79 A.D., Vesuvius erupted, completely destroying the famous city of Pompeii. Under masses of ashes and lava was another clue to the mystery: on one of the walls a Roman child had scratched a drawing of a maze. Underneath, written in his own hand, were the words: "Labyrinth! Here dwells the Minotaur." So this Roman child was familiar with the Cretan labyrinth and the story of the Minotaur. We know something else as well: in the curriculum of Roman schools this "fairy tale" was still a matter of history.

King Minos' architect, the man who built the palace at Knossos and invented the labyrinth, supposedly was one Daedalus. Perhaps he was a real person. According to legend he seems to have been a kind of Leonardo, always surprising his royal master with new inventions and feats of ingenuity. He was also a sculptor of genius. It is said that when King Minos imprisoned him and his son Icarus in the impenetrable labyrinth, he contrived wings for them both, with which they soared over the walls of the labyrinth and flew away far above the sea.

Icarus died on the flight as a result of climbing too near to the sun, but Daedalus landed in Sicily, where he introduced the culture of Crete and executed some magnificent statues, among them a marble relief of Minos' daughter, Ariadne, dancing. These works are said to have existed as late as 200 A.D., and the Greeks never doubted the historicity of Daedalus.

It is also possible that the legend of Theseus and Ariadne really happened. Once every nine years King Minos is said to have required the city of Athens to provide seven girls and seven young men as a sacrifice to the Minotaur. On one such occasion Theseus, son of King Aegeus, volunteered to go to Crete as one of these victims because he planned to slay the monster. But King Minos' daughter Ariadne no sooner set eyes on the young Athenian prince than she fell in love with him. She gave him a sword and showed him how to unwind a reel of thread behind him as he advanced into the labyrinth, so that he could find his way out. Theseus killed the Minotaur, followed Ariadne's thread out of the labyrinth, and escaped with the king's daughter to Naxos. He married her as he had promised, but then sailed away with his companions while she was asleep.

Stories like the one about Theseus and Ariadne are hardly ever sheer invention, and tales of buildings as complex as the labyrinth are seldom the products of fantasy. But it is still not clear exactly when the laby-

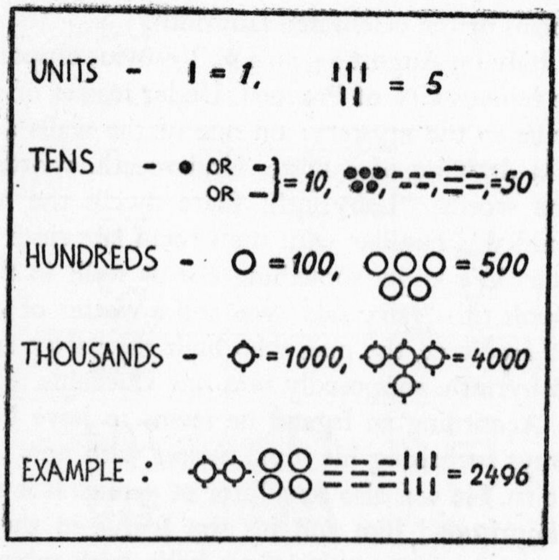

Cretan numbers. It is evident that by this system any figure, no matter how large, can be written. Our own system comes from the Arabs.

rinth was built, and if the people of Knossos knew it or only remembered it dimly and therefore did not know if it was square or round.

Since Minos reigned in the palace at Knossos and was the ruler of a large maritime empire, and because his name was very possibly a royal title—as Pharaoh was for the Egyptians—Evans named the culture of ancient Crete the Minoan civilization. He established through his excavations that the late Stone Age lasted here until about 3400 B.C., when the Bronze Age began, and he divided Minoan civilization into three periods: early Minoan (3400-2100), middle Minoan (2100-1580), and late Minoan (1580-1250). This classification, incidentally, was extremely difficult to arrive at, since the Minoans left no chronological data behind them. But the Egyptians have supplied us with very accurate dates, and it is thanks to the commercial and cultural relations between Egypt and ancient Crete that certain historical events in Crete can be fixed with reasonable accuracy.

About 2100 B.C. the princes of Knossos, Phaistos and Mallia erected massive palaces rising to a height of several stories and containing

[illegible]	[illegible]	ta
[illegible]	[illegible]	ti
[illegible]	[illegible]	pa
[illegible]	[illegible]	po
[illegible]	[illegible]	lo
[illegible]	[illegible]	ra
[illegible]		ni
[illegible]		re
[illegible]	[illegible]	ma
[illegible]	[illegible]	mi

Oldest alphabets of Europe. Left: Cretan; Middle: Cypriot; Right: Pronunciation as deciphered by Ernst Sittig.

innumerable rooms, workshops, store chambers, courtyards, staircases and balustrades. Altars and temples were built, as well as intricate water-supply systems. The walls of the various palaces were adorned with brilliantly colored frescoes, and a linear script evolved from the hieroglyphics of the past millennia.

In 1700 B.C. there seems to have been a great catastrophe, and the palace at Knossos was destroyed. Was it by an earthquake, or had the people of the rival city of Phaistos attacked the city? This is at least a possibility because curiously enough the palace at Phaistos did not collapse until a later date. While we still do not know the answer, the earth is yielding up one clue after another. Some time afterward more Cretan cities collapsed, including Mochlos, Gournia, Palaikastro and many others. Then, about 1600 B.C., life started afresh. New buildings rose from the ruins, grander and more beautiful palaces were built at Knossos, Phaistos, Tylissos, Hagia Triada and Gournia. A wealth and luxury now developed such as Greece would not know until a thousand years later. Plays were performed in the palace courtyards, gladiators fought wild beasts, the people's tastes became more and more sophisticated, craftsmanship and literature flourished and the wealthy discovered more and more outlets for their extravagance. Between 1600 and 1400 B.C. Crete and the Minoan civilization enjoyed a golden age, and the whole Aegean Sea glowed in the warmth of the Cretan sun. Then, about 1400 B.C., everything suddenly disintegrated. Some appalling catastrophe annihilated everything that human ingenuity, thought and endeavor had taken thousands of years to create.

What had happened?

THE MYSTERIOUS DOWNFALL

Woe unto the inhabitants of the sea coast, the nation of the Cherethites!
Zephaniah 2.5

ABOUT 1400 B.C. Minoan civilization fell apart as if it had been smashed by some superhuman fist. The catastrophe that demolished the cities of Crete was all-embracing: Knossos, Phaistos, Hagia Triada, Gournia, Mochlos, Mallia and Zakros, all these cities, large and small, show traces of simultaneous demolition and fire, while other towns, like Palaikastro, Pseira and Tylissos, collapsed without burning.

No firsthand account of this 3,350-year-old disaster has been left us; there apparently were no contemporary descriptions of the collapse of advanced Minoan civilization, and we have no exact date. All we can rely on is the research of the archaeologists. Amazingly, although archaeology can supply us only with the approximate year in which the catastrophe occurred, scholars have been able to name the exact month.

The year 1400 B.C. was established after an extremely careful examination of the individual layers of subterranean debris, and was confirmed by the last descriptions of the Cretans (Kefti) found in Egypt and dating from the time of Pharaoh Amenophis III (1401-1375). This estimate may be a few years off, but if the great disaster did not precisely take place in 1400 B.C., it certainly happened shortly thereafter.

We come now to the traces of the fire, or, rather, the smoke stains which are still clearly visible on the walls of the excavated ruins. We can actually *see* the wind that swept the clouds of smoke through the burning palace. The smoke has left such clear traces on the blocks of masonry that we can establish that the fire and billowing smoke racing along the tottering walls was driven from the southwest to northeast by a southwesterly storm. Modern Moslems call this southwest wind *gharbis,* and it blows in the spring months, bringing with it vast clouds of sand from the distant Sahara and reaching its full force in March. Only a *gharbis* of enormous power could have left the traces of smoke which were found on the walls of Knossos, and thus we are quite certain the city was destroyed in March. For only in March could so many cities have gone up in flame at the same time, since only a very strong wind could have assisted the fires so effectively.

But how did these fires break out? Evans is convinced that Knossos, like the other cities in Crete, collapsed during a great earthquake, followed by a terrible conflagration. Everything points to a swift end which took the inhabitants completely by surprise. The most sacred place in Knossos, the throne room, showed signs of an extraordinary drama that was enacted there at the last moment. Alabaster oil jars used solely for the most sacred ceremonies were standing in readiness at the very moment of disaster. Apparently the catastrophe coincided with some sacred ritual. The city's workshops also show that her craftsmen and artists were overtaken by disaster in the midst of their work. If an enemy had been approaching the island, the surprise would not have been so complete—at least in Evans' perceptive opinion, and his arguments carry great conviction.

Another noted archaeologist, J. D. S. Pendlebury, who knows Knossos extremely well, has a different theory. He holds that in ancient times earthquakes were not inevitably followed by fire, but that fire is primarily the result of modern gas and electricity—the great earthquake at Tokyo in 1923 being a case in point. Furthermore, an earthquake would have also destroyed the great staircase at Knossos; yet it is established that this structure survived for a long time after the date of the alleged disaster. Pendlebury believes that all the evidence points to intentional destruction by human hands.

Let us assume that in 1400 B.C. it was no longer Crete which ruled the mainland, but the mainland—or modern Greece—which ruled the island of Crete. It then becomes conceivable that the cities of the island, conscious of their own ancient civilization, one day tired of this foreign domination and decided to shake it off by a concerted revolt against all foreign elements. We know that the Cretans rebuilt their cities after the disaster and lived on relatively undisturbed, and we also know that two hundred years later they accepted even less foreign culture than they had before. All these facts are substantiated by excavations, and so the revolution theory seems perfectly plausible.

If, on the other hand, Crete still controlled the whole Aegean realm in 1400 B.C., and if her dominions decided to break the hegemony of the mother country, then a landing and subsequent invasion by the Mycenaean Greeks become conceivable. In that case, the hostile armada that destroyed the cities of Crete must have been brilliantly organized. The motive for this planned devastation would seem to have been exclusively political, with no intention to settle down and colonize, for as soon as the destruction was complete the enemy must have abandoned the island, leaving the Cretans to rebuild their cities and lead a shadowy existence for another 200 years. This second theory, the invasion theory, is the one favored by Pendlebury who pointed out that the Mycenaean Greeks succeeded to Crete's hegemony in the Aegean, and it fits in well with the legend of Theseus.

If Crete really did demand a number of young Athenian men and girls at certain regular intervals to be sacrificed at Knossos, and if there really was such a person as Theseus who decided to kill the man-eating Minotaur in the labyrinth at Knossos, the Theseus adventure may well have been a retaliatory campaign against Crete transformed into myth. In any case, Crete had fallen. After vegetating for another two centuries as a satellite of the Greek world, she was strangled by the greater vigor of Hellenic culture and assimilated into a new world whose life had only just begun.

The Cretans were a Mediterranean race, a seafaring people who maintained commercial relations with Egypt, the Near East and all the Aegean and Mediterranean communities as far west as Italy and Spain. Their navy was so powerful that they never felt the need to fortify Knossos.

The Cretans never wore beards, which alone should be enough to discourage the ever recurrent speculation about Cretan-Mycenaean civilization, for the Mycenaean Greeks were addicted to beards. The Cretans, on the other hand, were so attached to their razors that they took them along with them into their graves.

The ladies of the Minoan civilization wore large conical hats, white leather shoes with ornaments (if they were well-to-do), and lovely narrow-waisted gowns that covered their bodies completely—except for their breasts. Waists had to be extremely slim, and the ladies who lived in Crete 4,000 years ago laced themselves up tightly in elegant bodices. Their skirts were stiffened with metal ribs to keep them flared out, just like crinolines. The colors of their dresses were expertly matched, their coiffures were very elaborate, and their pretty faces painted and powdered with a finesse that could scarcely be rivaled today. Youths and men also narrowed their waists with metal belts, but otherwise they wore only a loincloth, and by Greek standards were very scantily clad.

Cretan women wore valuable jewelry, a form of adornment which the men themselves did not disdain. The men of ancient Crete seem to have held their women in great esteem, because even the ladies of Egypt were seldom groomed with such sophisticated taste. It is no mere coincidence that the supreme member of the Cretan pantheon was a mother goddess.

One cannot fail to be amazed by the towns which have been excavated in Crete, with their well-kept streets, their facilities for water supply, baths and drainage, their shops, their smithies, potteries, carpenters' and shoemakers' workshops, their oil refineries and textile factories. Knossos had houses up to five stories high, with folding doors and artificial lighting supplied by oil lamps. The Cretans used to play an interesting game similar to chess. In their art they show a gay, constructive striving toward graceful and delicate effects. It was particularly in the small things that the Cretans showed their skills, for they delighted in the precious, pretty minutiae of everyday life.

Thus Sir Arthur Evans succeeded in presenting us with a highly developed European civilization which was 3,500 years old and yet surprisingly modern. But he did not merely intend to revive Europe's *prehistory*. He had a much bolder vision: he wanted to expand European *history* by a thousand years. History always begins with writing, and the known history of Greece then began in 776 B.C. Therefore, if Evans wanted to push the frontiers of European history back into the past, he would have to find much older examples of a European script than had existed hitherto. In fact it was the wish to discover European documents that prompted him to visit Crete in the first place.

And, indeed, he found two types of script, which he named "Linear A" and "Linear B." Linear A was apparently used on the island of Crete as early as 1600 B.C. This fact alone enlarged the written history of Europe by 800 years.

Linear A was discovered at fourteen places on the island. Thirteen of these sites produced a total of fifty-one different inscriptions, while the fourteenth, at Hagia Triada, yielded one hundred and sixty-eight. Of the group of fifty-one, all of which are quite brief, fourteen were found on terracotta tablets, eight on terracotta vases, six on sacrificial tables, and another six on seals, and so on. Of the one hundred and sixty-eight inscriptions found at Hagia Triada, in a prince's summer villa near the center of Crete's south coast, one hundred and fifty-four were scratched into clay tablets. They are trivial little memoranda about managing the villa, written in crude and sketchy characters that certainly do not reveal a flowing hand. In fact, it may be said that there is not one fine piece of handwriting in Linear A.

Why were so few examples found? If Linear A was only discovered at fourteen sites and on seventeen different kinds of objects, it is fair to assume that we possess only an infinitesimal fraction of all that was ever written in that script. Moreover, we do not know if any sort of paper or ink had been invented and if only the less perishable specimens have survived. The Cretans probably wrote on palm leaves, as Pliny the Elder informs us in his *Natural History*. Yet if so much more was written than our finds indicate, it is hard to understand why the characters in the inscriptions seem to have been executed by very inexperienced hands, if not by raw beginners. We probably come closer to the truth if we assume that throughout Crete the art of writing was practiced only by a select few.

Besides, in spite of a very high culture and equally high artistic standards in Crete during this period–*i.e.*, between 1600 and 1400 B.C. –writing obviously was regarded as fit only for bureaucrats. The fact that the script was employed only for trivial housekeeping records suggests that it was considered as unimportant. All this would explain why not many examples of Linear A exist. Neither was it "exported" anywhere. Linear A has rarely been found elsewhere in the Aegean area, two inscriptions at Melos and one at Thera being the only ones that were unearthed outside Crete. Therefore, the negligible finds of Linear A on Crete can scarcely be blamed on insufficient excavations.

An even greater mystery surrounds the script known as Linear B. Whereas Linear A was used all over the island from 1600 B.C. on, Linear B first appeared in 1450 B.C., but only in one place: in the palace at Knossos. All Linear B inscriptions found *in Crete* come from this palace, and all date from the period immediately preceding 1400. They therefore represent the government records of one generation, at the most. While the rest of Crete went on using Linear A, the palace scribes at Knossos used Linear B for making calculations, inventories and recording various transactions. All the examples we have found are bookkeeping entries, calculations or accounts relating to financial administration. Evans found 2,000 small oval clay tablets in the palace, all bearing Linear B inscriptions. They were stored in sealed wooden chests.

In 1939 the American archaeologist Carl W. Blegen and his Greek associate Kourouniotis dug up a set of archives very similar to those at Knossos, and comprising 600 clay tablets on the mainland, in western Messenia. This sensational discovery was made eleven miles north of the city of Pylos, and the ruined palace at Pylos yielded items similar to those at Knossos, including business statements, bills and labels, all drawn up in Linear B and dating from the fourteenth century B.C.

Blegen found another 400 tablets in 1952 and over fifty more in 1954, or a total of approximately 1050 tablets at this site.

Finally, in 1952, the English archaeologist Alan Wace discovered further examples of Linear B in the "House of the Wine Merchant" at Mycenae. They were the tradesman's accounts. Wace thinks that we can expect to find such tablets in every house and palace of this period —1300-1200 B.C.

All these tablets—the 2,000 Knossos tablets, the 1,050 Pylos tablets and the forty-two Mycenae tablets—display marked similarities—and all three groups are in Linear B. Before 1400, when Linear B first turned up on the mainland, the Greeks had no script of any kind. Then in 1300 or perhaps even about 1400, the people on the mainland began to write. But in 1100 B.C. writing in Greece died out again while in Crete, the disaster of 1400 destroyed both Linear A and Linear B. Greece represents the only case in the history of Europe where the art of writing completely disappeared after several centuries of use, for it was not until 800 B.C. that the Greeks adopted another script, this time from the Phoenicians of Thera on the island of Santorin.

For decades the Cretan notations remained unread since no one had managed to decipher their script. In 1928 the German historian of antiquity, Eduard Meyer, wrote: "Whether the discovery of a successful combination will one day make it possible for us to decipher this script remains uncertain, and what makes it even more problematical is that we know absolutely nothing about the basic language or even the names. . . ."

The English philologist Michael Ventris said in 1940: "The Minoan inscriptions of Knossos and elsewhere remain . . . the only wide-spread script in the ancient world which can neither be read nor understood."

The American philologist Kober stated in 1948: "We are dealing with three unknown quantities: language, script and meaning. . . . An unknown language written in an unknown script cannot be deciphered, either with or without a bilingual text."

Together with other scholars of many nationalities, the German philologist Ernst Sittig endeavored to decipher the Cretan script. His studies of the classical, Semitic, Slavonic, Etruscan, Cyprian and other rare idioms, including those of Asia Minor, made him admirably suited for his task.

As Evans, Myres and Sundwall before him, Sittig presumed a similarity between the script of ancient Crete and a Cypriote script. In Cyprus, this ancient syllabic script was used for another 1,000 years, almost exclusively for a Greek dialect but also for a pre-Greek language for which originally it must have been intended. On the basis of the individual characters, Sittig methodically compared the structure of this pre-Greek language with ancient Cretan, established their similarity and thus obtained reliable phonetic values for a number of Cretan syllabic symbols. By doing so, Sittig laid the foundations of a technique for deciphering the Minoan script of ancient Crete and ancient Cyprus.

In 1951 the Pylos inscriptions were published in America by Bennett, followed in 1952 by the Knossos inscriptions taken from Evans' papers after his death and published by John Myres, who was his friend. Then in 1953, a sensational development came from London: J. Chadwick and Michael Ventris demonstrated that the basic language on the tablets at Knossos, Pylos and Mycenae was not only Indo-European but *Greek*. Ventris and Chadwick deciphered sixty-five out of an approximate total of eighty symbols, and their interpretations have recently been corrected and amplified by Hans L. Stoltenberg of Giessen.

Without wishing to minimize the accomplishments of Ventris, it must be said that, considering all previous research, the assumption of Greek as the basic language behind the Linear B symbols was not as daring as it might seem. For example, if one combined three Minoan symbols whose value Sittig had already discovered–*ti*, *ri*, (or *re*, as the case might be), and *po*, which produced the word *tiripo* or *tripos*, namely, the Greek for tripod, it was fairly clear that some Greek idiom or other was involved, especially since on one of the Pylos inscriptions a tripod was painted behind these three symbols. The assumption made by Wace and Blegen on historical grounds–namely, that a Greek language was spoken in Mycenae and Pylos and perhaps even Tiryns, *i.e.*, in the fortified towns of the Mycenaean period–had now been proved beyond all reasonable doubt.

But how did the Linear B script get from Knossos to Pylos and Mycenae? What had happened in 1400 B.C.?

Apparently some people in Knossos had taken Linear A and evolved it into a script which could express Greek words. The result of this adaptation was Linear B. For the first time a script had been adapted for the Greek language, and since the Cretans were not of Greek origin the question arises as to who inhabited Knossos at that time, and who was interested in inventing a script for the Greek language.

It seems likely that by 1400, at the latest, rulers from the Greek mainland lived at Knossos, that a mainland dynasty had conquered

Knossos but no other city on the island, and that these rulers introduced the new invention to Pylos and Mycenae.

It might also be argued that the new script, Linear B, was brought to Knossos from the mainland. What militates against this theory, however, is that Linear B is related to the earlier Cretan Linear A script (in fact, nearly half the symbols of Linear A also appear in Linear B), and that Linear B thus must necessarily have evolved from Linear A. The additional fact that most of the clay tablets written in Linear B were found at Knossos—2,000 as against the 1,050 found at Pylos—also speaks for its Cretan origin. So Linear B was adapted for the Greek from Linear A, a script originally conceived for Cretan, a foreign language with no resemblance to Greek.

But what sort of Greek was spoken at that time?

We would expect the inhabitants of Pylos and Mycenae to have spoken an ancient Achaean dialect. And, in fact, the language on these little clay tablets is early Achaean of the early Arcadian variety.

The Minoans knew the decimal system, derived either from the Egyptians or from their own ten fingers. And if they had no single symbol for "five," we must remember that even our own Arabic 5 consists of five separate symbols. The Minoans had no nought sign, either. For 1, they used a simple vertical stroke |, for 2, two strokes ||, for 3, three strokes |||, for 4 two strokes on top and two below ¦¦. 8 was represented by four vertical strokes with another four beneath ¦¦¦¦, 9 by three groups of three strokes one beneath the other ⁞⁞⁞. If they wanted to change 9 to 8, they did not strike out one of the nine strokes, but erased all nine and replaced them by four strokes on top of another four. 10 was a horizontal stroke —, 20 was expressed by two horizontal strokes =, and so on up to 10,000, -①- the Greek myriad. Numerous miscalculations were discovered on the clay tablets. Some tablets also have crosses that look like our own multiplication sign ×. However, these were only marks made by those who checked the figures. The marks were found on thirty-nine Linear B documents.

With this clumsy system the Minoans could not pursue higher mathematics, but the system was quite adequate for lists of tribute payments, accounts and registers of craftsmen and laborers.

Ventris announced, after spending years on this script: "The more one studies Linear B, the more amazed one becomes at the stereotyped nature of the tablets, which goes far beyond the similarity of characters and language." Ventris assumes the existence of a permanent writing tradition with a common origin and environment. As long as

Linear B continued in use in Knossos, Pylos and Mycenae, the people retained the awkward characters without modifying them, and in this respect were far more conservative than the Phoenicians after them. Minoan civilization can hardly be described as "literary." This highly artistic people left no other literature behind except bookkeeping entries.

However, the deciphering of Linear B will gradually familiarize us with a pre-Homeric Greece, a Greece almost a thousand years older than the one we have known. This will have a tremendous influence on our knowledge of the early days of Greece, and the day will come when her history will no longer begin in 776 B.C., but in 1400 B.C., at the very latest.

Editor's Note:

As this book goes to press Professor Cyrus H. Gordon of Brandeis University, Waltham, Massachusetts, has announced that, using the deciphering framework built by Michael Ventris, he has decoded samples of Minoan Linear A and that the language on the samples is Akkadian, the Semitic tongue of Babylon. Although this solves the problem of Linear A, the indigenous language of Crete remains as much of a mystery as ever.

Reproduction of the characters on a tablet inscribed in "Linear B." Carl W. Blegen and K. Kourouniotis found hundreds of such tablets in West Messinia in 1939.

THE CITY OF PRIAM

So then I said: 'Father, if such walls were there at one time, they cannot have been completely destroyed, but are probably hidden beneath the dust and rubble of centuries.'

Heinrich Schliemann, at the age of eight

TWO AND A HALF miles from the shores of the Dardanelles is a hill which the Turks call Hissarlik. It is an ideal site for a fortress, citadel or town, since it stands some distance from the sea and is not directly exposed to naval attack, yet it commands the approaches to the Dardanelles. And it is no surprise therefore that the ruins of ten towns and villages lie buried beneath the hill of Hissarlik. It was originally believed that the hill contained only nine different layers, but archaeologists later realized that the seventh layer was made up of two distinct kinds of rubble, and so they divided it into two categories, VIIa and VIIb.

The lowest layer was composed of ruins at least 5,000 years old. The second layer, or Troy II, contains the ruins of a town which was burned down by some enemy hand about 4,200 years ago. The third, fourth and fifth layers–Troy III-V–covered the period 2200-1750 B.C., while Troy VI is a vanished civilization which flourished between 1750 and 1300 B.C. According to the American archaeologist Blegen, the giant walls of this particular period, which are still in relatively good condition, were demolished by an earthquake; an assumption he based on the fact that numerous unconnected walls all exhibit cracks running in the same direction. The archaeologist Wilhelm Dörpfeld took Troy VI for the Troy of Homer, but he was mistaken.

Troy VIIa was destroyed about 1200 B.C., which would agree with the ancient tradition which sets the date of Troy's destruction at 1185 B.C. Blegen presumes that Homer's city lies in that layer, and indeed it would seem that this is where the sources for one of the greatest heroic epics in human history lie buried. Professor Brandenstein of Graz also holds layer VIIa to be the Homeric Troy. Unlike Dörpfeld, he was not misled by the much more impressive walls in the sixth layer. The remaining three layers, Troy VIIb-IX, embrace the period 1200 B.C.-400A.D.

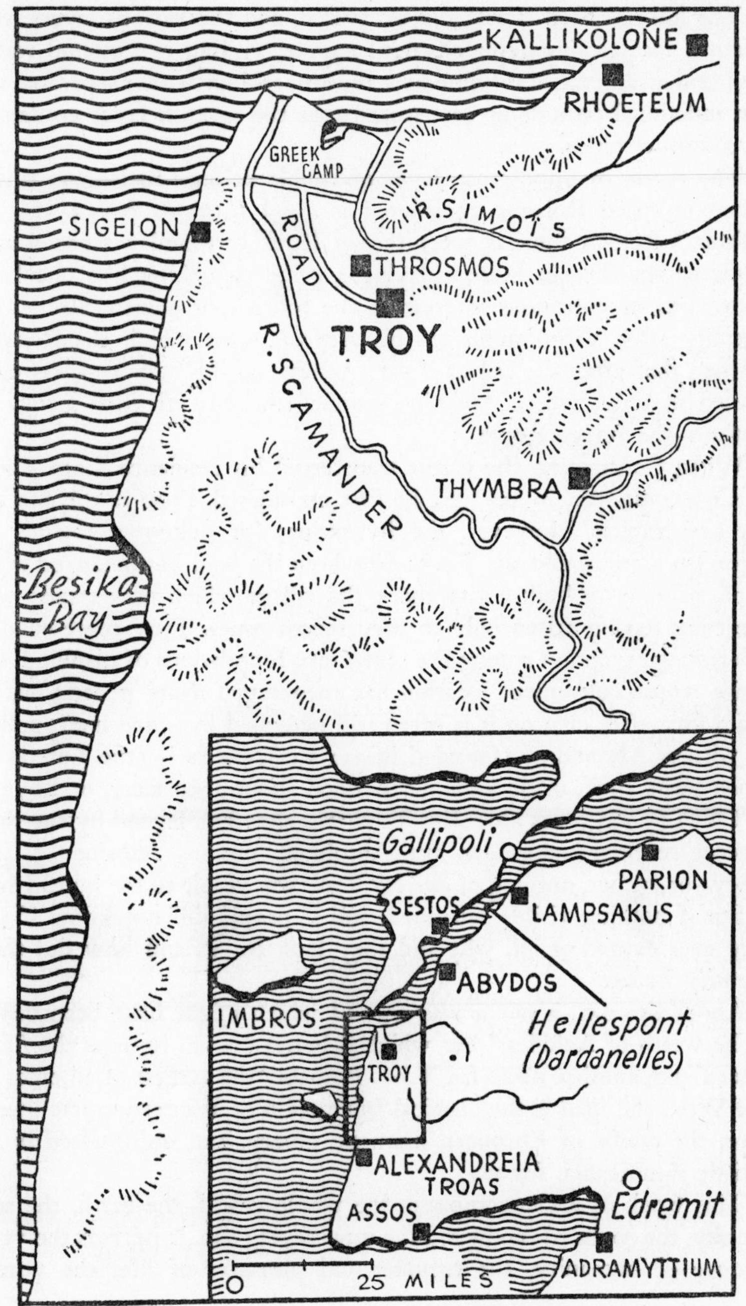
KALLIKOLONE
RHOETEUM
GREEK CAMP
SIGEION
R. SIMOIS
ROAD
THROSMOS
TROY
R. SCAMANDER
THYMBRA
Besika Bay
Gallipoli
PARION
SESTOS
LAMPSAKUS
ABYDOS
IMBROS
Hellespont (Dardanelles)
TROY
ALEXANDREIA TROAS
Edremit
ASSOS
ADRAMYTTIUM
0 25 MILES

The hill has been repeatedly excavated, and the various layers have become inextricably mingled, until anyone visiting the mound today will find it difficult to imagine how the archaeologists ever separated the ten individual periods or recognized that the seventh layer contained two distinct cities.

The tenth, or uppermost, layer of rubble belongs to Roman times; when cultured Romans considered it good form to pay a visit to "Troia." Roman tourists were shown Paris' lyre and a stone which depicted the Trojan heroes playing a game something like checkers. Troy was of enormous interest to the tourists of ancient Rome, especially after Virgil published his *Aeneid*, from which the Romans learned that after the fall of Troy, Aeneas and his son Ascanius emigrated to Italy, where Ascanius founded the city of Alba Longa in Latium—the future Rome.

When Constantine the Great transferred his residence from Rome to Constantinople, in 350 A.D., he first considered Troy as the site for his new capital. However, the Byzantines for unknown reasons let Troy go to ruin, and the Turks, to whom the land has belonged since 1306, have never built a city there, the village which now stands near the ruins having arisen only in very recent times. Troy represents an interesting exception among the oldest city foundations of mankind, for a site whose convenient location has encouraged many generations to build city after city on it is often still occupied by some metropolis—as witness Alexandria (founded in 332 B.C.), or Paris (the Lutetia of 3,000 years ago), or Jerusalem (founded about 2000 B.C.), or Loyang in China (5,000 years old). But Troy was already a legend by the time Greece reached her golden age. Absolutely nothing remained of her glory—or, rather, nothing of *ancient* Troy was visible to the human eye.

But if nothing visible remained, and if people did not know if the city ever existed at all, why did they look for it, and how did they identify its site?

About 850 B.C., a poem was created which might have been called "The wrath of Achilles," but which is better known to us as the *Iliad*, after Ilium, another name for Troy. Probably the earliest of all epics of the West, the *Iliad* is the classical foundation of Western world literature; the cradle of European dramatic poetry, and unsurpassed in its artistic significance for us.

This work of art encompasses the whole world—the earth, the sea, the sky, the rounded moon and the unwearying sun. It mirrors the very essence of humanity, the troubles and pleasures of life, the yearly round of toil on the land, the daily chores of the herdsman, fisherman and woodcutter, the moments of ecstasy in the graceful dance of maidens or the poet's song. From the sublime reality of the gods to the depths of the netherworld, from war, rage, delusion and bitter harshness to the most sensitive impulses of sympathy, friendship and conjugal love—there is nothing that lies outside the scope of this monumental work of epic poetry.

The *Iliad* is always regarded as the work of the poet Homer. But who was this Homer? Did he exist? And did he alone create this gigantic work, or were there countless other contributors?

In spite of all interpolations made at a later date, the *Iliad* is so homogeneous in style and composition that we must assume that only *one* genius was involved in this "enacted truth of an ever-present past," as Goethe called the giant epic.

The earliest mention of Homer's name is found in Xenophanes of Colophon, a Greek poet and philosopher who lived between 570 and 480 B.C. And Herodotus, the "father of history" we have so often quoted here, writes: "Homer lived four hundred years before my time." That would have been about 850 B.C.

It is astonishing that we know extremely little about the two greatest poets produced by the Western world—Homer and Shakespeare. Even in ancient times, there was very little certainty about the person of Homer. No less than seven cities wrangled over the honor of having been his birthplace. He was undoubtedly a Greek, and probably lived in Asia Minor. It is possible that he was born in the Greek town of Smyrna in Asia Minor, and perhaps he was blind, which, according to the Greek historian Ephorus, is what his name signifies. Even the number of Homer's works is a matter for controversy; it is even arguable whether he wrote both the *Iliad* and the *Odyssey*, since the two works are about a hundred years apart in time.

The *Iliad* describes the war for Troy. However, the poet does not deal with the whole ten years from the arrival of the Greeks to the fall of Troy, but only with fifty-one days, during which we live through the whole war up to and including the destruction of the city. But the division of the *Iliad* into twenty-four books was not Homer's idea: it was the Alexandrine scholars of a later age who split it up according to the number of letters in the Greek alphabet. This organization is, as it were, unprofessional, and the blind genius would have shaken his head at these literary amateurs. It is also likely that the ancient *Iliad* was somewhat shorter than its present Alexandrine version, and that it was expanded at Athens as early as Pisistratus' day, or 550 B.C. A mass of varied material has undoubtedly found its way into the work, including, for instance, some legends originating in the southern part of Asia Minor.

Just as Shakespeare culled the plots for most of his plays from old tales or historical works, so Homer created his remarkable epic from ancient folklore and tradition. The military events described in Homer's *Iliad* must have taken place in 1184 B.C., the year which the scholars of antiquity have set for Troy's destruction.

Homer's genius fell prey to the pardonable temptation of painting his compatriots in a more favorable light than their enemies. When the casualties of the two warring races are counted, for instance, the Greeks only lose 50 dead as compared with the Trojans' 200. Even the Trojans' victories are never entirely on the level—the valiant Greeks are often stabbed in the back or ambushed by concealed bowmen.

In the European imagination Troy was associated with Homer's poetry, and the ruins of the city slept undisturbed beneath the hill of Hissarlik. Nevertheless, since the long Trojan war could not merely have been invented by Homer; since so many details had to have some historical basis; since both Greeks and Romans assumed that the Homeric Troy must lie near the hill which much later became known as Hissarlik, the ancient city almost certainly had to be somewhere near there.

It was the local peasants who declared that Troy lay beneath Hissarlik, and Frank Calvert, an Englishman acting as United States consul in the Dardanelles, eventually bought part of the hill of Hissarlik with a view to excavating it. The project involved considerable expense, however, and when the British Museum declined to participate in the test diggings, Calvert abandoned his idea. Then, one day, he was visited by a millionaire, a strange man who told him unceremoniously that he wanted to excavate Troy and find King Priam's treasure. Calvert was delighted to be relieved of his worries by this odd stranger whose name was Heinrich Schliemann.

Schliemann was one of the most interesting personalities of the last century. A German who became an American citizen, a poor man who became a millionaire, he was at once businessman and scholar, visionary and realist, genius and pedant, a restless globetrotter and one of the most tenacious archaeologists who ever excavated the site of his youthful dreams: Troy.

His daughter, significantly named Andromache, once related an incident which occurred in her childhood. She remembered her father asking her for what she was reading. "*Ivanhoe*, by Sir Walter Scott," she replied. "Read me a sentence," said her father. But Andromache had scarcely read a few words when her father interrupted her and began to recite page after page of the book from memory. He had learned the entire book by heart when he was nineteen, and even at the age of sixty he remembered it word for word.

Heinrich Schliemann's biography reads like a fairy tale. A poor parson's son from Neu-Buckow in Mecklenburg-Schwerin, as a youth he fell in love with a girl of fourteen named Minna Meincke. Furthermore, she returned his affections, a happy circumstance which fired his ambition enormously. Heinrich was a shop assistant in a small general store in Fürstenberg, but later he went to Hamburg, where he signed on as cabin boy on the brig *Dorothea.* The ship sailed from Hamburg on November 28, 1841, but during the night of December 12 it sank. Schliemann was rescued, and later was employed by a commercial house in Amsterdam. A Brussels calligrapher taught him how to write.

Now he began to devote himself to the study of foreign languages, learning first Dutch, then English, French, Spanish, Portuguese, Italian, Swedish, Polish and Russian. To his impatient mind it all seemed to take far too long even though he learned these languages in a matter of months.

Schliemann was eventually doing so well as a commercial representative in St. Petersburg that he decided to propose to Minna, only to learn that his childhood sweetheart had married a few days before. He journeyed to the United States, and on July 4, 1850, during his stay in California, the territory achieved statehood and all the people who were there on that day—including Schliemann—became American citizens. In 1852, back in Europe, he opened an agency in Moscow to handle wholesale purchases of indigo, dye woods, saltpeter, sulphur and lead. And in his spare time he learned Greek and read all the classics (in particular the *Iliad* and the *Odyssey*) over and over again in ancient Greek. To his dying day, Schliemann knew both the *Iliad* and the *Odyssey* by heart.

By this time Schliemann had become an extremely wealthy man, so he retired from business and began for the first time in his life to take a good look at the world. Starting in Sweden, he traveled to Denmark, Germany, Italy, Egypt and Nubia. He speedily learned Arabic. He visited Syria and Smyrna, the Cyclades, Athens and the island of Ithaca. And when his Russian wife refused to leave her native land to travel with him, he divorced her, advertised in the papers for a Greek wife, and, at the age of 47, picked out a 19-year-old Greek girl from one of the photographs he received. He christened their son Agamemnon.

In 1864 he traveled to Tunis and visited the ruins of Carthage. Then, revisiting Egypt on the way, he journeyed to Ceylon, Madras, Calcutta, Benares, Agra, Lucknow, Delhi, the Himalayas, Java, Saigon and China. Schliemann climbed the Great Wall, traveled on to Japan, and then sailed off across the Pacific to San Francisco. During the passage, which lasted fifty days, he wrote his first book, *China and Japan.* From then on he settled down in Paris and devoted himself to the study of archaeology.

Then came the day when the millionaire met Frank Calvert, the man who owned half the hill of Hissarlik. On October 11, 1871, Schliemann began the first of his four extensive excavations of the mound. They covered eleven months out of the next two years, and by the end of that time Troy had been rediscovered.

In the course of his explorations, the brilliant scholar made an error. He worked his way through all the layers of Troy down to the lowest, and along the way came upon some fortifications—the ruins of a very ancient city which had burned down—and found immense treasures of gold and jewels. Schliemann dubbed this find "the treasure of Priam" (the collection was almost completely destroyed in Berlin during the last war), and thought he had discovered Homeric Troy. And although his city belonged to a much earlier period, he had in fact found Troy; his only error lay in confusing the layers with which he was dealing. Astonishing as it may seem, Schielmann had dug down *past* Homer's Troy (VIIa), for the gold and silver and the ruined palace he found belonged to Troy II, destroyed about 2200 B.C. However, he had gained his main objective: he had found out where the legendary city had been sleeping. It was only shortly before his death that Schliemann realized his error, too late for him to start digging again.

Before the end of his fascinating life, Schliemann carried out excavations at Mycenae, Ithaca and Orchomenos. He unearthed a portion of Tiryns and intended to excavate the palace of Minos in Crete. But one lifetime is not long enough, he had to leave it to others to complete the project he had started or planned.

Schliemann's closest associate was Wilhelm Dörpfeld, the brilliant archaeologist who died as recently as 1940, at the age of eighty-six. It was Dörpfeld who excavated ancient Olympia and Pergamum and who carried on Schliemann's work at Hissarlik with such perseverance that, stone by stone, Troy came to life under his hands. This gifted man invented a methodology for excavations which is now used by archaeologists all over the world.

Schliemann was buried in Athens, which was appropriate enough, for he was the man who proved what for centuries had been only dimly suspected—that Troy and the heroic epic called the *Iliad* were not merely the products of Homer's wild imagination. They really existed —in stone and gold, flesh and blood.

GRAVES TELL SECRETS

Agamemnon really lived, and so did Hercules, the strongest man in all history. Mycenae was not mere legend, nor Tiryns mere imagination. The entire prehistory of Greece, with all its legendary figures and Homeric cities, is being excavated stone by stone. It was all true.

HISTORY is the written past. And it can take us back only as far as writings and inscriptions exist to tell us of man's activities on earth.

Yet, by far the greater fraction of humanity's past lies in those dim times when there was no writing but only oral tradition. It is these interminable ages which precede our written sources of historical information and are thus without written records or fixed chronology which we call prehistory. Only the soil can tell us what happened in those times, and the real experts of prehistory are the field archaeologists.

Modern techniques have now reached the stage where we can obtain from a single fragment of pottery, by the specific way in which a stone is chipped, and especially by the radio-carbon method (C_{14}) evolved by Professor Libby of Chicago, a pretty accurate idea of dates. The archaeologists, the explorers of the soil, are the detectives who uncover the good and—seemingly more frequently—the evil deeds that men have committed in far distant times. The tiniest clue may lead to the discovery of strange religious beliefs, superstitions, or other aspects of human activity—in short, to the deeds and misdeeds, large and small, which make up what is known as prehistory.

The history of Greece as it emerges from written documents covers only a span of about 600 years. It begins with the first Olympiad in 776 B.C. and ends in 146 B.C., when Greece was placed under the general supervision of the Roman Governor of Macedonia.

Before this time lies a much longer era, embracing approximately 3,000 years, which is lost in a fog of legends, myths and heroic sagas which were passed on by word of mouth and not written down until much later.

On the basis of the materials man used to make his tools and weapons, science has divided prehistory into the following main categories: the Paleolithic Age, the Neolithic Age, the Bronze Age and the Iron Age.

At first, men fashioned their weapons and implements out of stone. Then they invented pottery and learned how to bake clay vessels, and finally they discovered the use of metals and their alloys. Stone preceded bronze and bronze preceded iron: this was the same the world over.

Greece apparently was not inhabited during the Paleolithic Age, and it was Achilles' native land, fertile Thessaly, which played a decisive role in settling the area. During the Neolithic Age a number of tribes from Asia Minor arrived in Thessaly, and settled there. The earliest civilization found in Greece is known as the Sesklo civilization and was discovered in Thessaly. It lasted from 3000 to 2800 B.C., during which time it expanded over all of Greece.

The next immigrant invasion came from the lands along the Danube, and arrived in two waves. Some authorities have attempted, on insufficient grounds, to classify these immigrants as proto-Indo-Europeans. The first wave never got beyond Thessaly where their culture is known as the Dimini civilization, after the main site of its discovery. The second wave, however, reached the northern Peloponnesus. The rest of Greece was at that time in its early Helladic stage which lasted roughly from 2500 to 2400 B.C., and marked the transition to the age of metals.

The two succeeding stages are merely evolutionary, and are known as Early Helladic II and III (2400-1900 B.C.); they represent the link with the Bronze Age. Then in 1900 B.C. a new race appeared from the north and devastated many settlements. This time there is reasonable justification for assuming that the invaders were Indo-Europeans, but there is no proof that they were, properly speaking, Greeks. This was the beginning of the pre-Mycenaean Bronze (also known as Middle Helladic) Age, and the cultural transition to the Late Helladic period, or Mycenaean Bronze Age, followed about 1600 B.C. And the appearance of the so-called war chariot—a light, two-wheeled racing and fighting vehicle introduced into the Near East by way of India at about that time—probably indicates that a new race had indeed arrived: the Mycenaean Greeks, the same people who produced Homer's heroes.

Mycenaean civilization, which was strongly influenced by Crete, was completely wiped out about 1200 B.C. by the so-called Aegean migration. This cataclysmic event was undoubtedly connected with the greatest of all prehistoric migrations, that of the Urn-Field People—so named by scholars of prehistory because these people cremated their dead and buried their remains in large urns which were sunk into the ground in regular cemeteries, forming the large urn fields which are the only legacy these people left us. The great migration originated in central Germany, and eventually caused an upheaval in almost every civilization of the contemporary world as one race after another was set in motion. About 1200 B.C. all of Greece was razed by these invaders. Later, the Dorian Greeks wandered into the country together with Illyrian tribes.

Two cities were pre-eminent during the Bronze Age of prehistoric Greece: Mycenae and Tiryns. Both were in the Argolis region of the Peloponnesus, and modern archaeologists might never have looked for either of them had Homer not mentioned them in his *Iliad*. According to Homer, Mycenae was the stronghold of Agamemnon, the prince who besieged Troy.

It has long been disputed whether Agamemnon was a historical personage or merely a legendary figure, for many Greek myths originated in the Mycenaean period, a prehistoric era between 1,000 and 2,000 years before the birth of Christ. But during the past hundred years archaeologists have transposed one legendary city and one mythological hero after another from shadowy existence into reality. We know today that Agamemnon, the man who besieged Troy, really lived: Alan J. B. Wace dates him at about 1200 B.C. Homer has given us the names of Agamemnon's father, Atreus, and of his brother, Menelaus. These men, too, must have been historical figures.

Legend also tells us of Hercules (the Greek Heracles), whose descendants, the Heraclidae, were the heroes of the Dorian migration, the last major influx of people to pour into Greece. Hercules settled down at Tiryns in the service of the lord of Mycenae, who was his wicked uncle Eurystheus. Hercules was reputedly the strongest man in the world. Even in Roman times the school children were still told about the feats of Hercules. It appears that Eurystheus of Mycenae felt uneasy about having such a strong vassal as Hercules virtually on his doorstep, for Tiryns was but nine miles away from Mycenae. So Eurystheus in an effort to destroy his nephew set him twelve tasks, each more difficult than the last. Hercules' labors eventually took him as far as the Straits of Gibraltar, the gateway to the Atlantic, which the ancients came to call the "Pillars of Hercules."

It would seem obvious that a city linked with such names as Eurystheus and Hercules, Atreus and Agamemnon, must have stood *somewhere*, but its alleged site was now covered by a nondescript hill. Undiscouraged, two Englishmen (Lord Elgin and Lord Sligo) and

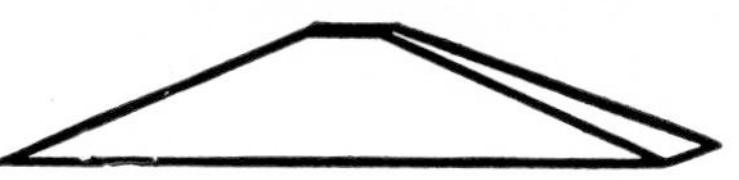

(a) *The pyramid at Cholula, Mexico.* Its cubic capacity (38,820,000 cubic yards) is larger than that of the Pyramid of Cheops.

(b) *The sun pyramid at Teotihuacán,* the ruined city's largest building (drawn to scale).

(c) *The moon pyramid at Teotihuacán,* probably the city's most important building.

(d) *The Pyramid of Cheops, Egypt.* Its capacity is about 35,402,790 cubic yards.

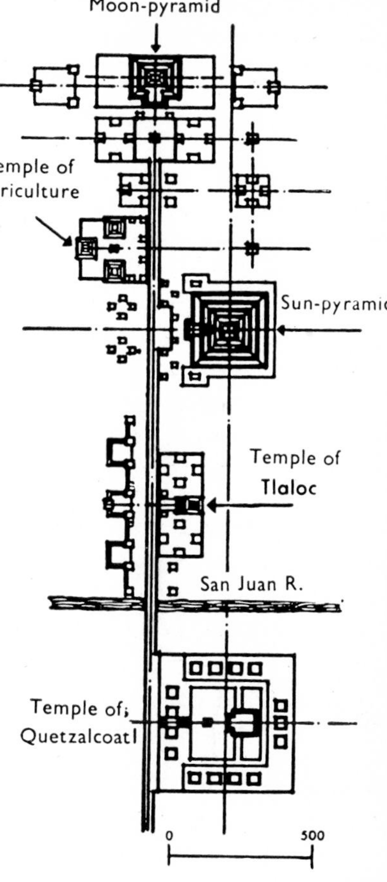

Plan of Teotihuacan

This overgrown hill is really the pyramid of Cholula, in cubic capacity the largest building in the world. It is now surmounted by the church of Los Remedios.

Mexican mummy from Comatlan, showing typical hunched up position.

A Knossos "creation," 2000 B.C. Skirt adorned with crocuses, bodice vertically striped, waist narrow.

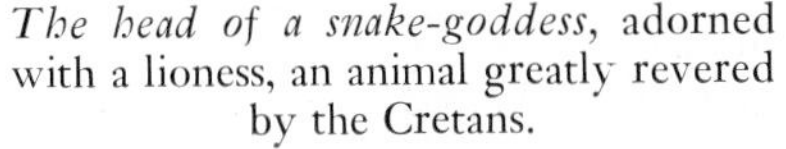

The head of a snake-goddess, adorned with a lioness, an animal greatly revered by the Cretans.

Tight bodices were the height of fashion. Note the wealth of beautiful embroidery.

A gown with six flounces, surmounted by a short hip-piece and a sort of apron. The beautiful long black hair is carefully dressed.

Limestone figure of a Minoan snake-goddess dates from 1500 B.C. The Cretans had a household snake-cult, and there was a snake-room in the palace at Knossos.

In the Minoan civilization women's clothing displayed great opulence and refinement of taste. The waist was kept very slim, and elaborate corsets were worn, but the breasts were always exposed. This was the Goddess of Sport.

Ivory carving found at Mycenae, in the Peloponnesus. It probably dates from the late Bronze Age, or about 3,500 years ago. This period produced some remarkably fine workmanship in ivory.

Left: a two-drachma piece in silver with Nike's head. *Center:* a Syracusan ten-drachma piece from the year 405 B.C. (a bull cost about five drachmas). *Right:* an Achaean two-drachma piece bearing the head of the goddess Artemis.

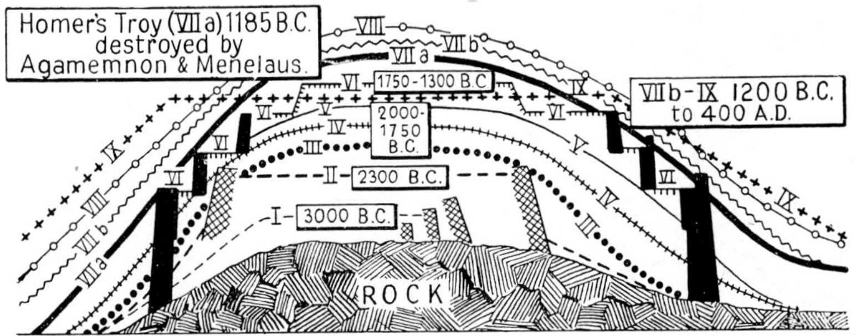

Layer VIIa is believed by Professor Brandenstein of Graz and the American archaeologist Carl Blegen to contain the city of Troy which Homer described in his *Iliad*.

The hill of Hissarlik, two and a half miles from the shores of the Dardanelles in Turkey. Under it was found the debris of ten separate Trojan settlements.

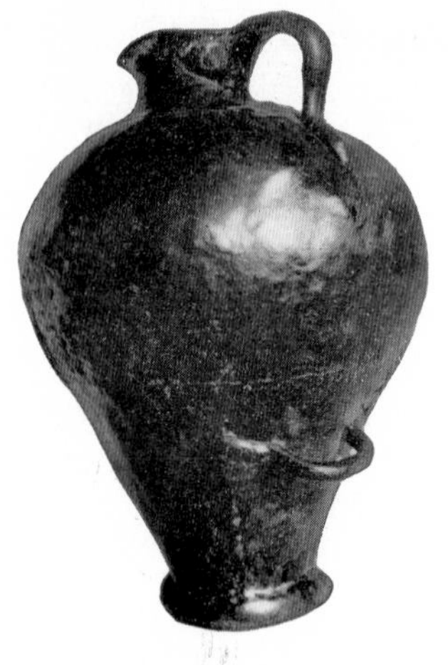

Large copper water-jug from Grave IV in the citadel of Mycenae. The jug had been repaired.

This golden beaker also came from Grave IV at Mycenae, which contained five bodies.

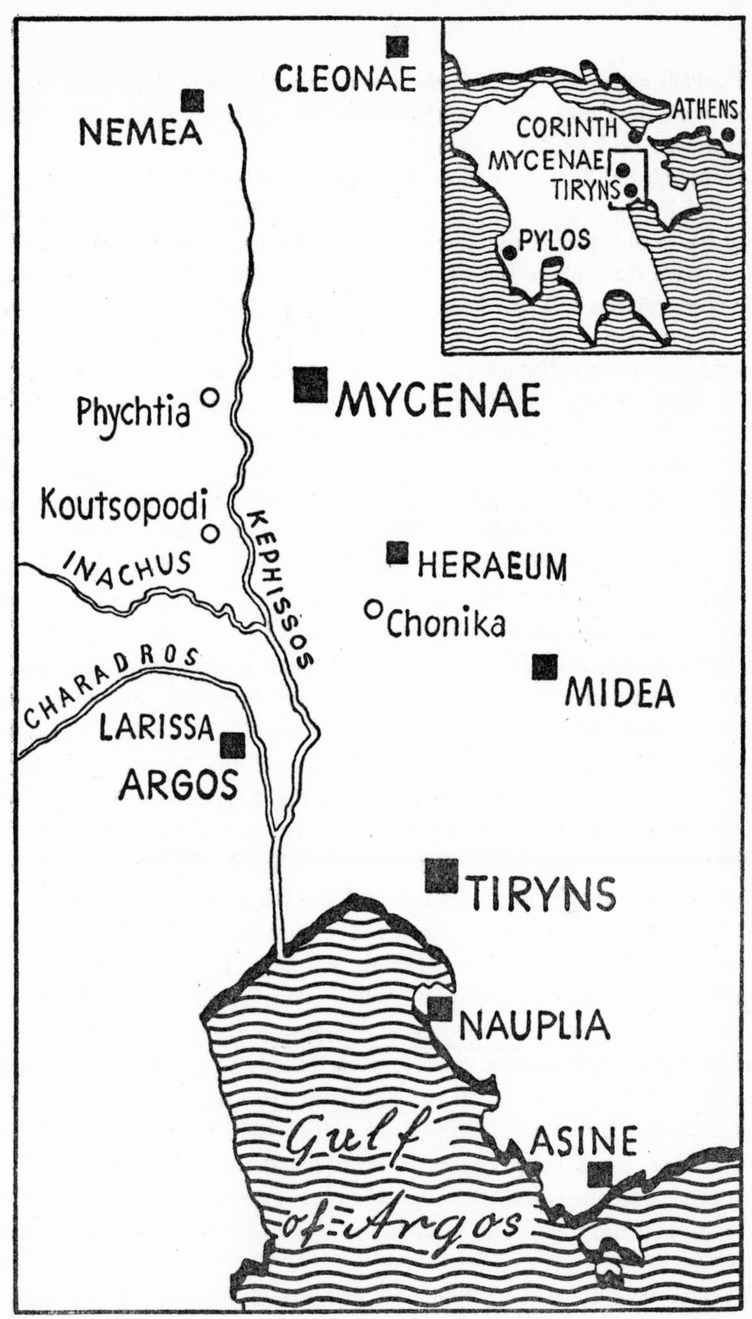

The large fortified towns of the Mycenaean period.

a Turkish governor (Veli Pasha) began to dig there. But these gentlemen were less concerned with prehistoric research than with finding sculptures, and ancient treasures.

Heinrich Schliemann had other motives: respect for mythology, and a belief in the basic truth of prehistoric tradition. He was convinced that he could prove the historicity of Homer's descriptions, and in 1874, with the excavation of Troy already behind him, he started test diggings on the hill at Mycenae, hoping to find Agamemnon's grave and the treasure of Atreus. It was a bold undertaking: who today would set out to dig up the famous hoard of the Nibelungs?

In 1876, when Schliemann began his excavations in earnest, he opened up a whole new world for archaeology. He found five royal graves dating from the sixteenth century B.C., graves damaged only by the ravages of time and not by human hand; they had neither been broken open nor plundered. Schliemann's excavations were costing him a fortune—his own money, too—but he knew almost too well that his fame was guaranteed for all time to come. He wrote: "I could not abandon the excavations at Mycenae before I had thoroughly explored all the royal graves. It is well known what a wonderful measure of success attended my excavations, and how immense and remarkable were the treasures with which I enriched the Greek nation. Far in the distant future, travelers from all quarters of the world will still be flocking into the Greek capital to visit the Mycenaean Museum and marvel at and study the fruits of my disinterested labors."

Between 1877 and 1878, the Greek archaeologist Stamatakes continued Schliemann's work and found a sixth grave which he named the "Grave of Agamemnon or the Treasure of Atreus." At the turn of the century yet another Greek scholar, Tsountas, followed in Schliemann's footsteps, and now a fairly accurate picture of Mycenaean civilization began to take shape. Keramopoullos and the German archaeologist Rodenwaldt also set their spades to the task; the British School at Athens worked on the hill from 1920 on, and finally the site was explored by that phenomenally gifted British archaeologist Alan J. B. Wace, the man who clearly recognized that Mycenaean culture between 1400 and 1200 B.C. was an early expression of the spirit of Greece—and the same man who found the forty-two tablets in Linear B script.

Thus archaeology shed light first on prehistory and then on people who had left written records.

The citadel at Mycenae was already inhabited by men in 3000 B.C.—5,000 years ago. Many centuries later the first Greek tribes apparently immigrated about 2000 B.C.—their arrival marking the beginning of the city's golden age. Gradually Mycenae established relations with Crete and adopted the island's customs, habits, art, technical knowledge and script—in short, everything we define as culture. Nevertheless, it was only after Crete's power had been broken and the mainland states were free to develop independently that Mycenaean civilization attained its greatest heights. In 1350 B.C. the city was expanded, and the legendary Cyclopean walls with their Lion Gate were built. Later Greek generations did not believe that ordinary mortals could have piled up such massive stone blocks, and so they ascribed the work to giants; one-eyed titans whom they called Cyclops, or "round eyes." The citadel of Tiryns was surrounded by similar Cyclopean walls, and Tiryns and Mycenae are probably the earliest large fortified towns in Europe.

A whole chain of fortresses extended across the region of Argolis, from Tiryns via Nauplia, Asine, Midaea, Argos and Prosymna to Mycenae, largest and strongest of them all. Most of these sites show evidence of violent destruction which must have occurred about 1100 B.C. The fortresses were first pillaged and then burned to the ground. We do not know how long Mycenae remained unoccupied, but people were living there again somewhere between 1100 and 750 B.C. In 468 B.C. Mycenae was attacked by her jealous neighbor Argos and eventually razed. When the Greek geographer Pausanias visited the site in the second century A.D., he found it in ruins. And oddly enough, the town was never rebuilt but remained buried under rubble, eventually turning into just another hill like Troy.

It is astonishing how many details of a people's daily life are revealed by graves. Schliemann's six Mycenaean shaft graves dating from the sixteenth century B.C. tell the story of a whole civilization. The human skeletons lay stretched out on their backs, most of them with their heads pointing east. The men were buried with their weapons, their faces covered by golden masks. These masks are, as Hermann Bengtson has pointed out, the first attempts at portraiture in Europe. And while the skulls had crumbled, the masks survived, so that we can see the faces of the Mycenaean princes as they looked in life. They belong either to a Nordic or a Mediterranean race, and the varying beard styles are clearly distinguishable. Similar golden masks, dating from the sixth century B.C., were found at Trebenishtshe in southern Jugoslavia.

The shaft graves of Mycenae contained numerous fragments of gold leaf scattered about, above and below the skeletons. These little pieces of gold leaf had obviously been sewn onto the cloths which once swathed the corpses. Weapons and implements lying beside the dead included metal receptacles, clay utensils, breastplates, swords, daggers, knives and chisels. The graves were obviously family vaults, and grave IV contained the bodies of five adults and two children. The three corpses in grave III were smothered under golden ornaments. Large golden crowns were found on two of the skulls. Thirty-five arrowheads lay in a heap, and the corpses of two babies were completely encased in gold, evidence that the children had been laid to rest with loving care.

The women of the Mycenaean civilization set great store by cosmetics, as their silvery tweezers and little cosmetic jars and spoons prove. A semicircular ivory comb, earrings, necklaces, finger rings and thirty-seven golden buttons in an alabaster bowl all indicate that jewelry and dainty fashion accessories were in vogue here 3,500 years ago. However, it seems that the ladies of Mycenae seldom if ever looked at themselves in the mirror. One single mirror-metal was found, and archaeologists even doubt if the object was a mirror at all.

The men wore short aprons or trousers. Nakedness was considered unseemly, and women of the upper class wore long chemises and tight, short-sleeved jackets which, however, sometimes left the breasts bare. We know nothing about the footwear of the early and middle Bronze Age, but strangely enough fragments of linen have been preserved for all this time. Among other things which the graves yielded up were pieces of wood (mainly tiny fragments of cypress), razors, a checker board, fasteners for leggings, helmet crests in gold and a thousand articles for daily use.

We know that the Mycenaeans were familiar with eagles, swallows, butterflies, the nautilus and the octopus. And sea monsters seem to have played an important part in their lives. The stone walls of their burial places bore the earliest representations of a two-wheeled war chariot to be found in Hellas. Oxen, sheep, pigs, goats and donkeys were the principal domestic animals, but chickens, ducks and geese were also kept, and many pictures of horses have been found. It appears that the dog was always man's most loyal companion: the rulers of those ancient days used to take their favorite dog along with them into the graves, as the presence of canine skeletons indicate.

The graves have disclosed a life of amazing diversity and richness. The heroes of antiquity have thrown off their shrouds of dust, debris and ruins, and a prehistoric world 4,000 years old, which had long remained in the realm of legend, is again coming to life.

THE WORLD'S FIRST DEMOCRACY

We Athenians fought the Persian at Marathon singlehanded. When he returned, and we were not strong enough to defend ourselves against him on land, we boarded our ships one and all, and in company with the other Greeks, fought the sea battle at Salamis.

Thucydides I, 73

GREECE is a rocky peninsula, largely treeless and barren, lying insignificant, small and forlorn in a distant corner of the Mediterranean. Yet the *history* of this peninsula forms the basis of Western civilization–regardless of whether we think of it in terms of six centuries, according to former tradition, or in terms of some 1,300 years, as the latest excavations strongly suggest.

As we have said, the history of Greece traditionally began in 776 B.C., with the first Olympiad, and ended in 146 B.C., when the Greek world passed under Roman domination. In these 600 years the Greeks created more history than any other people of the Western world. In the beginning was Greece: twenty centuries have lived off the fruits of her experience.

It was here that a relatively small group of men dethroned the blind and unpredictable deities of the East which had ruled the world for thousands of years. The Greeks fought their way through the tangled misconceptions of oriental mythology to the conviction that the universe is ordered, and that by using reason man can comprehend it. The Greeks recognized the concept of virtue. The Greeks were the first to make scientific truth the goal of all thought. It is to the Greeks that we owe our ideas of political freedom and equality before the law. Two thousand years have done nothing to pale the glory of this inexhaustible heritage. It is this bedrock of extraordinary historical vitality, this classical civilization at the very beginning of European thought, this intellectual miracle that was Greece, which forever forms the indispensable basis for understanding the present.

The Greeks passed on their store of knowledge to the Romans, and in Rome the spiritual order of Greece was fused with Christianity. It is this unity which supports the edifice of Western civilization—which *is* Western civilization, for without this foundation we would plunge back 2,000 years in time.

In the second millennium B.C., wave upon wave of immigrants invaded Greece—Indo-European mountain tribes who pushed further and further south until they eventually occupied the Peloponnesus. The Achaeans were followed by the Aeolians and Ionians and, finally, by the Dorians, ancestors of the Greeks of classical times, who settled in the Peloponnesus as well as on Crete, Rhodes and many other islands. This Dorian migration overwhelmed the ancient civilizations of the Minoans and Mycenaeans and also conquered the Achaeans who had arrived several centuries earlier.

The numerous Greek tribes never established one common state, but they nevertheless regarded themselves as one people to whom all others were *barbaroi*, or foreigners. Despite all their differences, the Greek tribes were united by a common language, common religious beliefs, the oracle at Delphi, a kind of league of nations (the Amphictyonic League) and their great national festivals—the Olympic, Isthmian, Nemean and Pythian games—the most famous being the Olympic games. One and all, the tribes which spoke Greek and were linked by Delphi, the League and the games, called themselves Hellenes, and their country, Hellas. The word "Greek" by which we know them comes from Italy, where the first people to build a Greek city on Italian soil were probably the Graiei. The Latin version of this name was "Graeci," and it is this which is the basis of our own word "Greek."

Most historical works merely tell us about the amazing progress of the Greek peoples. But if we wish to understand the secret of Greece's immense cultural achievements, we must try to analyze the characteristics of her two predominant tribes, the Dorians and Ionians. The Dorians were mountain people. The Ionians inhabited the seacoasts. The Dorians—as shown by Sparta—were a practical, hardy, conservative, helpful and, on the whole, good-natured people. The Ionians were probably more temperamental and imaginative. They were seafarers, merchants, cosmopolitans, and it was they who provided the intellectual element of the blend. They traveled widely, saw a great deal of the world, talked about their experiences and embroidered on them, and invented the drama. It was these two largest, and very different, tribes which determined the ultimate destiny and success of Greece. They were as fortunate a combination as the Anglo-Saxons and Celts in the United Kingdom—the English and Scots of today.

Gradually the Greeks founded colonies on the coasts of Asia Minor, in southern Italy and Sicily, and on the northern shores of Africa.

They even went as far as Gibraltar. The Italian settlements of Tarentum, Sybaris, Croton, Cumae and Neapolis were all founded by the Greeks, as were Syracuse in Sicily and Cyrene on the North African coast. Massilia (modern Marseilles) was also a Greek commercial center.

The Greeks' homeland, however, was not Hellas–or Greece–but the *polis*, or city-state. Greece was split up into hundreds of such political microcosms which in general passed through four phases. They began as monarchies, but in the eighth and seventh centuries B.C. the kings were on their way out, and the monarchy was replaced by an oligarchy, or "government by the few." The oligarchy in turn gave way to tyranny, but one social group or another was always discontented. A tyrant would rise to power on the strength of his program, and when he had broken every one of his promises he was overthrown (and usually assassinated), and then it was the people's turn: a democracy, or "government by the people," was formed. Greek history has shown that the *tyrannis*, or rule by a tyrant, is the most reliable preliminary phase for a democracy, and that a tyrant often stands between oligarchy and democracy.

In 527 B.C., before the aged tyrant Pisistratus died a natural death at Athens, he handed over the reins of government to his two sons, Hippias and Hipparchus. Hippias, the elder, devoted himself to state affairs, but Hipparchus preferred to concentrate on poetry and love.

At that time there lived in Athens a handsome young man named Harmodius, who was in love with a citizen named Aristogeiton. These two Athenians were linked by a passionate friendship, until one day Hipparchus took a fancy to Harmodius' exceptional charms. Harmodius rebuked him and reported the whole story to his friend Aristogeiton, who immediately flew into a jealous rage.

When Hipparchus' overtures were rejected a second time, he resolved to take revenge. It so happened that the object of his infatuation had a young and virginal sister who was chosen to "carry the basket" in the religious procession during the great Panathenaea of 514 B.C. Hipparchus saw to it that this honor was withdrawn from the young girl on the grounds that "she was far too wicked for it." This insult roused Harmodius and his friend Aristogeiton to such a pitch of anger that they decided to wait only for the day of the Panathenaea to avenge themselves on Hipparchus and overthrow the tyranny. It was an ideal occasion since anyone attending the festival could carry arms without arousing suspicion, and when the time came they fell upon Hipparchus furiously and stabbed him to death.

Aristogeiton managed to escape temporarily, but Harmodius was killed on the spot. Now if two tryrants are in power—and they are brothers to boot—there is little point in killing only one of them, and unfortunately an attempt on the elder brother's life miscarried in the general confusion. Hippias now became cautious and frightened: he had numerous Athenians executed and Aristogeiton was tortured to death. It is said that a beautiful girl, Leaena, was also in love with the handsome Harmodius. She, too, was subjected to torture, but refused to reveal the names of the other conspirators. Instead, she purportedly bit off her tongue and spat it in the faces of her tormentors.

The tyrant Hippias governed for another three years until he was forced to abdicate in 510 B.C. Under a close escort, he managed to reach the court of the Persian king, Darius, and twenty years later when he was a very old man he had occasion to see the striking power of a democracy in action when, from the Persian ranks, he watched his Athenians win the battle of Marathon. Harmodius' and Aristogeiton's heroic act became the symbol of Athenian liberty. When Cleisthenes took Athens he gave her the first democratic government in world history. That was in 508 B.C. From then on, dangerous persons—*i.e.*, those who showed any signs of becoming demagogues or tyrants—could be exiled, and any citizen whom a majority of at least 6,000 votes declared to be dangerous was forced to leave the country for ten years. The people cast their votes by scratching their own names on pieces of clay.

Meanwhile, Sparta had grown into the most powerful military state in Greece. Still clinging to a primitive monarchical form of government and adhering to the strict laws initiated by Lycurgus, she watched her democratic rival, Athens, with mounting jealousy.

It was at about this time that the Greeks began to develop the twin talents which were to make them unique in the history of the world: science and philosophy.

Thales, the first Greek philosopher, was a citizen of Miletus who won universal admiration in Greece by predicting a solar eclipse for May 28, 585 B.C., which duly occurred. Thales believed that plants, metals and animals possessed an immortal soul, just as human beings did. When he was asked what he regarded as difficult, Thales answered:

"To know myself." And when he was asked what he regarded as easy, he replied: "To give advice."

Pythagoras, who was born on the island of Samus, was also a Greek philosopher, but from 529 B.C. on he lived at Croton in Italy. He is reported to have been the most indefatigable scholar of his time. At Croton he became the center of a sort of religious brotherhood devoted as much to philosophy as to a new moral order. It is worthy of note that, five centuries before the birth of Christ, Pythagoras' most important precept was the immortality of the soul. His amazing intellect was not concerned with mathematics and geometry alone. He established rules for music, studied harmony and was an astronomer of repute.

Heraclitus was a recluse and a meditator from Ephesus who lived between 540 and 475 B.C. He was possibly the father of metaphysics, or the doctrine of the ultimate unity and coherence of all life. To him, heat and cold, good and evil, day and night, all formed a unity and were merely complementary halves of one and the same thing. Fire was the basic substance and rhythm, the reason of the universe.

Heraclitus' lonely life, his contempt for humanity, the depth of his philosophy and his dark, oracular pronouncements caused him to be named "the dark philosopher," while Democritus of Abdera who lived about 450 B.C. in Thrace was called by the Greeks "the laughing philosopher." Democritus' genius produced seventy-two works whose subjects included the study of atoms and cosmology, the origins of the universe, the soul, emotions, ethics and theology. He believed that the upper regions of the air were peopled by creatures composed of the tiniest atoms, and hence far less susceptible to decay than humans, but nonetheless mortal.

The Greeks' greatest poetess was Sappho, who was born about 635 B.C. on Lesbos, the island of wine and flowers. She is said to have composed nine books of poems, epigrams and elegiac verse, but until recently her compositions were known to us only from quotations of ancient authors. It is only in the last fifty years that papyrus rolls were found in Egypt, bearing authentic texts of Sappho's works. Fragments of these rolls are now in Oxford, Berlin, London, Florence, Halle and Graz.

Sappho was one of the great lovers of history. But she literally devoted her life in giving love to others, and was perhaps the first woman in Europe who, by keeping aloof from men, consumed herself entirely in the service of Aphrodite and immortalized that love in verse. She was at once priestess and poetess. On Lesbos, young girls had formed sacred societies called *thiasoi*, to prepare for marriage. They worshiped Aphrodite, prepared future brides for marriage, guided their education, and cultivated all the fine arts, including music, singing and the choral dance. These consecrated societies were also schools for deportment, grace and charm. There were several such schools at Mytilene, the capital of Lesbos, and Sappho directed the most important of these. She enjoyed a world-wide reputation, for—in spite of all the vilification heaped on her name in later centuries—she was perhaps the greatest and most dedicated teacher of womanhood in history. And in her devotion to the refinement and education of young girls, she was the first to experience the calvary and transfiguration which is the lot of all women teachers. She saw the eternal failings of humanity and knew how to forgive them. She worried and grieved, yearned and prayed—and was patient, gentle in her reprimands, and ever ready to console. She saw her girls come and go, while she alone remained solitary and unfulfilled, yet she was always stirred and fascinated by the lives of others.

The famous Greek geographer Strabo (63 B.C.-19 A.D.) said of Sappho: "There is, to our knowledge, no other poetess in the long ages of history to equal her." Plato called her "the tenth Muse." And on her death at Mytilene she was accorded the honor of a hero's burial. The work of this great woman is a fragment shattered by time so that the verses of "pure, gently smiling Sappho," as the Greek poet Alcaeus called her, will never be known to us in their entirety. But our own era, which trusts nobody and believes in virtually nothing, has once more taken Sappho's sensitive love and pure devotion, her secret life of dreams and visions, her fragile body which yearned for eternal love and goodness, and burned it on the funeral pyre of abuse and misrepresentation. It was not until 1897 that Grenfell and Hunt discovered some burial shrouds made of papier-mâché at Oxyrhynchus in Egypt. This material was composed of ancient papyrus rolls that contained the texts of some of Sappho's poems.

With the Greek spirit and Grecian statecraft well on the way to immortality, ominous storm clouds began to gather in the East. Persia, the great Asiatic power of the day, had observed the awakening of the free peoples of Greece, for Athens had been aiding the oppressed Greeks in Asia Minor. The ensuing wars between Persia and Greece were a dramatic climax to the conflict between the two great world powers and their ideologies.

There was neither sympathy nor understanding between the peoples of Greece and Persia, and to the Greeks their victories over the Persians under Datis and Artaphernes in 490 B.C. were simply the result of their better moral cause. They felt that the subjects of a dictator must always ultimately prove inferior to the citizens of free states. The Persians fought under duress, the Greeks out of conviction.

The battles of Marathon, Thermopylae, Salamis, Plateaea and Mycale were contests between the Persian giant and the Greek midget. And in the end the midget won. Why? Because he was morally and intellectually superior to the giant.

Germany's great classical scholar Ulrich von Wilamowitz-Möllendorff wrote: "The days of Marathon and Salamis were epoch-making. They determined, for the moment and for perpetuity, that there would be an individual European culture and a political and social order at once superior to and unlike any which the East–its Aryans as well as its Semites–had ever possessed."

THE AGE OF PERICLES

That is what earthly immortality means—that one of the great ages of civilization be designated by the name of Pericles. Men of great superiority are anyway irreplaceable.

Leopold von Ranke, 1795-1886

THEMISTOCLES was the greatest of the Greek statesmen, one of the first outstanding personalities to appear on the stage of European history, and the man who laid the cornerstone of Athens' world-wide importance. Gifted to a degree where his wisdom became foolhardy and bordered on high treason, he was often unscrupulous in the means he employed to gain his goal. He had an unusually flexible mind. And if no one before him had ever rendered Athens such great services, no one before him had ever demanded and exacted such high payment for them either. He was regarded as egotistical, greedy, unpredictable and cunning. Even as a young man he was avid for fame. After the battle of Marathon when he walked around lost in melancholy thought during the day and was unable to sleep at night, friends asked him what was wrong. He replied that he could not stop brooding about the reputation Miltiades had won by his victory.

Themistocles was probably born in 514 B.C., but almost nothing is known about his early years. Later, however, he elbowed his way ruthlessly into power, for he had certain ideas and was determined to carry them out. All Greece could see the danger that threatened her from the East, where, with all the vast resources at its disposal, the Persian Empire was building up powerful armies and fleets. But Themistocles alone knew what had to be done. He alone devised effective countermeasures. He talked the Athenians into building two hundred ships, fortifying their harbor and erecting higher walls. He decreed that Athens should devote all her energies to becoming a naval power. And so the Piraeus became a naval stronghold, Athens a first-class naval power, and Themistocles the first statesman of Greece.

Soon Athenian merchant ships sailed off all over the known world—to Asia, and as far west as the Pillars of Hercules. The city's coffers began to fill with gold. And outside, even women and children worked on the new walls, for every minute was precious. Huge quays and warehouses arose, together with shipyards and the first dry docks in the world.

The Spartans watched Athens' growing strength with mixed emotions, but Themistocles' diplomacy proved more than a match for Spartan envy. And then Themistocles won the naval battle at Salamis. When the immense Persian fleet approached, like some inexorable catastrophe, the Athenians desperately turned to the Delphic oracle which had prophesied that all was lost. As they consulted it for the last time, it replied that Athens should take refuge behind wooden walls. Themistocles, never at a loss, had an immediate interpretation ready: the wooden walls were ships, and all Athens must go on board. Thousands of Athenians abandoned their homes, leaving the Persians free to land and burn down the Acropolis with its temples and sacred trees.

Xerxes, King of the Persians, had his throne set high up on the cliffs overlooking the Bay of Salamis, from which vantage point he hoped to witness with his own eyes the final blow against Hellas, the sinking of the Greek fleet, and the victory of his own Phoenician ships. But the large Persian fleet could not deploy properly in the narrow gulf–it fell into disorder and confusion, and soon the day was lost.

Although the Greeks showered Themistocles with honors after his victory, they soon began to have their doubts about him. It was the Spartans, Athens' greatest rivals, who finally managed to discredit the statesman. They discovered that their ruler Pausanias had been conducting a clandestine correspondence with the Persians, and asserted that Themistocles was also involved in a conspiracy with the Persian king. This information was passed on to the Athenians, and a warrant was issued for Themistocles' arrest–and Sparta had its revenge on the great Athenian wall-builder. As for King Pausanias, he was incarcerated in the temple of Athena Chalcioicos where the Spartans left him to starve to death.

Themistocles fled to Asia Minor and informed Artaxerxes, Xerxes' son, that he was being persecuted by the Greeks because of his friendship for the Persians. The oriental king admired Themistocles' sharp mind (the Greek had meanwhile learned to speak Persian), consented to receive him, and made him prince of several cities in Asia Minor. In return, Themistocles promised the Persian king that he would act as his adviser in helping him to conquer all of Greece. However, before he could realize his final plans for revenge against his native country, he died at Magnesia in about 460 B.C.

Themistocles was about sixty-five years old when he died, the object of warm admiration and violent hatred throughout the Mediterranean world. The people of Magnesia deified him and erected a magnificent memorial in his honor. The Greeks would not permit his body to be buried in his native soil, but some friends secretly brought his remains home to Attica, and his grave at the Piraeus was later decorated and honored.

The Athenian historian Thucydides, writing approximately forty years after Themistocles' death, felt that the statesman deserved only the greatest of praise. He pointed out that Themistocles could reach swift decisions when faced by sudden disaster, that he possessed a gift for accurately forecasting events, and that even in a field where he had no immediate experience his judgment was almost invariably extremely sound. Thucydides also stated that Themistocles probably poisoned himself because he could not keep his promise to the Persian king—to subjugate all Greece. Thucydides was a Greek, and it is understandable that he was not overanxious to mourn Themistocles the "Persophile," despite his great admiration for the victor of Salamis. It is more probable, therefore, that the founder of Greek sea power died a natural death surrounded by great wealth and comfort.

Teachers can exert a great influence on the development of their pupils, but the intellectual stature of the pupil is often just as important as his instructor's. The Greek philosopher Anaxagoras, who was born about 500 B.C., had a pupil who epitomizes this truth.

We all know that anxiety is the chain which each of us drags along behind throughout life. Anaxagoras taught that the things which fill us with apprehension about the unknown future are all really quite natural events; and that thus, they need not be feared any more than nature itself, and should never be allowed to disrupt our peace of mind. His pupil, Pericles, absorbed this philosophy at an early age and grew up to be a man who was free from superstition, free from anxiety, and reasonably free from doubt. It is not surprising that a man who followed the great philosopher's teachings so faithfully would rise quickly to the top of the political ladder. Pericles was a democrat, and he regarded *demos,* the people, as an entity whose sympathy and consent had to be won over and over again. It was certainly not easy to guide and influence the people of Athens. Thucydides tells us that Pericles never followed the masses but that the masses followed him.

Power was vested in the people, but Pericles guided the assembly in such a way that he made the power of the people the basis for his own authority. Such constructive co-operation between the people and the individual has scarcely ever been equaled in history.

Pericles knew no other road than the one leading from his house to the assembly, where he spoke better than any man before him. He constantly prayed that no unseemly word should ever escape his lips, and he never indulged in temperamental outbursts or emotions. He must have been the Churchill of his day, a brilliant parliamentarian who ignored abuse and insults and never digressed from his purpose. He was usually one of the ten *strategoi*, *i.e.*, the commanders and highest officials in the administration. He was responsible for maintaining peace and order in the city-state, he had to conduct public festivals—a very important function—and, even more important, he controlled the public treasury.

Like Themistocles before him, Pericles realized that to Athens, sea power was more important than land power, and that a permanently mobilized fleet was indispensable to Athens' security.

Under Pericles, the plastic arts in Greece reached a peak never attained before or after. It was during his golden time that the Athenians rebuilt the Acropolis which the Persians had destroyed.

A miraculous building arose on this Acropolis between 447 and 437 B.C., under the supervision of Callicrates and Ictinus. It was the Parthenon, the great new marble temple dedicated to Athena Parthenos, the tutelary goddess of Athens, and it is probably the most perfect example of architecture Europe has ever produced. The horizontal lines of the steps that formed its substructure were given a slight upward curve in the center to counteract the optical illusion which otherwise would have made them seem slightly concave. Nor were the Parthenon's pillars completely perpendicular but leaned slightly inward, for perpendicular pillars give the impression they are slanting outward. In 438 B.C. a colossal statue of the goddess Athena, nearly forty feet high—a work in wood, gold and ivory by the sculptor Phidias—was placed in the temple's inner sanctum. (After the banning of all heathen cults by the Emperor Theodosius II, the statue was taken to Constantinople in 435 A.D. Since then, it has disappeared without a trace.)

The bas-reliefs of the Parthenon were executed by sculptors from every studio in Athens, working under the direction of Phidias. The Greeks held important national festivals at Olympia, Delphi, Nemea and on the Isthmus of Corinth–and Athens had her own festival, the Panathenaea, which took place every four years and became an event of world renown. It is not surprising, therefore, that it was the ceremonial procession of the Panathenaea which furnished the theme for the Parthenon's frieze. Originally 525 feet long, only a portion of the narrow western side now survives *in situ*, for the greater part of the frieze, together with most of the remaining sculptures, was dismantled and taken to London in 1816 by Lord Elgin. It is now in the British Museum.

The Erechtheum on the Acropolis was named after King Erechtheus. At one time there were several shrines on the site of this ancient royal palace: Athena's sacred olive tree, the spot where Poseidon reputedly split the rock, the tomb of King Cecrops, and altars dedicated to Athena, Poseidon and Erechtheus himself. Pericles meant to unify all these holy places within a single structure, the Erechtheum, but his plan was not carried out until after his death, between 421 and 406 B.C.

Pericles also built the Propylaea, the large gateway that formed the entrance and western façade of the Acropolis. He entrusted this task to his architect, Mnesicles, and it became the prototype for all gate constructions down to very recent times.

Northwest of the Acropolis, on the market hill, arose the Theseum, a shrine dedicated to Hephaestus and at first mistaken for the temple of Theseus–hence its name. It is the best preserved temple in Greece. To the southeast, at the foot of the citadel, the Odeum was erected. This hall was considered Athens' most beautiful building and was for the performances relating to the Greek Dionysus cult. The Odeum was excavated, but only its foundations have survived.

The Athenians, like all members of the Attic League, made great financial sacrifices to pay for building these shrines. From building costs which have been preserved for us, chiseled in stone, we know that the Parthenon alone cost 469 talents, or about $500,000–the ephemeral countervalue for an eternal work of art.

Our terms "gymnasium," "lyceum" and "academy" all originated in Greece. Under Pericles, these institutions, which were dedicated to the mental and physical education of youth, sprang up stone by stone on the barren Athenian soil and blazed an educational trail for all Western civilization. While other places in Greece remained large villages or towns, Athens became a true metropolis, small though it was in comparison with our large modern cities. Numerous men of genius and talent were responsible for transforming Athens into a cultural wonder of the world during the Periclean age. And in the forefront of all these engineers and artists stood Phidias, who created so many glorious statues, supervised the progress of the building on the Acropolis, and executed most of the sculptures in the Parthenon with the aid of his pupils. But always behind him stood Pericles, determined that his buildings should outshine the palaces at Persepolis—another facet in the rivalry between Greece and Persia.

The history books show us Pericles' many-sided genius, describing him as a man of great self-control, wisdom and discretion, but they neglect the human angle. Pericles' first marriage apparently was not the happiest. It had obviously never occurred to him that he might one day fall in love with a non-Athenian woman, for at one time he sponsored a law prohibiting marriages between Athenians and non-Athenians. Yet when he separated from his first wife, he took up with a woman from Miletus named Aspasia. He now became victimized by his own legislation because, being a non-Athenian, Aspasia could never become his wife, and it was only natural that the Athenians should gossip forever about this relationship. She was a foreigner, and perhaps it was true that before her friendship with Pericles she had pursued the disreputable profession of maintaining a large establishment of *hetaerae*. These *hetaerae* were girls without any family life, but often of great intellectual attainments.

Aspasia was a beautiful and cultured woman. She opened a school of rhetoric and philosophy, attracted young girls, women and men into her orbit, and became such a famous hostess that even the philosopher Socrates declared he had learned the art of speaking from her. Aspasia gathered around her all the important scientists, artists and scholars of her day, not to mention the Sophists, "those impudent innovators who disputed the ancient beliefs," as Eduard Meyer put it.

The historian Herodotus, the great poet Sophocles, the philosopher Anaxagoras of Clazomenae, the most progressive city-planner of his day, Hippodamus of Miletus, the greatest sculptor, Phidias—one and all belonged to Pericles' and Aspasia's circle. Although women had little or no share in Attic society, Aspasia, the foreigner, set the style in Athens. The poet Cratinus called her "beloved," and she became so world-famous that Cyrus the Younger, the pretender to the Persian throne, renamed his favorite mistress after her.

The last two years of Pericles' life lay in the shadow of the war between Athens and Sparta, which lasted from 431 until 404 B.C., and in which Sparta ultimately gained supremacy. The true victor, however, was a third party: the Persian Empire.

In Thucydides, the great struggle found a chronicler who for the first time treated history as a science—"not necessarily pleasant or amusing," as he put it, but "reliable, profitable, and of lasting usefulness." Hegel went so far as to declare that Thucydides' work is the profit humanity gained from the Peloponnesian War which otherwise produced such upheavals, atrocities, disease and misery, that from then on Greece virtually withdrew from the world stage and watched from the wings while Persia, Macedonia and, finally, Italy stepped into the limelight to play their part in the pre-Christian drama of mankind.

The war was all the more tragic because neither Sparta nor Athens wanted to fight. Sparta's population was decreasing, and she feared fresh uprisings among her helots, or serfs. Furthermore her economic and financial condition was insecure, and her Peloponnesian League was less reliable than Athens' maritime Attic League. It seems obvious that Sparta did not go to war of her own volition.

On the Athenian side, Pericles was equally reluctant to fight. The instigators of the war were clearly Corinth and her allies, who could not tolerate Athens' thriving world trade. But Corinth forced Sparta to go along with her, and Pericles could not avoid a conflict without great humiliation to Athens. Such were the immediate causes. The underlying causes, however, must be sought in the rivalry between Athens and Sparta, and in their contrasting political systems.

In the second year of this suicidal conflict Pericles' object was already limited to the defense of Athens. And since Sparta was the land power and Athens commanded the sea, Pericles decided to sacrifice the open country to the enemy. Accordingly he ordered the country people to abandon their farms and take to the triangular area enclosed by the two long walls linking Athens with the Piraeus and Phaleron. So long as the Athenian fleet remained undefeated this immense twin stronghold could never be successfully blockaded, since its only exposed flank—toward the sea—could be supplied and protected by naval forces. A great migration began as, laden with their goods and chattels, thousands of people poured into Athens to take refuge behind the walls. Many of them had dismantled their houses and dragged them into the safety zone.

Then Athens was overtaken by a fate which no one could have foreseen: an epidemic broke out among the inhabitants of the Piraeus. The exact nature of the disease is still in dispute, but at all events it began with "high fever, redness and smarting of the eyes, a raw throat, and a foul and fetid-smelling breath." The next symptoms, according to Thucydides, were "hoarseness, a racking cough, secretions of bile, great pain and convulsions," followed by "tumors in the abdomen, diarrhea, exhaustion" and death. Many sufferers lost their limbs, others their eyesight, and still others their memories—all these symptoms are listed by Thucydides. The sick had such high fevers that they were desperate for cold water, and in their torment threw themselves into the water tanks, racked by unquenchable thirst. The epidemic spread with lightning speed: soon there were too many sick to nurse, too many dead to bury. People were afraid to come near those who had been afflicted, and many households were completely wiped out. It was hot in that dreadful summer in 430 B.C., and the huts were cramped, small and stifling. Corpses lay everywhere, even in the temples, and men and women in their last throes tottered along the streets and thronged around the fountains. In their panic men turned into animals, raided other people's funeral pyres and laid their own dead upon them, or threw them onto the first pyre whose flames caught their eyes.

Almost everyone succumbed to the temptation to have one last fling at life; no longer was anyone ashamed to exhibit his most latent vices, indulge in a frenzy of sensuality, or hastily squander his money. None feared the gods any longer, since they spared no one, and no one respected the laws, since it seemed unlikely that anyone would live long enough to be punished for breaking them. Yet, throughout this turmoil the courts continued to function, and the daily round of accusations and counteraccusations continued even in the face of imminent death. Dense clouds of smoke from the funeral pyres hung over the center of the city day and night, and the plague spread to the Athenian fleet.

Curiously enough, Sparta and the Peloponnesus remained unaffected by the epidemic, but the Peloponnesians refused to take prisoners, killing everyone who fell into their hands for fear of catching the plague. And during the same time another epidemic was raging in an unknown town in Italy—clearly the same sickness which had attacked Athens. This insignificant township was Rome.

What with the second Peloponnesian invasion and the new devastation it caused, the general hardships of war and the particular hardships brought on by disease, the Athenians lapsed into a mood of apathetic despair. And almost inevitably they began to regard Pericles

Skoplje
0
50 MILES
AXIOS
Lake Ochrid
L. Megali Prespa
MACEDONIA
AEGAE
PELLA
EUPORIA
PHILIPPI
ABDERA
AMPHIPOLIS
THASOS
CHALCIDICE
ALIAKMON
PYDNA
OLYNTHUS
DION
EPIRUS
NEA POTIDHAIA
DION
MENDE
TORONE
THESSALIA
OZYA
TRIKKALA
LARISSA
DODONA
CRANNON
VOLOS
PHARSALUS
ARTA
SCYROS
ARGOS
HERACLEA
OREUS
EUBOIA
THYREUM
AETOLIA
THERMOPYLAE
LEUCAS
STRATUS
AGRINION
AMPHISSA
BG DELPHI
CHALCIS
CALYDON
NAUPACTUS
DELPHI
OPUS
ERETRIA
ITHACA
THEBES
LEUCTRA
ATTICA
CEPHALLENIA
PATRAE
PLATAEA
MARATHON
CARYSTUS
MEGARA
ATHENAE
CORINTH
SALAMIS
PIRAEUS
ANDROS
ELIS
ARGOLIS
OLYMPIA
MYCENAE
SUNIUM
ORCHOMENUS
ARGOS
TIRYNS
NAUPLIA
ZACYNTHUS
MANTINEA
ASINE
CEOS
MEGALOPOLIS
THYREA
CYTHNOS
PELOPONNESUS
SERIPHOS
ITHOME
SPARTA
SIPHNOS
PYLOS
YITHION
MELOS
CYTHERA

as the man who was responsible for their predicament. Had he not advised them to go to war? Had he not described the risks as slight? Had he not underestimated the Spartans' war potential?

For all the danger, Pericles kept his head. He was still guided by his genius. Above all, he still had Aspasia. But the Athenians would not leave her alone. Comic dramatists poked fun at her. Lewd jokes were whispered about her. She was even brought to trial for alleged impiety and procuration, charges against which Pericles himself defended her with burning eloquence. Aspasia was acquitted, but from then on Pericles seemed to have lost some of his old integrity, infallibility and power of persuasion. The Athenians were really an extremely difficult and critical people who time and again wore down their greatest men by their never-ending fondness for intrigues, slanders and accusations.

And since Phidias was a friend of Pericles and had many rivals, the next attempt to undermine Pericles' reputation took the form of a lawsuit against the sculptor who was accused of embezzling certain funds in regard to his statue of Athena. He was convicted, and died in prison. Then the Athenians turned on the philosopher Anaxagoras, who had ascribed the creation of the universe not to chance, but to pure, disinterested reason. He was charged with propagating atheistic doctrines, and although Pericles defended his friend, Anaxagoras was convicted and had to pay a fine of 5 talents, or about $5,000.

By now, the people of Athens were so desperate that they were willing to lend an ear to any kind of slander, and finally even the incorruptible Pericles was convicted of embezzlement. He was relieved of his office in the autumn of 430 B.C., after the terrible summer of the plague, and ceased to be a *strategos* of Athens. However, only one year passed before he was reinstated, for in their hour of need, the Athenians realized that he was their ablest man. "What with the people being what they are," says Thucydides, "they made him *strategos* once more and entrusted him with the administration of all affairs." But Pericles' strength was gone. The plague had robbed him of two sons, and now it attacked him and carried him off in the midst of his labors—in 429 B.C.

ATHENS' MOST DANGEROUS FRIEND

Everyone loved him, but he loved only two people: himself and Socrates.

THEMISTOCLES was Greece's greatest statesman, the savior of Athens, the victor of Salamis, and the man who banished the Asiatic peril, Persia. Pericles was Athens' greatest builder, an aristocrat by birth and nature, Greece's most brilliant parliamentarian, and the man who gave his country's golden age its name, "the Periclean age." Alcibiades, on the other hand, was Athens' idol, Athens' Mephistopheles, Athens' seducer, and Athens' destroyer. All three men were impeached and betrayed by Athens, but Pericles alone remained true to himself and true to Athens. Themistocles and Alcibiades died on Persian soil, enemies of their native land.

Alcibiades was an uncommonly handsome person and he never lost his power to be fascinating and to endear himself to others. He combined a magnificent physique with an extraordinary number of physical and mental abilities. And while he had a lisp, the Athenians found everything about him charming—even his lisp—and the whole city sought to imitate him.

He was passionate and impetuous, hot-blooded and ambitious. But basically Alcibiades despised the Athenians. And while everyone loved him, he loved only two people: himself and Socrates, the greatest Greek philosopher. Everyone flattered the youth and sought his company and his friendship, but he kept his rich and aristocratic admirers at arm's length while he dined frequently with Socrates, practiced wrestling with him, and shared his tent with him on military campaigns. With all others he remained defiant and aloof.

Alcibiades' mad escapades knew no bounds—and the only time he wept was when Socrates reproved him. If he tried to run away from Socrates, the old philosopher chased after him and caught him, and then Alcibiades was ashamed and afraid. Socrates even saved his pupil's life on two occasions; once during the campaign against Potidaea, and another time in the battle of Delion.

In return for a box on the ears, Alcibiades received a wife. He slapped Hipponicus, a rich and highly respected Athenian, to win a bet he had made with some friends. The next morning he knocked on the affronted man's door and announced that he was ready to be thrashed for what he had done. The rich man was so touched by this that he offered Alcibiades his daughter Hipparete in marriage. The worthy girl was virtuous and loved her husband dearly, but he carried on such a lively association with the hetaerae of Athens that she eventually sought refuge in her brother's house. But as Hipparete appeared before the magistrates to sue for divorce, Alcibiades arrived, grabbed her, and carried her home across the market place. From then on she stayed with him, contenting herself with the occasional crumbs of his affection, until she died soon afterward.

Alcibiades was a brilliant speaker, but since he insisted on using only the best possible words or expressions, which did not always occur to him, he would often stop in the middle of a speech, and remain silent for a while, without a trace of embarrassment, only to continue as eloquently as before.

From the very beginning of his career, Alcibiades had some powerful rivals. The most important among them was Nicias, a much older man who was regarded as the ablest general of Athens, and who the Greeks insisted would have successfully terminated the war against Sparta if he had been in command. Alcibiades, in his jealousy, decided to break the armistice with Sparta. He succeeded admirably. The public assembly could always be relied upon to applaud him, and every speech he made won their unanimous approval.

Even in the time of Pericles the island of Sicily had been the object of Athens' dreams and aspirations. But Sicily was in part dominated by the city of Syracuse. Knowing the attraction Sicily held for the Athenians, Alcibiades advised them to send a great fleet to conquer the island, painting a glowing picture of the future. From Sicily the Athenians could go on, conquering Carthage, Africa, Italy, and control the treasures of the entire western Mediterranean. And while Nicias pointed out the difficulties of such an undertaking, the enthusiasm of the young men for Alcibiades' plans could not be shaken.

Socrates, too, advised against the campaign, and when the astronomer and astrologer Meton heard of Alcibiades' mad plans, he was so outraged that he seized a burning torch and set fire to his own house. But the Athenians went ahead, and eventually entrusted the leadership of the expedition to Alcibiades, Nicias and a third general, Lamachus.

All was ready, when something happened which was ultimately to mean defeat for Athens.

In front of the houses of the citizens and before the doors of the temples stood sacred statues called Hermae. They were merely stone pillars surmounted by a head, and of no particular beauty, but the Athenians venerated them greatly. And on the night of the Adonia, a festival dedicated to Aphrodite and Adonis, the sacred stone images were mutilated by an unknown hand.

Since Alcibiades had many enemies in Athens, the blame was laid on him and his companions. He asked to be allowed to defend himself, but his enemies knew that if he once got up to make a speech, they would be overwhelmed. They therefore declared that it would be inappropriate to bring the leader of a projected expedition before a court. Alcibiades did not like the idea of setting out under such a cloud of suspicion, but he received orders to embark, and so 140 galleys weighed anchor. Reaching Italy, he captured Rhegium, and crossing over to Sicily, forced Catania to surrender.

At this juncture, the Athenians recalled Alcibiades to face a judicial inquiry. Absence is always a dangerous thing in such circumstances, for slanderous rumors spring up like mushrooms. A ship arrived to pick him up, and at once the morale of the Greek soldiers in Sicily dropped. Once aboard, Alcibiades found out that the Athenians had condemned him to death *in absentia*, and he decided to show them that he was very much alive. When he reached Rhuri he slipped ashore, traveled across the Peloponnesus and sought asylum in Sparta, promising to help the Spartans against Athens and advising them to send a general to Sicily to help crush Athenian naval power. At the same time he began to incite them to war on Athens herself. It was not long before he became an object of respect and admiration among the Spartans.

Alcibiades was a great actor who could adapt himself to any situation whatsoever. And since life in Sparta was simple, plain and frugal—in other words, *Spartan*—the fastidious Alcibiades had his hair shaved—bathed in cold water and ate barley bread and the famous black blood soup. People were astounded to see that the same man who once employed the best chef and perfumer in Athens, suddenly lived a more Spartan life than the Spartans themselves. Alcibiades enjoyed playing this part, but unfortunately he could not long control his sensuality. His roving eye lighted upon Timaea, the wife of Agis, the Spartan king. This "hero" had dashed out of his wife's bedroom during an earthquake, and the experience so unnerved him that he did not touch her for ten months. Alcibiades took advantage of Timaea's enforced solitude to seduce her, and when she gave birth to a son there was no doubt about the infant's paternity. Moreover, Timaea was so smitten with her lover that she whispered to all her women friends that the child should really be named Alcibiades.

Meanwhile, the Athenians in Sicily had suffered a terrible defeat. What was more, Alcibiades had managed to alienate all Ionia from Athens. But King Agis was in a rage, first because of Alcibiades' great fame, and secondly, because of his wife's adultery. Thus Alcibiades' position in Sparta was no longer secure, and he betook himself to the Persian satrap Tissaphernes, a cruel barbarian who was greatly feared and who hated the Greeks. His new guest's poise and cunning appealed to Tissaphernes, and Alcibiades now exerted all his eloquence and powers of persuasion to incite the satrap against Sparta. Simultaneously, he began to conspire with the Council of the Four Hundred, the body which only recently had been established by a revolution to rule Athens.

All of Athens' naval power was now concentrated at Samos, where her fleet was engaged in crushing her former allies that had defected and in defending Athens' possessions. Alcibiades joined the Athenian fleet and eventually became commander of a naval squadron on the Hellespont. He defeated the Spartan navy three times and conquered Chalcedon and Byzantium. Then, with all these victories behind him, he decided to show his face once more in Athens.

It was a triumphal home-coming. All his ships were decorated with captured enemy shields. Yet Alcibiades did not dare leave his galley until many of his most trusted friends arrived to welcome him. He was accompanied through the city amid great rejoicing, the Athenians decking him with garlands and holding their children up to see the great hero. Before a special assembly Alcibiades, with tears in his eyes, described the injustice he had suffered. And the people presented him with golden crowns and appointed him supreme commander of their land and sea forces.

But if ever a man was undone by his own fame, it was Alcibiades. The Athenians regarded him as infallible and believed that he would succeed in any and every undertaking. Actually a single failure destroyed him.

The Spartans had ordered their fleet to sea under the command of Lysander. Seeking to raise funds to pay his seamen, Alcibiades temporarily handed over his command of the Greek fleet to a helmsman named Antiochus, with strict injunctions not to engage the Spartans in battle during his absence. Antiochus disregarded this warning, however, and was defeated, losing his life in the process. Thanks to the Athenians' traditional fickleness, Alcibiades immediately fell into disgrace and was forced to take to his heels once more. Lysander surprised the Greek fleet at Aegostpotami (405 B.C.), besieged Athens, starved the city out and captured it. He burned all Athenian ships and had the protective walls dismantled. The destiny of Greece had run its course. Athens fell—and dragged all Hellas down with her.

Alcibiades could expect nothing from the Athenians, and now he had the Spartans to fear as well. Then he remembered Themistocles, who had found asylum with the king of Persia, and he traveled across Phrygia to see the Persian satrap Pharnabazus, hoping to receive a recommendation to the Persian king.

But Alcibiades was not the sort of man the world leaves in peace. As long as he was alive, the Spartans could never feel sure that their conquest of Athens was complete. So Lysander requested Pharnabazus to have Alcibiades murdered.

The men who were assigned to kill Alcibiades did not dare to attack him in hand-to-hand combat. Instead, they surrounded his house and set it ablaze. Inside, Alcibiades hastily bundled clothing and rugs together to smother the flames. When the smoke threatened to choke him, he wrapped his cloak about his left hand; then, taking his sword in his right, he plunged out through the inferno. The barbarians shrank back before the lone figure, the most dangerous man in Greece. Not one of them dared to stop him or oppose him, but when he was at a safe distance they shot arrows and threw spears after him. Alcibiades fell, blood streaming from a dozen wounds. He died in 404 B.C., when he was about fifty years old.

Torn by dissension and petty rivalries between the city-states, the strength of Greece was dissipated and she fell an easy prey, first to Alexander the Great of Macedon, then to the new rising power in the West. But although Greece fell before the Roman legions, through Rome, Greek thought, art and culture created the civilization of Western Europe.

SOCRATES—A SAINTLY MAN

You will put me to death heedlessly and then go on sleeping out your lives, unless God in His mercy sends you another.

Socrates in 399 B.C. (Plato's *Apology*)

IN 470 B.C. a man was born who by his life raised insight, reason, intellect and morality to heights never attained before him. He brought mankind closer by several hundred years to true humanitarian civilization and to God.

Socrates' father was Sophroniscus, a sculptor and a solid, law-abiding citizen. His mother was a midwife named Phainarete. Both parents died as obscurely as they had lived, but their son came into conflict with the law, was sentenced to death—and became immortal.

Our sources for information about the life of Socrates are the Greek historian Xenophon and the Greek philosopher Plato. But since both were some forty-five years younger than Socrates, their accounts—factual or poetic—were based upon personal contact with him only over the last ten or twelve years of his life.

Xenophon was a passionate sportsman, a landowner and an officer. Being an aristocrat, he did not feel at home in democratic Athens, so he went off to Persia and took part in one of the campaigns of the younger Cyrus. He later fought for the Spartans, and for this was exiled from Athens. When he died in 354 B.C., he left behind an extensive library of books he had written, including a history of Hellas; a work on the Spartan State; the *Cyropaedia*, a novel with a pedagogic-*cum*-political bias; the famous *Anabasis*, which describes the march home from Persia to Thrace made by 10,000 Greek mercenaries; a textbook on the duties of a cavalry officer; the *Banquet*, a work on domestic science and the duties of a housewife; and four volumes of memoirs, the *Apommemoneumata*. In these last, Xenophon defends Socrates against the charges leveled at him. But these books do not do justice to Socrates, for they tend to lessen the philosopher's stature, whereas Plato heightens and enhances it. For Xenophon was a man of moderate talents, while Plato was one of the great thinkers in the history of the world.

Almost all of Plato's works are written in dialogue form, and, with one exception, Socrates is always the protagonist. With Plato it is often difficult to distinguish between imagination and actual experience, but his portrayal of the philosopher rings so true and is so convincing that he would have been as great a genius as Socrates if he had invented it all. Like his teacher, Plato was ever in search of a firm basis for his thinking. All his prose works have survived, and they form a gigantic edifice of human insight, as well as the greatest memorial to Socrates.

Socrates himself never wrote, but he knew something about geometry and astronomy. Yet he refused to undertake any scholarly studies, for he wished to devote himself entirely to the study of ethics and the betterment of the individual. He also tried to steer clear of politics, and successfully managed to avoid holding any state office, declaring that a public appointment would force him to compromise his integrity. And compromise was not for Socrates. The man who wishes to fight for justice, he said, must lead a private, not a public life. "For it is certain, Athenians, that if I had taken part in public affairs, I should long ago have been done away with, and thus been of no more use either to you or to myself."

The poets of Athens poked fun at Socrates' poverty in their comedies. He obviously cared nothing for personal property. He probably did not marry Xanthippe, who bore him three sons, until quite late in life. And while the legend that Socrates was henpecked and that Xanthippe was a shrew may not be authentic, Xenophon tells us that she had a somewhat tempestuous disposition.

Although Socrates was a good soldier (he took part in three campaigns), his physical appearance seems to have been rather grotesque, for he was small and rotund, with prominent eyes, a flattened nose, wide nostrils, and a large mouth. Inwardly, however, "this wisest and most intelligent man of the whole era," as Plato described him, seethed and sparkled, shone and glowed with a mysterious fire. His self-control and powers of endurance were impressive, for he had practiced self-denial to such a point that he was content with the very barest necessities of life. At the same time, he was no ascetic. He was familiar with the so-called pleasures of life even if he rarely pursued them (it is recorded in Plato's *Symposium*, however, that Socrates drank all present under the table!), and he could be so gay and witty when he was at a banquet or with friends that he was always the center of attention. He was firmly convinced that he was as imperfect as the next man, and he considered it his god-given mission in life to serve his fellow men by showing them the way to reason, and therefore to goodness. He was well aware that the best way to persuade people was to gain their friendship and confidence. Moreover, he had compassion for the weak, the mediocre, and the meek in spirit.

Socrates spent nearly all of his life in the open air, in the streets and the market place or at the gymnasium. But he had no taste for country life. He said of himself: "I know that I know nothing." And when he spoke with people who fancied they were wise, and deduced from their conversations that they could offer no logical proof of their wisdom, he became convinced that he was after all wiser than anybody else, since he alone was conscious of his ignorance. Knowledge—that to Socrates was the supreme attainment, and he was so completely absorbed in his mission to explain the meaning of knowledge and insight to all men that everything else seemed of little importance. Poverty, hunger, mocking laughter—he endured them all with the same splendid equanimity, and he would rather have suffered death than betray his convictions. He wore neither shirt nor shoes, and the only cloak he owned served him all year around. He was completely indifferent to the thousand and one things his fellow men found so important, so it is little wonder than his contemporary Antiphon said that even a slave would have run away if he were forced to live like Socrates.

Socrates was a loyal son of his native Athens, a true patriot, and a man of uncommonly high moral courage. Disregarding all popular trends and traditional opinions, all ingrained habits of thought and action that marked his time, Socrates resolutely took up his lone stand and taught that the only source of all concepts and all ethical ideas was the human mind. Unaware of the god-seekers of Mesopotamia and Israel, he recognized that there were some phenomena that only God could understand and that a single divine intelligence was at work in all phenomena. And, to Socrates, one of the creations of this supreme intelligence, and one which was related to the gods, was the human mind.

There was something else, something mysterious that could only be surmised but not known—an invisible link between the human and the divine, a measure of which Socrates felt he could detect in his own identity. And there was another thing that warned him whenever he went astray—his soul. Socrates firmly believed that the soul was immortal. Four hundred years before Christ, he brought Greek thinking remarkably close to the New Testament, and it is no accident that

Western civilization is rooted in the Christian religion and in Socrates, who unwittingly laid the ethical foundation for their ultimate union.

Before Socrates, philosophy had been exclusively concerned with the study of natural phenomena. After he appeared, philosophers were obliged to deal with virtue, with man's actions and conduct. And Socrates strove not only for knowledge for himself but also used it for enlightening others. He taught that the sole goal of all study was the improvement of man, and he was the first to pluck philosophy out of the clouds and implant it in the hearts of men. He became the founder of philosophical ethics, which derives from the Greek word *ethos*, meaning decent attitudes, morality and character.

During Socrates' lifetime a school of philosophers flourished in Athens who created an important intellectual movement called sophism. The Greek word *sophistes* means "man of wisdom," and these Sophists were itinerant teachers who provided instruction in return for high fees. Hence this form of education was available only to the wealthier classes. They taught philosophy, literature, art, grammar, mathematics, astronomy and, above all, political science, and turned their pupils into men well qualified for private and public careers.

In the Sophists' opinion there was no such thing as absolute truth or absolute morality, and their teaching eliminated the ties that linked the individual with religion and society. The Sophists' insistence on specialization finally became almost as dangerous as overspecialization is today. Egotism got out of hand, and people followed the materialistic precept that "whatever is useful is permitted." The Sophists taught their students to argue convincingly for or against any given proposition. But by such methods the wrong cause could be as successfully defended as the right, and in the end public morality was threatened by a universal collapse—a development the Sophists had not intended at all. Socrates, however, had recognized this danger and went into action against the Sophists.

It should not be forgotten that during Socrates' lifetime Greece still worshiped her ancient gods. What was more, her gods were endowed with extremely human and extremely immoral characteristics. Fables and legends told of the wildest love affairs and amorous intrigues on Mount Olympus, and Greece was filled with strange and mysterious cults. The Athenians' fury at the mutilation of their Hermae, and the fact that Alcibiades' enemies chose this particular "most dangerous" crime to rid themselves of him, prove that the people were still deeply entrenched in a primitive polytheism. Socrates was thus far ahead of his time when he publicly declared that all Greek mythology was poetic fiction. Buttonholing everyone he met, he demonstrated with inexorable logic that the only source of knowledge was the human intellect, and that the only thing superior to human knowledge was God. Socrates became the terror of the city, admired and revered by only a small number of followers. The rest of Athens misunderstood him and laughed at him. Aristophanes, the greatest comic dramatist of his age, misrepresented the barefooted philosopher in his comedy, *The Clouds,* which was intended to show how Socrates was leading Athenian youth down the road to corruption and godlessness.

Yet the Athenians could have somehow tolerated all that Socrates said if only he had not come out against the basic tenet of democracy. If morality is the product of enlightened reason—as King Solomon taught in the Old Testament—then, said Socrates, only the most enlightened man should rule, and never the people. Perhaps it was Socrates' ill luck that he lived at a time when no ruler of such superlative intelligence could be found. Certainly Alcibiades did not correspond to this ideal.

In 404 B.C. Sparta forced Athens to capitulate, and the walls of Athens were razed. Sparta had triumphed.

In 403 B.C. there was a universal amnesty and Socrates could not be indicted for acts committed prior to that date. His indictment in 399 B.C. was therefore couched in very general terms: "Corrupting the young, scorning the old gods and worshiping new ones."

The prosecutor Meletus was an insignificant and obscure person, but behind Meletus were the responsible, democratic leaders who had disinterestedly risked their own lives to free Athens in 403 B.C.

Just as great lovers become exalted and immortal in the memory of mankind only when they have put death as a seal to their love, so it appears that, before people will believe them, the world's great moral teachers must also pay for their efforts with death—death by torture, at the stake, in the arena, or on the cross. Socrates had to drink a cup of hemlock. But the nobility he displayed in the market place and in the streets of Athens has served as a pattern for succeeding generations. Four hundred and thirty years after Socrates' execution, the selfsame cry rang through the narrow streets of Jerusalem: "Crucify him!" And another 1,500 years later it was heard in Rouen: "To the stake with the witch!"

Like Joan of Arc, Socrates was executed for heresy. Actually, of

Statue of the goddess Persephone from the period 540-530 B.C., on the Acropolis, the sacred citadel of Athens.

An Attic mixing-bowl from the middle of the 6th century B.C., now in the Musco Archeologico, Florence. It represents a Babylonian hunting scene, chariot battle for Patroclus' body, a cortege of gods going to the wedding of Thetis, Achilles pursuing Troilus, and pygmies fighting.

◀ *This statue was erected in the Temple of Zeus* at Olympia in 460 B.C., ten years after the birth of Socrates. It shows a Lapithae girl, one of the legendary people of Thessaly. At the wedding of their king, Peirithoos, the guests included some centaurs (creatures half horse, half man), who got drunk and tried to rape the ladies. The disembodied hand of a centaur is still in the girl's hair.

A Greek painting dating from 440 B.C., in the lifetime of Themistocles.

►

Boeotian terracotta statuette of a cape-dancer dating from the middle of the 3rd century B.C. [Antikensammlungen, Munich. *Photograph:* Hirmer.

Relief from the Attic tomb of the courtesan Mnesarete, circa 380 B.C.

►

The Parthenon on the Acropolis at Athens was dedicated to the virgin goddess Athena. Ictinus built it for Pericles, using plans drawn up by Phidias. The building was completed in the year 438 B.C.

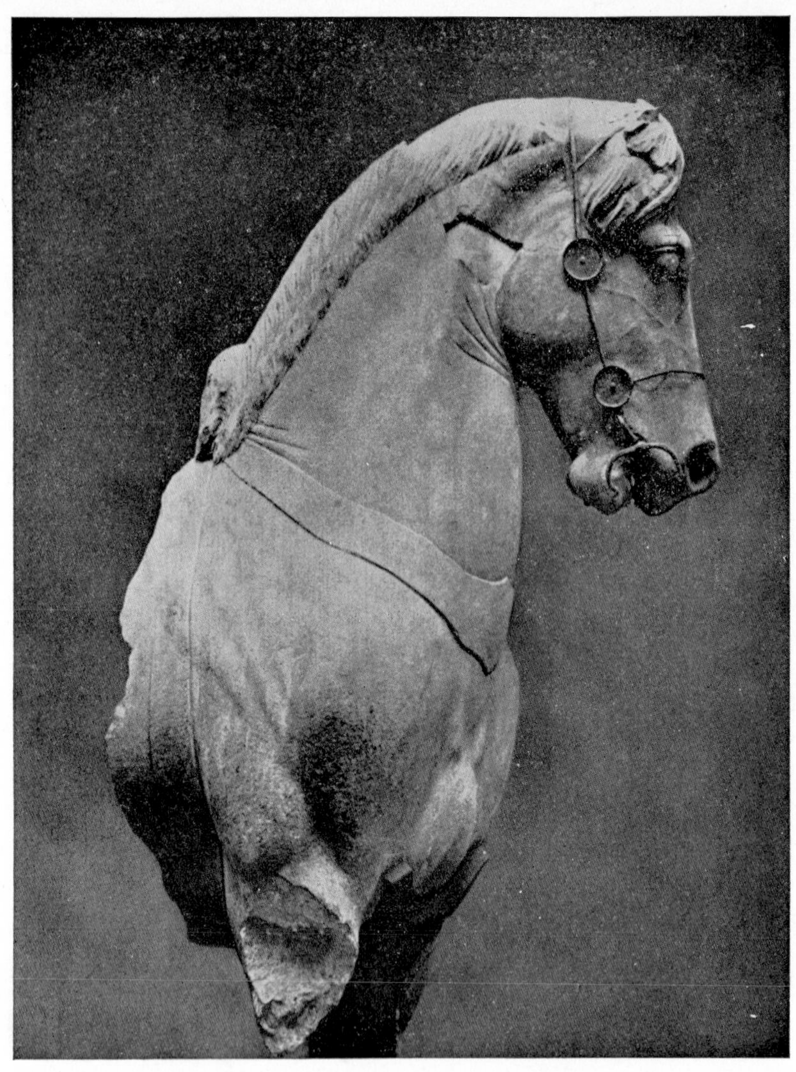

Torso of a horse from the apex of the tomb of Mausolus at Halicarnassus. Circa 350 B.C. Attributed to Pythios, it is now in the British Museum.

course, the term "heresy" had not yet been invented, but he was accused of refusing to acknowledge the gods worshiped by Athens, and of serving others of his own in their stead. What the prosecutors called "other gods" was the inner voice which Socrates obeyed, the inner voice which spoke to him in dreams, and which he took for a divine message. He called this heavenly sign his *daimonion.* The indictment against him also referred to his corruption of the young. If it was really corruption to seek to set virtue—and not mere natural science—as the supreme goal of philosophy, then the prosecutors were right.

Death was the punishment demanded, and the trial resulted in a verdict of guilty (by 281 votes to 220), and a death sentence (by 300 votes to 201). In Plato's famous *Apology* we find the full text of Socrates' defense which he conducted in such a manner as to virtually compel his judges to find him guilty and at the same time demonstrate that they were in the wrong. He forced his judges to condemn him despite his innocence, so that his teachings would be etched into the hearts of men for all time, and by doing so he ranged himself among the great souls of this world. Socrates' speech, as Plato has handed it down to us, is one of the grandest and most stirring vindications of a lonely genius, whose sole crime was his refusal to compromise in his struggle for a better world.

During the thirty days following his sentencing, Socrates lived in his customary fashion, and conducted his usual discourses. In fact he was quite content with his confinement because the prison and its fetters were conducive to philosophical thought. "You see," he said, "when I was in the market place I was distracted by all kinds of people."

On his last day, after he had bathed and they had brought his children and the women of his family to see him, he spoke to them in the presence of his friend Crito, who had tried to arrange his escape, and told them his last wishes. Then he bade them depart. It was close to sunset when the jailer came to him and said: "O Socrates, I know that I shall not have to complain about you as I have to about others. They are angry with me and curse me when I summon them to drink the poison. In my eyes, you are the noblest, gentlest and most admirable of all those who have ever been here. Farewell, and try to bear what must be as lightly as you can." The warden turned away weeping and went out, leaving Socrates looking after him. "How courteous the man is! He has treated me well all the time I have been here, and now he weeps for me."

Crito said: "The sun is still shining on the hills. It has not yet gone down. I know that other men do not take the poisoned cup until quite late. They dine and drink heartily, and some even have girls brought to them. So do not be overhasty; there is time enough."

But Socrates replied: "The men you mention were quite right to do as they did, for by doing so they thought to gain something. But I do not think to gain anything by drinking a little later. I should only seem ridiculous in my own eyes if I clung to life."

Crito motioned to his slave, who went out and soon came back with the man who was to administer the poison to Socrates. He held the potion before him in a cup, and when Socrates saw him, he said: "Well, my good friend, I expect you understand how one does these things?"

"You have only to drink this," the man replied. "When you have drunk it, walk around until your legs become heavy, and then lie down. It will act of itself." So saying, he handed the cup to Socrates, who took it confidently, without the slightest tremor or change of expression.

"I suppose that I may, and must, pray to the gods that my journey hence be prosperous. That is my prayer: let it be so." And saying this, he put the goblet to his lips and quietly drained it.

BRIDES, WIVES AND MISTRESSES

Why do you trouble to write long letters? I need fifty gold pieces, not epistles. If you love me, give!
The hetaera Philomene to Crito

A CHANCE stroke of good fortune has preserved for us a dainty little shoe which, 2,400 years ago, belonged to a Greek streetwalker. Nailed onto the sole of this shoe are the words "Follow me," set in such a manner that this pert invitation was imprinted in the soft dirt of the streets as the girl strolled along. The Greeks were an ingenious people, and they were certainly not prudes. "Yearning Love was there, and Desire, sweet Dalliance and ingratiating Entreaty, which infatuates even the wise." So Homer wrote of Aphrodite, and his words might well have applied to the Greeks as a race.

In Homer's time, about 800 B.C., it appears that women occupied a much more respected position, both at home and in public, than the women of Greece's later historical period.

How did it happen that the position of Greek woman gradually worsened until she was left almost like her oriental counterpart?

How did it happen that Greek womanhood was held in contempt by its men?

These questions have never been fully answered, but it is evident that within the span of a few centuries the status of the women of Greece had fallen from that of "subject" to that of "object." The best way of ascertaining the standing of women in any given era is to study marriage customs. In Homer's day, a girl still had to be bought from her parents. But as time went by, the price of brides fell, until finally the positions were reversed; the father either provided his daughter with a dowry—or had to keep her.

The men of Greece set great store by their freedom, and as man's personal liberty increased, so woman lost hers. At the same time, pederasty came into fashion—a sexual aberration unknown in Homer's day.

The Athenian male spent his life in the open air, in the *agora* or market place, in the gymnasium, at his place of business, or at public assemblies. Athenian women, on the other hand, spent most of their lives shut up at home. Girls and young women were not permitted to see any men, nor be seen by them. Hence they never had an opportunity to fall in love, and very few marriages were love matches. The only time amorous glances were exchanged was at public festivals, religious ceremonies, burials or during temple sacrifices. That was why Greek girls were just as excited over the prospect of a funeral as a sheltered modern girl might be over a party. And certainly a girl was never asked whom she *wanted* to marry. The only thing that mattered was that she should be married young, preferably between fifteen and twenty. Greek men, on the other hand, were not considered ready for marriage until they had reached the age of thirty or thirty-five, so that as a rule the men were twice as old as their brides.

The Greek philosopher Aristoxenus, who lived in the fourth century B.C., held that boys should be kept so effectively occupied and fatigued by every kind of sport that they would never feel any interest in sex until they were twenty. And even after they reached that age, they should indulge in the pleasures of love only at rare intervals.

During the Classical period the Greeks regarded women as inferior—intellectually and otherwise—incapable of contributing to public life, and fit only for gratifying the senses and producing children. Nature, it was believed, had allotted women a position far beneath that of men, and except in their own homes the activities of women were unimportant. A woman was expected to obey her husband, bring up her children, supervise the household slaves, spin, weave, embroider and keep herself as attractive as possible. The Athenian woman had no civil rights and was treated throughout her life like a minor. And nothing a man did at the advice or request of a woman carried any legal validity.

The education of girls was left to their mothers and to female attendants, which meant that cultured women were a rarity. While the "woman chamber," or *gynaeconitis*, was not exactly a prison or a sealed harem, it was still a confined space to which the women were assigned for the rest of their lives. Girls were kept under lock and key up to their marriage, and a young wife could never leave the house without her husband's permission. A husband could lock his wife up, and her company would thus be limited to her women slaves. In Sparta, however, it was the other way around: girls were intentionally left free to associate with men, although married women had to live in seclusion. The symbol of captive Athenian womanhood was the tortoise, which the sculptor Phidias placed under the feet of his Urania who crushed the creature. Many Greeks kept their wives completely out of sight and as an added precaution carefully sealed the door of the *gynaeconitis*.

All this seclusion, particularly among young girls, produced inexperience, timidity and exaggerated reserve. Yet it also lent the youthful Athenian woman a certain charm, a spirit of patient submissiveness found today only among Japanese women. Certainly the shyness of the Attic virgin was in sharp contrast to the forward behavior of her Spartan and barbarian sisters. It will be remembered that the Greeks divided their world into Hellenes and barbarians—with anyone who did not speak Greek automatically being classified as a barbarian, regardless of whether he was a savage Thracian tribesman, a highly civilized Egyptian or a sophisticated Persian. To the Greeks, all languages of the non-Greek world sounded like *bar-bar*, and Barbara was a name originally given to foreign slave girls.

A married Athenian woman would blush and draw back from her window if a man's glance fell upon her. But the respect for marriage and propriety was so universal that men did not often cast their glances in the direction of upper windows.

It was a girl's lot to be given in lifelong marriage to a man she did not know, to bear his children, and to form part of his "estate" when he died. On the eve of their marriage, the brides—generally fifteen, sixteen or seventeen years old—used to bring their dolls and a lock of their hair to the temple and sacrifice them to Artemis.

The Greeks regarded the physical aspect of love as a sort of sickness, a more or less violent form of madness. Love, they thought, was a disturbance of the equilibrium of body and soul, and erotic desire was a temporary clouding of the mind. Of course, this did not stop the Greeks from openly admitting to this "clouding of the mind" nor from giving it free rein. Numerous Greek texts describe intimate associations with hetaerae, hired women who were public mistresses. The term hetaerae means "comrade" or "companion" and, while that was the nicer term for them, there were also "bridge girls," or girls who hung around the bridges, "strollers" who roamed the streets, "she-wolves," "street sweepers" and "dice" who passed from hand to hand. Some hetaerae were highly educated women of genuine intellectual achievement. No stigma attached to an association with them, and it was in their company that the men of Greece found the mental stimulation they lacked at home.

Probably the most intelligent hetaera of all was Aspasia of Miletus, who became Pericles' mistress. Glycera (literally, "sweet one") was the poet Menander's lover. The hetaera Gnathaena ("little cheek") liked to be seen in the streets with her young granddaughter, on whom she set a price twice as high as the charge for her own services. And the whole of Greece "languished," to use Propertius' expression, before the door of the famous Lais.

Phryne, whose real name was Mnesarete, was the most beautiful and celebrated as well as the most dangerous of all Athenian hetaerae. Even the great sculptor Praxiteles succumbed to her beauty and used her as a model for his statue of Aphrodite. Her scandalous affairs were the talk of the town. Indicted for sacrilege, she was defended by the orator Hypereides, who, seeing that all his oratory was getting him nowhere, tore his beautiful client's robe from her body—and the judges dared not convict "the priestess of Aphrodite." Phryne wore the *chiton*, a clinging chemise, and never appeared in the public baths. But on one occasion, when all the people of Greece were assembled for the festival of Poseidon, she took off her clothes in full view of the public, loosened her hair and stepped naked into the sea. This sight reputedly inspired the painter Apelles to create his foam-born Aphrodite rising from the waves.

The hetaerae were of course not faithful to any one man. They frequently changed their lovers, caused great emotional turmoil among their clients and, by and large, had a frankly commercial outlook. The hetaera Philomene, for example, wrote to Crito: "Why do you trouble to write long letters? I need fifty gold pieces, not epistles. If you love me, give! But if you love your money, then do not trouble me further. With that, farewell!"

The hetaerae curled their hair, manicured their nails, and wore handsome purple robes. Aristophanes has left us an inventory of feminine toilet articles, the stock-in-trade of Athenian hetaerae. It included scarves, ribbons, mirrors and scissors, veils and hair nets, sashes and pyjamas, dressing gowns, chemises and dresses with trains, wax cosmetics, soda, white lead, pumice stone and rouge, ankle bangles, beauty patches, ear pendants, jeweled necklaces, precious stones and a hundred other aids to beauty.

There were regular handbooks for hetaerae, and we find one of them instructing her charges as follows: "Above all, you must never be faithful. You must learn the art of lying and hypocrisy. And as for shame—you do not know the meaning of the word. If your lover raves and tears out your hair, reconciliation must be purchased with gifts. Let your doorkeeper be well-schooled. He must shut out the poor and open only to the rich. Even slaves are not to be disdained, providing their pockets are well-lined. What good is a poet who adorns you only with verses, but not with gifts?"

Yet even a poet sometimes had his uses, and the fair Archeanassa, a hetaera from Colophon, achieved immortality through an epigram purportedly, but not certainly, authored by Plato, who was in love with her. Although a hetaera's professional efforts fell far short of earning her immortality, Pythionice was another who gained posthumous fame. After her death, the governor Harpalus erected two memorials—one at Athens and another at Babylon—in honor of the girl who had so extravagantly squandered her favors during her lifetime. He dedicated a shrine, a temple precinct, a temple and an altar to her and, overcome with grief, inscribed the words "Pythionice Aphrodite" on the marble.

Even though the role of the hetaerae was important, the Greeks also loved their wives, and they have left us many fine examples of conjugal fidelity. No matter how many millennia may go by, this epitaph from the 2nd century A.D. of one Marathonis to his wife Nicopolis will never cease to stir our feelings: "Under this stone Marathonis laid his Nicopolis to rest and spilled tears upon the marble coffin. They were useless. For what remains for a man whose wife has departed, leaving him alone in the world?"

CURSING THEIR MASTER BEHIND HIS BACK

Divine power reposes in slaves' hearts, too.
Aeschylus

OTHER peoples saw only themselves, stared at their royal citadels, prayed in their temples, danced about their idols, sacrificed to their own particular Moloch. The Greeks, by contrast, tried to understand not only their own nature but that of others as well. Without them, we would have only the scantiest information about early times.

The Greeks had an unerring instinct for the things that matter. In their eyes, the supreme attainment was freedom, and everything the Greeks did or endured, they did and endured in freedom. This was yet another respect in which they differed from all of their contemporaries. They regarded personal liberty as the greatest blessing on earth.

They also tried to be just, and if they did not always succeed, perhaps it was because the question "What is justice?" was as nearly unanswerable then as it is today. Yet the people which more than any other had recognized the value of personal liberty deprived millions of others of their freedom, and reduced them to mere tools or useful domestic animals—a marketable merchandise. For the Greeks were incapable of conceiving of a world without slaves. Born and bred in humiliation, generation after generation, the slaves formed a social stratum of their own. Without slaves, the Greeks thought, neither the individual nor the state could exist. But the question of *just* or *unjust* in connection with slavery never even presented itself.

Where did the Greeks obtain their slaves?

Some slaves were born into slavery. But this was not the most productive source of supply, for there were for fewer female than male slaves, and it was cheaper to buy a slave than to raise one from birth. Children could be sold into slavery by free parents, a practice which was universally permitted except in Attica. Foundlings became slaves, free men could sell themselves into slavery, and until the time of Solon (638-588 B.C.), a debtor who went bankrupt automatically became his creditor's slave. But the most important source of slaves was war, which furnished prisoners. Eventually there were not only

Asiatic and Thracian slaves but Greek slaves as well—men who had been captured during the numerous fratricidal wars which racked Greece. Kidnapers and pirates were also forever on the lookout for marketable human prey, and life on the coasts of the Mediterranean was quite precarious. Through the years the slave trade flourished, the principal exporting countries being Syria, Pontus, Lydia, Galatia and, in particular, Thrace, although Egypt, Ethiopia and Italy also supplied this human merchandise. Asiatics were the most popular slaves because they were considered adaptable and expert at making all sort of luxurious articles, but Greek slaves were the most expensive. The slave trade also furnished the courts of eastern potentates with courtesans, female musicians and dancers. Athens was an important slave market, and the state imposed a high sales tax on such transactions. Other important slave centers existed on the islands of Cyprus and Rhodes, at Ephesus and, above all, on the island of Chios.

Slaves who were put up for sale were either exhibited naked or forced to disrobe for the benefit of the purchaser, for a trader was not allowed to conceal the physical defects of his human wares. Prices varied according to age, competence and character, a male or female slave costing between 1 and 10 minas.

And what did an Athenian pay for a slave? There were 100 drachmas to a mina, and a drachma's purchasing power at the time of Pericles roughly corresponded to that of $5.00 today, which would make a Periclean mina worth about $500. On that basis, a slave cost between $500 and $5,000. There were relatively far fewer poor people in those days than there are now, and any well-to-do family maintained seven slaves at the very least. Indeed, to possess only seven slaves was an indication of poverty. It was considered unseemly if the lady of the house was accompanied by a mere four female slaves when she went out, and to go for a walk without any slave attendants was regarded as a sign of complete destitution. When the wife of a certain Phocion was seen with only one woman slave, people were scandalized to the point of discussing the matter in the theatre. Men, too, were often attended by three or more slaves, especially when traveling.

Plato thought it was normal that a man should own fifty slaves or more. Nicias hired out 1,000 of his slaves to the mines of Attica. As a matter of fact, most Greek slaves were laborers whom their owners hired out to factories, farms or building contractors: they were regarded as a form of capital investment. And slaves who were manual laborers were, in general, more independent than household slaves.

The lot of the Greek slave was better than that of his Roman counterpart, and in Athens there probably was a better relationship between slave and master than later prevailed in Italy. Plutarch, for example, speaks of the "mute obedience" of the Roman slave and the "familiar garrulity" of the Greek. Everything depended of course on the temperament of the master. Aristotle, for example, recommended that slaves should be treated neither with excessive harshness nor excessive familiarity. The Athenians felt that masters or mistresses should never jest with their slaves, since this would weaken their authority. And Plato said that a man should act with the utmost formality toward his slaves. It was advisable that slaves should always be allowed to hope for emancipation, as a final reward. This hope was invariably cherished—and surprisingly often fulfilled.

A master could beat, chain or punish his slave. And while he was not allowed to kill him, he could hand him over to a magistrate for punishment. If a slave had his own complaints, he could put in a request to be sold, but he could not appeal to the courts. If his master treated him very cruelly, his only recourse was to flee to the temple and seek sanctuary at the altars of the gods, waiting until his owner was compelled to sell him. Household slaves were often beaten, regardless of their sex, but the slaves who suffered worst were those in the workshops, where the overseers and foremen were slaves like themselves.

Slaves who worked on the land or in the mines often were fettered, not as a form of punishment but to prevent their escape. There were also inter-state agreements regulating the recapture and extradition of runaway slaves, while those who had escaped once were branded to prevent any further attempts. Unlike Rome, Greece had no educated slaves engaged in scholarly work for Greek teachers were always freemen, never slaves. However, reliable slaves, and those unfit for heavy work, were entrusted with the care of children, which often resulted in close and affectionate relationships between such slaves and their charges. Luxury slaves—like musicians, dancers or actors—did not come into fashion until later, when Roman influence began to be felt throughout Greece. Negroes and eunuchs, however, were very popular with the wealthy. People were vain and liked to parade their slaves, and eunuchs were particularly in demand. And since they were regarded as especially trustworthy, they often handled their masters' finances. On the other hand, there is no evidence that they were ever entrusted with the custody of women.

Some women kept slaves as lovers, for the Greek poet Herondas, who lived in the third century B.C., has left us some descriptions of everyday life in which he tells about a jealous woman who accused her slave-lover of infidelity. She had him shackled and he was given 2,000 lashes.

Although there were far fewer female than male slaves, much of the work in every prosperous household was performed by women slaves. They were responsible for maintaining order and cleanliness, they cooked and spun, served as nurses and attendants, and waited on the lady of the house.

Particularly sad was the lot of the girls who had to operate the handmills for grinding grain; the characteristic hum of these gadgets filled the air in every Greek village. These poor girls often worked until they dropped because their overseers had forgotten all about them, and the handmill was the constant nightmare of every woman slave in Greece.

It was not uncommon for free men to live with women slaves, but their children were free only in rare cases. Slaves were regarded as mere tools of the free, and the virtue of a male or female slave (the Greeks were quite positive about this) ranked far below that of the free—about as far as animals are below human beings. This attitude was partly due to the fact that people of some of the Greek states were in exaggerated perpetual fear of the slave population. Whenever a war broke out the Spartans, for example, always felt the threat of a slave uprising behind the front line. And after the Athenian army was defeated in Sicily and Deceleia occupied in 413 B.C. by the Spartans under King Agis, 20,000 slaves, largely from the mines, did desert the Athenians in Attica in one mass exodus.

There was also constant friction between the various city-states caused by one of them giving asylum to escaped slaves from another city-state. And in wartime attempts were always made to incite the enemy's slaves to desert, so that generally speaking it was only in times of complete peace and quiet that the Greek city-states could feel secure about their slaves and exploit their manpower to the fullest.

Slaves who showed bravery in battle were frequently rewarded with freedom. And yet Greek literature is full of stories about slaves who murdered their masters. Xenophon tells us that the citizens set up a defense committee, on a volunteer basis, to combat the slave menace, and the owner of an estate felt safe only if he was the first to rise in the morning and the last to retire at night.

On the other hand, the characteristics of the institution of slavery varied enormously from Greek state to Greek state. Thus no blanket generalizations can truthfully be made. The Athenians, for example, did not exhibit the psychology of a people who feared their slaves or slave revolts. Other states, however, certainly did fear their slaves.

The dialogue between Xanthias and Aeacus in the celebrated *Frogs*, by the comic dramatist Aristophanes, gives us some indication of what slaves thought and felt. "They stick their finger into every pie, listen to what their master says, and then start a rumor or two. They grumble outside after they have been beaten, and their greatest delight is in cursing their master behind his back."

THE MYSTERIOUS ETRUSCANS

They passed many peoples until they came to the Umbrians, where they founded cities and have dwelt ever since.
Herodotus

ROUGHLY 3,000 years ago, an alien people landed on the western shores of Italy and, gradually overrunning the present provinces of Tuscany and Umbria, founded cities, evolved a culture of their own, engaged in astrology, built gigantic walls and produced unique sculptures and paintings, some of which still survive. They were the first people to create an advanced civilization on Italian soil.

These Etruscans were a strange people, most of whose fascinating secrets remain unknown to us since nobody yet has managed to decipher their writing. They lasted for 700 years, and then vanished from history. And the more modern scientists have excavated, the more they have explored, the more they have striven to understand the forgotten language of the Etruscans, the harder it has become to comprehend the true nature of this people. If the Etruscans recorded their history such records have not been found. What brought them to Italy? Whence did they come?

About 1200 B.C., as we have mentioned before, something happened in the countries of the eastern Mediterranean which convulsed the entire known world. It was a catastrophe beneath whose impact governments collapsed, peoples were scattered, and cities tumbled into dust and ashes. Whole populations migrated on a scale hitherto unknown, and an incessant stream of invaders surged from the north to the south. Assyrian inscriptions, the Old Testament and Egyptian sources shed but scanty light on this vast upheavel, which is known as the Aegean migration because the area about the Aegean Sea was particularly affected. The migrating peoples carried along all their goods and chattels.

This Aegean migration brought the Dorians into Greece, and resulted in the destruction of the ancient Mycenaean civilization. Due to this same population pressure from the north, a people was set in motion whom the Greeks called the Tyrsanoi and from whom the Etruscans of Italy descended.

Our earliest and virtually only information about the origins of the Etruscans again comes from the Greek historian Herodotus, who tells us that in the time of King Atys a great famine broke out in the land of the Lydians. (Lydia lay on the Aegean Sea, almost in the center of the western coast of modern Turkey.) The famine lasted for eighteen years, and in order to end it, the king of the Lydians commanded half his subjects to emigrate, appointing his son Tyrsanus as their leader. These homeless people procured ships at Smyrna, loaded them with all their household equipment, and sailed across the open seas to look for a new home. "After sojourning with many nations in turn, they came to the Umbrikoi, and here they founded cities and have dwelt ever since. They no longer called themselves Lydians, however, but Tyrsanians, after the name of the king's son who had led them thither.

Who were these Tyrsanoi, Tyrsenoi or Tyrrhenoi, as the Greeks variously spelled the name? The Greeks themselves did not always exclusively connect them with Tyrsanus, the king's son, but also with *tyrsis*, a word meaning "fortress." The Etruscans built walled cities, and some of these walls may still be seen as at Volterra.

Scholars have become increasingly convinced that the Tyrsanians, or Etruscans, were foreign immigrants from Asia Minor. And this means that we are back to the old theory about a long sea voyage—back, in fact, to Herodotus. Etruscan culture, art, religion and mythology all point toward an origin in Asia Minor. Their art resembles that of Mesopotamia, Syria, Crete, Cyprus and Egypt, while their gods and mythological figures appear to be the heroes and gods of the Asiatic legends. Their chronology corresponds to Chaldean conceptions, while the reading of livers and their various configurations—which lies at the heart of their religious rites—is found only among the Babylonians and Hittites. Etruscan towns were laid out in terraces after the Babylonian manner, and their burial customs, which included preserving the ashes of the dead in cloths and open receptacles, has its roots in Asia Minor. Furthermore, dome-shaped tombs were unknown in Italy before the Etruscans arrived, yet the Mycenaeans did build such graves. And, finally, the Etruscan language also appears to come from Asia. But here we are confronted with mysteries that have not yet been solved.

There already exists an extensive literature on the Etruscan language and script, and the tomes written by the numerous scholars who have attacked this problem with great perspicacity and enthusiasm would fill a large library. Although we can identify those letters of the Etruscan alphabet which are derived from early Greek, the meaning

Most important settlements of the Etruscans.

of the inscriptions carved in stone, scratched on clay, or engraved in metal has remained a mystery.

Today we possess some 9,000 Etruscan inscriptions, most of them just names, brief title deeds or epitaphs. The only text of any length we have is the so-called Zagreb "mummy shroud." This is a linen roll with some 1,500 words—a sacrificial calendar. This linen was used for embalming an Egyptian princess, and it now is at the Zagreb Museum.

The Berlin Museum owns a clay tablet from Santa Maria di Capua with about 300 words on it, apparently sacrificial instructions. A large stone from Perugia carries what is apparently a family agreement about the use of a burial vault. The bronze liver from Piacenza, with its numerous names of gods, is particularly important since it gives us an idea of Etruscan methods of divining from animal livers. Recent successes in elucidating these inscriptions are based on an interpretation of Etruscan numerical terms as used in recording death statistics.

The scholars who believed that Etruscan belonged to the Indo-European languages were mistaken for the structure of Etruscan is similar to that of the Ural-Altaic (Finno-Ugric) group of languages. We know that Etruscan had some influence on the Italian language, and even the name of Rome, Italy's capital, has been traced back to the Etruscan.

The Roman emperor Claudius, who was born in 10 B.C., wrote a twenty-volume Etruscan history, a work which unfortunately has been lost. But even if it still existed, its value would be doubtful, since Etruria flourished more than 500 years before Claudius' time. Moreover, the emperor could scarcely have drawn on Etruscan sources, since, as far as we know, the Etruscans left no recorded history.

The Etruscans were the first people in Italy, however, to establish towns, usually in terraces on the slopes of hills. Cortona, Chiusi (Clusium), Volterra and Perugia are examples of such hillside cities. And whenever the Etruscans built a town above a river, they built their necropolis, or city of the dead, on the opposite bank, so that the abode of the dead was always within sight of the living—as at Vulci, Cerveteri (Caere) and Tarquinia. Massive walls enclosed each town and, just as in Babylonia, the temple was always in the center. So that the living could commune with their dead, shafts were sunk deep into the ground to enable them to be near to the departed.

Italy was still densely wooded in Etruscan times, and almost everything the Etruscans built was made of wood: their houses, their temples, their bridges and their sacred precincts.

The Romans described Etruscan men as a race of fat, drunken, dissolute gluttons. We should not forget, however, that the Romans spent hundreds of years fighting against the Etruscans, and were never exactly fond of their hardy enemies. Veii, the most important city in southern Etruria, was besieged by the Romans for ten years before it fell into their hands in 396 B.C. And although fierce fighting continued for another 300 years, the city's capture really marked the beginning of the end for the Etruscans.

At the battles of Fidenae (426 B.C.) and Sutrium (356 B.C.), the Etruscans were led by priests who charged at the Romans with a reckless, desperate courage, brandishing live snakes and flaming torches. Later the Romans fought bitterly for eight years against the city of Tarquinia where the Etruscans sacrificed 307 Roman prisoners of war to their gods. The Romans retaliated in 353 B.C. by stoning and decapitating 358 members of the Etruscan aristocracy in the Forum. It was not until 265 B.C., however, that the Romans finally captured the Etruscan town of Volsini, and not until 89 B.C. that the Etruscans were given Roman citizenship. But even after that time a few isolated Etruscan cities continued to resist, and it took Sulla three years of savage fighting before he finally subdued Populonia and Volaterrae in 79 B.C. The Etruscan people certainly put up a heroic defense, and it seems improbable that such men could have been as flabby and self-indulgent as the Romans said they were.

Etruscan women enjoyed equal rights with their men and took part in festivals, games and assemblies. Many sculptures and paintings testify to the death-transcending love and harmony that existed between Etruscan married couples, and it has even been suggested that Etruscan society was matriarchal. There was an Etruscan queen of Rome, Tanaquil, who seems to have been one of the truly great women of the ancient world. She had the gift of clairvoyance, and allegedly had magical powers that enabled her to guide the passions of Rome's young brides as she pleased. Etruscan women were famous for their beauty.

The whole earthly life of the Etruscans was governed by the life to come, and the Etruscans did not live carelessly from day to day, but kept the thought of death constantly before their eyes. Just as in Babylon and Egypt, the citizenry were ruled and guided by a powerful priesthood, and all streets, temples, gates and public squares were consecrated to one or another of the three most important gods, Tina, Uni and Minerva.

Funerals were marked by great festivals held in honor of the dead, by competitive sports, dancing, flute playing, and pantomimes. Actually much of our knowledge of Etruscan civilization has been revealed to us by their habit of thinking in terms of eternity and their building, modeling and painting for their dead. The necropolises at Cerveteri and Tarquinia, for example, disclosed complete homes for the dead hewn out of the ground. Precious objects, glorious vases, golden ornaments and magnificent paintings were brought to light from the cemeteries of Etruria, and whereas Roman slaves were buried in communal graves, the remains of Etruscan slaves were often found in funeral urns grouped around their master's sarcophagus.

Whatever wisdom and culture Rome may have taken over from the East was owed mainly to the Etruscans. From them the Romans learned the art of building cities. And the Romans also adopted the realism of Etruscan sculpture, while Rome's artistic life was heavily influenced by Etruscan fashions, music and drama. And it was the Etruscans who introduced divination, astrology, natural science and a well-reasoned theory about lightning into Italy. The influence of the Etruscans thus survived long after their cities had been destroyed by the Romans. The Roman emperors Galba, Vespasian, Hadrian, Alexander Severus and Diocletian were all followers of the Etruscan theories of divination by means of animal entrails. And, much later, Dante, whose features were supposedly Etruscan, drew upon murals of Etruscan burial vaults for his visions of Hell.

Etruscan hegemony in Italy lasted only 700 years, yet the culture of this mysterious race of seers and diviners lives on. More and more of their graves are being opened. The highly intelligent faces sculpted on their sarcophagi smile at us and seem to look into eternity. There is much wisdom in these faces, much nobility and a hint of irony. Their mute lips seem to whisper: "Your life, too, will last but one day. And to whom belongs eternity?"

LAND OF CALVES

At the foot of the Palatine, one of the seven hills of Rome, lay a marsh where the first Romans used to bury their dead. This burial ground was the site of the later Forum. A few years ago, the urns of men who had been dead for 3,000 years were dug up there—Eternal Rome!

THE history of Rome, and with it the history of a world empire, begins with a bridge.

About twelve miles from the Tyrrhenian Sea, the Tiber meets a small but stubborn obstruction: an island which has been there from time immemorial. From here, over a wooden bridge, people could cross the Tiber in comfort. It was a very old bridge, older even than the Bronze Age which was succeeded by the Iron Age about 1000 B.C. Not a single nail was driven into the bridge and nothing but wood was used for its construction, for wood was still vested with the sanctity which Europe's great forests once possessed in the misty obscurity of prehistoric times. It still held the magic properties of the sacred trees once worshiped by the white inhabitants of primeval Europe.

There, at the left end of the bridge and in the heart of the fertile plain of Latium, rose the eternal city of Rome. It was there that Roman dancers used to gather each spring to prance about in wild war dances, while their weapons clanged, the woodwork groaned, and weird songs floated across the river to the opposite bank. Priests guarded the sanctity of this bridge and supervised its cults, and one of these priests was the bridge-maker, or the *pontifex*.

That was over a thousand years before Christ's birth; and yet today, 3,000 years later, the man who builds the bridge between earth and heaven, which all true believers must cross, is still called *pontifex*. And the Pope resides in the same Rome where the first bridge was once thrown across the Tiber. Rome is truly an eternal city.

Looking down from the streets of modern Rome onto the ancient *Forum Romanum*—that jumble of ruined marble columns, Roman arches and stonework—we are almost frighteningly reminded of the city's eternal past. As we stand there, it seems as though the clock were racing irresistibly backward in time—thousands of years toward the moment when the first stone was laid—and we are struck by a thought which has probably occurred to countless millions of men in countless ages: 2,000 or 3,000 years ago people like ourselves walked across these same stones, people with cares and joys, good and evil thoughts, much like our own. We have to look down a little to see the Forum, for it lies slightly below modern street level, proving once again that cities not only grow downward into the depths of their burial vaults and catacombs, but upward as well, rising above the debris left behind by generation after generation.

Yet we are struck by another thought. How small was ancient Rome—in spite of her magnificent buildings—and how cramped and confined!

Of the seven hills of Rome (they are now partially flattened) one was called the Palatine and the other, the Capitoline. Between them was a valley, and in the valley lay a dismal marsh and three ponds. To the northeast of the Capitoline was the Quirinal Hill. The Quirinal was inhabited by a tribe known as the Sabines, and the Palatine by the Latins. But these people were not yet townsmen, and Rome was still far from being a city. Her people lived in mud huts with thatched roofs, and the smoke of their fires drifted out through the doors. The living quarters were surrounded by stables, and cattle wandered in the roads. They were actually a race of sturdy peasants, these ancestors of the future masters of the world!

In the valley below the Palatine Hill, on the present site of the Forum, there was a burial ground, and the Romans of Cicero's time knew that underneath their Forum lay an ancient necropolis, a place known as the Doliola. On this particular spot it was forbidden to spit on the ground or raise one's voice, for far below lay the sinister potsherds of prehistoric times, the funeral urns of the first inhabitants of Rome.

It was this ancient tradition which encouraged the Italian archaeologist Giacomo Boni (d. 1925) to dig there. On the northern edge of the valley, at the foot of the temple of Antoninus and Faustina, he unearthed a burial ground dating from the early Iron Age (ninth to sixth centuries B.C.). It is the earliest evidence of human presence in the Forum.

But to return to the Latins on the Palatine and the Sabines on the Quirinal: Wars were waged between the two hills just as they were later waged between towns, principalities and, eventually, between countries. However, there came a day when the inhabitants of the two hills made peace, and, after that, they drained the marsh below the two hills. The villages expanded and eventually the center of the marsh became a communal market place—the Forum.

On the rocks projecting from the lower slopes of the Capitoline Hill the early Romans erected altars to their gods Saturn and Vulcan, and on the Palatine Hill they built a shrine for the goddess Vesta and a house for her priestesses, the vestal virgins.

The early people of Rome had a curious collection of gods: Pales, the tutelary god of cattle; Deverra, the goddess of the broomstick, and Janus, the twin-headed god who guarded the front door, which was itself sacred. Then there was Faunus, a woodland god whose sacred festival, the Lupercalia, was celebrated by wolf-men who danced naked on the Palatine Hill and lashed the women with thongs to stimulate fertility and easy delivery.

The wolf-men ... that is a story all by itself.

Italy was then a land of virgin forests from which wolves would stray into the town, howl eerily at night on the slopes of the seven hills, and occasionally steal a child or two. The twin brothers Romulus and Remus, to whom legend attributes the founding of Rome in 753 B.C., were reputedly suckled by a she-wolf.

The Romans of those days were a wild people who wore clothes and caps made of skins. And although they were familiar with altars and shrines they had not yet started to build temples or set up idols. Just as the cattle of Homer's Greece served as a form of money (about 1000 B.C.), so they did in Rome, and *pecunia*, the Roman word for "money," stems from *pecus*, meaning "ox." At a time when Greek civilization was in its prime, the Latins were still forging primitive weapons of bronze and sacrificing bulls on the Mons Albanus. The tribe that spoke the language we now call Latin was probably more ingenious than its neighbors, yet the idioms spoken by all these tribes were so closely related that they are now classified as Italic, and the people themselves became known as Italians.

The early Italians were primarily cattle breeders, and according to ancient tradition this is how Italy obtained its name: *italos* is the Greek for "bull calf"; it followed that "Italia" was "the land of calves."

* * *

The boundary between the Latins and the Etruscans was the Tiber River, and since the Etruscans were constantly attacking the village of Rome, the Romans learned the arts of defense and warfare at an early stage in their history. It was from the Etruscans that they adopted the phalanx, an infantry battle formation of heavily armed troops wearing helmets and armor and carrying spears and shields. The Etruscans, in their turn, had taken over this battle formation from the Greeks.

As late as 700 B.C. the Romans could neither read nor write. This was another art they learned from the Etruscans, for they patterned their own letters on the Etruscans' Greek alphabet, although, unlike the Etruscans, they wrote from left to right. And it is this Roman modification of the Greek alphabet which we ourselves finally inherited.

In 600 B.C. the Latins fell completely under the sway of their neighbors, and the Etruscan Tarquins became the first kings of Rome. In 509 B.C., however, these kings were overthrown and Rome became a republic.

But if the Romans had succeeded in throwing off Etruscan domination, southern Italy and the island of Sicily were still occupied by Greek colonists. This portion of the peninsula was known as Magna Graecia, or Greater Greece, and Tarentum, Heraclea, Rhegium and Locri were all Greek cities during this period.

But how could these cities maintain their strength when their Greek motherland was weary and on the verge of collapse and when the all-conquering warrior of Macedonia, Alexander the Great, had been carried to his grave? Greece, and the East in general, still had many artists, scholars and poets, and the Greek theatre produced magnificent performances. But when the actors are better than their playwrights, the end is usually near. Greece and the countries of the eastern Mediterranean had never held more spendid banquets, never eaten finer food, never enjoyed more sophisticated pleasures. Trade was flourishing. Yet, militarily, the Orient was weak. And Rome had already gained the upper hand in the Greek portion of southern Italy.

It was at this juncture—before little Rome, the future ruler of the world, burst upon the scene—that she encountered Pyrrhus, the last of the great Greek generals.

Pyrrhus was the king of Epirus and a relative of Olympias, the mother of Alexander the Great. Throughout his life (318-272 B.C.), Pyrrhus referred to himself as a descendant of Achilles, the hero who fought at Troy. Pyrrhus, too, was a hero, but he was that ultimate tragedy, a man born too late, a man at heart still one with the glories of ancient Greece, but who belonged to an age when Greece had spent herself and was going down.

Pyrrhus was a boy when he came to the throne, and the school of life made him wise and adaptable. Later he was brought by Demetrius to the court of Ptolemy as a hostage. Ptolemy, who had been one of Alexander the Great's confidantes and generals, was another man who occupied a throne which had once ruled the world. He founded the Ptolemaic dynasty in Egypt. It was at his court that Pyrrhus married Antigone, Ptolemy's stepdaughter.

The stronghold of Hellenism in Italy—the pride of all the Greek colonial outposts—was the splendid city of Tarentum. And in 281 B.C. Tarentum was attacked by Rome. Tarentum immediately appealed to the mother country for aid, whereupon Pyrrhus was dispatched to Italy and marched to the attack with 25,000 men, including cavalry and elephants. He engaged the Romans at Heraclea, and in the ensuing battle defeated the Roman consul Valerius Laevinus. The encounter cost him so many casualties, however, that to this day a costly triumph is known as a "Pyrrhic victory."

Pyrrhus almost reached the outskirts of Rome and defeated the Roman legions again, but the Romans obstinately refused to sue for peace. And in the end, the gallant Pyrrhus gained so many victories that he was completely exhausted. He crossed over to Sicily, planning to drive the Carthaginians from that island, but the Romans allied themselves with the Carthaginians and the Sicilian cities rebelled against the Greek general's tyrannical methods. Pyrrhus stayed in Sicily for three years before trying his luck in Italy once more, only to be held to a drawn battle at Beneventum in 275 B.C. Five years later, in 270 B.C., all of southern Italy was under Roman control.

Before Pyrrhus, discouraged, left Italy to make his way home, he made a most interesting prophecy: he foretold the dreadful struggle which was later to ensue between Rome and Carthage. Looking eleven years ahead, he saw a war which was destined to drag on for more than a century. "What a battlefield I am bequeathing to Rome and Carthage!" he said. It has always been so in world history: first, two powers unite against a common enemy, but once that enemy has been disposed of, a conflict inevitably arises between the victors. It was true with Rome and Carthage; it is still true today.

The Romans captured so much booty in their wars against Pyrrhus that they could afford to build the most famous aqueduct in the world. It was over thirty-four miles long, and brought fresh water to Rome from the mountains. It was so solidly built, so firmly supported by the Roman arches that carried it on its lofty journey through the countryside, that large sections of it have survived for more than 2,200 years to the present day.

For centuries the Romans drank water that traveled along this canal in the sky, and even today people are lost in wonder before this miracle wrought by a people on the ascendant, before this symbol of a strength which clothed itself in beauty and passed it on to later European millennia as civilization and culture.

ELEPHANTS AND GALLEYS

They dwelt careless, after the manner of the Zidonians, quiet and secure.
Book of Judges

"FROM now on there can be no more progress," people said. "We have reached the zenith of knowledge, wisdom and ingenuity." That was in 300 B.C.

Berossus, the Babylonian priest, historian, astrologer and astronomer, was constructing a giant sundial. In the "Bright Hall" at Athens the Stoics were discoursing on the meaning of life, and on virtue as the only source of happiness. The Greek astronomer Aristarchus recognized that the sun is the center of our planetary system, but he made an even greater discovery: the earth does not merely rotate upon its own axis, but whirls around the sun as well. Manetho, the Egyptian priest and historian, was striving to communicate Egypt's former greatness to the West. In Rome, the Forum shook with crowds jubilant because from then on plebeians could hold state appointments.

A mysterious race invaded Rome's northern territories, plundered them and finally settled there: they were the Celts. Meanwhile, the fields of Central Europe witnessed the appearance of a strange new invention; an iron plow with round contraptions attached to it—the first wheels the northern Occident had ever seen.

Three hundred years before Christ!

The Carthaginians lolled on the terraced roofs of their six-storied houses, sipping wine from the island of Samos and feeling that they were the masters of the world. It was inconceivable to them than anyone could be richer, more powerful or more magnificent than they were. The zenith of progress had indeed been reached.

Italy and the island of Sicily divide the Mediterranean into an eastern and a western half. At the point where North Africa juts out closest to Sicily lies the Gulf of Tunis, and by the shores of this bay, a dozen miles from the modern city of Tunis, the coastline has always been broken by a hill. Today this hill is the site of the French Convent of the White Fathers, the Cathedral of St. Louis, an archaeological museum housing the treasures of ancient Carthage which were excavated by Père Delattre.

Our word "purse" has an interesting etymology. The Greek word *byrsa* meant "leather" or "leather money pouch." Later the term was applied to the actual site of commercial transactions (cf. the French *Bourse*), and so it is easy to see how the heart of Carthage, the largest commercial city in the Mediterranean, came to be called Byrsa. Byrsa was the name of the hill, the citadel of Carthage, the oldest part of this amazing metropolis. It was there that the earliest Punic graves were found. For the Carthaginians were Punians, the same people whom we know as Phoenicians or Poeni, from the adjective *punicus*. They were descendants of the same Semites who called their original home Chanaan, after the Canaan of the Bible, and whose oldest capital cities were Tyre and Sidon. Carthage was founded by Phoenician colonists from Tyre about 800 B.C., and its name literally means "new city."

Anyone visiting Tunis today should make that short trip to the shore and climb the hill of Byrsa. It is only a little under 200 feet high, but the view from its summit is most rewarding. What immediately strikes us is the decisive command Carthage must have had over the sea and the undulating hinterland which stretches westward to Tunis and the Lake of Tunis.

The Greek author Polybius, who wrote a forty-volume world history about 150 B.C., described Carthage as the wealthiest city in the world. It was the Phoenicians' most important commercial center, and had spacious harbors protected against the most violent storms. Walls over sixty feet high have been dug up on the hill of Byrsa. At the height of its power the city dominated the entire North African coast from Egypt to Gibraltar, including southern Spain, the islands of Sardinia and Corsica and the western half of Sicily. From Sicily to Gibraltar, the Mediterranean was indeed a "Carthaginian sea." Through the warehouses of Carthage passed the gold and pearls of the East, purple from Tyre, ivory, lion and leopard skins from the African interior, incense from Arabia, linen from Egypt, ceramics and aromatic wines from Greece, copper from Cyprus, silver from Spain, tin from England, iron from Elba. Her ships sailed far out into the Atlantic, putting in at the Canary Islands and probably the Azores, too. Was it any wonder that Carthage became a world power?

About 300 B.C. the citizens of Carthage were a detached, cultured and, one might almost say, slightly sated people whose city could look back on 500 years of wealth and splendor. Foreign visitors stared in awe at the marble temples with their gold and silver pillars and gilded statues of Greek workmanship, at the largest harbor installations in the contemporary world, the wharves and docks, the warehouses, workshops and factories. (The magnificent cathedral at Pisa was constructed from blocks of marble brought to Italy from the ruins of Carthage.) The Carthaginians had business corporations, developed the most up-to-date financial economy in the ancient world, knew all about government loans, and invented the first "banknotes" made of a substance of only nominal value. They owned well-stocked arsenals, knew how to build machinery, and manufactured weapons—quite possibly the earliest artillery in the world—and there were stables for 300 elephants. The sturdiest Negro slaves and the loveliest slave girls in Africa were sold in the city's market. Carthaginian planters owned the fertile land of Libya and used chain gangs to work it. A few citizens owned as many as 20,000 slaves.

There were villas and palaces at Carthage, as well as tall blocks of apartment and office buildings, and the city had a rectangular street system just like Manhattan's, each block measuring 36 yards by 136. The astonishing symmetry of this network came to light during archaeological excavations. There were berths for 220 warships in the port of Carthage, while in the middle of the harbor there was an island from which the Punic admiral could conveniently review his fleet.

If ever there was such a thing as a plutocracy, a government by the rich, it was Carthage. The wealthiest families made the laws and directed all policy, and the two presidents who were elected annually well knew that gold and silver were the decisive factors in war. It was gold and silver which enabled the Carthaginians to build ships and recruit foreign mercenaries willing to sacrifice their lives for their wealthy masters; gold and silver which allowed them to win sea battles without exposing themselves to the risks necessarily connected with such unpleasant work. A few aristocratic families supplied the admirals, but by and large the millionaires of Carthage preferred to stay comfortably at home on their roof gardens, fanned by slave girls and admiring the purple robes of their elegantly gowned women.

There was no doubt about it—Carthage was the richest city in the world. Her inhabitants had implicit faith in the power of gold, and it was only in times of great danger that the masters of the world in their towering houses were ready to make sacrifices beyond gold. In such cases, the Carthaginians cremated their children alive to placate Baal Moloch and appease the hunger of the goddess Tanit. Generally speaking, however, the Carthaginians knew of better ways to win wars than by the sickly-sweet smell of burning human flesh. They relied on the courage of hired barbarians, on large war-trained elephant corps, on their splendid navy, and on gold—especially on gold.

How did this commercial metropolis become so wealthy?

It was quite simple. Foreign ships—and, in particular, Roman ships—were permitted to trade with Carthage direct, but not with her colonies. Thanks to this shrewd measure, all merchandise passed through the city's books. Any ships that disregarded the embargo on direct colonial trade were seized and their crews thrown overboard. One Carthaginian admiral said with pride: "The Romans cannot even wash their hands in the Mediterranean without our permission."

Three wars were ultimately fought between Carthage and Rome, the celebrated Punic wars which covered a span of 119 years. The dreadful bloodletting began in 264 B.C. By 146 B.C. it was over. Carthage was destroyed and her territory became a Roman province in Africa.

Were the people of Carthage cowards? Did this city of merchants have no heroes left?

It required stout hearts to sail across the charted, let alone uncharted, seas of the world in those days, and the Phoenicians proved their daring time and again. These Semites (Mommsen calls them Aramaeans) "defended their national integrity against all the lures of Greek civilization as well as against all the coercive methods of oriental and occidental despots with a stubbornness unequaled by any Indo-European people, both with the weapons of the spirit and with their blood."

What the Carthaginians lacked was political organization. We read in the Bible: "They dwelt careless, after the manner of the Zidonians, quiet and secure." (Judges.) The men who experienced the first Punic war, and those who fought in the second, were long dead when Rome was finally victorious.

How did the wars start in the first place?

The city of Messina in Sicily supplied the immediate cause. First the Roman tribune Caius Claudius landed there and arrested the Carthaginian general Hanno. Then the Carthaginians, after lengthy deliberations, declared war.

The Roman Senate was naturally well aware that any interference in Sicily might mean war with Carthage. However, the war party in Rome gained the upper hand, and thus began one of the bloodiest chapters in world history, which ended in Roman supremacy in the Mediterranean.

The Carthaginians were at that time superior to every other people in the world when it came to ship building. They built powerful quinqueremes, ships with five banks of oars manned by government-owned slaves. These galley slaves were excellently drilled, and the ships' captains were skillful and daring men.

The Romans on the other hand were still little more than peasants and had no knowledge of how to build warships. However, there came a day when a Carthaginian ship was stranded on the Roman coast. With this wreckage as a model, the Romans before long had constructed 120 galleys, each manned by 300 oarsmen and 120 soldiers.

At that time, naval engagements were won by ramming and thus sinking enemy ships, a maneuver which demanded considerable experience. And naval experience was precisely what the Romans lacked. But necessity is the mother of invention, and the Romans hit upon one of the most important inventions in their history. On the forward part of their galleys they installed flying bridges, triple ramps which could be let down over the prow or on either side. If an enemy ship rammed a Roman galley, the Romans threw the bridge across the enemy deck, where it stayed, fastened by an iron spike which became embedded in the woodwork. The Carthaginian captains, who were only schooled in the ramming technique, had some 300 oarsmen and a mere handful of soldiers on board. Once the Romans had driven hooks into the enemy deck, some 120 legionaries charged across the gangway and fought with their swords. Thus the Romans turned the sea battle of Mylae (260 B.C.) into a sort of land battle. The date is important, for it marks the Romans' first great naval victory.

For all that, the Roman admirals lost one fleet after another as time went by, until 700 Roman ships and 200,000 men lay on the bottom of the Mediterranean. But Rome summoned up her last reserves, built a new fleet, defeated the Punians, and Carthage surrendered, bringing the first Punic war to an end in 241 B.C. It had lasted twenty-four years. Carthage had to pay 3,200 gold talents in reparations, and her possessions in western Sicily were annexed by Rome. It looked as if Carthage was finished: her naval power was shattered–mutiny broke out, and flames painted the sky above the city a sinister red. Gradually, however, order was restored and the Carthaginians went back to sipping wine on their terraces in the cool of the evening.

The man who quelled the postwar mutiny was a general named Hamilcar who, his work at home done, set sail with his young son for southern Spain and defiantly began to fortify and extend the Carthaginian overseas possessions. This was the only means of retaliation.

Hannibal, the nine-year-old boy at Hamilcar's side, solemnly swore lasting hatred to Rome at the command of his father. And the future of the project was ensured.

Hamilcar died, and young Hannibal rose in the world as no other Carthaginian before him. At the age of twenty he was a cavalry general, at twenty-five commander-in-chief of the Carthaginian army in Spain. He conquered large territories and eventually besieged Saguntum, a city south of the Ebro. But since Saguntum had a defense treaty with Rome, Roman envoys warned him that the city was a Roman sphere of interest. Hannibal was undeterred, however, and after eight months Saguntum fell into his hands. Shortly thereafter a Roman delegation appeared in Carthage and demanded satisfaction. Bunching his robe together, the Roman spokesman declared that it contained peace or war and that it was for Carthage to choose. The shrewd Carthaginians answered that they would leave the decision to the Romans. The Roman envoy was no diplomat: he chose war. The Carthaginians nodded assent, and the second Punic war had begun.

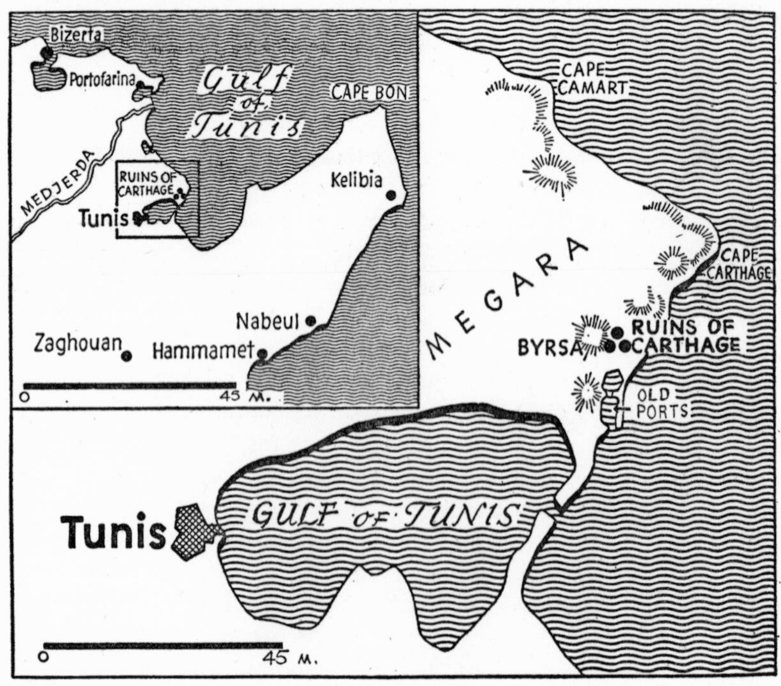

Rome at once shipped troops to Spain and simultaneously prepared to attack Carthage herself. But Hannibal devised an even bolder plan. At the head of his battle-tried veterans, he marched through Spain, across the Pyrenees, through southern France, and finally across the Alps into Italy, taking an elephant corps with him. Thousands of his soldiers, accustomed as they were to the warm climates of Spain and Africa, died of cold and hunger on the high Alpine passes. Even so, Hannibal eventually reached the Po valley with half his army intact.

This enterprise is one of the most interesting military achievements in world history which nowadays we would describe as a masterpiece of logistics. Hannibal's crossing of the Alps has been so hotly debated by geographers, historians, military experts and ethnologists that it is well worth the trouble to pause to accompany the great cavalry general, organizer and strategist on his journey across the snow-covered heights of what was perhaps the St. Bernard Pass.

THE TRAGEDY OF HANNIBAL

By the way, I am of the opinion that Carthage must be destroyed.

Cato in the Roman Senate

THE Roman historian Titus Livius, a contemporary of Christ, left behind a monumental work in 142 volumes. Livy, as he is known to us, was born in 59 B.C. and died in the seventeenth year of our era. Thirty-five of his books have survived.

A Roman to the core, Livy extolled the traditional Roman virtues, idealized Rome's past, and produced what the ancient world regarded as the crowning glory of Roman historiography. And as a patriotic Roman, Livy must have had good reason to praise Hannibal, the most dangerous enemy his country ever had. (Most other Roman and Greek historians, by the way, wrote about Hannibal with a mixture of hatred and envy.) Let us listen to what Livy says about the Carthaginian general:

"Hannibal met dangers with the most painstaking precautions, but conducted himself in moments of emergency with complete equanimity. He never allowed any difficulties to fatigue his body or curb his spirits. He ate and drank only what was absolutely necessary, never for pleasure. His times of rising and retiring were independent of the day or night. He rested when he had time, and needed neither a soft bed nor quiet for sleep. He could often be seen lying on the ground between guard posts, wrapped only in a short military cape. His dress scarcely differed from that of his men, but his weapons and his charger were the objects of universal admiration. He was always by far the best cavalryman and by far the best foot soldier in his great army. He rode into action ahead of everyone, and was the last to leave the battlefield."

The Romans' plan was to transport their main army from Sicily to Africa by sea and attack Carthage, meanwhile sending a second army to Spain to keep the enemy occupied there. Under no circumstances did they want to fight on Italian soil. But Hannibal resolved to carry the war to the very gates of Rome.

It was a daring and dangerous undertaking, for ever since Rome's victory in the first Punic war her navy had been far superior to that of Carthage. Hannibal was thus faced with the problem of carrying

The so-called Athena Lemnia in the Museo Civico, Bologna, commissioned by Athenian settlers in Lemnos, the bronze original was considered to be Phidias' finest work. This is a copy. [*Photograph:* Alinari.

A very early copy of the bronze statue erected by remorseful Athenians in 380 B.C., nineteen years after Socrates' execution.

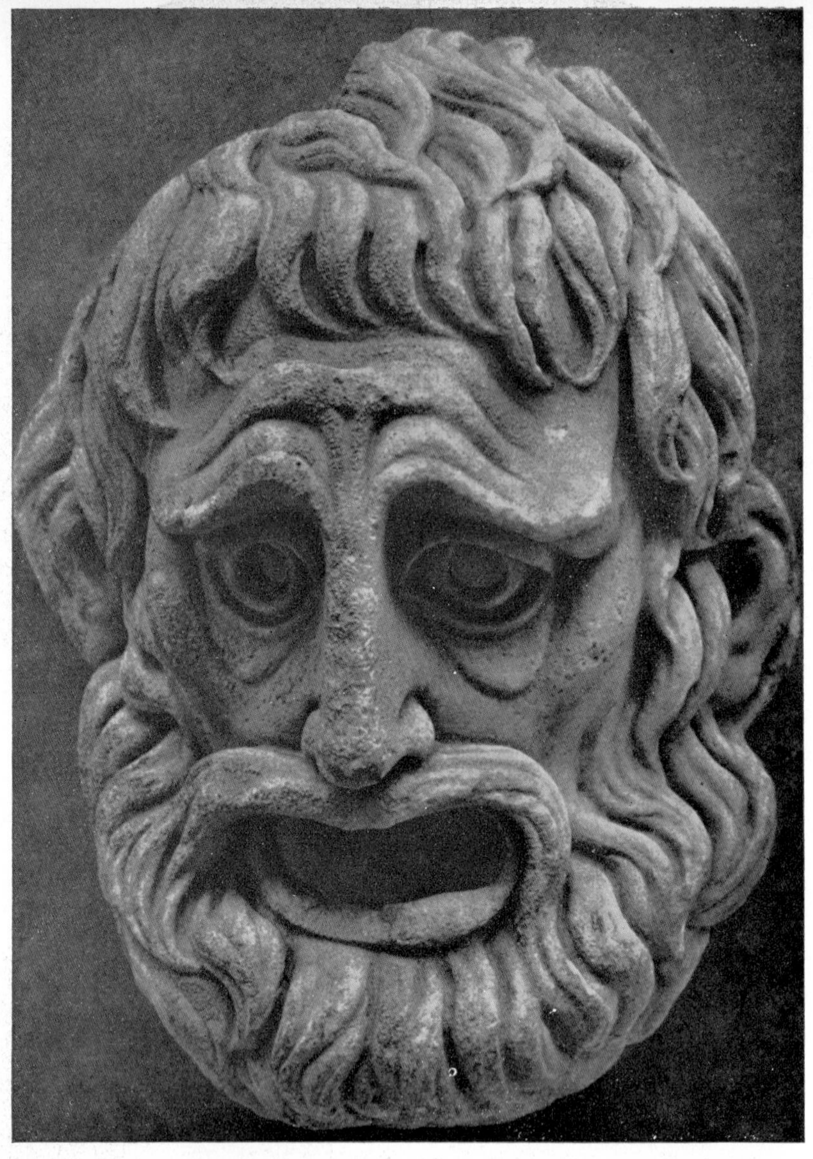

Grecian mask for a tragic actor, from the 4th-3rd century B.C. The marble original is in the Metropolitan Museum in New York. In the mouth opening of many of these masks there was a sort of speaking tube which increased the resonance of the voice. The mask prevented any change of expression, but it must be remembered that the onlooker usually saw and heard the actors from a considerable distance.

►

Head of Athena from the eastern pediment of the Temple of Aphaea on the island of Aegina. In 490 B.C., Aphaea (Britomartis) was the island's tutelary goddess. [Antikensammlungen, Munich.

This painting of an Etruscan woman is presumably a portrait of the deceased person buried in the "Golden Tomb" in the Etruscan city of Tarquinia.

►

This Etruscan married couple adorns the terracotta sarcophagus in a tomb in the ancient Etruscan town of Caere. The Etruscans reclined on cushions in this fashion while banqueting.

►

Top of a tomb portraying a stout Etruscan, found at Chiusi, on the route from Rome to Florence. Date: possibly 3rd century B.C. [In Florence Museum. *Photograph:* Carlo G. Mundt.

Bronze head of an African, 350 B.C. These were the sort of men who worked as government-owned slaves in the wooden galleys of the Carthaginians.

A Roman trireme in the time of the Punic Wars. The heavy ship was propelled by slaves rowing sixty a side, and the deck was manned by legionaries armed with spears and shields. During the course of the Punic Wars, these ancient "ships of the line" were superseded by quinqueremes, five-deckers capable of greater speeds.

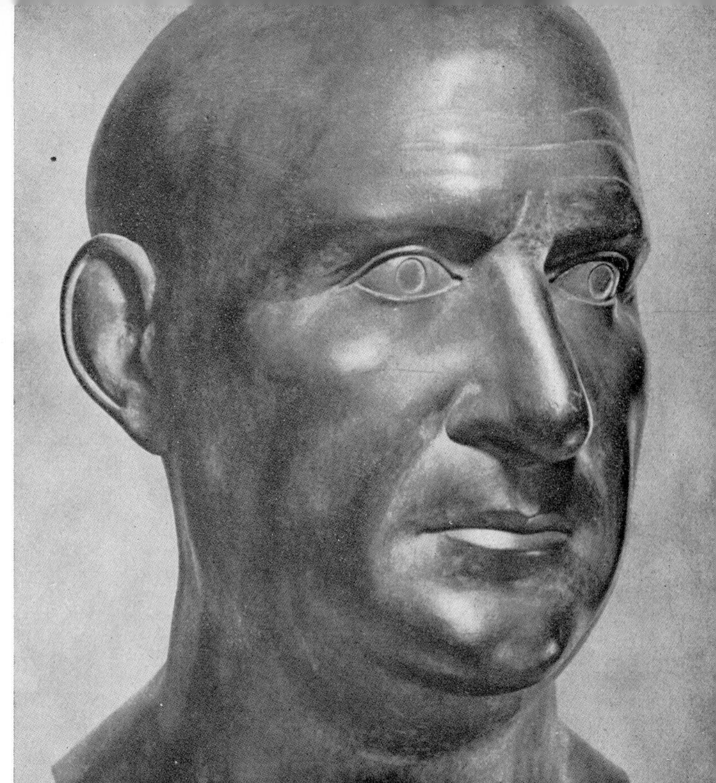

Publius Cornelius Scipio (237-183 B.C.), who defeated Hannibal, was the first really outstanding figure in Roman history.

1 and 2. *Golden stater.* 1 stater = 2 drachmas. Obverse: the nymph Arethusa with dolphins.

3 and 4. *Silver tetradrachm*, or four-drachma piece, Sicily.

5 and 6. *Golden double-stater* minted in Africa, showing the head of Demeter. Punic script on the reverse.

Fresco of a married couple found in Pompeii. Now in the National Museum at Naples.

the war to Italy without shipping his soldiers across the Mediterranean. He devised a plan—remember this was in 218 B.C.!—which must be numbered among the most audacious projects of military strategy in world history. If he could march an army across Spain and southern France, over the Alps and down into the valley of the Po, he would cause the Romans so much trouble that they would have to abandon the idea of attacking Carthage.

Hannibal did not, however, plunge blindly into his vast undertaking, but pondered it carefully, planning it down to the last detail. Indeed, he prepared his Italian expedition with much greater care than Alexander the Great ever devoted to his Asian campaigns. There was one thing in his favor: the north of Italy was occupied by the Gauls who were a source of constant irritation to the Romans. If he could only reach the southern side of the Alps he would be able to count on Gallic support.

Hannibal assembled a powerful army in Spain, and he refused to rely on mercenaries but collected veteran Carthaginian soldiers whom he equipped with the most up-to-date weapons. He sent scouts across the Alps to explore various routes and passes, for the area was then scarcely known, and dispatched envoys to the Gauls of northern Italy to interest them in his plans long before he himself arrived. He concluded friendship pacts with numerous Gallic tribes, established embassies among them, and sent them financial aid. He never underestimated the immense risks he was running, but he also realized the advantage of surprise.

The Romans were subtle in small details but careless in important matters. They had given Carthage twenty years in which to recuperate, twenty years in which they could have attacked Africa, and the respite was sufficiently long to revive the Carthaginians' spirit of aggression. And Rome failed to recognize the dangers of the Punic conquest of Spain. She neglected to put down the Celts and secure the Alpine passes. Her only resolve was to fight the next Punic war on African soil, and she went on nursing that idea until the Carthaginians selected their own battleground.

In May of 218 B.C., Hannibal was thirty-one years old as he led his splendid army out of New Carthage, the present Cartagena. The core of this force was composed of Carthaginian veterans, Libyans and Spaniards. Two-thirds of it were Carthaginian Africans, battle-hardened, disciplined men who were absolutely devoted to their leader. It is fully in keeping with our picture of this tough general, with his strength of character and self-discipline, that he sent his beautiful Spanish wife Imilcea and his little son back to Carthage before he left. Sixteen years were to pass before he embraced them again.

At the end of May, Hannibal crossed the Ebro and marched on over the Pyrenees. Crossing the Rhône, he passed through the valley of the upper Isère and reached the High Alps at a point near the Little St. Bernard Pass. Throughout this march, and especially in the mountains of Tarentaise, he was incessantly attacked by hostile Celtic tribes.

Historians and geographers have fiercely debated which pass Hannibal used when he crossed the Alps. As distinguished a scholar of antiquity as Professor Gaetano de Sanctis of the University of Rome believes that Hannibal used the Alpine pass of Mont Genèvre. This must be an error, however, and the *Encyclopaedia Britannica* would do well to amend its article on the subject. Our most reliable source is the Greek historian Polybius, who was born in 201 B.C., actually saw Carthage burning in 146 B.C., and died in 120 B.C. His treatment of the second Punic war contains very precise details regarding the distances Hannibal covered on his march. Livy, too, describes Hannibal's march across the Alps, but he lived 200 years after the event and his account is much too beautifully written to be entirely true. Polybius, however, was interested in military affairs, and he wrote at least two generations after Hannibal's campaign. Not too long ago Lieutenant Colonel Theodore Ayrault Dodge, an American, took the trouble to follow both Polybius' and Livy's accounts, clambering over the Alpine passes with their texts in his hand, until he finally settled for the Little St. Bernard Pass. Dodge then wrote a first-rate book on Hannibal, in which he refuted even Napoleon, who understandably enough was vastly interested in Hannibal's route but concluded that Hannibal chose the pass over Mont Cénis.

At the foot of the St. Bernard rises the celebrated White Rock, *La Roche Blanche*, a chalk cliff commanding the approaches to the pass. It was here that Hannibal camped with his infantry and spent a whole night covering the laborious ascent of his cavalry, pack mules and elephants. There was a good deal of bloody fighting during the night, but the top of the pass was reached on the following day. There, by the shores of a small lake at the source of the Doria, Hannibal allowed his army to rest.

This army originally consisted of roughly 50,000 infantry, 9,000 cavalry, and a corps of thirty-seven elephants. These elephants, incidentally, present us with another interesting historical problem. The

Carthaginians had adopted the war-trained elephant from the Greek kings, perhaps from Pyrrhus or even Alexander. They used African, not Indian elephants, although the drivers were Indians. Perhaps the territory of the wild elephant extended further north than it does now, or else the Carthaginians had them brought from Central Africa along the caravan routes leading through the Sahara.

This much is certain: Hannibal took these elephants along primarily to intimidate the Celts and Gauls rather than to use them in battle where one could never be too sure how long the beasts would behave. For while they struck terror into peoples who had never seen any before, if they turned savage they were very often more dangerous to the Carthaginians than to their foes. That was why elephant drivers in the second Punic war always kept heavy mallets and long iron pegs handy, so that they could drive them behind their beast's ear and kill it if it threatened to get out of control.

Hannibal had crossed the Alps, but he had lost more than half his army en route and could only muster 20,000 infantry, 6,000 cavalry and fifteen to twenty elephants. What was worse, he was now in a country which, theoretically, could mobilize 280,000 men and recruit about twice that number among its allies. However, the Romans had only 40,000 men under arms, and no sooner had the first Roman army taken up its stand in the Po valley than the Carthaginians overwhelmed it.

The Gauls had joined forces with Hannibal, according to plan, which doubled his striking power, and now he annihilated a second Roman army at Lake Trasimenus. It was in this hour of emergency that the Romans hastily levied some more troops and put them under the command of the dictator Fabius, a cautious aristocrat who had gone down in history as *Cunctator*, or "delayer" for, although he followed Hannibal's army wherever it went, he never dared engage it in pitched battle.

Rome finally gave the supreme command to two Consuls, who were ordered to annihilate Hannibal once and for all. Battle was joined in a narrow plain near Cannae in 216 B.C., with the Romans greatly outnumbering the Carthaginians, although Hannibal was the greater strategist and had better cavalry. Taking the Roman army in the flank—a tactic which deprived the heavily armed Roman soldiery of their maneuverability and turned them into an impotent mass—he butchered it. On that day 50,000 Roman and allied soldiers were slain, and 10,000 were captured.

When the news reached Rome, the Senate decreed that the women who had lost their fathers, husbands and sons were not allowed to weep, and the city prepared for a siege. But Hannibal never appeared. While his cavalry could win battles, they could not charge walls, and he had not been able to carry along any catapults or battering rams on his long-range expedition.

As usually happens in an emergency, some of Rome's allies such as the large cities of Syracuse and Capua deserted her. But the Roman Senate remained imperturbable. While Hannibal was marching through Italy and devastating the country, the Romans were mustering more and more legions each year. But Italy's fields were devastated, and grain had to be imported at wartime prices. Eventually the Romans besieged Capua and Syracuse, as an object lesson and to keep their other allies in line. Capua was starved out, Syracuse was looted and her glorious marble statues borne away to Rome.

Then, in her hour of need, Rome found a young and brilliant general—Publius Cornelius Scipio, the man who captured Cartagena in Spain.

Hannibal was now in southern Italy, waiting for Rome to capitulate and for his younger brother Hasdrubal to arrive from Spain with reinforcements. Hasdrubal did indeed cross the Alps in Hannibal's footsteps, only to be defeated and slain by the Roman legions at the Metaurus. By now the Romans were so embittered by their years of defeat that they catapulted Hasdrubal's head right into Hannibal's camp.

Hannibal waited. He was undefeated, but without reinforcements he was growing weaker year by year. In Spain, young Scipio annihilated one batch of reinforcements after another, and finally returned to Rome in triumph, after which he was given an army and a fleet, and sailed off to attack Carthage. Now the tables were turned, and Scipio the Roman soon stood before the gates of Carthage. Carthage was forced to capitulate, sue for peace and recall Hannibal from Italy. In fifteen years in Italy Hannibal had not lost a single battle. On one occasion he had come within three miles of Rome. Nothing but weeds grew in the fields of Italy. Hundreds of towns lay in ruins. The bones of Carthaginian soldiers and pack animals bleached on the Alpine passes. Hundreds of thousands of Romans and Roman allies had been killed. All this Hannibal had achieved. He was one of the greatest military geniuses of the ancient world, perhaps second only to Alexander the Great. And it had all been in vain.

Hannibal returned to Carthage and immediately persuaded the men who ruled his country that the war must continue. He engaged Scipio at Zama, and suffered the first defeat of his career. Now Carthage was forced to pay the fabulous sum of 10,000 talents, and had to relinquish all her warships and all her elephants except for ten. Furthermore, she had to pledge that she would never again go to war without Roman sanction, and to forfeit all her possessions in Spain.

Hannibal was given an important government post at Carthage, but the Romans insisted that he be banished. He made his way to the East, still maintaining his hatred of Rome. The Romans pursued their implacable enemy, and in order not to fall into Roman hands Hannibal finally took poison.

Fifty years later, the history of Carthage came to an end. The Carthaginians had grown rich once more and had also regained their courage. They attacked Massinissa, the king of Numidia, who was a friend of Rome. And in Rome at that time there lived an old man, a member of a wealthy plebeian family. His name was Cato and he discharged his duties as censor with the utmost severity, hounding everyone whose conduct offended his standards of respectability and engaging in endless tirades against any Roman who was interested in Greek culture, philosophy or any form of luxury. He wanted Rome to be a city of nothing but peasants and tough soldiers. Women lived to work and obey, he thought, and slaves should be sold as soon as they become old and weak. He traveled to Carthage, convinced himself of the remarkable economic recovery Rome's former enemy had made, and brought back some Carthaginian agricultural products. From then on he constantly advocated war against the Romans' dangerous rival, concluding every speech he made with the words:

"Carthage must be destroyed."

In the end, the Romans followed his advice. When Carthage rose against Massinissa they sent their legions to Africa, and the third Punic war began. The Carthaginians offered the Romans 300 of their most prominent citizens as hostages, but the Romans insisted that Carthage should be demolished. The Carthaginians could build a new city, they said, but it must be at least ten miles inland. As the result of this request, the Carthaginians started forging every rusty nail they had into a weapon. Once more they summoned up their courage and resisted fiercely. The Romans besieged the city for two years, and in the third year they stormed it.

The Carthaginians defended their city house by house and block by block. Nor did this miraculous metropolis, inhabited by nearly 500,000 people, surrender until everything was drowned in blood and ruins and only 50,000 Carthaginians survived to be sold into slavery. Everything went up in flames. Houses, temples and splendid terraces tottered and crashed. Jetties crumbled and lighthouses collapsed. Carthage was not to rise again until it was re-founded as a Roman colony something more than a hundred years later by Julius Caesar.

So ended the last Punic war—in 146 B.C. If Carthage had not been destroyed, if she had remained a world power, the Carthaginians would have handed down to us the ancient Mediterranean civilizations. As it was, world supremacy passed to the Romans, and Rome became the cultural link between the Mediterranean heritage and modern Europe.

260,000 SPECTATORS AT THE CIRCUS MAXIMUS

He who loves shall do well. He who knows not how to love shall perish. He who forbids love shall perish twice. (Scribbled on a wall at Pompeii, before the city was destroyed in 79 A.D.)

TO achieve world domination is hard, to maintain it even harder. The Romans had become the masters of the world, but the day came when this domination slipped away from them as it had from all other world empires in history. Obviously no country or people can rule forever, but its spirit and culture can survive in those that take over.

Before Rome, the stage of world history was set in the East; Rome carried it to the north and the west. Neither Babylon nor Thebes, neither the Hittite mountain fortress of Hattusas nor Sparta and Athens, neither Alexandria nor Carthage ruled the whole Mediterranean and unified the Western world. The only city to succeed was Rome, the eternal city. No other city has been more enduring, or radiated more energy, than this ancient center of Western culture–including Knossos, Athens, Byzantium, Milan, Aachen and Vienna. Rome is the oldest capital of the Occident, and has remained a spiritual metropolis to this day. Rome drew almost all of Europe into its spiritual orbit, and it was Rome which civilized our own–the Western–world.

After the Punic wars, the whole Orient was talking of a powerful Republic in the West, where no one wore a crown. Something had appeared that had never existed before: here was a Republic that dominated the known world.

To quote the Roman historian Livy, a contemporary of Christ, as he admiringly evoked the era of the Republic:

There never was a state that was greater, or richer in honors and men of exemplary conduct. There never was a city that lived for so long in harmony and integrity before greed and waste undermined it. There never was a place where poverty and thriftiness were esteemed so highly and so lastingly. The less the people possessed, the less they coveted. But it is not so very long ago that the wealth among us generated avarice, and that the desire for luxuries, for gratifying any and all forms of sensuality, for opulence and debauchery, destroyed everything and everyone.

The golden age of the Republic was brief. Slave insurrections and bloody civil wars broke out. Tiberius and Gaius Gracchus were too far ahead of their times in fighting for a better world. They lived and worked for the peasants, for the underprivileged classes of Italy, and died for their ideals. Whenever Cornelia, the mother of the Gracchi, spoke of her sons she shed no tears; she recounted their accomplishments as if they had happened in some prehistoric age. She raised eleven children, all of whom died before her, and she was the first woman for whom Rome erected a monument to honor her grief.

But then, inevitably, came the day when a Roman donned the purple robe and reached for the crown: Julius Caesar, who carried the dying Republic over into the monarchy. His far-flung campaigns kept him so occupied that between 49 and 44 B.C. he stayed in his capital off and on for no more than fifteen months. In these brief intervals of his astounding career he settled the destiny of his own time—and, one might say, of the future. Western civilization took over from Caesar innumerable ideas about administration, government and law. Our vocabulary owes him the name for the month of July, and it was he who introduced the modern calendar.

To some extent it may be said that Caesar merged the disparate concepts of a free democracy and absolutism effectively. But the era of the emperors who followed him showed that fire and water do not mix. Caesar had ordered that his own statue be erected next to those of the seven ancient kings on the Capitoline Hill, and when he appeared in public he wore the robes of the former kings of Alba Longa. But the royal title itself was stigmatized by the despotism and tyranny of many oriental rulers, and while Caesar was determined to exercise the powers of a king he preferred to do so under a different title. On February 9, 44 B.C., he was nominated dictator for life. Politically speaking, this was really tantamount to being king, although the discredited word itself was avoided.

Before Caesar, no living person had ever had his profile appear on any coin; Caesar broke with that precedent. In the final years of his life, people thought it was so important to be close to him that the rents in the quarter where Caesar lived rose sky-high. Had he not been murdered on March 15, 44 B.C., the West's spiritual unification would have been strengthened. As it was, Caesar's premature death split the Occident in half—into a western and an eastern part.

It was Octavianus Augustus who initiated the era of the Roman emperors. Next to Philip II of Macedon, Augustus was probably the greatest statesman of antiquity—and a far wiser ruler than Caesar, although the latter perhaps had greater genius. But without the genuine humaneness of this man who protected freedom and prosperity, without this extraordinary ruler who governed the known world for forty-four years, the Roman imperial era could not have lasted for so many years.

With Augustus' reign of freedom, Rome attained the greatest heights of statecraft. Under Augustus, Rome's spirit and creative energy reached their culmination. The people's ears were still ringing with the lament and accusations of the incomparable oratory of Cicero who, before he was murdered in 43 B.C., gave greatness to the Latin language. This was the time of the poet Ovid, a true child of the big city, with an almost uncanny awareness of his own gifts; the man who wrote the great *Metamorphoses*, fifteen books composed in hexameters. This was the time when Horace, a lifelong bachelor, sang about love and wine, the grandeur of Rome and the beauty of nature. This was the time when the timid Virgil recited before Augustus and Octavia several books of his *Aeneid*, Rome's greatest national epic, which according to the poet's wishes was to be burned on his death but which Augustus saved from the flames. This was the time when the historian Livy wrote his monumental work consisting of one hundred and forty-two books of which thirty-five remain. The sensitive Catullus of Verona had, before this era, bared his throbbing heart to the radiantly beautiful but slightly disreputable Lesbia, thus creating the greatest verses of love that exist in the Latin language. And later, the philosopher Seneca tried to impart some of his own wisdom to Nero, Rome's *enfant terrible*.

In the afternoon of August 19, 14 A.D., the seventy-six-year-old Augustus died in his wife's arms. "If I have played my role well," he said, "then give me your applause." And in his final agony he whispered: "Livia, think of our happy marriage—and farewell." For Rome, some fifty years of uninterrupted stability and splendor had ended.

Although there were some worthy and outstanding personalities among Rome's emperors, the city also was governed by some truly terrifying figures. Through Rome's history have passed rulers of the most varying temperament and character: bloodthirsty maniacs, irresponsible singers and dancers, geniuses, fearless warriors, philosophers, and organizers of the first magnitude. The aged Tiberius who cowered away much of his reign in his palace on the isle of Capri was more like a cruel specter than a human being. He had greater fear of individuals than of masses, and the trials of his victims, recorded in the historical works of Tacitus, accuse him to this day. Like a thief he, the emperor, would sneak from his island to the walls of Rome to listen to what people were whispering in the city.

The Emperor Caligula used to stroll through the jails of his metropolis, and personally select prisoners to be thrown to the wild beasts in the circus. The Emperor Claudius loved to play the judge and also ordered executions, but he frequently could not remember whom he had ordered slain. One day, after his wife Messalina had been murdered, he asked absent-mindedly, "Why does the Empress not appear at table?" And several times men he had had executed were summoned by him to hold council or play a game of draughts. Since of course they could no longer appear, he sent them messengers to tell them they were incurable dullards. Nero—actor, singer, pyromaniac, persecutor of Christians, and in spite of all this a true poet—was reddish-blond, bullnecked and extremely nearsighted. It was he who built the largest house in Rome, the famed Golden House, whose vaults have been excavated and can be visited today.

But occasionally the Roman world was ruled by such noble and magnanimous figures as the Emperor Titus, who seems truly like the sun in the dark sky of Rome's imperial history. He was perpetually concerned about his vast empire and the welfare of its people. Unfortunately, during his reign the volcano Vesuvius erupted in 79 A.D. and turned Pompeii, Herculaneum and Stabiae to ashes. This cataclysm was followed by a devastating plague and, finally, by a conflagration in Rome itself.

The Emperor Nerva was kind and thrifty, but no more than that, while Trajan was one of the most impressive personalities of Roman history. He built the magnificent Imperial Forum, the ports of Ancona, Ostia and Civitavecchia, and threw powerful bridges across the Danube so that the Roman Legions could cross easily to keep down the hostile Dacian tribes. In Africa he founded the city of Thamugadi (Thimgad), whose ruins have been preserved in the desert sand. He built a road through the Pontine Marshes, as well as forts and river crossings in Germania. Under him, the Roman Empire achieved its greatest extent: stretching from Portugal and Morocco across the Euphrates and Tigris to the borders of Parthia; from Greece deep into the Sahara desert and beyond the first Nile cataract in Egypt. To anyone traveling along the borders of this former empire—through Europe, Asia and Africa—and seeing the aqueducts, canals, baths, amphitheaters, houses and palaces, market places, gates, walls, towers and fortresses which the Romans built wherever they went, it seems amazing that such a relatively small city could have had such a widespread influence. Truly Trajan was "The Best," or *Optimus*, as the Roman Senate called him.

Hadrian, Grecophile and prince of peace, was another emperor who immortalized his name with magnificent buildings. Technically, perhaps one of the most perfect structures of world architecture is his Roman Pantheon: the temple of all the gods, which has been preserved to this day. The circular hall in its center is one of the most majestic and inspiring rooms ever conceived, and no description can do justice to its symmetrical beauty. Under Hadrian, the temple of Zeus Olympios at Athens, which had taken six hundred years to build, was completed. And for himself he built a magnificent villa near Tibur, the modern Tivoli. Even its ground plans reveal the elegance of this palace. And finally Hadrian erected his own tomb—the most colossal mausoleum of the Roman world. It was built so solidly that for centuries it served as an unassailable bastion. Today it is the Fort of St. Angelo.

Antoninus Pius was frugal and modest, always striving to preserve peace. And if this emperor had not himself raised a protest against being so honored, our months of September and October would now be known as Antonini and Faustini, after himself and his wife Faustina.

In the long and lonely nights during his campaigns against the Marcomanni and other tribes of Bohemia and Austria, Marcus Aurelius, perhaps the most truly enlightened of all the Roman emperors, wrestled constantly with one problem: "How does man attain peace of mind?" He even left us a fine book on the subject—what we know as his *Meditations*, bearing the title "To one's self." And under Septimius Severus, North Africa experienced an unprecedented flowering. Severus himself was descended from the seafaring Semitic Phoenicians. He was a Punian, spoke Latin with a Punic accent, and turned Carthage once more into a metropolis. In Asia Minor he even erected a monument in honor of Hannibal.

Then, again, the Roman empire was ruled by a vicious megalomaniac, the fratricidal Caracalla. Severus Alexander, however, had virtue and integrity, and was loved by everyone; a model figure, he reputedly always obeyed his mother, with whom he was ultimately assassinated. From the desert city of Palmyra, Aurelian brought the famous Queen Zenobia back to Rome in triumph, in golden chains and as part of his booty. Diocletian, the greatest organizational genius of antiquity, built a palace at Salona (the modern Split, in Yugoslavia), which was so vast that during the Middle Ages a whole town was built inside it. But it fell to Constantine to become the world's first Christian emperor.

People from East and West alike were magnetically attracted to Rome, the city of forums, marble arches and basilicas, gigantic amphitheaters, circuses, twenty-eight libraries, three theaters, thirty-seven gates, eleven vast *thermae*, eight hundred and fifty-six baths, two capitols and two market places, eight large squares—the city of permanent games and entertainments, the city where scandals mushroomed and emperors often died violently. On the Palatine Hill, west of the Forum and near the Tiber, lay the residential section where the wealthy families lived in splendor. But we can no longer view these dwellings for they lie under the palace built there by the Emperor Domitian. Only the house of Livia, the wife of Augustus, has been partially preserved—an identification made possible by the fact that the lead pipes of the drainage system that was found here bear her name. To this day we can walk through some of the rooms and recall the words of the Roman historian Suetonius who reported, somewhat cattily, that the house was distinguished neither by its spaciousness nor its splendor.

The rooms had no marble adornments but they did have beautiful mosaic floors. For more than forty years Augustus lived there, summer and winter, in the same room. Augustus was born on the Palatine Hill, and here, in one of the most magnificent houses of Rome, lived Cicero and the politician Crassus; here the emperors built their palaces, which is why the Palatine Hill has given its name to all princely residences in the world—"palace." Judging from a letter of Pliny the Younger who describes his villa Laurentum, some sixteen miles south of Rome, by the sea near the modern Casale di Capocotta, the well-to-do Romans lived in the greatest comfort. A mere hundred years after Christ was born, this country home had a D-shaped colonnade with glass windows and several dining halls, one of which fronted the sea so that when there was a southwesterly wind, the surf would beat against its outer walls. There were reception rooms, libraries, several bedrooms, rest rooms, a wind-protected hall where slaves practiced calisthenics, three bathrooms overlooking the sea, special massage rooms, a room for ball games and spacious wine cellars. It was provided with central heating, and verandas and gardens surrounded the property. Thus when Pliny asks, "Do you not think that I have every reason to regard this country seat as my favorite residence?" we can readily agree with him.

But Rome was not merely the city of the Flavian amphitheater seat-ing 55,000 people, or the Circus Maximus, a giant stadium capable of holding up to 260,000 spectators, with its dangerous racing track where chariots raced around and gladiators fought to the death; Rome was not merely the city of the magnificent imperial forums, the Jupiter temple and the Marcellian theater, or the city that operated the *thermae* of Diocletian and Caracalla, the largest public baths on earth equipped with a kind of air conditioning which regulated the temperature in the individual rooms by releasing heated air through openings in the walls. Rome also had quite another face.

Overpopulated, its narrow streets crowded with a screaming multitude, Rome was a noisy and dangerous city. According to the latest estimates of modern research, Rome at the time of Augustus had 1,200,000 inhabitants. Carts piled high with timber careened along, barrels were rolled willy-nilly through the streets and other loads clattered along on wagon wheels. Marble from the coast of Liguria (now the Genoa region) was hauled through the streets, endangering the pedestrians—an axle would break, a load crash and spill on the passers-by. "Who will find the limbs, the bones, the dead body of the plebeian?" asked the Roman poet Juvenal. A rod would strike someone on the head, a nail imbed itself in someone else's toe; there was the splintering of glass, or the leaking of a vessel that dripped from an open window. "You are irresponsible," Juvenal said, "if you walk through the streets of Rome by night without making your will beforehand." The city was so noisy that people could not sleep at night. The healthy lost their health, and the ailing their lives. Apartment rents were high, the rooms small, dank and dark. Wagons were forever rolling past, and sometimes a bellowing herd of cattle would be trapped by the traffic in the middle of the street.

But the wealthy were borne high above the heads of the throng by tall Liburnian slaves. These slaves from Liburnia (in Illyria) were so strong that the Romans used them as load carriers, messengers and bodyguards. The wealthy reclined in their sedan chairs, dozing or scribbling, but always swaying on four, six or even eight human necks through the city. Poorer citizens were carried by only two slaves.

This overcrowding became particularly dangerous when a fire broke out—and Rome lived in eternal fear of fires, especially at night. Smoke would pour from the third floor of some house, someone could be seen dragging his household goods from a building, and no sooner had he reached the street level than the upper floor had burned down. Some houses in Herculaneum, which were preserved by the ashes of Vesuvius in 79 A.D., have been excavated, and here the old wooden stairways, floors, tables and wardrobes can still be seen. Virtuvius, an architect and engineer of the Emperor Augustus, has left us the only document of antiquity dealing with building techniques and machinery construction. He reports that once a fire started, these frame houses turned into "regular torches." Roman real estate brokers and architects preferred this method of building because it was cheap and fast, but the houses also collapsed just as fast. Augustus prohibited the building of any dwellings higher than seventy feet or so (about the height of a modern four-story house), but he was unable to eliminate the frame houses by legislation.

However, Augustus did erect a fireproof wall, about forty yards high, betwen his Forum and the densely populated Subura quarter. Then one day so many fires broke out simultaneously in different places that there was not enough manpower to extinguish them. Therefore Augustus organized a fire brigade of 7,000 men which he financed by levying a four per cent tax on the sale of slaves.

The Subura, located at the foot of the Caelian and Esquiline hills, was always crowded, noisy and foul-smelling. All kinds of food were sold there. And from three o'clock in the afternoon on, the streetwalkers could be seen sitting on high chairs, either completely naked or clad in transparent silken gowns. This quarter was infamous as a hideout for thieves, and many a murder was plotted here, but it was also the quarter where the slaves bought their household necessities. There were innumerable stalls operated by wool merchants, linen weavers, goldsmiths, wig makers, barbers. And always the policeman stood ready, his club "dripping with blood," as the Roman writer Martial put it.

The prominent and wealthy Romans, on the other hand, made their purchases on the edge of the Campus Martius, near the Forum, in the Septae district. Here, Rome offered its treasures; the most valuable slaves, exhibited not in the open but in closed booths; ivory and tortoise shell; crystal goblets; beautiful bowls; jewels set in gold; ear pendants; onyx and jaspis and all the precious stones of the Orient. Here the sophisticated ladies and gentlemen of Rome strolled and lovers whispered under the nearby arcades.

Rome truly had many faces. Rome was warmhearted, hospitable and generous, receiving all foreigners with open arms, absorbing the Greek spirit, Greek art, Greek literature, science and philosophy—in fact, the entire Hellenistic culture. There they promenaded on the Forum—the Greeks from the islands of Andros and Samos, from Alabanda in

Caria where people lived in pleasure and extravagance; or from Tralles (the modern Aidin in western Turkey). These Greeks were adaptable, intelligent and versatile, competent in every profession. They were orators, grammarians, magicians, painters, ointment experts, masseurs, tightrope walkers. They soon made money and many were received by Rome's most distinguished families. Then, there were so many orientals in the city that Juvenal thought one might as well say that "Syria's river" (the Euphrates) "empties into the Tiber." They came from everywhere—Armenia, Cappadocia, Syria—and brought along their own peculiarities and customs: flute playing, Syrian harps with slanting strings, drums, tambourins, and girls of easy virtue wearing embroidered caps and loitering with burning eyes in front of the Circus Maximus. These foreigners could do as they pleased, except for one thing: they could not wear the toga, for this was a Roman's privilege. And yet the day came when even Syrians and Africans became emperors of Rome.

Rome was cruel, sensual and licentious, forever insatiable in its boundless passions. Innumerable delicacies passed through the stomachs of the ancient Romans: thrushes and flamingo tongues; peacocks, cranes and storks; goose livers and capons; dormice, wild asses and boars; flounders and sturgeons, and untold millions of gallons of the finest Falernian wine. Oysters were imported to Brundisium from Rutupiae (today Richborough, Kent), and one bite into an oyster was enough for the fat gourmet Montanus, who shared Nero's nightly drinking orgies, to know whether it came from Bajae or from the oysterbeds of the English coast. Silver dishes piled high with lobsters and asparagus were served by slaves and the most delicious fish sizzled in the finest oil from the city of Venafrum.

Rome was gorgeous and radiant, but Rome was also disorderly and irresponsible, often leering, arrogant and pitiless. Its slaves were exploited in Etruria and Lucania, in the ore pits, pitch huts and the Spanish mines, during the grape and olive picking season. And when the night finally relieved them, they had to languish in the slave jail or Ergastulum. But the slaves were dangerous, too; those who were freed became the cruelest masters, and Juvenal says that "the larger a house, the more impudent its slaves."

Young slave girls were forever condemned to grind the hand mills. And if they became obstreperous in the household, the mistress' rod soon broke on their backs. Some luckless slave girls were kept by rich Roman women to care for their skin and hair. They worked with the upper parts of their bodies bare, and if a single one of their mistress' curls was not exactly in the right place, they were beaten with a cowhide whip.

Rome was bloodthirsty, cold and inhuman. For years on end prisoners of war were locked up in barracks and prepared for the battle to the death in the circus or amphitheater. Here they were trained with iron rigor, by trainers who were without pity. In the Flavian amphitheater, in the Circus Maximus, the Circus Flaminius, thousands of eyes would look down on the gladiators who had pledged themselves to kill or be killed.

The Romans were unpredictable. When a wounded gladiator looked up at the sea of screaming faces above him—when he was bleeding and weary to death—he was trying to discern if they were waving their handkerchiefs, which meant his life would be saved, or if their thumbs were turned downward, which meant he had only a few more seconds to live . . . a final look at the sun—and amid the roars of the spectators his opponent's weapon would strike him down.

When the net fighter stood in the arena, when he tried to throw the net over his opponent to entangle him so he could slay him with his three-forked javelin, the eyes of the Emperor Claudius gleamed with morbid pleasure. If the net fighter's opponent—the man with shield and sword or with an iron ball swinging at the end of a leather thong—was victorious, Claudius invariably ordered the net fighter killed: because he fought without helmet or visor—and one could look into his face as he died.

The Romans would howl with pleasure when they saw the spectacle of Icarus—a man condemned to death and sent crashing into the dust from a great height, his artificial wings torn to shreds. Panthers, tigers, lions and bears, starved and provoked to the point of utter ferocity, were released from their subterranean cages underneath the circus. Imperial Rome was not going to waste a single drop of blood. The masses had to savor everything and executions became public spectacles, with the dying as the stars of the tragedy. Some criminals who were sentenced to death were torn limb from limb.

Anyone who was young and spirited would attend these horror scenes—the chariot races as well as the gladiator fights. The youth of Rome, the rich and the poor, the pompous and the parvenus, but above all their imperial majesties, basked in the festive glory that overshadowed even death and murder. Ovid suggested to the young Romans that they visit the Circus to meet beautiful women; or "to sit with virtuous young girls," as Juvenal put it.

The Roman woman was somewhat freer than her Greek counterpart, and certainly not hermetically sealed off in the oriental style. If she rarely drank wine, and was not allowed to recline at banquets like the men, she could go out shopping, and now and then she would accompany her husband to the Circus.

The daughters of the elite had little opportunity for flirting for they married young, and their fathers picked the husbands. They took their dolls to the household gods, the *lares*, and then played the game of abduction with the groom, in commemoration of the rape of the Sabines. Girls of good families were taught not only reading, writing and arithmetic, but also to sing, dance and play the zither. They were further instructed in Greek and Latin literature. The married women busied themselves with embroidery, and supervised the slaves and the household in general. Wicked and cruel women were the exception among the Romans; most of them were frank and simple, loyal, decent and friendly. And they were wonderful mothers. Wealthy Aurelia, Caesar's mother, and Atia, the mother of Augustus, would not commit their sons to the care of slaves but brought them up themselves.

The scribblings on the walls of Pompeii, Herculaneum and Stabiae—no matter whether they were found on sacred, worldly, public or private buildings—bring the Romans as close to us as if they had lived yesterday. "Here lives Felicitas." Was this an introduction of sorts? Or had the lover merely marked the house so he would find it again? What was in the mind of the man who scrawled on a wall: "I want to break the ribs of Venus!"? And what was the nature of the girl for whom some young man was pining: "My life, my love, let us play a little!" Carried away by sentimental enthusiasm, some anonymous man scribbled for all eternity to read: "If there is anyone who has not seen the Venus painted by Apelles, let him look at my love!" And another wrote: "If there is faithfulness among people, then I have loved you, and you alone, ever since we met." Perhaps it was a woman who suffered so much that she had to write: "If you can, but do not want to, why, then, do you postpone the pleasures and give me hope? Why do you always promise to return tomorrow? Force me to die, then, since you are forcing me to live without you. Please do not torment me. What hope has taken away, hope will also give back to the one who loves."

But the buried cities also tell us of the sordid side of human passions.

"I have loved a beautiful girl, praised by many—but underneath I found only filth." And three words were found that seem to turn the destruction of Pompeii into a divine judgment—three simple words that even 2,000 years later make us thoughtful: "Sodom and Gomorrah." Was it a spark of foreknowledge which enabled someone to visualize the day of doom? Whoever it was must have heard of these cities of ancient sin which perished in flames and sulphurous rain, like Pompeii and Herculaneum—and yet he was 2,000 years removed in time from the catastrophe which occurred north of the Dead Sea.

But what are a few millennia when computed by the clock of eternity that measures the rhythm of human development? Everything we do, think and create is based on the vast foundation of the ancient civilizations. The magnificent works of Greece would have been inconceivable without the ancient Orient—without Sumer, Babylon, Assyria, Egypt. The life of the Greeks, their grandiose imagination and creative energy, radiated across the eastern Mediterranean to Italy. It is solely because Rome handed Greek culture down to us that the spirit of Greece could spread across the entire Western world. In the plastic arts, in literature and science, a great many other peoples of antiquity accomplished far more than the Romans. But the Romans surpassed them all in the art of statecraft which they strengthened by a unifying culture. To unite all the countries around the Mediterranean in an all-encompassing peace—this Rome alone could do. The Romans experienced life with such immediacy, they were so practically oriented, they were such great statesmen and political organizers that their artistic imagination necessarily remained of secondary importance. Artistically, they were not as gifted as the Greeks or Egyptians, but politically they were probably the most able people who have ever lived on earth.

The wheels of history continue to roll across the globe, the scene forever changes, civilizations come and go. Generations after generations march along the endless road through the millennia. This road passes by the amazing civilizations of Mesopotamia; the pyramids of Egypt's IV Dynasty and the kings who were gods; the commercial aristocrats of Phoenicia; the palaces of Persepolis and the harem of Xerxes; the promise of redemption that Palestine gave to mankind; the mysterious cities of Mohenjo-Daro; the 40,000 towers of the Great Wall of China; the labyrinth of King Minos; the artistic consummation of Greece, the classicism which admits of no further improvement.

Man spends himself in great accomplishments; states to which we owe a tremendous heritage perish; lost empires teach us the fickleness of fate and the eternal cycle of all life on earth.

What an immense road of human experiences! We would like to stand still for a moment, to turn back and look, to learn from it all. But the road is too wide, too long, and man is weak and powerless —no more than a speck in a cosmos which remains forever beyond his comprehension.

INDICES

INDICES

1. Names

[Gods, Persons, Religions, Battles, Races, etc.]

2. Place Names

[Countries, Districts, Cities and Towns, Rivers, etc.]

3. Miscellaneous

4. Authorities

Gaetano de Sanctis, Italian historian
Gardner, E. W., British archaeologist
Garstang, John, British archaeologist
Ghoneim, Zakaria, Egyptian archaeologist
Grotefend, Georg Friedrich, German historian

Haberlandt, Michael, Austrian ethnographer
Hall, British ancient historian
Helmolt, Hans F., German historian
Herzfeld, E., archaeologist
Heyerdahl, Thor, Norwegian zoologist, student of Polynesia
Humboldt, Alexander, German scientist

Junker, Hermann, Austrian Egyptologist

Kämpfer, Engelbert, Assyriologist
Keramopoullos, Greek archaeologist
Kingsborough, Edward King, Irish archaeologist
Kober, American philologist
Kramer, Samuel Noah, American Assyriologist
Kraus, F. R., Dutch Assyriologist
Krause-Marquet, British archaeologist
Kourouniotis, K., Greek archaeologist

Layard, Austen Henry, British archaeologist
Libby, American archaeologist
Loftus, British archaeologist

Mallowan, British archaeologist
Marshall, Sir John, British Indologist
Menghin, Oswald, Austrian ethnologist
Métraux, Alfred, French student of Polynesia
Meyer, Eduard, German ancient historian
Mommsen, Theodor, German historian
Monetet, French archaeologist
Mouhot, Henri, French Sinologist
Myres, John, British ancient historian

O'Neale, Lila Morris, American archaeologist
Oppert, Jules, French Assyriologist
Osborne, Henry Fairfield, American authority on Asia

Pendlebury, J. D., British archaeologist
Posnansky, Arthur, German Americanist
Prescott, William Hickling, American authority on Peru

Ranke, Leopold, German historian
Rawlinson, Henry, British Assyriologist
Rémusat, Abel, French Sinologist
Roberts, C. H., British papyrologist
Rodenwaldt, German archaeologist
Routledge, Katherine, ethnologist

Schachermeyer, Fritz, German authority on the Etruscans
Scharff, Alex, German ancient historian
Schliemann, Heinrich, German archaeologist
Schmidt, Erich, German archaeologist
Schultze Jena, Leonhard, German geographer
Sittig, Ernst, German philologist
Skeat, T. C., British papyrologist
Smith, Edwin, Egyptologist
Speiser, E. A., American archaeologist
Stamatakes, Greek archaeologist

Taylor, British archaeologist
Thomson, American authority on Polynesia
Tsountas, Greek archaeologist

Ventris, Michael, British philologist

Wace, Alan J. B., British archaeologist
Wheeler, Sir Mortimer, British Indologist
Wilamowitz-Möllendorff, Ulrich v., German ancient historian
Woolley, Sir Leonard, British archaeologist

Yeivin, Egyptologist

5. Illustrations

6. *Maps and Drawings*

BIBLIOGRAPHY

7. *Bibliography*

MESOPOTAMIA

BALTRUSAITIS M., Art sumérien, art roman, Paris 1934. – CHRISTIAN V., Altertumskunde des Zweistromlandes, Leipzig 1940. – CONTENAU G., Manuel d'archéologie orientale I–IV, Paris 1927–47. – CONTENAU G., La vie quotidienne à Babylonie et en Assyrie, Paris 1953. – DEIMEL A., POHL A., FOLLET R., Codex Hammurabi, Rom 1950. – DELAPORTE L., Geschichte der Babylonier, Assyrer, Perser und Phöniker [Geschichte der führenden Völker, Bd. 3], Freiburg 1933. – EBELING E., Babylonisch-assyrische Texte: Altorientalische Texte und Bilder zum Alten Testament, herausgegeben von Hugo Gressmann, Berlin-Leipzig 1926, S. 108ff. – FALKENSTEIN-VON SODEN, Sumerische und akkadische Hymnen und Gebete, Zürich und Stuttgart 1953. – FRANKFORT H., Cylinder Seals, London 1939. – FRANKFORT H., Art and Architecture of the Ancient Orient, Harmondsworth 1954. – FRITZ-ANDRAE, Der babylonische Turm, Leipzig 1932. – KING L. W., A History of Sumer and Akkad, London 1923. – KOHLER J. und PEISER F. E., Hammurabi's Gesetz, Bd. I, Leipzig 1904, Bd. II, 1909. – KRAMER S. N., Sumerian Mythology, Philadelphia 1944. – KRAMER S. N., Inannas Descent to the Nether World, Journal of Cuneiform Studies, Bd. 5, 1951, S. 1ff. – KRAMER S. N., Enmerkar and the Lord of Aratta, Philadelphia 1952. – LENZEN H., Die Summerer, Berlin 1948. – MEISSNER B., Die Keilschrift, Berlin-Leipzig 1922. – MEISSNER B., Die babylonisch-assyrische Literatur, Wildpark-Potsdam 1928. – MEYER E., Geschichte des Altertums I, 2. Stuttgart und Berlin 1926, S. 331ff. – MOORTGAT A., Die Entstehung der sumerischen Hochkultur [Der Alte Orient, Bd. 43], Leipzig 1945. – MOORTGAT A., Geschichte Vorderasiens bis zum Hellenismus [SCHARFF-MOORTGAT. Ägypten und Vorderasien im Altertum], München 1950. – OLMSTEAD A., History of Assyria, New York-London 1923. – PARROT A., Archéologie mésopotamienne. Les étapes, Paris 1946. – PARROT A., Tello, Paris 1948. – PARROT A., Ziggurats et Tour de Babel, Paris 1949. – PARROT A., Mari, Neuchâtel 1953. – PARROT A., La Tour de Babel, Neuchâtel und Paris 1953. – WETZEL F., Die Stadtmauer von Babylon, WVDOG 48, 1930. – WOOLLEY L., Ur Excavations II, The Royal Cemetery, London-Philadelphia 1934. – WOOLLEY L., Ur Excavations V., The Ziggurat and its Surroundings, 1939. – WOOLLEY L., Excavations at Ur, London 1954.

EGYPT

ANTHES R., Ägypten [Historia Mundi], München 1953, Bd. II, S. 130ff. – BISSING FR. W. v., Der Anteil Ägyptens am Kunstleben der Völker, München 1912 [Festrede, gelesen in der öffentlichen Sitzung der Kunstakademie der Wissenschaften, 9. März 1912]. – BONNET H., Reallexikon der ägyptischen Religionsgeschichte, Berlin 1952. – BREASTED J. H., Geschichte Ägyptens, Leipzig 1936. – BREASTED J. H., Ancient Records of Egypt, 1906. – BREASTED J. H., RANKE H., Geschichte Ägyptens, Berlin 1911. – CAPART J., L'Art égyptien, Brüssel 1924. – CARTER H., Tut-Ench-Amun, Leipzig 1924–34. – ERMAN A., RANKE H., Ägypten und ägyptisches Leben im Altertum, Tübingen 1923. – ERMAN A., Die Literatur der Ägypter, Leipzig 1923. – ERMAN A., Die Religion der Ägypter, Berlin 1934. – FRANKFORT H.,

Ancient Egyptian Religion, New York 1948. – KEES H., Der Götterglaube im alten Ägypten, Leipzig 1941. – MASPERO G., Das alte Ägypten, Berlin 1921. – MASPERO G., Histoire ancienne des peuples de l'Orient classique, Paris 1895–1899. – MEYER E., Geschichte des Altertums, Stuttgart und Berlin 1921–1944. – MORET A., Le Nil et la Civilisation égyptienne, Paris 1926 und 1937. – OTTO E., Ägypten, Stuttgart 1953. – PETRIE F., The Arts and Crafts of Ancient Egypt, London 1910. – RANKE H., Ägyptische Texte: Altorientalische Texte und Bilder zum Alten Testament, herausgegeben von Hugo Gressmann, Berlin-Leipzig 1926, S. 1ff. – SCHAEFER H., Von Ägyptischer Kunst, Leipzig 1930. – SCHARFF A., Ägypten [W. Otto, Handbuch der Altertumswissenschaft I, München 1939, S. 433ff.]. – SCHARFF A., Der Bericht über das Streitgespräch eines Lebensmüden mit seiner Seele, München 1937 [Sitzungsbericht der Bayerischen Akademie der Wissenschaften, Jg. 1937, Heft 9]. – SCHARFF A., Geschichte Ägyptens [Scharff-Moortgat, Ägypten und Vorderasien im Altertum], München 1950. – STIER H. E., Geschichte Ägyptens [Propyläen-Weltgeschichte, Bd. I, Berlin o.J.]. – THAUSING G., Der Auferstehungsgedanke in ägyptischen religiösen Texten, Leipzig 1943. – VANDIER J., La religion égyptienne, Paris 1944 und 1949. – VIGNEAU A., Le Musée du Caire [Encyclopédie photographique de l'Art], Paris 1949. – WEILL R., Les Origines de l'Egypte pharaonique, Paris 1908. – *Egypt and Babylonia* [The Cambridge Ancient History, Bd. I. The Egyptian and Hittite Empires, Bd. II].

ANATOLIA

The Hittites

BITTEL, K., Grundzüge der Vor- und Frühgeschichte Kleinasiens, Tübingen 1950. – BITTEL, K. u. NAUMANN, R., Bogazköy-Hattusa in Wissenschaftliche Veröffentlichungen der Deutschen Orient-Gesellschaft, 63, Stuttgart 1952. – CAVAIGNAC, E., Le probleme hittite, Paris 1936. – CONTENEAU, G., La civilisation des Hittites et des Mitanniens, Paris 1934. – DELLAPORTE, L., Les Hittites, Paris 1936. – FRANKFORT, H., Asia Minor and the Hittites in The Art and Architecture of the Ancient Orient [The Pelican History of Art], Baltimore 1954. – FRIEDRICH, J., Entzifferung verschollener Schriften und Sprachen, Berlin-Göttingen-Heidelberg, 1954. – GELB, I. J., The contribution of the new cilician bilinguis to the decipherment of hieroglyphic Hittite, Chicago 1950. – GÜTERBOCK, H. G., Hittite Religion, Forgotten Religions ed. by Vergilius Ferm, New York 1950. – GÜTERBOCK, H. G., Authority and Law in the Hittite Kingdom, reprinted from Journal of the American Oriental Society, Suppl. No. 17, July - September 1954. – GÜTERBOCK, H. G., The deeds of Suppiluliuma as told by his son, Mursili II, reprinted from the Journal of Cuneiform Studies, Vol. X, 1956. – GÜTERBOCK, H. G., Besprechung von Die Welt der Hethiter von M. Riemschneider in Orientalische Literatur Zeitung 1956, Nr. 11/12, S. 513ff. – GURNEY, O. R., The Hittites [Pelican Books], Baltimore 1954. – Hethitische Texte, herausg. von FERDINAND SOMMER in Mitteilungen der Vorderasiatischen-Aegyptischen Gesellschaft, 1925 u. folg. Jahre. – Hettitische Gesetze in Altorientalische Texte zum Alten Testament, herausg. von HUGO GRESSMANN, Berlin u. Leipzig 1926, S. 423 ff. – LAROCHE, E., Recherches sur les Noms des Dieux Hittites, Paris 1947. – MOORTGAT, A., Das Reich der Hethiter in Ägypten und Vorderasien im Altertum von A. SCHARF u. A. MOORTGAT, München 1950, S. 349 ff. – OTTEN, H., Zu den Anfängen der hethitischen Geschichte, in Mitteilungen der Deutschen Orient Gesellschaft, Nr. 83, Berlin 1951, S. 33 ff. – Schaeffer, C. F. A., Ugaritica III, Paris 1956. – Sommer, F., Hethiter und Hethitisch, Stuttgart 1947. – Sommer, F., und Falkenstein, A., Die hethitisch-akkadische Bilingue des Hattusili I [Labarna II.], München 1938. – Wooley, L. und Barnett, R. D., Carchemish, Report on the Excavations at Jerablus on Behalf of the British Museum, London 1952.

PHOENICIA

Autran C., Les Phéniciens, 1920. – Bérard U., Les Phéniciens et l'Odyssee, 1902–1903. – Bruston, Etudes Phén, 1903. – Contenau G., La civilisation phénicienne, Paris 1939, 3. Auflage. – Eissfeldt O., Phoiniker: Pauly-Wissowa, Realenzyklopädie der klassischen Altertumswissenschaft, Bd. XX, 1, 1941. – Hill G. F., Catalogue of Phœnicia, 1910. – Landau Freiherr v., Die Bedeutung der Phönizier im Völkerleben: Ex Oriente Lux I, Leipzig 1905. – Pietschmann R., Geschichte der Phönizier, Berlin 1889. – Scharff A., Moortgat A., Ägypten und Vorderasien im Altertum, München 1950. – Winkler H., Altorientalische Forschungen, 1893–1906. – Woolley C. L., La Phénicie et les peuples égéens, Syria 1921. – *The Cambridge Ancient History,* Vol. III, Cambridge 1924.

PERSIA

Andrae E. W., Vorderasien [Handbuch der Altertumswissenschaft, München 1939, 6. Abt., I. Textbd., S. 734 ff.]. – Cameron G. G., History of early Iran, Chicago 1936. – Cameron G. G., Persepolis Treasure Tablets, Chicago 1948. – Cowley A., Aramaic papyri of the fifth century B. C., Oxford 1923 [Die Elephantine-Papyri]. Driver G. R., Aramaic Documents of the fifth century B. C., Oxford 1954 [Die Briefe an Arsames]. – Frankfort H., The Art of Ancient Persia [The Art and Architecture of the Ancient Orient, London-Baltimore-Melbourne 1954, S. 202ff.]. Herzfeld E., Altpersische Inschriften [Ergänzungsband zu den Archäologischen Mitteilungen aus Iran], Berlin 1938. – Herzfeld E., Archaeological History of Iran [The Schweich Lectures of the British Academy 1934], London 1935. – Junge P. J., Saka-Studien [Klio-Beiheft 24], Leipzig 1939. – Kornemann E., Weltgeschichte des Mittelmeer-Raumes, München 1948, Bd. I., S. 15ff. – Kraeling E. G., The Brooklyn Museum: Aramaic papyri, New Haven 1953 [weitere Papyri aus Elephantine]. – Justi F., Geschichte des alten Persiens, Berlin 1879. – Meyer E., Geschichte des Altertums, Stuttgart 1954, 4. Bd., 1. Abt., S. 14ff., 3. Bd., S. 181ff. – Moortgat A., Bronzegerät aus Luristan, Berlin 1932. – Nyberg H. S., Das Reich der Achämeniden [Historia Mundi, München 1954, Bd. III, S. 56ff.]. – Nyberg H. S., Die Religionen des alten Iran. Deutsch von H. H. Schaefer [Mitteilungen der vorderasiatisch-ägyptischen Gesellschaft, 43. Bd.], Leipzig 1938. – Prasek J. V., Geschichte der Meder und Perser [Handbücher der Alten Geschichte, II. Bd., Gotha 1910]. – Sarre F. und Herzfeld E., Iranische Felsreliefs, Berlin 1910. – Schmidt E., Persepolis, Chicago 1953. – *The Persian Empire and the West* [Cambridge Ancient History, Cambridge 1939, Bd. IV].

PALESTINE

Abramowski R., Das Buch des betenden Volkes, Stuttgart 1938. – Abramowski R., Das Buch des betenden Gottesknechtes, Stuttgart 1939. – Albright W. F., From the

Stone Age to Christianity, 1946. – ALBRIGHT W. F., The Archaeology of Palestine, England 1951. – BAETHGEN F., Die Psalmen, Göttingen 1892. – BUDE K., Das Buch Hiob, Göttingen 1913. – DELITZSCH F., Die poetischen Bücher des Alten Testaments, 1864. – DUHM B., Das Buch Hiob, Freiburg 1897. – EWAIN Mc., The Permanent element in Old Testament Prophecy, 1946. – FICHTNER J., Weisheit Salomos, Tübingen 1938. – GEMSER B., Sprüche Salomos, Tübingen 1937. – HALLER M., Die Fünf Megilloth, Tübingen 1940. – HAMILTON E., Spokesmen for God, New York 1949. – HAUSS F., Biblische Gestalten, Hamburg 1952. – KITTEL R., Die Psalmen, Leipzig 1922. – LAMPARTER H., Das Buch der Auferstehung, Stuttgart 1951. – LANDAUER G., Palästina, München 1925. – MEINHOLD J., Einführung in das Alte Testament, Giessen 1926. – NOTH M., Die Welt des Alten Testaments, Berlin 1953. – NOTH M., Geschichte Israels, Göttingen 1954. – OESTERLEY W., Hebrew Religion, London 1930. – PETERS N., Das Buch Job. Münster 1928. – ROTH C., Geschichte der Juden, Stuttgart 1954. – ROWLEY H. H., The Servant of the Lord and other Essays on the Old Testament, London 1952. – UMBREIT F. W., Das Buch Hiob, Heidelberg 1832. – WRIGHT G. E., The Westminster Historical Atlas to the Bible, 1947.

INDIA

Hindu Culture: BASHAM A. L., The Wonder That Was India, London 1954. – LANGDON S., The Script of Harappā and Mohenjo-Daro and its Connection with other Scripts, London 1934. – MACKAY E., Early Indus Civilization, 2nd ed., revised and enlarged, London 1948. – MACKAY, E., Die Induskultur, Leipzig 1938. – MACKAY E. J. H., Chanhu-Daro Excavations 1935-1936, New Haven, Conn. 1943. – MACKAY E. J. H., Further Excavations at Mohenjo-Daro, 2 Bde., Delhi 1937–1938. – MADHO SARUP VATS, Excavations at Harappā, 2 Bde., Delhi 1940. – MARSHALL SIR JOHN, Mohenjo-Daro and the Indus Civilization, 3 Bde., London 1931. – MODE H., Indische Frühkulturen und ihre Beziehungen zum Westen, Basel 1944. – PIGGOT S., Prehistoric India to 1000 B. C. [Penguin Books], Harmondsworth 1950. – RENOU L., FILLIOZAT J., L'Inde Classique, Paris I. 1947, II. 1953. [Alles bisher Erschienene]. – ROWLAND B., The Art and Architecture of India [The Pelican History of Art, 1954]. – WADDELL L. A., The Indo-Sumerian Seals Deciphered, London 1925. – WHEELER R. E. M. Five Thousand Years of Pakistan, London 1950. – WHEELER SIR MORTIMER, The Indus Civilization [The Cambridge History of India. Supplementary Volume, Cambridge 1953].

Buddhist Culture: BECKH H., Buddhismus. Buddha und seine Lehre [Sammlung Göschen], 3. Aufl., 2 Bde., Berlin-Leipzig 1928. – BENIMADHAB BARMA, Barhut, 3 Bde., Calcutta 1924–1927. – BLEICHSTEINER R., Die Gelbe Kirche. Entstehung/Geschichte/Kultur, Wien 1937. – DASGUPTY S., A History of Indian Philosophy, bis jetzt 4 Bde., Cambridge 1949–1952. – DAVID-NEEL A., Vom Leiden zur Erlösung. Sinn und Lehre des Buddhismus, Leipzig 1937. – DAVIDS R., Sakya or Buddhist Origins, London 1931. – ELIOT SIR CHARLES, Hinduism and Buddhism, Reprinted, 3 Bde., London 1954. – FOUCHER A., La Vie du Bouddha d'après les Textes et les Monuments de L'Inde, Paris 1949. – FOUCHER A., The Beginnings of Buddhist Art, Paris-London 1917. – FOUCHER A., MARSHALL SIR JOHN, The Monuments of Sāñchī, 3 Bde., Calcutta 1940. – FRAUWALLNER E., Geschichte der Indischen Philosophie, I. Bd., besonders S. 147–246, Salzburg 1953. – GLASENAPP H. v., Buddhistische Mysterien, Stuttgart 1940. – GLASENAPP H. v., Die Philosophie der Inder [Krönersche

Taschenausgabe], Stuttgart 1949. – Glasnapp H. v., Entwicklungsstufen des indischen Denkens, Halle 1940. – Godard A., Godard Y., Hackin J., Les Antiquités Bouddhiques de Bāmiyān, Paris-Bruxelles 1928. – Grünwedel A., Mythologie des Buddhismus in Tibet und der Mongolei, Leipzig 1900. – Grünwedel-Waldschmidt, Buddhistische Kunst in Indien, I. Teil, Berlin 1932. [Alles Erschienene.] – Oldenberg H., Buddha – Sein Leben, Seine Lehre, Seine Gemeinde, 6. Auflage, Stuttgart-Berlin 1914. – Oldenberg H., Reden des Buddha. Lehre/Verse/Erzählungen, München 1922. – Rosenberg O., Die Probleme der Buddhistischen Philosophie [Materialien zur Kunde des Buddhismus, Heft 7/8], Heidelberg 1924. – Thomas E. J., The Life of The Buddha as Legend and History, London 1931. – Waddell L. A., The Buddhism of Tibet or Lamaism, 2nd ed. Cambridge 1934. – Waldschmidt E., Gandhara-Kutscha-Turfan, Leipzig 1925. – Winternitz M., Der Ältere Buddhismus [Religionsgeschichte, Lesebuch, 2. Auflage, Heft 11], Tübingen 1929. – Winternitz M., A History of Indian Literature, Vol. II. Calcutta 1933. – Winternitz M., Geschichte der Indischen Literatur, Bd. II. Die buddhistische Literatur, Leipzig 1913. – *Ajanta.* The Colour and Monochrome Reproduction of the Ajanta *Frescoes based on Photography.* With an Explanatory Text by Yazdani. Published under the special Authority of His Exalted Highness the Nizam. Bis jetzt 6 Bände.

CAMBODIA

Aymonier E., Le Cambodge, Bd. III, Le groupe d'Angkor, Paris 1904. – Beylié L. de, L'architecture Hindoue en Extrême-Orient, Paris 1902. – Carpeaux Ch., Les ruines d'Angkor, 1908. – Coèdes G., Les Bas-reliefs d'Angkor-Vat, 1911. – Commaille J., Guide aux ruines d'Angkor, Paris 1912. – Commaille J., Angkor: Ostasiatische Zeitschrift, I. 1913, II. 1914. – Coomaraswamy A. K., Geschichte der indischen und indonesischen Kunst, Leipzig 1927. – Cordier H., Biblitotheca Indosinica, 4 Vol., Paris 1914. – Delaporte, Les Monuments du Cambodge. – Fergusson J., History of Indian and Eastern Architecture, I und II, London 1910. – Fournereau L., Les Ruines Khmères, Cambodge et Siam, Paris 1890. – Fournereau L., Les Ruines d'Angkor, Paris 1890. – Groslier G., Arts et Archéologie Khmères, 1926. – Groslier G., Angkor, 1924. – Grousset R., Histoire de l'Extrême-Orient, 2 Vol., Paris 1929. – Krug H.-J., Götterthrone im Urwald, Berlin 1943. – Leclère Adhémard, Histoire du Cambodge, Paris 1914. – Lunet de Lajonquière E., Inventaire descriptif des Monuments du Cambodge, Paris I. 1892, II. 1897. – Marchal H., Guide archéologique aux Temples d'Angkor, Paris et Bruxelles 1928. – Marchal S., Costumes et Patrures Khmèrs, Paris 1927. – Maspero G., L'Empire Khmèr, 1904. – Maspero G., L'Indochine, I und II, Paris und Bruxelles 1929-30. – Parmentier H., Origine commune des Architectures Hindoues dans l'Inde et en Extrême-Orient, Paris 1915. – Pelliot P., Le Fou-nan: BEFEO 1903. – Percheron M. und Teston M. R., L'Indochine, Paris 1939. – Stern P., Le Bayon d'Angkor, 1927. – BEFEO = Bulletin de l'Ecole Française d'Extrême-Orient, Hanoi ab 1901.

CHINA

General History: Andersson J. G., Children of the Yellow Earth, London 1934. – Bishop C. W., The Chronology of Ancient China [Journal American Oriental Society 52], 1932. – Bishop C. W., The Rise of civilisation in China [Geographical Review 22], 1932. – Chavannes E., Les Mémoires Historiques de Se-ma

Ts'ien, 5 Bde., Paris 1895. – CREEL H. G., The Birth of China, London 1936. – CREEL H. G., Confucius, the Man and the Myth, London 1951. – CREEL H. G., Studies in early Chinese culture, Baltimore 1937. – EBERHARD W., Chinas Geschichte, Berlin 1948. – ERKES E., Chinesisch-Amerikanische Mythenparallelen: T'oung Pao 24, 1926. – FRANKE O., Geschichte des Chinesischen Reiches, 3 Bde., 1930. – FRANKE O., Studien zur Geschichte des Konfuzianischen Dogmas, Hamburg 1920. – FORKE A., Geschichte der Chinesischen Philosophie, 3 Bde. – FORKE A., World Conception of the Chinese, London 1925. – FUNG Y. L., History of Chinese Philosophy. – GILES H. A., Chuang Tzu, London 1889. – GRANET M., La Pensée Chinoise, Paris 1934. – GROOT J. J. M. de, The Religious System of China, 6 Bde., Leiden 1892. – GROUSSETT R., Histoire de l'Extrême-Orient. – GROUSSETT R., La Chine, [Les Civilisations de l'Orient, Tome III], 1930. – HSÜ L. S., The Political Philosophy of Confucius, London 1932. – KARLGREN B., Philology and Ancient China, Oslo 1926. – LEGGE J., Chinese Classics, Bd. I bis V. – LEGGE J., The life and Works of Mencius, London 1875. – LEGGE J., The Texts of Aoism, London 1891. – MASPERO H., La Chine Antique, Paris 1927. – MASPERO H., Le Taoïsme, Paris 1950. – ROSS J., The Origin of the Chinese People, London 1916. – ROSTOVTZEFF M., The Animal Style in South Russia and China, 1929. – SAWAKICHI K., Grundriss der Ju-Lehre. – TSUI CHI, Geschichte Chinas, Zürich 1946. – WALEY A., The way and its Power, London 1934. – WALEY A., Lebensweisheit im Alten China, Hamburg. – WALEY A., The Analects of Confucius, London 1938. – WERNER E., Myths and Legends of China, London 1922. – WILHELM R., Die Chinesische Literatur, 1926. – WILHELM R., Laotse, Jena 1910. – WILHELM R., Kung Futse, Gespräche, Jena 1911. – WILHELM R., Dschuang Dsi, Jena 1912. – WILHELM R., Kung Tse, Leben und Werk, Stuttgart 1925. – WILHELM R., Geschichte der Chinesischen Kultur, München 1928. – WU G. D., Prehistoric Pottery in China, London 1938. – ZENKER E., Chinesische Philosophie, 1926. – *Bulletin Museum Far Eastern Antiquities*, Stockholm [Zeitschrift für Archäologie und Paläographie Chinas].

The Great Wall: GEIL W. E., The Great Wall of China, London 1909. – GROOT DE J. J. M., Chinesische Urkunden zur Geschichte Asiens, Berlin 1921–26. – HAYES L. N., The Great Wall of China, 1929. – MÖLLENDORF O. F. v., Die Grosse Mauer von China [Zeitschrift der Deutschen Morgenländischen Gesellschaft, 1881]. – STEIN A., Ruins of Desert Cathay, London 1912.

Li T'ai-po: AYSCOUGH F., Fir Flower Tablets, Boston 1921. – BERNHARDI A., Li-T'ai-Po, MSOS, S. 105–138. – CRANMER-BYNG L., A Lute of Jade, London 1911. – FLORENZ K., Gedichte von Li Taipe [Mitteilungen der Gesellschaft für Natur-Völkerkunde Ostasiens, 1889, S. 44–61]. – FORKE A., Blüthen Chinesischer Dichtung, Magdeburg 1899. – GILES, H., A Chinese Biographical Dictionary, London 1900, s. v. – GILES H., A History of Chinese Literature, London 1901. – GRUBE W., Geschichte der Chinesischen Literatur, Leipzig 1902. – OBATA S., The Works of Li-Po, London 1923. – WALEY A., Li T'ai-Po [Asiatic Review, London, Oktober 1919]. – WALEY A., More Translation from the Chinese, New York 1919. – WALEY A., The Poetry and Career of Li-Po, New York 1950.

Peking: ARLINGTON L. C. und LEWISOHN W., In Search of Old Peking, 1935. – BODDE D., Anual customs and festivals in Peking, Peiping 1936. – BODDE D., Peking-Tagebuch, Wiesbaden 1952. – BOERSCHMANN E., Baukunst und Landschaft in China, Berlin 1923. – BOERSCHMANN E., Chinesische Architektur, Berlin 1925. – BOERSCHMANN E., Chinesische Pagoden, Berlin 1931. – BREDON J., Peking, 1931. – BRETSCHNEIDER E., Recherches archéologiques et historiques sur Pékin et ses environs, Paris 1879. – BURGESS J. S., The Guilds of Peking, New York 1928. – BURGESS J. S. und GAMBLE S. D., Peking: a social Survey, 1921. – CATLEEN E., Peking Studies. – COMBAZ G., Les sépultures impériales de la Chine, Brüssel 1907. – FAVIER A., Pékin: Histoire et description, 1897. – GEIL W. E., Eighteen Capitals of China, London 1911. – GRUBE W., Zur Pekinger Volkskunde, Berlin 1901. – HUBRECHT A., Grandeur et Suprématie de Pékin, 1928. – MEERSCHEIDT-HÜLLESEM, In und um Peking, Berlin 1902. – PLAYFAIR G. M. F., The Cities and Towns of China, Shanghai 1910. – SWALLOW R. W., Sidelights on Peking Life, 1930.

CENTRAL ASIA

BACHFELD, Die Mongolen in Polen, Böhmen und Mähren, Innsbruck 1899. – BALODIS, Alt Sarai und Neu Sarai, die Hauptstädte der Goldenen Horde, Riga 1926. – BARTHOLD W., Turkestan down to the Mongol Invasion, London 1928. – BARTHOLD W., Zwölf Vorlesungen über die Geschichte der Türken Mittelasiens, Berlin 1935. – BLOCHET E., Introduction à l'histoire des Mongols de Fadl Allah Rashid ed-Din, Leiden, London 1910. – BOUVAT L., Essai sur la civilisation timouride, Paris 1926 [Journal asiatique 208]. – BOUVAT L., L'Empire mongol, Paris 1927. – CURTIN J., The Mongols, Boston 1908. – CURTIN J., The Mongols in Russia, London 1908. – CZAPLINA, The Turks of Central Asia, Oxford 1918. – DEGUIGNES J., Histoire générale des Huns, des Turcs, des Mongols et des autres Tartares occidentaux, ouvrage tiré des livres chinois, Paris 1756–1758. – DOUGLAS, The Life of Jenghis Khan, London 1877. – ERDMANN F., Temudschin der Unerschütterliche, 1862. – FRANKE O., Geschichte des chinesischen Reiches, Berlin 1930–1952, IV. und V. Bd. – GRASMANN S., Einfall der Mongolen in Mitteleuropa, Innsbruck 1893. – GROUSSET R., Histoire de L'Asie, Paris 1922. – GROUSSET R., Histoire de l'Extrême-Orient, Paris 1929. – GROUSSET R., L'Empire des steppes, Paris 1939. – GROUSSET R., L'Empire mongol, Paris 1941. – HAENISCH E., Die Geheime Geschichte der Mongolen aus einer mongolischen Niederschrift des Jahres 1240, Leipzig 1941. – HAENISCH E., Die letzten Feldzüge Cinggis Han's [Asia Major IX, 1933: 503–551]. – HERRMANN A., Atlas of China, Karte 49 und 54/55, Cambridge, Mass. 1935. – HOWORTH H. H., History of the Mongols from the 9th to the 19th Cenutry, London 1876–1888. – KLIUTSCHEWSKIJ W., Geschichte Russlands, Stuttgart 1925. – KOROSTOVETZ I. J., Von Cinggis Khan zur Sowjetrepublik, Berlin 1926. – KRAUSE F. C. A., Cingis Han, Heidelberg 1922. – KRAUSE F. C. A., Die Epoche der Mongolen, Mitt. Seminars für Orientalische Sprachen, Berlin 1924. – LAMB H., Genghis Khan, New York 1927. – LAMB H., Tamerlane, New York 1928. – LÉVINE J., La Mongolie, Paris 1937. – MOREL CAP. H., Les campagnes mongoles [Revue militaire française Juni-Juli 1922]. – MOULE A. C., Tabelle der mongolischen Herrscher [Journal North China Branch Royal Asiatic Society XLV: 124]. – OHSSON A. C. MOURADGEA D', Histoire des Mongols depuis Tchioguis-Khan jusqu'à Timour Bey ou Tamerlan, 2. Auflage, Amsterdam 1852. – PELLIOT P. und MOULE A. C., Marco Polo, The description of the World, London, 1938. – PELLIOT und HAMBIS, Histoire des campagnes de Gengis Khan, Bd. I, Leiden 1951. – PRAWDIN M., Tschingis Chan, Stuttgart 1938. – SMOLIK J., Die Timuridischen Baudenkmäler in Samarkand, Wien 1929. – SPULER

B., Die Mongolen in Iran, Leipzig 1939. – SPULER B., Die Goldene Horde, Leipzig 1943. – SPULER B., Die Mongolenzeit, Handbuch der Orientalistik, Berlin 1948. – STRANGE LE, Mesopotamia and Persia under the Mongols, London 1934. – STÜBE R., Tschinghiz-Chan, seine Staatsbildung und seine Persönlichkeit [Neue Jahrbücher für Klassisches Altertum, 1908]. TOGAN A. ZEKI VELIDI, Bugünkü Türkili [Türkistan] ve yakintarihi [Das heutige Westturkistan und seine letztvergangene Geschichte], Istanbul 1942–1947. – VLADIMIRCOV B. J., Tchingis-Chan, Paris 1929. – VLADIMIRCOV B. J., Obščestvennyj stroj Mongolov. Mongol'skij kočevoj feodalizm [Der soziale Aufbau der Mongolen. Das mongolisch-nomadische Lebenssystem], Leningrad 1934. – VLADIMIRCOV B. J., The Life of Chingis-Khan, London 1930 [Französisch, Paris 1947].

JAPAN

Ainus: BATCHELOR J., The Ainu and their folklore, London 1901. – DRÖBER W., Die Ainos, München 1909. – HAAS H., Die Ainu und ihre Religion, Leipzig 1925. – HITCHCOCK R., The Ainos of Yezo, Washington. – MACRITCHIE D., The Ainos, Leiden 1892. – MONTANDON G., La civilisation Ainou, Paris 1937. – SCHEUBE, Die Ainos [Mitteilungen der Gesellschaft für Natur- und Völkerkunde Ostasiens, Bd. 26].

General History: ABEGG L., Ostasien denkt anders, Zürich 1949. – AISABURO AKIYAMA, Shinto and its architecture, Kyoto 1936. – ANEZAKI, History of Religion in Japan, London 1930. – ASTON W. G., Early Japanese History, Tokio 1888. – ASTON W. G., Shinto: The Way of the Gods, 1905. – ASTON W. G., History of Japanese Literature, London 1909. – BRINCKMANN J., Kunst und Kunsthandwerk in Japan, Berlin 1889. – CHAMBERLAIN B. H., Things Japanese, London 1891. – FLORENZ K., Geschichte der japanischen Literatur, Leipzig 1906, 2. Auflaga 1909. – GUNDERT W., Die Japanische Literatur, Potsdam 1929. – GUNDERT W., Japanische Religionsgeschichte, Stuttgart 1935. – HARADA J., A Glimpse of Japanese Ideals, Tokio 1937. – HAUSHOFER K., Japan und die Japaner, Leipzig 1923. – HOLTOM D. C., The Japanese Enthronement Ceremonies, Tokio 1928. – HONJO E., The Social and Economic History of Japan, Kyoto 1935. – MATSUMOTO N., Essai sur la Mythologie Japonaise, Paris 1928. – MUNRO N. G., Prehistoric Japan, Yokohama 1908. – MURDOCH J., A History of Japan, 3 Bde., Kobe 1903 und London 1926. – NACHOD O., Geschichte von Japan, Leipzig 1929–30. – SANSOM G. B., Japan, A Short Cultural History, London 1931. – TETSURO YOSHIDA, Das Japanische Wohnhaus, Berlin 1935. – Japan Year Book 1936.

Masters of the Japanese Print: BINGON L. und O'BRIEN SEXTAN J. J., Japanese Colour Prints, London. – BOLLER W., Meister des japanischen Farbholzschnittes, Bern 1947. – HILLIER J., Japanese Masters of the Colour Print, London 1954. – KURTH J., Utamaro, Leipzig 1907. – KURTH J., Der Japanische Holzschnitt, München 1911. – KURTH J., Suzuki Harunobu, München 1923. – KURTH J., Die Geschichte des japanischen Holzschnitts, 3 Bde., Leipzig 1925. – MICHENER J. A., The Floating World, New York 1954. – PRIESTLEY A. F., How to know Japanese Colour Prints, New York 1827. – SEIDITZ W. v., Geschichte des japanischen Farbenholzschnitts, Dresden 1897. – SHIZNYA PUJIKAKE, Japanese Wood-Block Prints [Tourist Library, Vol. 10], Tokio 1953. – STEWART B., Subjects Portrayed in Japanese Colour-Prints,

London 1922. – STRANGE E. F., The Colour Prints of Hiroshige, London 1925. – SUCCO F., Utagawa Toyokumi und seine Zeit, I. Bd., München 1913. – SUCCO F., Utagawa Toyokumi und seine Zeit, II. Bd., München 1914.

AUSTRALIA

BASEDOW H., The Australian aboriginal, Adelaide 1925. – BECK W., Das Individuum bei den Australiern, Leipzig 1925. – BERNDT R. M., Kunapipi. A study of an Australian aboriginal religions cult, Melbourne 1951. – ELKIN, A. P., The Australian aborigines. How to understand them, Sydney 1948. – HAMBLEY W. D., Primitive hunters of Australia, Chicago 1932. – HORNE G., Savage life in Central Australia, London 1924. – HOWITT A. W., The native tribes of South East Australia, London 1904. – KNABENHANS A., Die politische Organisation bei den australischen Eingeborenen, Berlin 1910. – LOMMEL A., Die Unambal, Hamburg 1952. – MOUNTFORD CH. P., Brown men and red sand. Journeying in wild Australia, Melbourne 1948. – ROTH H. L., The aborigines of Tasmania, Halifax 1899. – SEMON R., Im australischen Busch und an den Küsten des Korallenmeeres, Leipzig 1903. – SPENCER B., Native tribes of Northern territory of Australia, London 1914. – SPENCER B., GILLEN F. J., The Arunta, 2 Bde., London 1927. – SIMPSON C., Adam in ochre. Inside aboriginal Australia, Sydney 1951. – STREHLOW C., Die Aranda- und Loritja-Stämme in Zentral-Australien, Frankfurt/Main 1907–20. – THOMAS N. W., Natives of Australia, London 1906. – VATTER E., Der australische Totemismus [Mitteilungen aus dem Museum für Völkerkunde, Hamburg, Bd. 10, Hamburg 1925].

POLYNESIA

General: ANDERSEN J. C., Myths and legends of the Polynesians, London 1928. – BEAGLEHOLE J. C., Polynesian anthropology, Washington 1937. – BECKWITH M., Hawaiian mythology, New Haven 1940. – BEST E., Polynesian voyagers, Dominion Museum Monograph 5, Wellington, N. Z. 1923. – BEST E., The Maori, 2 Bde., Wellington, N. Z. 1924. – CHURCHILL W., Polynesian wanderings, Washington 1911. – DUFF R., The Mao-hunter period of Maori culture, Wellington, N. Z. 1950. – FIRTH R., Primitive Polynesian economy, London 1939. – FRIEDERICI G., Malaio-polynesische Wanderungen, Leipzig 1914. – FRIEDERICI G., Zu den vorkolumbischen Verbindungen der Südsee-Völker mit Amerika, Anthropos Bd. 24, Mödling/Wien 1929. – HANDY E. S. C., The native culture of the Marquesas. Bernice P. Bishop Museum Bulletin 9, Honolulu 1923. – HANDY E. S. C., Polynesian religion. Bernice P. Bishop Museum Bulletin 34, Honolulu 1927. – HENRY T., Ancient Tahiti-Bernice P. Bishop Museum Bulletin 48, Honolulu 1928. – HIROA, TE RANGI, Vikings of the sunrise, New York 1938. – HIROA, TE RANGI, Ethnology of Mangareva. Bernice P. Bishop Museum, Bulletin 157. Honolulu 1938. – HIROA, TE RANGI, An introduction to Polynesian anthropology. Bernice P. Bishop Museum Bulletin 187, Honolulu 1945. – HIROA, TE RANGI, The coming of the Maori, Wellington N. Z. 1950. – HIROA, TE RANGI, Explores of the Pacific, Honolulu 1953. – HOGBIN H. J., Law and order in Polynesia, London 1934. – KRÄMER A., Die Samoa-Inseln, 2 Bde., Stuttgart 1903. – LEHMANN R., Die polynesischen Tabusitten, Leipzig 1930. – MEAD M., Coming of age in Samoa, London 1929. – MALO D., Hawaiian antiquities, Honolulu 1952. – NEVERMANN H., Götter der Südsee, Stuttgart 1947. – RECHE E., Tangaloa. Ein Beitrig zur geistigen Kultur der Polynesier, München

1926. – SMITH P. S., Hawaiki. The original home of the Maori, London 1921. – STEINEN K. v. D., Die Marquesaner und ihre Kunst, 3 Bde., Berlin 1928. – TREGEAR E., The Maori race, Wanganui N. Z. 1926. – WILLIAMSON R. W., Essays in Polynesian ethnology, Cambridge 1939. – WILLIAMSON R. W., Religion and social organization in Central Polynesia, Cambridge 1937.

Easter Island: BROWN J. M., The riddle of the Pacific, London 1924. – CHAUVET ST., L'île de Pâques et ses mystères, Paris 1936. – ENGLERT, La tierra de Hotu Matna. Historia, Etnologia y lengua de la Isla de Pascua, Padre las Casas 1948. – GEISELER, Die Osterinsel, Berlin 1883. – HEINER-GELDERN R. v., Die Osterinselschrift, Anthropos Bd. 33, Wien/Mödling 1938. – JAUSSEN T., Les bois parlants de l'ile de Pâques [Bulletin de la Société des études Océaniennes, Bd. 5], Papeete 1936. – KNOCHE W., Die Osterinsel, Concepcion 1925. – LAVACHERY H., L'Ile de Pâques, Paris 1935. – MÉTRAUC A., The Proto-Indian script and the Easter Island tablets, Anthropos Bd. 33, Wien/Mödling 1938. – MÉTRAUC A., Ethnology of Easter Island, Bernice P. Bishop Museum Bulletin 160, Honolulu 1940. – MÉTRAUC A., Easter Island sanctuaries. Etnologiska studier, Göteborg 1937. – ROUTLEDGE C. S., The Mystery of Easter Island, London 1919. – SCHMIDT H., Die Steinbilder-Typen der Osterinsel und ihre Chronologie, Hamburg 1927. – SCHULZE-MAIZIER F., Die Osterinsel, Leipzig. – SKINNER H. D., The Easter Island script, Journal of the Polynesian Society, Bd. 41, Wellington N. Z. 1932. – THOMSON W. J., Te pito te henua, or Easter Island, Report of National Museum, Washington 1888/89.

MELANESIA

BLACKWOOD B., Both sides of Buka passage, Oxford 1935. – BROWN G., Melanesians and Polynesians, London 1910. – BROWN J. M., Peoples and problems of the Pacific, London 1927. – DEACON A. B., Malekula. A vanishing people in the New-Hebrides, London 1934. – HOGBIN H. J., Peoples of the Southwest Pacific, New York 1945. – IVENS W. G., The Melanesians of South East Solomon Islands, London 1927. – KRÄMER-BANNOW E., Bei kunstsinnigen Kannibalen der Südsee, Berlin 1916. – LEENHARDT M., Notes d'ethnologie Néo-Calédonienne, Paris 1930. – LEWIS A. B., The Melanesians. People of the South Pacific, Chicago 1951. – LANDTMANN G., The Kiwai Papuans of British New Guinea, London 1927. – LAYARD J., Stone men of Malekula, London 1942. – MALINOWSKI B., Argonauts of the Western Pacific, London 1922. – MALINOWSKI B., Coral gardens and their magic, 2 Bde., London 1935. – NEVERMANN H., Masken und Geheimbünde in Melanesien, Berlin 1933. – NEUHAUSS R., Deutsch-Neuguinea, 3 Bde., Berlin 1911. – PARKINSON R., Dreissig Jahre in der Südsee, Stuttgart 1907 – RIESENFELD A., The megalithic culture of Melanesia, Leiden 1950. – RIBBE C., Zwei Jahre unter den Kannibalen der Salomo-Inseln, Dresden 1903. – RIVERS W. H. R., History of Melanesia society, 2 Bde., London 1914. – SARASIN F., Ethnologie der Neu-Caledonier und Loyalty-Insulaner, 2 Bde., München 1929. – SELIGMANN C. G., The Melanesians of British New Guinea, Cambridge 1911. – TISCHNER H., HEWICKER F., Kunst der Südsee, Hamburg 1954. – SPEISER F., Südsee, Urwald, Kannibalen, Stuttgart 1924. VICEDOM F. G., TISCHNER H., Die Mbowamb. Die Kultur der Hagenberg-Stämme im östlichen Zentral-Neuguinea, 3 Bde., Hamburg 1943–48. – WIRZ P., Dämonen und Wilde in Neuguinea, Stuttgart 1928.

BIBLIOGRAPHY

NORTH AMERICA

Broderick A. H., Early man, London 1948. – Collier J., Indians of the Americas, New York 1947. – Gruimby M., Indians before Columbus, Chicago 1947. – Wissler C., The American Indian, New York 1950. – Wissler C., Das Leben und Sterben der Indianer, Wien 1948.

SOUTH AMERICA

Baessler A., Altperuanische Metallgeräte, Berlin 1906. – Baudin L., L'empire socialiste des Incas, Paris 1928. – Bahdin L., Die Inka von Peru, Essen 1947. – Bennett W. C., und Bird J. B., Andean Culture history, New York 1949. Bennett W. C., Ancient arts of the Andes, New York 1954. – Bingham H., Machu Picchu, a citadel of the Incas, New Haven 1930. – Doering H. U., Auf den Königsstrassen der Inka, Berlin 1941. – Doering H. U., Kunst im Reiche der Inka, Tübingen 1952 – Joyce Th., South American Archaeology, London 1912. – Karsten R., Das altperuanische Inkareich, Leipzig 1949. – Kutscher G., Chimu. Eine altindianische Hochkultur, Berlin 1950. – Markham C. R., The Incas of Peru, London 1910. Mead Ch. W., Old Civilizations of Inca Land, New York 1932. Means P. A., Ancient civilizations of the Andes, New York 1931. – Means P. A., Fall of the Inca Empire, New York 1932. – Nordenskiöld E., The copper and bronze ages in South America, Göteborg 1921. – Posnansky A., Eine Prähistorische Metropole in Südamerika, Berlin 1914. – Prescott W., Die Eroberung von Peru, Wien 1937. – Schmidt M., Kunst und Kultur von Peru, Berlin 1929. – Stübe A. und Uhle M., Die Ruinenstätte von Tiahuanaco, Leipzig 1892. – Uhle M., Kultur und Industrie der Südamerikanichen Völker, Berlin 1889/90. – *Handbook of South American Indians,* 6 Bde., Washington 1946 bis 1951.

MEXICO

Cerwin H., These are the Mexicans, New York 1947. – Danzel T. W., Mexiko, Darmstadt 1922. – Farnsworth D., The Americas before Columbus, 1947. – Gann T., Ancient cities and modern tribes, London 1926. – Gann T., Mexico, London 1936. – Hagen W. v., Maya Explorer, Oklahoma 1948. – Hoyningen-Huene, Mexican Heritage, New York 1946. – Joyce T. A., Mexican Archeology, London 1914. – Joyce T. A., Maya and Mexican Art, London 1927. – Kroeber A. L., Anthropology, New York 1948. – Lehmann W., Aus den Ruinenstätten Alt-Mexikos, Berlin. – Madariaga S. de, The Fall of the Spanish American Empire, 1947. – Marquina J., Arquitectura prehispánica, Mexiko 1951. – Mitchell J. L., The Conquest of the Maya, London 1934. – Morley S. G., The ancient Maya, Stanford 1946. – Prescott W., Die Eroberung von Mexiko, Wien 1937. – Radin P., Histoire de la Civilisation Indienne, Paris 1935. – Redfield R., The Folk Culture of Yucatan, Chicago 1941. – Sanford T. E., The Story of Architecture in Mexico, New York 1947. – Seler E., Fray Bernardino de Sahagun, Stuttgart 1927. – Spinden H. J., Ancient Civilizations of Mexico, New York 1928. – Stirling M. W., Stone Monuments of South Mexico, 1943. – Strode H., Now in Mexico, New York 1947. – Strode H., Timeless Mexico, New York 1944. – Thompson E. H., The rise and fall of Maya civilization, Norman [Oklahoma] 1954. – Thompson E. H., People of the Serpent, London 1932. – Toor F., Mexican Folkways, New York 1950. – Tos-

CANO S., Arte Precolombino, Mexico 1952. – VAILLANT G. C., The Aztecs of Mexico, New York 1944.

CRETE

BOSSERT H. TH., Altkreta, 1937. – EMMET L., BENNETT J., The Pylos Tablets, Princeton 1951. – EVANS A., The Palace of Minos at Knossos, 7 Bde., London 1921–36. – EVANS A., Scripta Minoa, 2 Bde., Oxford 1909–52. – FIMMEN D., Die kretisch-mykenische Kultur, 1924. – GLOTZ G., La civilisation égéenne, Paris 1923. – MATZ F., Die Ägäis [Handbuch der Archäologie, Bd. 2], 1950. – PENDLEBURY J. D. S., The Archaeology of Crete, London 1939. – PERNIER L., BANTI L., Il Palazzo minoico di Festos, 2 Bde., Rom 1935–51. – SITTIG E., Sprachen die Minoer griechisch? [Minos, Vol. III, masc. 2], Salamanca 1954. – VENTRIS M., Chadwick J., Evidence for Greek Dialect in the Mycenaean. Archives [Journal of Hellenic Studies 73], 1953. – WACE A. J. B., Mycenae, Princeton 1949. – *Etudes crétoises,* 9 Bde., Paris 1928–53.

GREECE

AELIAN, Varia Historia, V. – ARISTOPHANES. – ARISTOTLE, Constitutio Atheniensis, XXIII–VIII; Politica, VIII [V]. – DIODORUS, XII. – HERODOTUS, III, V–IX. – NEPOS CORNELIUS, Alcibiades. – NEPOS CORNELIUS, Themistocles. – PAUSANIAS, Description of Greece. – PLATO, Symposium. – PLATO, Alcibiades. – PLUTARCH, Alcibiades, 1–16; Pericles, 9–12; Themistocles, 10. – STRABO, VII. – THUCYDIDES, I–III. – XENOPHON, Hellenica, I, III, V. – XENOPHON, Memorabilia.

ALTHEIM F., Weltgeschichte Asiens im griechischen Zeitalter, I. Bd., Halle 1947. – BAUMGARTEN F., POLAND F., WAGNER R., Die Hellenische Kultur, Leipzig und Berlin 1913. – BELOCH K. J., Die Bevölkerung der griechisch-römischen Welt, 1886. – BELOCH K. J., Griechische Geschichte, Bd. IV, Berlin-Leipzig 1925–27. – BENGTSON H., Griechische Geschichte [Handbuch der Altertumswissenschaft, III 2] 1950. – BERVE H., Sparta, 1944. – BERVE H., Griechische Geschichte, 2 Bde., 1951 bis 1952. – BITTEL K., Grundzüge der Vor- und Frühgeschichte Kleinasiens, 1950. – BLEGEN C. W., Troy, 2 Bde., London 1950–51. – BOSSERT H. TH., Altanatolien, Berlin 1942. – BURCKHARDT J., Griechische Kulturgeschichte, 3 Bde., 1953, herausgegeben von R. Marx. – BURR V., Nostrum Mare, Stuttgart 1932. – BURY J. B., History of Greece, New York. – CALDWELL W. E., The new popular history of the world, New York 1950. – CAVAIGNAC E., Histoire de l'Antiquité, Bd. II, Paris 1913. – CAVAIGNAC E., Histoire de l'Antiquité, Bd. III, Paris 1914. – CICOTTI E., Der Untergang der Sklaverei im Altertum, 1910. CLOCHÉ P., Le siècle de Périclès, Paris 1949. – COHEN R., La Grèce et l'Hellénisation du Monde Antique, Paris 1948. – DÖRPFELD W., Troja und Ilion, Athen 1902. – DUNBABIN T. J., The Western Greeks, Oxford 1948. – DURANT W., The Life of Greece, New York 1939. – EHRENBERG V., The People of Aristophanes, Oxford 1951. – FORBIGER A., Strabo's Erdbeschreibung [I.], Stuttgart 1856. – FORBIGER A., Strabo's Erdbescheibung [V.], Stuttgart 1858. – FRAENKEL H., Dichtung und Philosophie des frühen Griechentums, New York 1951. – GIGON O., Sokrates, Berlin 1947. – GLOTZ G., La cité grecque, Paris 1928. – GREGOR J., Perikles, München 1944. – GRUNDY B. G., The Great Persian War, London 1901. – GRUNDY B. G., Thucydides and the History of his Age, 2 Bde., London 1948. – HATZFELD J., Alcibiade, Paris 1951. – HENDERSON B. W., The Great War between Athens and Sparta, London 1927. – HERRE P., Der Kampf um die

Herrschaft im Mittelmeer, Leipzig 1909. – Herzog R., Dittrich P., Listmann K., Das Zeitalter des Hellenismus, 1 Bd., Leipzig 1932. – Holleaux M., Rome, la Grèce, et les monarchies hellénistiques au IIIe siècle av. J.-C. [273–205], Paris 1921. – Jacobi M., Thucydides, 1 Bd., Hamburg 1804. – Jacobi M., Thucydides, 2. Bd., Hamburg 1806. – Jacobi M., Thucydides, 3. Bd., Hamburg 1808. – Jones H. L., The Geography of Strabo [IV], London 1949. – Jouguet R., L'Impérialisme macédonien et l'hellénisation de l'Orient 1926. – Kaerst J., Geschichte des Hellenistischen Zeitalters, Bd. I und II, Leipzig 1901. – Kaerst J., Geschichte der Karthager, Berlin 1879–1913. – Karo G., Die Schachtgräber von Mykenai, 2 Bde., 1930–33. – Melber J., Olympia, 1936. – Meyer E., Geschichte von Troas, Leipzig 1877. – Michell H., The Economics of Ancient Greece, Cambridge 1940. – Michell H., Sparta, Cambridge 1942. – Miller W., Greece and the Greeks, New York 1941. – Nilsson M. P., Homer and Mycenae, London 1933. – Obst E., Der Feldzug des Xerxes, 1914. – Pohlenz M., Herodot, 1937. – Pritchett W. K., Meritt B. D., The Chronology of Hellenistic Athens, Cambridge 1940. – Ranke L. v., Perikles, Berlin 1942. – Rostovtzeff M., Geschichte der Alten Welt, Wiesbaden 1941. – Sanctis G. de, Pericle, Mailand-Messina 1944. – Schadewaldt W., Von Homers Welt und Werk, 1951. – Schliemann H., Mykenae, Leipzig 1878. – Schliemann H., Ilios, Leipzig 1881. – Schliemann H., Troja, Leipzig 1884. – Schliemann H., Tiryns, Leipzig 1886. – Taeger F., Alkibiades, 1943. – Westermann W. L., Sklaverei [Realenzyklopädie der klassischen Altertumswissenschaft, herausgegeben von Pauly-Wissowa, Suppl.-Bd. 6], 1935. – Wiesner J., Vor- und Frühzeit der Mittelmeerländer [I], Berlin 1943. – Wilamowitz-Moellendorff U. v., Platon, 2 Bde., 1919. – Wilamowitz-Moellendorff U. v., Der Glaube der Hellenen, 2 Bde., 1931–1932. – Willrich H., Perikles, Göttingen 1936. – Woodhause W. J., Solon the Liberator, Oxford 1938. – Zellwecker E., Troja, Zürich 1947. – *Hellenistic Civilization*, London 1927. – *Handbuch der Archaeologie*, Bd. IV, München.

ITALY

Akerström A., Studien über etruskische Gräber, Lund 1934. – Altheim F., Der Ursprung der Etrusker, Baden-Baden 1950. – Avrigemma S., Il R. Museo di Spina in Ferrara, Rom 1936. – Bauer H., Der Ursprung des Alphabets [Der alte Orient, Vorderasiatische und ägyptische Gesellschaft, 35. Bd.], Leipzig 1937. – Bennett E. L. jr., The Pylos Tablets, Princeton 1951. – Brandenstein W., Die Herkunft der Etrusker [Der alte Orient, Vorderasiatische und ägyptische Gesellschaft, 35. Bd.], Leipzig 1937. – Clemen C., Die Religion der Etrusker, Bonn 1936 [Untersuchungen zur allgemeinen Religionsgeschichte, Heft 7]. – Cles-Reden S., Das versunkene Volk, Innsbruck und Wien 1948. – Ducati P., Etruria antica, Torino 1925. – Ducati P., L'Italia antica, Bd. 1, Mailand. – Ducati P., Storia dell'Arte Etrusca, 2 Bde., Florenz 1927. – Ducati P. – Giglioli G. Qu., Arte etrusca, Rom-Mailand 1927. – Duhn F. v., Italische Gräberkunde I, Heidelberg 1924. – Goldmann E., Beiträge zur Lehre vom indogermanischen Charakter des Etruskischen I. und II., Heidelberg 1929 und 1930. – Neue Beiträge usw. Wien 1936 – [Klotho, Heft 3]. – Leisinger H., Malerei der Etrusker, Stuttgart. – Mühlestein H., Über die Herkunft der Etrusker, Berlin 1929. – Olzscha K., Die Sprache der Etrusker [Neue Jahrbücher 1936, 97–116]. – Pareti L., Le origini etrusche, Florenz 1926. – Pfister K., Die Etrusker, München 1940. – Randall D., MacIver, The Etruscans, Oxford 1927. – Riis P. J., Tyrrhenika, Kopenhagen 1941. Riis P. J., An Introduction to Etruscan Art, Kopenhagen 1953. – SCHACHENMEYER F., Etruskische Frühgeschichte, Berlin 1929. – SCHULTEN A., Tartessos, Hamburg 1950. – STOLTENBERG H. L., Übersetzung der Tontafeln von Capua [Studi Etruschi, Bd. XXII, Serie II], Florenz 1952–53. – *Corpus Inscriptionum Struscarum*, Leipzig ab 1893. – *The great King of Assyria*, Assyrian Reliefs in the Metropolitan Museum of Art.

CARTHAGE

General: ARNOLD T., The Second Punic War, London 1886. – CARY M., The origin of the Punic Wars, History, VII, 1922, p. 109. – DELBRÜCK H., Geschichte der Kriegskunst, II. Bd., Berlin 1908. – EHRENBERG V., Karthago, Leipzig 1927. – GSELL S., Histoire Ancienne de l'Afrique du Nord, vols. I to IV, Paris 1913–20. – KAHRSTEDT U., in Meltzers Geschichte der Karthager, Vol. III, Berlin 1913, pp. 143–362. – KROMAYER, Antike Schlachtfelder, III. Bd., Berlin 1912. – LAPEYRE G. G., Carthage, Paris 1942. – LAPEYRE G. G. und PELLEGRIN A., Carthage Punique, Paris 1942. – LAQUEUR R., Scipio Africanus und die Eroberung von Neukarthago, Hermes, LVI, 1921, p. 138. – LEHMANN K., Die Anfriffe der drei Barkiden auf Italien, Leipzig 1905. – MOMMSEN, Römische Geschichte, III. – NEUMANN, Das Zeitalter der punischen Kriege, Breslau 1883. – PAIS E., Storia di Roma durante le guerre Puniche, I, II, Rom 1927. – SCULLARD H. H., Scipio Africanus in the Second Punic War, Cambridge 1930. – TÄUBLER E., Die Vorgeschichte des zweiten punischen Krieges, Berlin 1921. – *Rom und Karthago*, Leipzig 1943.

Hannibal: APPIAN, 4–38. – BONUS A. R., Where Hannibal passed, London 1925. – CONSTANS L. A., La route d'Hannibal, Rev. des Etudes hist. CXLVII, 1924, p. 22. – DIODORUS, XXV, XXVI. – DODGE T. A., Hannibal, 2 vols., Boston 1891. – EGELHAAF G., Hannibal, 1922. – GROAG E., Hannibal als Politiker, Wien 1929. – HORAZ, Oden, I, IV. – JELUSISCH MIRKO, Hannibal, Siegen 1934. – KLOTZ A., Zu Hannibals Alpenübergang, Erlangen 1925. – LIVIUS, XXI-XXX, ed. Weissenborn; ed. Conway. – OVID, Fasti, I, II, III, IV, VI. – PLINIUS, II, III, VII, XXIII, XXXIV. – PLUTARCH, Q. FABIUS MAXIMUS, M. CLAUDIUS MARCELLUS; Apophtlegmata regum et imperatorium. – POLYBIUS, III, und Teile aus VII–XI, XIV–XV. – STRABO, III, V, VI. – TERRELL G., Hannibal's Pass over the Alps, C. J., XVIII, 1922.

ROME

ARNOBIUS: Adversus nationes, ed. by C. Marchesi, 2nd ed. Turin 1953. – AUGUSTUS: Imperatoris Caesaris Augusti operum fragmenta, ed. by Henrica Malcovati, 3rd ed. Turin 1948. – HISTORIA AUGUSTA: Scriptores Historiae Augustae, ed. by E. Hohl, 2 vols., Leipzig 1927. – CAESAR: C. Juli Caesaris Commentarii, De bello Gallico and De bello civili, ed. by A. Klotz, Leipzig 1950 and 1952. – CASSIUS DIO: Cassius Dio Cocceianus, ed. by Ph. U. Boissevain, 4 vols, 2nd ed. Berlin 1955. – CICERO: M. Tulli Ciceronis scripta quae manserunt omnia, Leipzig 1923 sq. The Correspondence of M. Tullius Cicero, arranged according to its chronological order, with a revision of the text, comment., and introduct. Essays by R. Y. Tyrrell and I. C. Purser, Dublin and London, Vol. I, 1904. Vol. II 1906, Vol. III 1914, Vol. IV 1918, Vol V 1915, Vol. VI 1899, Vol VII 1901. – HORACE: O. Keller and A. Holder (with Index Verborum), ed. 2, 2 vols. Leipzig 1899–1925. – INSCRIPTIONES: Pompeji, Herculaneum, Stabiae, Corpus Inscriptionum Latinarum, Vol. X, 1883. –

BIBLIOGRAPHY

INSCRIPTIONES: Pompeianische Wandinschriften und Verwandtes ed. by Ernst Diehl, 2nd ed. Berlin 1930. – INSCRIPTIONES: Inscriptiones Graecae, Vol. I-XIV, Berlin 1890 sq. and Corpus Inscriptionum Latinarum, Vol. I-XVI, Berlin 1893 sq. – JUVENAL: D. Junii Juvenalis Saturae, ed. by A. E. Housman, Cambridge 1938. – G. Highet, Juvenal the Satirist, Oxford 1954. – D. Junius Juvenalis, Saturae, ed. U. Knoche, Munich 1950. – LIVY: R. S. Conway and C. F. Walters, Oxford, 1914. – MARTIAL: ed. W. M. Lindsay, Martinalis, 2nd ed. London 1929. – M. Valerii Martialis epigrammatonn libri, ed. by L. Friedlaender Leipzig 1886. – OVID: Ed. R. Merkel, R. Ehwald, F. Levy and F. W. Lenz, 1880–1932, Leipzig 3 vols, in 4. – PLINY THE YOUNGER: Gaius Plinus Caecilius Secundus, Spistulae and Panegyricus, ed. M. Schuster, Leipzig 1933. – PROPERTIUS: Ed. C. Hosius, Leipzig 1932. – SALLUST: Sallusti Catilina, Iugurtha, Fragmenta ampliora, ed. by A. W. Ahlberg – A. Kurfess, 2nd ed. Leipzig 1955. Appendix Sallustiana (epistulae, invectivae), ed. by A. Kurfess, 2 vols. Leipzig 1950–55. – SUETONIUS: Gaius Suetonius Tranquillus, Devita Caesarum, ed. by I. Lana, Turino, 1952. – TACITUS: Cornelii Taciti Annales, ed. by C. D. Fisher. Opera minora ed. by H. Furneaux in Scriporum classicorum bibliotheca Oxoniensis, London 1952. – TIBULLUS: Ed. F. W. Levy, Leipzig, 1927. – VIRGIL: J. W. Mackail, The Aeneid, Oxford 1930.

GENERAL BIBLIOGRAPHY

ALBERTINI, E.: L'empire romain, 3me edit., Paris 1938. – BENGTSON, H.: Einführung in die Alte Geschichte. 2nd Ed. Munich 1953. – The Cambridge Ancient History, ed. by S. A. Cook, F. E. Adcock, M. P. Charlesworth, IX Cambridge 1951, X Cambridge 1952, XI Cambridge 1936, XII Cambridge 1939. – DESSAU, H.: Geschichte der Römischen Kaiserzeit, 2 Vols. 3 parts, Berlin 1924–30. – FRANK, T.: Economic History of Rome, 2nd Ed., Baltimore 1927. – FRIEDLÄNDER, L.: Darstellungen aus der Sittengeschichte Roms, ed. by G. Wissowa, 4 Vols. 9th and 10th Ed. Leipzig 1920–22. – GELZER, M.: Das Römertum als Kulturmacht, Hist. Zeitschrift, 126, 1922. – GIBBON, E.: Decline and Fall of the Roman Empire [in Everyman Library, 434], six volumes, London 1954. – GLOTZ, G.: Histoire generale, Histoire romaine II–IV, Paris 1933–47. – HOMO, L.: Les institutions politiques romaines, l'evolution de l'humanite, Vol. 18, Paris 1933. – L'empire romain, Paris 1925. – La civilisation romaine, Paris 1930. – Les empereurs romains et le christianisme, Paris 1931. – Le haut empire [collection Histoire generale, Glotz] Paris 1933. – JEFFERSON LOANE, H.: Industry and Commerce of the city of Rome, Baltimore 1938. – KORNEMANN, E.: Römische Geschichte, 2 vols. 3rd ed., ed. by H. Bengtson, Stuttgart 1954. – Weltgeschichte des Mittelmeer-Raumes, ed. by H. Bengtson, 2 vols. Munich 1949. – MATTINGLY, H., SYDENHAM, E. A.: The Roman Imperial Coinage, 5 vols., London 1923–33. – MOMMSEN, TH.: Römische Geschichte, I-III, Leipzig 1854–56, V, 1885. – The Oxford Classical Dictionary, ed. by M. Cary, J. D. Denniston, J. Wight Duff, A. D. Nock, W. D. Ross, H. H. Scullard, Oxford 1953. – PAOLI, U. E.: Vita Romana, Firenze, 5th ed., 1947. – PARIBENI, R.: L'Italia imperiale, Storia d'Italia illustrata, 1938. – PAULEY, A., WISSOWA, G.: Real-Encyclopädie der classischen Altertumswissenschaft, neue Bearbeitung, Stuttgart 1894 sq. – PIGANIOL, A.: Histoire de Rome, 3rd Edition, Paris 1949. – RODENWALDT, G.: Die Kunst der Antike, Hellas und Rom, Berlin 1927. – ROSTOVTZEFF, M.: A History of the Ancient World, 2 vols. Oxford 1926 and 1927. – DE RUGIERO, E.: CARDINALI, G.: Dizionaro epigrafico di antichita romane, Roma

1886, sq. – SALMON, E. T.: A history of the Roman World from 30 B.C. to A.D. 138, London 1944. – SEECK, O.: Geschichte des Untergangs der antiken Welt, 6 vols., Berlin 1920–21. – DE TILLEMONT, M. L.: Histoire des Empereurs, 3 vols., Paris 1911. – WAGENVOORT, H.: Roman Dynamism, Studies in Ancient Roman Thought, Language and Custom, Oxford 1947.